The Life-Death Instinct

Throughout this enlightening collection, Neil Maizels considers the helical tandem between the Life Instinct and the Death drive in the light of canonical literary figures like Thomas Hardy, Patricia Highsmith, Sylvia Plath and Shakespeare, classic filmmakers like Hitchcock and contemporary television shows such as *Curb Your Enthusiasm*, *The West Wing* and *Succession*.

This light is filtered through intricate clinical work whereby Maizels seeks to illustrate and expound on the strength and indefatigability of the Life Instinct. He makes a case for it as the relentless driver of integration and "binding" in the ever-growing, expansive psyche. He considers both Freud's original equation of the Life Instinct with Eros and a widening interconnecting love of mankind, and Melanie Klein's with gratitude and creative reparation. This book is a multi-layered presentation of the clinical and theoretical work of Neil Maizels as it has evolved and convolved over several decades. It places the *feeling through* of one's conflicts at the heart of the mind's generation of a unique identity, equipped to evolve its own unique form of creative spirit in the face of life's most pressing psychological challenges: the limitation of time, and reciprocated beauty.

The Life-Death Instinct: Feeling Through Creative-Clinical Moments is important reading for anyone seeking to expand their knowledge in this fascinating intersection of psychoanalysis and the arts.

Neil Maizels has been a psychoanalytic psychotherapist and clinical psychologist with children, teens and adults for over four decades, and has published internationally in journal papers and book chapters. With a special interest in the arts and psychoanalysis, he is also a professional composer and artist. He lives in Melbourne, Australia.

The Life-Death Instinct

Feeling Through Creative-Clinical Moments

Neil Maizels

LONDON AND NEW YORK

Designed cover image: *Gathering Calm by* Neil Maizels

First published 2024
by Routledge
4 Park Square, Milton Park, Abingdon, Oxon OX14 4RN

and by Routledge
605 Third Avenue, New York, NY 10158

Routledge is an imprint of the Taylor & Francis Group, an informa business

© 2024 Neil Maizels

The right of Neil Maizels to be identified as author of this work has been asserted in accordance with sections 77 and 78 of the Copyright, Designs and Patents Act 1988.

All rights reserved. No part of this book may be reprinted or reproduced or utilised in any form or by any electronic, mechanical, or other means, now known or hereafter invented, including photocopying and recording, or in any information storage or retrieval system, without permission in writing from the publishers.

Trademark notice: Product or corporate names may be trademarks or registered trademarks, and are used only for identification and explanation without intent to infringe.

British Library Cataloguing-in-Publication Data
A catalogue record for this book is available from the British Library

Library of Congress Cataloging-in-Publication Data
Name: Maizels, Neil, author.
Title: The life-death instinct: feeling through creative-clinical moments / Neil Maizels.
Description: Abingdon, Oxon; New York, NY: Routledge, 2024. | Includes bibliographical references and index.
Identifiers: LCCN 2023027656 (print) | LCCN 2023027657 (ebook) | ISBN 9781032428932 (hardback) | ISBN 9781032428925 (paperback) | ISBN 9781003364788 (ebk)
Subjects: LCSH: Psychoanalysis—Philosophy. | Death instinct. | Psychoanalysis and the arts.
Classification: LCC BF175.M2648 2024 (print) | LCC BF175 (ebook) | DDC 150.19/5—dc23/eng/20230823
LC record available at https://lccn.loc.gov/2023027656

ISBN: 9781032428932 (hbk)
ISBN: 9781032428925 (pbk)
ISBN: 9781003364788 (ebk)

DOI: 10.4324/9781003364788

Typeset in Times New Roman
by codeMantra

Contents

	Introduction	*viii*
	Acknowledgement	*xvii*
1	**Inoculative identification in Alfred Hitchcock's *Strangers on a Train***	1
2	**Self-envy, the womb and the nature of goodness – a reappraisal of the death instinct**	13
3	**The destructive confounding of intra-uterine and post-uterine feeding as a factor against emotional growth**	24
4	**What could be better than nuclear warfare?: An essay on the quest for eirenarchic survival**	37
5	**Dreams Grown False: The "cannibalization" of alpha function**	47
6	**The role of *Disidentification* in the growth of personality and during the analytic termination phase**	58

Disidentification and disavowal 62
Eugenie Grandet and Catherine Sloper 63
Disidentification, the combined object and the depressive position 66
The Squid and the Whale 67
Transference and countertransference just prior to disidentification 69

A clinical fragment 72
Disidentification and termination 72
Higgins and Doolittle – separation, disidentification
  and the depressive position 74
Disidentification and the developing self 75
Further analyst-parent countertransference issues 76
Summary 77

7 **Working through, or beyond the depressive position? Achievements and defences of a *Spiritual* position** 79

The depressive position 81
Beyond the depressive position 85
Defences against the spiritual position 86
Discussion 94
The emergence of a feeling philosophical value system
  in the spiritual position 97
The "Merlin-Father" in the transformation of schizoid
  detachment into observing-ego-in-feeling 98
Psychoanalytic and artistic technique 101
A suggested metapsychological revision 103

8 **"I'm Miss Red!" Reworking a premature weaning in a lonely young girl** 106

9 **Loneliness and its amelioration through transformations of the Internal Father** 121

The female poet and her father 126
Loneliness and boredom 129

10 **Two Vices and a film review** 142

   (i) Sometimes a cigar ... on smokers and non-smokers 143

Death and the Marlboro 147
Holding it together: the crippled self and the little glowing
  cherry 147
Puffed-up Narcissism and contemptuous rage 148
Smoking in identification with an admired-and-hated
  father-figure 148
Oral-oedipal-genital fusion and confusion 149

The link with the sensual and the erotic 150
Evanescence 151

The significance of Swearing as a *proto-language*   156

Life and Death of a Planet in *Melancholia* – a film about depressive cynicism   172

11 **The wrecking and re-pairing of the internal couple: In clinical work and in Shakespeare's *Othello* and *The Winter's Tale***   179

Part II 183

12 **Trees of Knowledge in Thomas Hardy's *The Woodlanders***   199

13 **Distraction – as both an important manic defence, and yet also as a creative unconscious consolation when facing immense depressive or disintegrative states**   216

The changing concept of Manic *Defences 219*
Manic Denial compared to sublimatory reparation 221
Distraction in the socio-cultural matrix 223

14 **Narcissus Rejects: Unbearable Beauty and the urge to destroy it, in *The Comfort of Strangers***   228

Two clinical examples 230
Dangerous beauty in The Comfort of Strangers 235

15 **Inconclusive Conclusion: The resilient persistence of the Life-Death instinct through variations in its relationships with the drive to Death**   244

Index   *249*

Introduction

Psychoanalysis, with its longstanding focus on psychopathology, has achieved much in its understanding of the workings of the mind. But, with regard to a central (albeit controversial) concept – the interplay and conflict between Life and Death "instincts" – it has placed a heavy emphasis on the understanding and exploration of the latter of the two unconscious drives.

This book seeks to redress that imbalance and to explore the unconscious dynamic and fluid intertwined relationship between these drives in the mind's everlasting quest for growth and integration.

Through clinical work over forty years, and infusions from literature and the cinema, I will seek to describe and illustrate the strength and indefatigability of the Life Instinct as the driving force towards integration, creative propagation and transcendence in the potentially ever-growing psyche.

I will seek to elaborate Freud's original equation of Life Instinct with Eros and the reach for an interconnectedness of humanity through civilization, and Melanie Klein's expanded and somewhat modified understanding of this underlying conflictual duality.

Klein came to see unconscious spoiling envy as the hallmark of the death drive, and love, gratitude and reparative urges as the saving graces that allow for growth and creativity in the infant mind, and for the capacity to enjoin and enjoy relationships and Life's beneficence.

I will argue that the Life Instinct – in an intertwined, helical tandem with the death drive – may "co-opt" paranoid and schizoid tendencies in the personality for purposes of preservation, creativity and integrative mental development. This implies that it becomes crucial, in analytic work, to grasp the full context of unconscious aims before prematurely or simplistically labelling a particular behaviour, impulse or phantasy as merely "narcissistic," "manic" or "destructive." Doing so may lead the patient to withdraw, or to terminate and to feel "out in the cold" before their Life Instinct has been recognized and harnessed.

But, as a more complex, dialectic interweaving of the drives is illustrated, the clinical implications of this subtle interplay will call for a somewhat subtler technique – including a more balanced or holistic method of transference interpretation.

The Life and Death instincts were Freud's and Klein's attempt to abstract the workings of the mind to the large canvas – the biggest picture. Defences and impulses could be seen as over-arched by the particular lines of confederacy that these supposed polarities of Life versus Death enlisted. The conception of these drives served as a holding concept where the theories of love, hate and intense curiosity could nestle and coalesce for further clinical observation and reflection. (Bion preferred to speak of "minus" feelings rather than death instinct.)

Freud's and Klein's attempt to abstract the workings of the mind through defences and "propulsions" could be seen as over-arched by the particular lines of confederacy that *Eros* and *Thanatos* enlisted.

However, I am suggesting that these defensive-propulsive loops and struggles in personality formation are far more complex in their interactions, and that the language of psychic growth is built upon their effervescing interface and pendular interaction – resembling an ocean of mutually interacting cross-currents that thrive on ambiguity – so that no particular action or thought or feeling is ever totally or exactly what it seems to be if taken in mere isolation.

The mind is a very big place.

But, in its broadest infinite sense, its Life is as is poetry, an ongoing interconnectedness – of molecules, cells, organs, intentions and thoughts and feelings and feeling thoughts that may spread and develop and deepen.

Against this tide of inter-outer-reaching flows the swell of dismantling complexity and purpose – the drive back to atomic humming and droning of muons, gluons and the solitary, undeveloped, un-enriched soulless, mindless unmated narcissism, in all its tragic destruction and impossibly painful loneliness – with only the "dark matter" of envy and auto-immune defence as its air. These are the feeling worlds of our lived experience that we dwell and swim in, and watch others swim (and sometimes drown) in.

One complication of this book is that it has grown out of a collective of papers. But rather than a "collected works" – having evolved over decades of clinical work, and the attempt to see a gestalt in those papers, its overarching themes gradually emerged from the fog of these seemingly disparate papers.

But, I now see it is a realization of sorts of my attempt at a whole-object integration of my models of mental-emotional life. The experiment is to see whether or not this is of any interest or help to anyone else, especially those working clinically with unconscious conflict.

Chapter overview

Rather than force a strictly chronological order onto my apparently jig-saw method of producing papers, I will re-assemble the whole picture through an attempted retrospective thematic order of chapters, and I will start with the paper that I feel most psycho-dramatically evokes the larval-hot fluid struggle between the drive for increasingly urgent integration of one's most psychotic inclinations and the drive to maintain "civility" – and I found that the novelist Patricia Highsmith and the director Alfred Hitchcock were most apt here. Apart, and together, they forged a cinematic dream language for expressing this fight to the death, or to Life. (I see cinema, in particular, as a form of public dreaming.)

Their stark and nail-biting evocation in the novel and film *Strangers on a Train* of the battle for integration of murderous psychotic impulses vs "playing it safe" is discussed and expanded in Chapter 1, ***Inoculative identification in Alfred Hitchcock's Strangers on a Train***. I use the film to illustrate the dangerous, but inescapable, psychological knife-edge between personality integration and murderous disintegration. A healthy, integrative but risky, form of projective identification is described – which challenges Melanie Klein's somewhat pessimistic view that the most psychotic parts of the mind cannot be integrated into the growing Self and is revisited, and questioned. Both the film and the book by Patricia Highsmith provide rather chilling illustrations of the dialectic interplay between life and death drives, with the book ending tracing through the annihilation of the mind. The closeness of battle is exemplified in the two different endings.

I don't think that the term "dialectical" really captures the scintillatingly alive and yet deathly erotic dance of impulses that the above auteurs are able to conjure in a short work of art.

Chapter 2, ***Self-envy, the womb and the nature of goodness – A reappraisal of the death instinct***, involves a bio-psychological re-alignment of the Freudian and Kleinian conceptions of the primal instinctual theory. It forms the first part of a trilogy on this theme, and proposes a model which attempts both to reconcile and to add to the difference between their instinctual theories, whilst making some suggestions about the "nature of goodness." That the pervasive, universal wish for goodness in one's personality could have its basis in instinctual conflict may seem surprising. Attention is focused on the phantasy of returning to the womb and its consequent anxieties to the growing, active ego. Such anxiety, *and its reverse*, can only be moderated by the introjection of an object which is capable of creatively resolving the resulting conflicts. The emphasis is shifted to the ever-wrestling interaction and restlessness between these life and death instincts.

Some suggestions and observations about the United Nations bring the possibility of extending these dynamics to a global, large-group level.

However, a broader perspective is enabled in this chapter, whereby a form of unconscious envy – Self-envy – is not *only* seen as Self-destructive. It is also a crucial pathway in which the Self unconsciously detects what needs to be incorporated for further growth and integration and then externalizes this into an object, producing both imminent danger and the chance for growth, simultaneously. (This theme is further developed in Chapter 13 – *Narcissus Rejects*.)

The destructive confounding of intra-uterine and post-uterine feeding as a factor against emotional growth suggests that some Kleinian concepts (projective identification, "toilet breast," ideal breast, splitting and death-instinctual attacks on the feeding relationship) might also be understood in terms of a "collision" between the world of the foetus and the world of the new-born baby impacting on the mind of the infant. The transition from the womb to the breasts-and-air as feeder and provider may be fraught with intense emotional conflict, and some further suggestions are made in relation to the vicissitudes of this conflict.

Speculations about the phantasy of "going through" and its importance for the necessity of establishing a viable relationship with the world outside the womb, particularly the maternal breasts, are supported by some literary (Proust, in particular) and cinematic examples. Attention is also given to the extremely destructive ways in which the transition from womb to breasts might be opposed, (often named "destructive narcissism") seriously threatening the possibility of emotional growth.

These themes are explored at the large-group level in the next chapter, *What could be better than nuclear warfare?*

In the late 1980's international nuclear annihilation, anxiety was at a frenzied peak. In the present day, approximately 2023, it is re-emerging towards a new pique. For many people, nuclear weaponry is the embodiment of the death drive at the Group level of mankind, par excellence. Some serious questions are raised about the structure of the United Nations in containing such anxieties and unconscious wishes. But, the main concern of this chapter is in detailing the deadly battle between life and death drives in the Group mind. Once again, this is no simple "head to head" combat. It involves a complex dialectic which must be understood, in order to be contained, or transcended. The United Nations is an early, if flawed, attempt to find such a containing structure – but, its structure and spirit are still dominated by bullying and a mis-conception of the word "United."

In *Dreams Grown False (The "cannibalization" of alpha function.)* I illustrate the very fine line between creativity and Life-Death desperation in the formation and digestion of emotionally charged symbols, in and out of dream-life. Bion's minus K, extended to minus narrative-alpha, and minus (omniscient) Dream-work – is explicated through a short story by Sylvia Plath, and some clinical material.

In Chapter 6, *Disidentification*, I use the musical *My Fair Lady* and the "battle" between Eliza Doolittle and Henry Higgins to emphasize the near-equal importance of **disidentification** with **identification** in the growth of the mind - a crucially neglected issue, particularly in relation to the *termination* of an analysis – akin to "leaving home." Far from being a negative, deathly failure of identification – *disidentification* involves the newly forming Self gradually learning about which internal objects to listen less to, and even the good objects may be rebelled against, sometimes, for the cause of growth. (Hence the old saying that "standing up to one's friends is harder than defying one's enemies.") A child needs to learn, always painfully, the distinction between its own aggressive destructive envy of the parents, and what are crucial identity formation and growth in the form of disidentification.

Chapter 7, *Working through, or beyond the depressive position? (Achievements and defences of a spiritual position* explore some conceptual and technical issues in relation to the terms "Depressive Position" and "Working Through of the Depressive Position," and in so doing, suggests a new concept – *"The Spiritual Position".*

It is proposed that this spiritual position has achievements, such as a capacity for "meta feeling," and defences, which are somewhat different, although related, to the Freudian-Kleinian models of mourning and reparation. Particular attention is paid to the development of the "whole-object Father" in the formation of an "observing-ego-in-feeling," and to the development of the "whole-object Mother" (Nature) in the formation of a "metamorphosis," feeling, philosophy of Life. I speculate that together, combined, these formations give the mind a "heart," which may come under attack from an omniscient, Tiresias-like internal object.

Some clinical material is used to illustrate these achievements and defences, and to highlight the difference of emphasis (as compared with the working through of the depressive position) that they imply. This spiritual-transcendent emotional position is necessary for the losses, setbacks, slings and arrows of later Life – where one's blessings must be weighed against one's wounds and insults, especially mortality and evanescence. If these can be held together in a bitter-sweet (sighing) feeling of gratitude and apprehension of beauty, then the death drive towards non-existence (uterine oblivion) may be held in abeyance – and not quite so feared.

Chapter 8, *"I'm Miss Red!"* – *Premature weaning in a lonely young girl* – discusses the infinite persistence and irrepressibility of the Life-Death instinct in re-presenting, relentlessly, the symbolism of loss and incomplete mourning, until the child is ready to "feel it like a child."

The themes of isolation, loneliness and the complexities of internal fathers are again gathered and re-thought in Chapter 9, **Loneliness – and its amelioration through transformations of the loving internal father.**

There I develop the idea that the internal father – for better or for worse – plays a crucial role in the mediation of a particular type of (inner) loneliness, and that the absence, corruption or destruction of this paternal object paralyzes the mind of the child in its ongoing attempts to work with its depressive pains associated with the separation, usually of a more non-verbal nature, from the primary maternal object. This is why an excruciatingly painful form of boredom is often part of the emotional experience of loneliness, beyond the pangs of longing for non-verbal closeness with the lost or absent primary maternal object. A clinical example and one chosen from the television drama *The West Wing* illustrate these pains and their liberation.

I also outline the evolution of the internal father from this harsh part-object superego – threatening castration and permanent exile from the mother – to unhelpfully disinterested, (but not aggressive), to an encouraging, patient and interested whole-object representation – acting as a "lap" for the child to climb up onto (perhaps represented, in America, by Lincoln's huge statue, using sign language – for his initials, A.L, indicating his role in finding language for symbolization.) Here the child can hear itself think, in the presence of an empathetic and sympathetic elicitor of reverie-in-words, if anxiety due to feared maternal jealousy is not overwhelming or distracting. This "lap of the father" is an evolution of the primary reverie initially provided by the mother, except in a more verbally eliciting fashion. The father here provides the steady "knees" of his own mind to let the child find its own words for its own inner experiences and shapeless feelings – giving these a local habitation and a place, in the emerging words of the child, for its own emotional experiences. Therefore, I am extending Klein's very intra-psychic model of loneliness by introducing some notions about the importance of the paternal object in strengthening the internal availability of the good feeding object, once words can be found for her absence. Much poetry seems to have this function, of finding words for the otherwise painfully ineffable longing for the primal object

I argue that there is another element that builds on the maternal capacity to tune in to the infant's unconscious (what Bion calls *reverie*) but which is more a (whole object) paternal function. It provides the patience and sustained interest necessary for the child's Self-reflective curiosity to bring unconscious feeling and desire out into the light of concepts and words (Bion's *alpha elements*), that can be worked on through transformational thought. I hold that the link with the **father** is often vital in helping the growing child to find a viable, different space – including this reflective space – away from the link already forged with the maternal object. This helps the child to focus attention on nascent 'dream-thoughts' that are not yet fully formed or *saturated* (Bion) as thinkable thoughts, potentially communicable as words. In that sense, the father is a kind of mental "midwife" (Plato) – symbolically, and often physically, putting the child on his lap and enquiring gently about his or her needs, thoughts and aspirations, so that they can be born into consciousness. This resembles Shakespeare's Yorrick playing with the child Hamlet – at least in Hamlet's memory – as a counterweight to the dangerous, revenge-driven narcissistically damaged King-Father. (I address the tragedy of the incestuous-fearing "defensively-indifferent" father in Chapter 14.)

Such a paternal (eliciting) reverie focuses more on invoking reverie in the growing child, as compared with maternal reverie, which helps the child to feel understood, through the concerned, attentive imaginativeness of the mother's mind, holding its fear of dying or disintegrating. Paternal reverie (which may often be initiated by non-male external figures) is involved with more actively seeking out (through sincere interest and curiosity) and eliciting inspirational and hopeful preconceptual thinking in the **child's** mind. But, impeding this is a draconian (if supposedly well-meaning) superego, continually confounding and discouraging any attempt in the infant mind to be sincere and honest about where its true passions lie. In addition to the (usual) emotional pains of excessive loneliness, such as boredom and a longing for the lost ideal maternal object (*Sehnsucht*), an underdevelopment of this internal paternal object may have marked effects on the child's capacity for initiatory thinking – most noticeable, but not exclusively isolated to, when the child is physically alone. This, in turn, heightens the aimless, depressed longing for the preverbal mother and the tiresome, paralyzing pangs of boredom.

Chapter 10, ***Two Vices and a film review*** consists of three sections:

A few odd thoughts about smokers and non-smokers.
Swearing as a proto-language.
Life and Death of a Planet in *Melancholia* – a film about Cynicism and Drugs.

Even apparent vices and addictions may have complex unconscious aims to enhance, or to assist in the emotional processing of unbearable thoughts and feelings in the struggle for the integration of distressed and regressive emotional states.

Chapter 11, ***The trees of knowledge in Thomas Hardy's The Woodlanders*** focusses on a particular array of characters to explore a complicated issue, which I think Bion may have avoided – the interrelationship between Eros and Curiosity, especially the urge to know another person. (Freud and particularly Klein found ways of talking about this relationship, but certainly emphasized the more aggressive and jealous aspects of curiosity.) ***The Woodlanders*** is a relatively unheralded novel of Hardy's – probably because the story seems so plain, on the surface – but I experience it as a profound and detailed meditation on the different ways that characters seek to **know** or to **avoid** knowing each other, often with lifelong, tragic consequences. I'd even suggest that the worst tragedies in the lives of all of Hardy's characters ("Jude" and "Tess" par excellence) are caused by failures in really getting to know the hearts and minds of others, particularly of their "well-beloved". I see "The Woodlanders" as Hardy's par excellence evocation of, and meditation on, the interplay between knowing and loving.

Distraction – as **both** an important **manic defence**, and yet also as a **consolation** when facing immense depressive or disintegrative states is the topic of Chapter 12. The chapter commences with a brief excerpt from the socially observant comedy *Curb Your Enthusiasm* which illustrates the hereto under-explored manic defence of distraction. The anti-hero (*schlemiel*) Larry David is in a therapy session, and cannot abide the perceived difference in comfortableness between the therapist's chair and the patient's, which (supposedly) distracts him away from what his (not very good) therapist is trying to tell him about his obsessional sexual frustration. The discussion is then extended to show that distraction is not only an important manic defence but that it may play a crucial role in obsessional states of mind (or mindlessness). In fact, before Melanie Klein's model of psychic "positions" was dovetailed into *paranoid-schizoid* and *depressive*, she had included "manic-obsessive" as a midpoint – before full depressive guilt was tolerated by the infant mind. A clinical example is presented, where (as with the Larry David snippet) the patient always seems to be focusing on the "wrong" things, in order to avoid thinking through the most important issues – but which would invoke the experience of guilt. This is the very essence of the manic-obsessive state – and yet, sometimes, it does offer the chance of some "light" for the developing infant mind, if not seen as purely distraction. Unconsciously, the distraction is often providing a new clue (link) in the mapping out of the conflict in its full extent.

Upon reflection, I can now see that the next chapter, appears to be a "twin" to the first chapter on *Strangers on a Train*. ***Narcissus Rejects* – Unbearable beauty and the urge to destroy, in *The Comfort of Strangers*** not only discusses a film, has a common ironic key-word but has several (disturbing) themes in common – particularly the dangers of trying to integrate the psychotic, murderous impulses through intimate (perverse) relationships with others, seemingly met by chance. But, this time I go into more detail about what is at the heart of the psychotic disturbance, which is very intricately traced in the film. The chapter illustrates the paradoxical experience of rejection, in the narcissistic frame. For the narcissist, all emotional attention is focused on one's complaints about being unfairly rejected – and yet the massive tendency to reject love, care, help and beauty remains entirely unconscious. An attempt is made to delineate the components that combine to produce an unconscious intolerance and sometimes hatred of beauty – a failure to "apprehend" it, as Meltzer and Harris Williams called it.

Chapter 14, **The wrecking** and **re-pairing of the internal couple** presents a model of the progress of the internal parents from a violent, **combined** object (Klein), with little differentiation, through to a *combining* harmonious and differentiated couple. Some clinical anecdotes and examples from Shakespeare's *Othello* and *The Winter's Tale* are discussed. There is also the hope of an enhanced understanding of Shakespeare, who, particularly in his later plays, beautifully illustrates the tragi-comical interleaving of life and death drives – as envy and jealousy are wrestled with. This wrestling produces two types of "thought" – *delusional* and *feeling*. But the intellectual-poetic force of his most challenging lines is still well ahead of our time and comprehension.

The Resilient Persistence of the Life-Death Instinct as the unceasing quest for Wholeness and Integration forms the concluding chapter of this book. "Whole-Object thinking" as a lifelong development is described – and this chapter is an attempt at just that. By developing Jung's concept of an evolving Self, and reconfiguring Bion's grid to supplant mathematical (calculus) integration with **feeling** integration, through emotional-symbolic abstraction, a growing poetic Self is seen to unfold. (Not unlike a giant space telescope unfolding to receive new data, of a more revealing, deeper nature.) This achieves combining melding of thinking and feeling, as a type of freed-up, exploratory thinking – often called intuitive, or inspirational – which most major "scientific-deductive" systems and artistic creations originated from. An example of the type of curious, reverent widening of abstraction might be William Blake's achievement in whole object thinking as applied to a Creator in his famous *Tyger* poem. At first we think that he is in awe of the tiger itself – then we are hit with the impactful realization that he is actually addressing his feelings about the one who created the tiger.

Finally, for the moment, I propose four basic templates for the interrelationship-entwinement of Life-Death drives. (I can see a passing resemblance to Bion's (1970) typology of container-contained relationships.) These are:

1 **Unified-Cooperative.** Promoting exploratory intercourse, creative artistic gestation.
2 **Sabotaging-Fearful.** When the drives become split apart, and fear each other as annihilatory enemies.
3 **Provocative-Catastrophic.** Where one drive pushes to the extreme, in a desperate attempt to get the other to take hold. This is very dangerous, but sometimes felt to be necessary, for the sake of integration. (Chapter 1 details the dynamics of this Life-Death struggle through *Strangers on a Train* and *Dr. Jekyll and Mr. Hyde*.)

4 **Transcendent-Spiritual**. The sighing attempt to reach emotional integration through revering the combining, creative – although often hijacked by a pious, cynical lack of faith in the strength of Life's reparative-renewing force. (The biblical story of *Job* is but one example.)

I don't claim any final knowledge of the unity and interplay of these two drives. But nor do I think that the Freud-Klein abstraction to these ultimate psychic forces that sculpt and fire the mind was trivial, senescent or ill-thought. In this book, I am merely pushing for us to further reflect on the nature of the interrelationship – and to explore the clinical usefulness of conceiving these instincts as unified in aim, even if they may at times be at war in the mind. But I do know that my understanding of all this is quite incomplete and beyond my full grasp. And that whilst the never-ending drive towards integration is relentlessly and brutally determined, whole-object abstraction towards the Godhead in the mind is ostensibly more a direction than a reachable destination. It must involve perpetual mourning for lost Selves, as well as for their external, fleshly, representatives as a cognitive-emotional development in the formation of an authentic identity. And, with each new person we are about to meet, we juggle an ardent desire to expand and change our Selves with the terror of unknown destruction or dismantling of what we have thus far attempted to hold onto, and all that we yet know. From that multiply charged flux of psychic transformations, defences and growth-reversing minus-formations (Bion), something (say an impulse, or phantasy or action, is always at the same time, something **else**. Instinctual aims are magnetic compass threads, but not the composite organic growing-forging fabric of the Self (in Jung's conception of a unified mind). And the mind's purpose is to guard the Self from stagnation or overwrought iron filings of psychotic disintegration and Self-alienation – the most painful form of all psychic loneliness.

In my view, we require a constantly revitalized perspective on the concept of primal instincts or drives – to perceive and respect their sacred commonality of purpose in the survival and promulgation of Earthly, mental, emotional and spiritual Life.

There is quite a lot at stake.

Acknowledgement

For those who brought me to Life.
  But, particularly:

   Aidan
   Linda
   Monty
   Bill
   Meg
   Margot
   Alison
   Gwen
   Cassie
   Jo Ann
   Rori
   Jodie
   Jim
   Don
   And Three Roses …

Chapter 1

Inoculative identification in Alfred Hitchcock's *Strangers on a Train*

Inoculate: *To propagate. Join or unite by insertion. To impregnate with the virus or germs of a disease for the purpose of inducing a milder form of the disease and thus rendering the subject immune.* (OED)

I am going to explore the possibility that the biomedical model of inoculation might provide a useful way of understanding some aspects of personality integration, and also its failure in the retreat of disintegrative destructive narcissism.

The importance of the concept of "taming" (*Bändigung*) as part of one's psychological development runs as a discontinuous but firm thread through Freud's work. This thread first appears in his "Project" of 1895. In a speculative description of emotional memory decay which bears close resemblance to what will become the concept of repression, Freud suggests that:

> In the end, then, it becomes possible to cathect the memory of the pain in such a way that it cannot exhibit any backward flow and can release only minimal unpleasure. It is now **tamed**, and by a thought-facilitation strong enough to exercise a permanent effect and to produce an inhibiting action once more at every later repetition of the memory. The pathway leading to the release of unpleasure will then, owing to disuse, gradually increase its resistance: for facilitations are subject to gradual decay (forgetting). Only after this is the memory a **tamed** memory like any other.
>
> (Freud, 1895, p. 382, my emphasis)

Then, in a letter to Fliess of 1897:

> ... If in this way we see that the unconscious never overcomes the existence of the conscious, then, too, we lose our expectation that in treatment the opposite will happen, to the extent of the unconscious being completely **tamed** by the conscious.
>
> (Freud, 1897, p. 260, my emphasis)

And a year later, in *The Economic Problem of Masochism* (1924)

> The libido has the task of making the **destroying instinct innocuous**, and it fulfils the task by diverting that instinct to a great extent outwards-soon with the help of a special organic system, the muscular apparatus-towards objects in the external world. The instinct is then called the destructive instinct, the instinct for mastery, or the will to power. A portion of the instinct is placed directly in the service of the sexual function, where it has an important part to play. This is sadism proper. Another portion does not share in this transposition outwards; it remains inside the organism and, with the help of the accompanying sexual excitation … (it) becomes libidinally bound there. It is in this portion that we have to recognise the original, erotogenic masochism.
>
> We are without any physiological understanding of the ways and means by which this taming of the death-instinct by the libido may be effected. So far as the psychoanalytic field of ideas is concerned, we can only assume that a very extensive fusion and amalgamation, in varying proportions, of the two classes on instincts take place, so **that we never have to deal with pure life instincts or pure death instincts but only with mixtures of them in different amounts**. Corresponding to a fusion of instincts of this kind, there may, as a result of certain influences, be a **de**fusion of them. How large the portions of the death instincts are which **refuse to be tamed** in this way by being bound to admixtures of libido we cannot at present guess.
>
> (Freud, 1924, pp. 163–164, my emphasis)

Still incomplete, but still important, the thread emerges again in 1937 with this clarification of psychoanalytic aims in *Analysis Terminable and Interminable*:

> … To avoid misunderstanding it is not unnecessary, perhaps, to explain more exactly what is meant by 'permanently disposing of an instinctual demand'. Certainly not 'causing the demand to disappear so that nothing more is ever heard from it again'. This is in general impossible, nor is it at all to be desired. No, we mean something else, something which may be roughly described as **'taming' of the instinct**. That is to say, the instinct is brought completely into the harmony of the ego, becomes accessible to all the influences of the other trends in the ego and no longer seeks to go its independent way to satisfaction. If we are asked by what methods and means this result is achieved, it is not easy to find an answer.
>
> (Freud, 1937, pp. 224–225)

However, over the ensuing twenty years an answer was forged by Melanie Klein with her concept of the "depressive position," later bulwarked by the idea of gratitude, ameliorating, and stimulated by, unconscious envy – the linchpin of the death instinct. The "answer" to Freud's question about the "mechanics" of taming was, according to Klein, far removed from a mechanical process, but was rooted in the development of emotional concern and love for the whole mother in the face of ruthless demands for instinctual gratification from her parts and compartments, and envious attacks on her creative and aesthetic integrity. However, Klein's 1958 "postlude" to "Envy and Gratitude," entitled "On the Development of Mental

Functioning," contains the sobering idea that there are some parts of the self which are felt to be so dangerous and destructive that the risk of "binding" them creatively with a "life instinct" cannot be taken by the ego for fear of psychotic disintegration. But to this, she adds:

> I attribute to the ego from the beginning of life a need and capacity not only to split but also to integrate itself ... Though the rejected aspects of the self and of internalised objects contribute to instability, they are also the source of inspiration in artistic productions and in various intellectual activities.
>
> (p. 245, my emphasis)

Since then, through the work of Bion (1963), Meltzer (1968), Rosenfeld (1971), Steiner (1987), Gold (1985) and Sohn (1985), further elaboration of the "parts of the self" resistant to "taming" (the depressive position) has been possible, with a resultant strengthening of therapeutic leverage in previously "hopeless" cases, such as addictions and perversions, where destructive narcissism had taken over the organizational life of the psyche and had become a kind of living organism on its own. In Freud's 1937 terms, going its "independent way to satisfaction," or to use Gold's (1985) Frankenstein analogy, becoming a "monster." This valuable work on the resistance and resilience to "taming," on the perseverance of destructive narcissism, has allowed us to penetrate more and more deeply into the psychotically destructive, "untamed" area of all patients – and yet there is, I feel, still a sense in which Freud's question remains unanswered. Although it seems clear that the emotional instigation for growth and constructiveness lies in the transformation of the depressive position, we are still far from clear about just how it is that we are able to gradually integrate and "harmonise" our untamed destructiveness. How is it that some people, through analysis or life, push for a heightened intensity of contact with their unconscious destructiveness in the hope and intention of taming it, for life? In other words, what is the healthy nature of the process which urges us to take the sometimes substantial risk of a potentially dangerous close contact and exploration of our destructive narcissism for the benefit of greater integrity?

I am going to suggest that the concept of inoculation might provide a suitable metaphor for an approach to this question.

As mentioned above, the word inoculate means to propagate to join, or unite by insertion – to impregnate with the virus or germs of a disease for the purpose of inducing a milder form of the disease and rendering the subject immune. David Lonie (1990) reminds us that medical science has provided a much more sophisticated model of how an organism protects itself from potentially lethal and overwhelming contact with the external environment (given that some osmotic interchange is vital) than Freud's 1895 notion of a *Stimulus Barrier*.

> At birth, the infant has a capacity to differentiate self from not-self. Taking in, or invasion of not-self elements leads to both defences against those elements, an acquired immune response, and an internal representation of what has been

taken in, an anti-idiotype network. The primitive ability to differentiate self from not-self is a protective screen which is functional and not rigid in the sense that it is not impermeable totally, but allows a partial interchange between the inner and the outer world. This partial interchange allows and facilitates the development of an internal representation of the external world. In order for it to become a more effective barrier, it needs some invasion from the outside – this allows the elements of the cellular or the psychic organism which recognise the outside stimuli to proliferate in such a way that the outside is recognised more effectively.

(p. 11)

Lonie suggests that one function of the immune system may be "to serve as a sensory organ," sensing stimuli that are not recognized by the central and peripheral nervous systems. This would be effected by the anti-idiotype network.

Anti-idiotypes are a record of the characteristic structure of the invading substance, so that there is not only a memory bank of cells which recognise the invading substance, antibodies to the antigen, but also a network of cells which carry the characteristics of the antigen. One way of putting this would be to say that there is both a negative model of the antigen, that is the antibody network, but also a model of the antigen itself, so that there is in the internal world a model of the external world, an internal object representation. Obviously, as we are prone to infection, the system cannot cope with a major invasion of its defences. However, at times the system goes wrong for other reasons - that is, that it fails in its differentiation of self from not-self or its response to this difference.

(p. 9)

What might in the right doses enable the immune system to build up a very effective recognition system preventing illness, in the wrong doses overwhelms the system ...

(p. 11)

I will now give two brief clinical fragments which, I think, bear some resemblance, psychologically, to this model of the immune response. This will be augmented by a more detailed example which draws on Alfred Hitchcock's film *Strangers on a Train*. I will be attempting to elucidate a very complex form of projective identification (Klein, 1946) which, as an abbreviation, I will call "inoculative identification". The final section of this chapter will raise the issue of how necessary and growthful this type of identificatory process may be, as weighed against its more dangerous and pathological potential.

Case 1

This patient had been living with his parents into his mid-thirties and complained of chronic lethargy and inability to realize any of his own projects and ambitions.

Every day-to-day task loomed as an impossible burden and wherever possible he would "arrange" (most strenuously) for others to make efforts on his behalf. This corresponded with an internal and external parasitic relationship with his mother who seemed quite happy for it to be so.

In stark contrast to his seemingly passive compliance to all requests made of him – although his compliance was always sabotaged by "mucking it up" – it was possible to detect the presence of a ruthless gang of bullies in his internal world, similar to those described by Rosenfeld (1971) and Meltzer (1968). It appeared that these bullies were the driving force behind his parasitic demands on the mother, and they coloured his character with a passive-aggressive timidity that was apparently infuriating to others, including his therapist. I will not go into details here about the more exact nature of the internal bullying because what I want to show is how he made unconscious moves to deal with (inoculate himself against) their attacking by "arranging" for external bullies to fight against – as if he needed an internal image of these external bullies in order to rally some courage. In fact, while walking alone along a dark alley one night he was attacked by some bullies, but the following months saw a dramatic change in his character. Although clearly under great duress, he mustered all his courage – the persecutory fear was enormous – for the court case. The gang, also responsible for attacks on others, had been apprehended, but to "make himself and the community less prone to such attacks in future" he was going to have to testify in court, in spite of the danger that the bullies might more seriously harm him.

I present this fragment here not to explore the nature of his destructive narcissism (which included vicious bullying attacks on the creative and helpful efforts of not only those upon whom he was dependent but also his own capacities to do what he could for himself), but to look at the manner in which he went about confronting it. It was as if he needed the "invasion from the outside" to get a recognizable image of dangerous, destructive bullying that was to be eventually confronted and inoculated against in his internal world. In this sense he was not just "using" the external bullies in order to deny his own destructiveness through projective identification, but was also attempting to get a recognizable image of his own destructiveness in a "dosage" that he could comprehend and fight.

Case 2

This cherubical young man in his mid-twenties sought help for his depression after he recognized a recurring pattern of masochistic humiliation and disappointment in a series of failed homosexual relationships. His "pathetic" alcoholic father had been "thrown out of the home" when he was six, and he had been nursing (he is in fact a nurse) a longstanding grudge and disappointment towards his mother for as long as he could remember.

> "She never listens to me, she always criticises me, she gives things to my sister and brother but not me, she never shows any interest in me whatsoever except to show me off to her friends, she cannot see anything good in me at all."

The convolutions of his complex identifications and projective identifications with both parents were traced painfully but productively for some years and it became very clear that his masochistic homosexual relationships had their basis in a turning away from the mother as the object of dependency. This was partly out of envy, and partly out of a healthy wish to avoid being the receptacle for her damaging projections, but above all else, to avoid the experience of rage towards her so fierce that he feared he would destroy her. But, to his dismay, the masochistic relationships just seemed to repeat the same tortuous sadomasochistic flavour of that with his mother. Despite the increasing clarity of this dilemma in the transference, we both seemed to know that there was something not quite bound within its circumference of understanding, and we got bogged down in an emotionally repetitive impasse, which was something like, "You, with your interpretations, are just like my mother trying to tell me what I should be like telling me that if I wasn't so angry and immature I'd be in a relationship with a woman." This was a particularly painful stalemate for the patient because consciously he did not view my help as being critical or dogmatic at all. In fact, he expressed the opposite and often told me that he felt relieved by my understanding of him and my lack of criticalness towards him.

One session, after telling me that he had just commenced a hopeful and apparently less sadomasochistic relationship with a man who really seemed to care about him (following two sessions where we gained a brief insight into the extent of his murderous phantasies towards his mother) he reported the following dream: He was in a room with me-it seemed like a hospital room – and I was telling him, in an uncritical but concerned tone, that he was a "homopath." On second thought, maybe I had said that he was a "homeopath." He felt some disappointment about this, but also some relief that at last I had been able to tell him what was "bugging" him. Then he saw a woman on the other side of the room and felt that he'd better decipher the difference between homopath and homeopath before she came any closer. A used syringe lay on the floor, and he thought that it was very dangerous to be injected these days because of viral threats.

His association with the word "homopath" was that it reminded him of a psychopath or psychopathic killer, and it upset him greatly in the dream when I diagnosed that as his problem. This could be traced to the previous sessions where we had been looking at his murderous wishes towards his mother and his sister. But when, in the dream, he thought that I had said he was a homeopath, this seemed to leave him with a feeling that I had a fuller, more sympathetic grasp of his struggles, although there was some concern that I might be having a dig at his homosexuality. His associations with the word "homeopath" were that they treated toxicity in sick people by giving them remedies which were very small doses of the sickness. (He seemed quite anxious to forget about the woman and the syringe.) I was able to make an interpretation along the lines that perhaps there was a concern that I was only seeing the defensiveness in his masochistic relations with men and his avoidance of women – that perhaps homosexuality was a way of dosing himself with manageable portions of his rage and disappointment so that he might eventually be capable of handling it where it was most strongly aroused and most capable of making him sick. Somewhat to my surprise, he began crying, his voice softened, and a tic in the musculature of his jaw disappeared as he told me that now, for the first time, he felt really understood. I do think that there was more to this than simple relief that I had seen something positive to balance the murderous feelings. It seemed that we had acknowledged some constructive, life-seeking "homeopath" in his internal world. Of course, the dangerous risk that this sort of immunization posed to his relationships and his mental health may have been referred to by the presence of the syringe. Interestingly, he was not only concerned about getting AIDS from it, probably a reference to his fear and hatred of his need for help (aid) from the internal parent-therapist, but also referring to a possible deathly breakdown of his immune system.

Strangers on a Train

There is a way of viewing Alfred Hitchcock's film *Strangers on a Train* which will help me to explore the issues raised above in a little more detail, with very compact material. I will give a brief account of the storyline as I proceed, but because of the complexity of cross-identification that takes place between all the characters in the film – a fact constantly marked out by Hitchcock's numerous verbal and visual usage of the concept of doubles, crossings and double-crossings –, I will simplify my account by making the "hero," Guy, the main focus of our attention. Guy seems at first to be a "nice enough Guy." But before long we are shown some features, or lack of, in his character – largely passivity and entitlement. The villainous Bruno is not exactly his nemesis, but these features make Guy an extremely vulnerable target for Bruno's murderous intrusiveness.

They meet by bumping feet on a train and Bruno recognizes Guy as a fairly successful tennis star. But what begins as polite flattery from Bruno, egged on by Guy's naivety and vulnerability, becomes his invitation to manipulate Guy into a partnership which aims to murder Guy's estranged wife (yet to be divorced and pregnant to another man) and Bruno's hated father. Bruno appears to hate his father because he threatens Bruno's psychotically symbiotic relationship with his mother, and because he wants to pressure him into "working for a living." At first we are made to feel that Guy is very innocent when Bruno questions and gibes his way into the inner sanctum of his private life, especially Guy's intention to marry the respectable and well to do Senator's daughter, Anne, when he has divorced his wife, Miriam. But as the conversation proceeds we are squirming less at Bruno's relentless questioning, and more at Guy's lack of resistance to the onslaught.

When Bruno "shows his cards" and frankly admits to wanting to swap murders with Guy – he'll murder Miriam if Guy will murder his father – Guy replies that murder is against the law. Now this suggests that Guy really doesn't have any moral stance against murder, just a "healthy" respect for law and order. A bit later, after a "double" whiskey, Guy says to Bruno: "Sure, I like your theory, it's okay." He does say not say "no." And to seal the unconscious collusion, Guy leaves his lighter behind in Bruno's possession. But even without the lighter Bruno has already invaded Guy's private world sufficiently to be able to implicate him in Miriam's undoing. Bruno does murder Miriam and then tries to hold Guy to his unconscious word. That is, to murder Bruno's father. The whole psychological grip of the movie will rest on our uncertainty about whether Guy would go that far, or rather, would let himself be that taken over by the Bruno part of himself. But before we get to that, we are shown some more of Guy's character or lack of it. Guy is unimpassioned, until his "cross" with Bruno. Things seem to happen to him. He lacks responsibility for himself and although he might be capable of love, he seems not to know about the seriousness of threats to his loving, particularly in the form of Bruno-like aspects of his own personality. For example, it is hinted that one aspect of his attraction to Anne might be his wish to "use" her in a parasitic sort of way for status, wealth and ambition. (He wants to be a politician.) But he doesn't think about these matters. In fact, he even leaves it up to Anne to express the loving feelings, and there is also a hint that he left it up to Miriam to express the more problematic feelings of sexuality and jealousy and envy. His innocence gradually becomes neglect and destructive naivety, and his "niceness" gradually betrays a man who lacks initiative, and who cannot harness his aggressiveness for constructive purposes, and to protect the one he loves. It is said of his tennis playing, that he plays "well within himself." He lacks bite when it is appropriate, or even vital. Guy is, therefore, vulnerable to intrusive identifications, and he is passive and naive in the face of external danger and aggressiveness.

But the clear presence of Bruno (the external invasion) in his internal world now gives some impetus for change in Guy. Now things are beginning to matter. He has to choose between life and death and he slowly begins to care about his fate. His tennis and expressiveness to Anne take on a passion and immediacy that were sadly lacking, and interestingly, as a counterbalance to his increasing determination to thwart Bruno, Bruno becomes clumsy and uncertain. Guy is no longer a willing "host." So Guy is able to resist the lure of murder when he stalks his way into the bedroom of Bruno's father, and there is a breathtaking scene on the stairway to this bedroom where Guy has to confront the large family dog. But the dog might also stand for Guy's increasing discriminatory prowess with this problem.

In the climactic scene, at a carnival, Guy and Bruno have to physically grapple with each other on a merry-go-round before Bruno is killed in the struggle. During this scene, the theme of the naive/brave boy struggling with his murderous baby feelings is reinforced. (The music of the merry-go-round is "Baby Face," and a young boy is caught up in the action and endangered by it. An older man risks his life in order to halt the merry-go-round, which is now spinning out of control.) So by the end of the film Guy has developed the beginnings of courage and a capacity to care about himself and his beloved. This means relinquishing his innocence about such feelings as murderous hatred towards the father, intrusive and murderous desires towards the mother capable of pregnancy, and intrusively jealous wishes to destroy the parental couple. In short, all the feelings that he is "forced" to confront in the hyper-real form of Bruno.

The little tag in the epilogue, where Guy is on a train with Anne and now so supersensitive to intrusion or invasion from another Bruno threat that he shifts carriages (with Anne) after an innocent question about his identity from a priest, suggests that Hitchcock is well aware of the "greenness" of Guy's mental transformation. He will see a Bruno in everyone for a while – the day-to-day working through lies ahead.

Discussion

So much has to be excluded from this brief depiction of a complex, multi-faceted film, that I am not able to discuss here the other characters in more detail. (Bruno warrants a case conference of his own.) But I want to discuss here the sometimes very fine line between the push for integration and the succumbing to destructive narcissism.

It could be said that Guy has achieved nothing more by the end of the film than a manic flight from his own destructiveness, that the final evasion of the curious priest is his attempt to deny, and flee from, his superego-father, and that he has "successfully" dis-identified with the projection of his own destructiveness into the now-killed Bruno.

I feel that there is a certain amount of truth in this assessment, and yet I believe that it completely overlooks the emotional and poetic tone of the film. Guy has a conversation with a Maths Professor, on yet another train, where the Professor asks Guy if he understands **integration**. Guy answers that he does, and I think that he is correct, at least unconsciously. He does know that he cannot easily be rid of Bruno and he does sense that he is going to have to change. (He has hinted earlier that one day he wants to make the transition from tennis to politics.) In a wider perspective, Guy does begin to feel passion and to take a more active responsibility for his life and his relationships. But we can see just how sharp that knife-edge between development and destructive narcissism is when we consider for a moment the fate of that other Guy, the Guy in Patricia Highsmith's (1953) novel upon which Hitchcock based, with great difficulty via Raymond Chandler's screenplay, his film version. The Guy in the novel is totally taken over by Bruno's influence and does in fact kill Bruno's father. His mental decline, including unbearable guilt and total cross-identification with Bruno, is lucidly depicted in Highsmith's chilling novel. That account seems more like the Guy who is trying to rid himself of responsibility for destructive feelings and who is terrified of retaliatory superego detectives and policemen.

But, I do not believe that Hitchcock was looking for an "easy way out" for his Guy. That does not tally with the psychological depictions in his other cinematic achievements. In my view he is exploring the necessity of Guy's personality coming to grips with Bruno in order to become integrated, and capable of coupling in a loving relationship. (So many Hitchcock films deal with a character on the verge of making an emotional commitment, usually marriage, and their life-death struggles with a murderous figure.)

So I am suggesting that in spite of the great danger that destructive narcissism – including murderous rage towards the object of dependency – might take hold, there is nonetheless an unconscious urge to confront these feelings or parts of the self. Patricia Highsmith's Guy wants "... to immerse himself in ugly, uncomfortable undignified living so that he gained new power to fight it in his work ..." But this can only be done if the "enemy" (invasion) can be recognized, the quicker the better. To recall Lonie's description again – we need some invasion from the outside to allow the elements of our psychic organism which recognize the outside stimuli to proliferate in such a way that the outside is recognized more effectively.

I think that this holds true even when the danger to life springs from internal sources and not just external ones. This might have something in common with Bion's (1963) idea of pre-conceptions having to be made recognizable through alpha processing which produces concepts. It is only when (Hitchcock's) Guy sees what Bruno is capable of, that is, when he recognizes what human beings, including himself, are capable of feeling, that he begins to understand integration and is moved to take action to protect himself and the internal couple. At the conclusion, we might say that the "boy" Guy saved from the Bruno in himself and is inoculated against blindness to his own capacity for destruction. Now it can be readily, perhaps too readily at first, recognized for what it is – a threat to life.

His love for Anne, and his wish for life in general, take on the immediacy and passion of a doomed invalid now miraculously offered a new lease of life. He is no longer indifferent or naive about the endangering of his good objects.

It seems that this is a necessary part of the resolution of the Oedipus Complex – that we must overcome our destructive jealousy, envy and murderous intrusiveness towards the internal parental couple before we are able to protect our own coupling. Otherwise, we are doomed to feeling and being the perpetually resentful outsider, like Bruno, who remains unrepentant to the last, an apt personification of Freud's idea about the portions of "death **instinct which refuse to be tamed** by admixtures of libido," or Meltzer's (1967) "... schizophrenic part which, if mental health is to be maintained, must be kept split-off and projected, since it is in its very nature impossible of integration with other parts of the personality" (p. 49). In the following chapters, I will link this to a "mental remnant" of the foetus. (Bruno hates the idea of earning his own living.)

Inoculative identification is positive and growth-inducing when it "co-opts" bad (anti-life) external objects in order to further the integration of loving and hateful feelings. But the process requires a kind of working through and bulwarking against the internal couple destructor through a type of protectively identified relationship with an external figure who represents that destructor, and yet who might be challenged or tackled or tamed or destroyed **if one's personality is capable of the steps required**.

Nothing less than unflinching courage, determination and fearlessness in the face of tyrannical threat will do, although these qualities are impossible without the full co-operation and benevolence of one's "good objects." (Depicted in the film as Anne, her sister and her father, who combine qualities of wit, thoughtfulness, trust, patience, boldness, ingenuity, and a wry sense of humour against the humourless, unimaginative and impatient Bruno.) It is therefore not difficult to see the process is fraught with the danger of being "hijacked" for the purposes of a destructively organized narcissistic takeover of the mind. Then, as with physiological inoculation, the infection may take hold and prove lethal, as it does with Highsmith's version of Guy.

If this is correct, then as "physicians of the psyche" we are perhaps both much more and much less vulnerable than we imagine. It also helps us to respect the level of fear that our patients must face when engaging in the psychoanalytical process, and the degree of courage and the wish to recover. Without such respect, our patients would probably never feel that we really know what they are talking about. I think that Donald Meltzer (1986) has put his views exceptionally clearly when, speculating about the danger and disapproval that the thinking, growing part of the mind faces from the non-thinking (Basic Assumption) "organization," he wonders whether the thinking parts might

> ... find that the privilege of immunological products had been cancelled and that everyday processes of defence against bodily enemies, external ones like bacteria, for instance, or internal enemies like primitive cell mutations, no longer operated. It would be similar to one's electricity or water being cut off. The house would soon become uninhabitable unless archaic modes of coping could be revived. But where would one find a well or n unpolluted river. Whose wood would one scavenge by hook or by crook?
>
> (p. 39)

I have concluded that growth through inoculative identification is fraught with risk, but perhaps vitally necessary where the struggle between love and hate is particularly torrid, or where parents are absent or unavailable, or where the "artistic" struggle with life pushes for deeper and deeper levels of integration of the personality. It may be that the consequence of not taking up this struggle is a personality which may be just a little too sane and "normal," and who never descends into the ties and affairs and passions of those who risk intimacy. This kind of constrained character remains so frightened of his or her megalomaniacal impulses ruling in a totally "untamed" manner that the price paid, of reduced intimacy and imaginative, mystical thinking, seems insignificant. (But imagine the Richard of Melanie Klein's "Narrative of a child analysis" (1961) without his struggle with the Hitler in himself.)

Two literary examples of this sort of well-intentioned but haughty character might be Lockwood from *Wuthering Heights (1905)*, and Utterson from *Dr. Jekyll and Mr. Hyde (1963)*.

Utterson really is as central to the story as Jekyll/Hyde, is.

> ... austere with himself; drank gin when he was alone, to mortify a taste for vintages; and though he enjoyed the theatre, had not crossed the doors of one for twenty years. But he had an approved tolerance for others; sometimes wondering, almost with envy, at the high pressure of spirits involved in their misdeeds; and in any extremity inclined to help rather than to reprove. 'I incline to Cain's heresy', he used to say quaintly: 'I let my brother go to the devil in his own way.'

In this character, it was frequently his fortune to be the last reputable acquaintance and the last good influence in the lives of downgoing men.

(p. 2)

It is as if Emily Bronte and Robert Louis Stevenson had stripped back the "comfortable" veneer of Lockwood and Utterson and said to them: "If you want your involvement with people to be really alive and passionate then you will have to deal with the Heathcliff and Hyde feelings that such involvement engenders, and which you are disavowing in yourself."

This is the challenge that Guy, and all of us, must face, but never completely answer.

References

Bion, W. R. (1963). *Elements of Psychoanalysis*. London: Tavistock.
Bronte, E. (1905). *Wuthering Heights*. London and Glasgow: Collins.
Freud, S. (1895). 'Project for a scientific psychology', SE 3. London: Hogarth Press.
———. (1897). 'Letter to Fliess' (September 21), SE 1.
———. (1924). 'The economic problem of masochism', SE 19.
———. (1937). 'Analysis terminable and interminable', SE 23.
Gold, S. (1985). Frankenstein and other monsters: An examination of the concepts of destructive narcissism, and perverse relationships between parts of the self as seen in the gothic novel. *Int. Rev. Psycho-Anal.*, 12: 101–108.
Highsmith, P. (1953). *Strangers on a Train*. Harmondsworth: Penguin.
Hitchcock, A. (1956). *Strangers on a Train*. Screen Gems Films.
Klein, M. (1946). Notes on some Schizoid mechanisms. In *Envy and Gratitude and Other Works* (1975). Ed. Money-Kyrle, R. New York: Dell. pp. 244–259.
———. (1961). Narrative of a child analysis. In *Envy and Gratitude and Other Works* (1975). Ed. Money-Kyrle, R. New York: Dell. pp. 361–453.
———. (1958). On the development of mental functioning. In *Envy and Gratitude and Other Works* (1975). Ed. Money-Kyrle, R. New York: Dell. pp. 128–142.
Lonie, D. (1990). 'The stimulus barrier: A matter of interpretation'. Paper given at the Psychotherapy Association of Australia Annual Meeting, Tasmania.
Meltzer, D. (1967). *The Psycho-analytical Process*. Perthshire: Clunie Press.
———. (1968). Terror, persecution and dread. *Int. J. Psycho-Anal.*, 49: 396–400.
———. (1986). *Studies in Extended Metapsychology*. Perthshire: Clunie Press.
Rosenfeld, H. (1971). A clinical approach to the psychanalytic theory of the life and death instincts: An investigation into the aggressive aspects of narcissism. *Int. J. Psycho-Anal.*, 52: 169–178.
Sohn, L. (1985). Narcissistic organization, projective identification and the formation of the Identificate. *Int. J. Psycho-Anal.*, 66: 201–214.
Steiner, J. (1987). The interplay between pathological organizations and the paranoid-schizoid and depressive position. *Int. J. Psycho-Anal.*, 68: 69–80.
Stevenson, R. L. (1886). *Dr. Jekyll and Mr. Hyde* (1963). London: Scholastic Books.

Chapter 2

Self-envy, the womb and the nature of goodness – a reappraisal of the death instinct

Both Freud and Klein finally came to identify the instinctual dualism underlying the conflicts in human emotional life as that of life and death instincts. One aim of this brief chapter is to further explore and clarify the dynamics of this "dualism."

Norman Brown (1959) notes that Freud postulated a constant irreconcilable conflict between the life instinct, which seeks to preserve and enrich life, and the death instinct which seeks to return life to the peace and inactivity of death. He thought that psychoanalysts after Freud who did not accept the life and death duality were not able to produce any alternative. "They content themselves with rejecting the death instinct, and thus drift into instinctual monism, as Jung did, or into that general theoretical scepticism or indifference which is so congenial to the practitioner-technician" (p. 81). Brown notes that Freud's essay "Analysis terminable and interminable," which analyses the factors preventing complete cure, contains the suggestion that the unconscious resistance to cure, a kind of psychical entropy, is grounded in (his hypothesis of) the eternal and irreconcilable struggle of life and death in the very organism, producing in every human being a spontaneous tendency to conflict.

Freud suggested that the death instinct had three major characteristics. First, the aim of achieving inactivity, passivity or sleep; second, the compulsion to repeat; and third, the primary masochistic tendency, which could be projected outwards in the form of aggression (Brown, 1959, p. 88).

In his later clinical writings Freud implied that the anxiety of separation (from the mother's womb and/or breasts) was the prototype of repression and neuroses, or as Brown puts it is "a lifelong fixation to the infantile pattern of dependence on other people" (p. 109).

In my view, the above characteristics of the death instinct may be subsumed under the "phantasy conglomeration" of wanting to re-enter mother's body forever and return to a state of sleep in her womb, thereby indirectly opposing or attaching (masochistically) an achieved or potential individuality, autonomy or sense of separateness. Although it seemed as if Freud was approaching recognition of the importance of this phantasy as the "core" of the death instinct, there is some evidence which suggests that he may have a "blind spot" to it.

One such piece of evidence is well known and has to do with the way he emphasized envy of the *male* genitals and de-emphasized or ignore the possibility of such feeling about *mother's* body (a bias which has now been well corrected due to the work of Karen Horney and Melanie Klein). But the examples I will give here have to do with the way Freud interpreted certain dreams.

It seems to me that Freud was well aware of the references to, and phantasies about the womb in dreams, but that he rather quickly tended to assume that these were what he called "birth dreams".

A large number of dreams, often accompanied by anxiety, having as their content such subjects as passing through narrow spaces or being in water are based upon fantasies of intra-uterine life, of existence in the womb and of the act of birth (1900, p. 399).

And here is a pretty water dream, dreamt by a woman patient, which served a special purpose in the treatment. At her summer holiday resort, by the lake of –, she dived into the dark water just where the pale moon was mirrored in it. Dreams like this one are birth dreams. Their interpretation is reached by *reversing* the event reported in the manifest dream; thus, instead of "diving into the water," we have "coming out of the water," i.e. being born. We can discover the locality from which a child is born by calling to mind the slang used in the word "*lune*" in French [viz. "bottom'"]. The pale moon was thus the white bottom which children are quick to guess that they come out of. What was the meaning of the patient's wishing to be born at her summer holiday resort? I asked her and she replied without hesitation: "Isn't it just as though I had been reborn through the treatment?" Thus the dream was an invitation to me to continue treating her at the holiday resort – that is, to visit her there. Perhaps there was a very timid hint in it, too, of the patient's wish to become a mother herself (p. 400, my italics).

Freud did not allow for the possibility that the dream contains a wish to dive into the womb (or in the transference *his* womb). A further example:

'In dreams as in mythology, the delivery of the child from the uterine waters is commonly presented by *distortion* as the entry of the child *into* water …' (p. 401, my italics). Freud goes on to give other examples, both from his own clinical experience and those of his colleagues, all of which show that he was reluctant to acknowledge the desire to enter the womb, as a possible phantasy wish in *itself*.

Melanie Klein wanted to emphasize the aggressive, destructive components of emotional life, and thereby expanded Freud's use of the term "death instinct," According to her, the death instinct was represented through phantasies of biting, tearing, and intruding into mother's body, particularly at times of frustration and/or into the absence of mother's body. However, Klein was eventually able to jettison a simple frustration-aggression model by attributing to the death instinct the characteristic of envy. This enabled her to account for the presence of such phantasies even when the mother was present and gratifying.

Although Klein wished to expand the content of Freud's conception of the death instinct, she still agreed with its necessity as a concept and underlined that "if Freud's conception of the two instincts is taken to its ultimate conclusion the interaction of the life and death instincts will be seen to govern the whole of mental life" (1958, p. 245).

Although Klein certainly does give importance to the phantasy of entering mother's womb, this is done in a particular context. More specifically, the death instinct is activated by particular events, which may be broadly divided into:

a Frustration away from the breast (separation), and
b Frustration at the breast (envy).

Without fully detailing Klein's theory here, it may be said that the infant responds to these frustrations with wishes to attack, control, and become the breast. However, Klein seems to juxtapose such phantasies (of projective identification) with a phantasy of intruding into mother's *womb* and attacking or eating rival babies which mother is thought to be producing. The purpose of this phantasy, although Klein did not emphasize it so much, seemed to be secure an exclusive state of being held in mother's womb. Klein did not really imply that such a wish may be present in *itself* as a *constant opposition* to the attainment of independence and separation from the mother,[1] (depressive position), but she did stress the anxiety caused to the growing ego (and therefore "life instinct") by the frequent activation of the "attaching" aspects of the phantasies. Her idea seems to be that the ego fears annihilation because of the retaliation of the internal and external objects, which, via projective phantasy, are imbued with these motives and intents.

My view is that the growing ego may fear these phantasies and wishes in themselves. More specifically, the infant "feels that" it cannot sleep inside mother's body and, at the same time become separate, independent and evolve its own ego. In order to expand this point of view, I will briefly describe some observations and conclusions drawn by Forrer (1969), in his book *Weaning and Human Development*.

Forrer takes the view that when the infant sucks on the breast during the pre-weaning period it enters into an involuntary psychological state of merging with, or dissolving into the mother and "losing itself."

> The contrast between the infant's capability of relating to objects outside himself with his utter abandonment of outside objects as he merges during the act of suckling becomes even more striking with the passage of time. At about the age of 1 month until the age of about 3 months one observes the emergence of a primitive ego, which, as maturation proceeds, becomes progressively more clearly-defined. The weaning period proper, has its beginnings during the time of early ego differentiation. It is the weaning process which is the principal subject of interest. This term has been used to indicate that the weaning of an infant is a complex time-consuming process rather than a parent-determined change of diet. Just prior to the weaning process the infant merged each time he suckled unaware of having undergone the experience of losing himself. The ego mechanism by which the awareness or merging can be realized coincides in its development with the commencement of the weaning process.

The merging, which up to the initiation of the weaning process had no meaning or particular significance to the infant, begins to confront an ego which increasingly appreciates its own expanding capacity to mediate between the demands from various sources made upon it. The infant now comes to perceive what before had gone unnoticed, namely, that when he merges during the act of suckling his ego boundaries crumble and cease to exist.

Examining the situation from the infant's viewpoint one can well imagine that it appears to him that each time he merges he ceases to exist, but the merging is not renounced on account of this impression. There is no intellect yet present to deal with what I believe to be an increasing concern and unavoidable anxiety-producing circumstance. Each time the infant nurses he merges and in so doing his barely-established ego boundaries dissolve ... this phenomenon of merging is not one of choice, is not a sometime thing. It is an omnipresent and obligate reaction which is part and parcel of the complex act of sucking.

(pp. 41–42)

Forrer goes on describe what he calls a transitional reaction *en route* to completion of the weaning process. He calls this reaction the state of "raptus" which gradually replaces merging. Raptus is characterized by "an open-eyed, fixed, unperceiving gaze, hypnotically fixed upon an object, often the mother's face" (p. 297). According to Forrer the weaning process is completed (psychologically) when the ego has developed enough to be able to relinquish "raptus' (as a remnant of the state of merging) and therefore is able to stay with its ego during feeding. I do not think that it is too far-fetched to suggest that feeding at the breast for the pre-weaned infant, through the processes of merging an/or raptus is a kind of replication, psychologically, of existence, or (more from the ego's point of view), non-existence in the womb. As Forrer suggests, this state of mind becomes more and more threatening as the ego develops, paving the way for completion of the weaning process. In that sense, the ego comes to feel the desire to merge or enter into a state of raptus as the equivalent of death threats. Thus Melanie Klein's belief that the first and most basic anxiety has to do with the ego's fear of annihilation by the death instinct has a meaning apart from its concerns about a "sizzling vortex" of aggressive impulses being turned against it (in Freud's view, primary masochism).

Grotstein (1982) has proposed a "dual-track theory" whereby the state of oneness with the mother (symbiotic/autistic state) "is an important state of relationship which normally persists on one level of mind long after the individual has achieved separation/individuation status in the depressive position of rapprochement" (p. 87). He therefore suggests that the mind continues to operate on the two "levels" of fusion and separateness throughout life.

Klein's concept of initial infant mental separateness collides with Mahler's (and others') conception of continuing postnatal primary narcissism or primary identification. The dual-track theory allows for each to be correct on two tracks - one of separateness, and one of continuing primary narcissism or primary identification. We can now think of normal autism and symbiosis as continuing permanent stages which exist side-by-side with states of separation-individuation throughout life.

The infant may go back and forth between the two tracks as playful mastery or states of danger motivate it (p. 88).

A model of psychological conflict

The model I suggest consists of the following hypotheses:

1 There exists a psychological tendency (←), in many ways corresponding to Freud's conception of the death instinct, towards achieving a permanent state of non-tension, non-effort, sleep, peace, passivity and oblivion, and the phantasy or mental representation of this tendency is of re-entering mother's womb.
2 With gradual physiological and ego development a new tendency "pushes" its way forwards. This tendency (→) is characterized by desires for autonomy, independence and the overcoming of frustrations in the external world through effort.
3 These two tendencies are often felt to be in a state of conflict, particularly prior to the working through of the depressive position.
4 The two tendencies exist in the psyche as if they were sub-personalities; that is, as if they had *feelings* and *attitudes* about the existence and/or activity of the other. For example, there may be attempts to dominate or even *kill off* the opposing tendency if it is thought to be threatening the existence of one of the tendencies.
5 The extent to which one tendency may want to dominate or kill off the opposing tendency will in turn depend on the degree to which that tendency is being gratified or denied at a particular time. At birth, since the ego is so underdeveloped, it is almost impossible (and unnecessary) for the autonomous tendency to make much opposition to the "sleep" tendency, but with the passage of time "retaliatory" attempts at independence can come into being.
6 When the 'active-autonomous tendency' (→) attempts to dominate the entire personality it does so by creating states of mind which foster omnipotence, pseudo-maturity and masturbatory attacks on dependency feelings (Meltzer, 1973). Such states of mind could be described variously as a *narcissistic organization* (Meltzer) or *false-self* (Winnicott) or *idealized self-image* (Horney). The endpoint is megalomania.
7 When the "sleep" tendency attempts to dominate the entire personality (and therefore to annihilate any feelings of autonomy or separateness) it generates, a 'morbid dependency' (Horney, 1950) and masochistically attacks any attempt at independence, individuation, responsibility or independent thinking. Its endpoint is suicide or mortal addiction or catatonia.
8 In early infancy, (especially) a viable balance between the two tendencies (↔) can *only* be achieved through a mediator (breast/mother/parent) who can set *limits* to ensure that neither tendency rules at the expense of the other. If the mediator has the capacity to do this then neither tendency needs to feel excessive fear of annihilation and will therefore reduce its attempts to dominate. Furthermore, the personality as a whole will feel the tensions within it have been contained (Bion, 1970) in a way that can be internalized and used later. (For example, when the "mediator" is not physically present.)

9 Objects (both internal and external) which strive to maintain a balance between the two tendencies, and therefore which facilitate the life and security of both tendencies, are felt to be *good* and inspire feelings of love. On the other hand, objects which seem to be undermining or not promoting such a balance are immediately felt to be persecutory in the sense that they are assumed to be aligned with a domination attempt. Such objects are felt to be *bad* and inspire *hatred* and *fear*.

10 When one tendency does dominate the personality, the person will *yearn* for and feel *envious* of any internal or external objects which *seem* to display characteristics of the non-dominant tendency (sub-personality). For example, someone who has kept themselves dependent and passive will be envious of and need to identify protectively with independent, active, achieving objects. On the other hand, the latter may in turn feel envious of someone who is able to gratify their own dependent or passive feelings.

Some comments on the model

At first, it may seem that I have merely replaced the Freudian or Kleinian concept of "instinct" with what I have called a 'tendency'. But my purpose is to clarify and underline the view that the terms "death" and "life" instincts ought to be reserved for emotional conditions whereby the two tendencies (a) try to kill each other off, or (b) live in balanced, non-violent, mutual enhancement.

This way of viewing emotional life yields a psychodynamic perspective where what counts most is the *balance*, *interplay* and *mutual tolerance* of the tendencies. It is not just a case of envious/destructive versus loving/grateful (Klein), or inactive/death versus active/sexual (Freud).

Through the model I have argued that a state of imbalance (where one tendency attempts to dominate or annihilate the other) can only be corrected by the availability, and eventually internalization of a mediating object (initially the breast). That is one which enables and brings about balancing and limiting of the death instinct – one's tendency to totally dominate the personality. It is not until this mediating function has been internalized (as a reliable good object, allied to and representing the balancing life instinct) that the "depressive position of separation-individuation" (Grotstein, 1982) and "weaning process' (Forrer, 1969) can be achieved.

One implication of the model is that there are two "basic" anxieties, one of which is felt by the tendency which is under the threat of domination by the other tendency. These are

1 Agoraphobic anxiety, based on the phantasy and fear of being trapped forever *outside* the womb (and therefore experienced by ← .
2 Claustrophobic anxiety, the phantasy and fear of being trapped forever inside the womb, experienced by →.

These anxieties, in addition to the experience of envy (as outlined in hypothesis (10), may be seen as the "warning signals" to the personality that may initiate and motivate increasingly more stable balances between the tendencies. If, however, these anxieties are not contained (according to hypotheses (8), and the experience of envy is excessively defended against (Klein, 1957), then a personality based on repression and denial of one of the tendencies will form (and firm). This will, of course, increase unconscious feelings of envy when the repressed characteristics are phantasized as being "alive" in the personalities of others.

I hope it is clear that when I use the terms claustrophobic and agoraphobic anxieties) I am referring to states of mind. For example, a personality suffering from the domination of → may or may not exhibit externally discernible behavioural characteristics commonly classed as agoraphobia. Nor is the preponderance of "passivity of mind" over "activity of mind" necessarily observable, (although it is quick to show in the transference).

I think that hypothesis (9) requires some explanation. I have really attempted to give a "functional" definition of how "goodness" is experienced and structured within the personality. I think that it closely approximates Klein's (1936) paradoxical suggestion to the mother that she "assist him (the child) to grow up to independence."

But I am saying more about the importance of good objects, or mothers. I am suggesting that good objects are not just important because they inspire feelings of love and security, but that they are "good *for*" the continuing expansion and integration of the personality, and in that sense absolutely essential.[2]

In the paranoid-schizoid position objects must be either for us or against us - it is life or death of the personality's unfolding. I think that the description of the nature of goodness in hypothesis (9) provides a criterion by which we assess the goodness of others and ourselves throughout life. That is, through *helping* others to achieve independence and responsibility for their own states of mind. Of course, the *ways* in which this may be done are infinite and different for every personality, but even the effort and willingness to achieve ↔ will inspire some loving feelings and, will somewhat reduce the "nameless dread" (Bion, 1962) of ς and Ω annihilating each other, (and therefore the *whole* personality). In conclusion, some brief clinical examples are given, although the next chapter will detail more fully the dynamics of *how* the ↔ functions might be experienced and internalized.

(In the following examples I have deleted biographical information about the patients where I did not think that such information adds to or is relevant to the points I wish to stress).

Patient 1

This patient transformed my consulting room into "a dark, damp enclosure - like being locked inside a coffin ... I just have to escape, its like I'll die, but like I'd still be alive, I know that, but I'd be trapped forever, I can't even *think* about it, it terrifies me ..." when she was in a session with me. But at the end of the session, and whilst waiting for the next session ...

> I can't bear to leave, it feels like I'm left on the outside; I want to get away from the outside world ... but if I imagine coming back into your woom (slip of tongue), I just want to get away again... it's just like with my mother and my husband, I know I want them to push me, but I'm afraid they'll take over and I'll just be dead like a robot. On the weekend I was at the beach and I thought how it would be to drown, just give myself up to the water, and it was sort of a good feeling, but I got really frightened, I ... I started to imagine it being dark and I was paralysed, I'm even feeling panicky now, like this is really stupid, I know it is, but I feel like jumping out of your window ...

This patient seems perched on a frightening see-saw of claustrophobic and agoraphobic anxieties. Her wish to be comfortable and passive in my 'woom' always causes an anxiety of being trapped inside my "will" at the expense of her own autonomous activity. Her anxiety was reduced when she began to internalize a way of thinking about these anxieties that linked them with her wishes for either total independence or total dependency.

Patient 2

The patient was a computer programmer who prided himself on his "capacity" to devise a way to make order out of chaos. "My ideal is to have my whole life under perfect control and not need anyone. I have this daydream of going through a long tunnel, like '2001. *A Space Odyssey*' and finally I'm reborn, totally self-sustaining, with the universe at my fingertips ..."

The patient spent many sessions quite contemptuously attacking his young brother, (whom he described as 'still with his thumb in his mouth ... he might just as well still be a foetus inside her (mother's) womb - I feel sick thinking about it" ...) before his envy of his brother's (and my own) ability to receive love and caring became clear. One day he was able to acknowledge a daydream about a woman at work and his secret wish that she would see through his "work-a-holic" front and "encase" him with a warm hug that would never end, whilst telling him that it was "all right" and he need never work again.

Patient 3

"I can't tell you how dead I feel when I'm watching TV, yet I feel I have to, like I'm hypnotized. I know it sort of feels good, like I'm floating, but I still feel like part of me is dying, trying to get out, but spellbound by the TV. I hate myself for watching it." The patient would also become fascinated by my eyes and resent himself for not being able to "get on with the session," whilst he thought only about them.

I think that his description of his emotional state whilst doing this, and watching television, corresponds well to what I (and Forrer) would describe as the ego's "feelings" about *"having"* to give way to a state of "raptus" or passivity of mind.

Patient 4

She had come for treatment because of her "sexual holding back" with her husband. After about two years of looking at her hatred of, and flight from dependency, (which was linked with intense envy of her husband and the "feeding" capacities of the breast and penis (me), we seemed to reach an impasse. There was no doubt that her relationship with me (and her husband and parents) had improved, but there was some incompleteness which, I think, was felt by both of us.

One day she was writing out a cheque to pay me and she asked me what the date was. The session had 'ended' and I would not usually ask questions, but I could not stop myself from asking whether she really did know the date since somehow I felt that her question was 'intrusive'. She flushed red with surprise and realized that "of course I knew the date, it's funny, but I automatically wanted you to do if for me ..." Next day she brought a dream. *She was living in a cave, but the rest of the tribe would go out and hunt for food. At the end of the day, she would fire arrows out of her cave and kill a hunter, then draw in his catch for herself. But one day she was firing an arrow out of the cave and suddenly realized that the "effort" and "skill" involved in her "hunting the hunters" meant that she really didn't need to stay in the cave - perhaps she could and should be outside doing her own hunting. She then saw a spider in the cave, and this confirmed her need to leave it.* Her associations were:

> It reminds me somehow of attacking (with arrows) my husband's doing his Ph.D. Actually that's when I started not being able to sleep with him; I was studying for a Master's degree, but I gave it up, to have kids - I wish *he'd* had the kids and I was still studying. I suppose really I could now, if I wanted to, I haven't let myself think about it - it'd require a lot of effort ... the cave's easy, I think, it must be my constricted life right now, hah, just like staying in the womb! Now I'm thinking about yesterday and how angry I was with you when you checked to see if I knew the date.

From this point on we were able to establish more links between her envy (and therefore hatred of dependency or needy feelings) and the way in which she denied or obliterated her own autonomous, exploratory urges. This led to a much improved, deeper relationship with me (and husband) where she was able to talk more freely and for greater lengths of time without demanding that I say something or reassure her. It also allowed an intensification and realization of her loving feelings, since I was no longer just the independent, envied rival, but someone who helped her to actualize her own independent capabilities and urges. Her pseudo-independence (giving rise to envious feelings towards people that she thought were *really* achieving something worthwhile) gave way gradually to a reassessment of what real achievements would be satisfying to her.

It is perhaps worth mentioning here the significance of spider imagery in dreams. I know that one must be careful when speculating about a constant meaning for a dream symbol across different people, but, in my experience, I have never heard of a "spider dream" where the spider did not seem to represent the *threat* to the active-autonomous tendency (ς or ego) posed by the (parasitic) sleep-passivity tendency (Ω, or return to womb). (In the above dream of patient 4 we can see that the recognition of the spider induces a recognition of her need to go outside and do some things for herself.)

This view of spider symbolism allows for the simultaneous veracity of interpretations which call the spider (a) the frightening, castrating engulfing mother, or (b) the threatening, sexually intrusive father who wants to get into the vagina. In my opinion, such interpretations are correct, at one level, but not "deep" enough at an "intra-psychic" level. More specifically, they focus too little on the way parts of the self cause anxiety in other parts (as I have outlined above). For example, Ogden (1982) states in reference to a clinical example) 'In the case under discussion, the spider is understood to represent a particular facet of the danger inherent in the earliest form of relatedness to the mother, namely, the danger involved in symbiotic union. The spiders surrounding the patient and suffocatingly entering his throat represent the mother of late symbiosis, who is alluring and yet threatening to haunt and suffuse the patient (or to be suffused by him) to the point the two dissolve into one another - thus annihilating the patient as a separate entity" (p. 196).

The above examples have been brief and are not an attempt at exhaustive testing of the model, although I hope that they convey some of its advantages.

In conclusion, I agree with Grotstein's (1982) "dual track" model, which "helps us to reconcile the existential polarities of being unique and ordinary (in the sense of being human) at the same time. Psychopathologically, it is difficult to keep both in balance" (p. 89). But in this chapter, I have wanted to say more about just *what* these difficulties are. As mentioned above, the next chapter will give more detail as to how the difficulties are tacked and resolved, in particular, by a fantasy of "going through."

Summary

The Freudian and Kleinian conceptions of the struggle between "life" and "death" instincts are not identical. This chapter puts forward a model which attempts both to reconcile and add to the difference between them, whilst making some suggestions about the "nature of goodness."

Attention is focused on the phantasy of returning to the womb and its consequent anxieties to the growing, active ego. Such anxiety, *and its reverse*, can only be moderated by the introjection of an object which is capable of creatively resolving the resulting conflicts. When envious feelings are not tolerated the impetus for such and introjection is reduced, which, in turn, increases the envy.

Notes

1 For example, Rosenfeld (1983) suggests that: "a similar view can be taken of those nirvana-like experiences, which involve a desire to live in a state of pleasurable fusion with an object. These probably involve a *regressive* phantasy of living happily inside the mother's womb and are often a defence against separateness and enable the avoidance of any feelings of envy" (p. 263).
2 When ↔ has been internalized as a functioning part of the personality then exploratory 'forays' into → can be made without ← becoming overly anxious and vice versa. Temporary dominations are not feared because there is a confidence that balance will always be restored in time. Then such forays can be made into deeper and deeper "psychic territory" (without a paralyzing anxiety about the disintegration of the personality), resulting in an increasing richness and growth of the personality as a whole.

References

Bion, W. R. (1962). *Learning from Experience*. London: Heinemann.
────── (1970). *Attention and Interpretation*. London: Tavistock.
Brown, N. O. (1959). *Life against Death: The Psychoanalytical Meaning of History*. Connecticut: Wesleyan University Press.
Forrer, G. R. (1969). *Weaning and Human Development*. New York: Libra.
Freud, S. (1900). The interpretation of dreams S.E. 5. London: Macmillan, 1963.
Grotstein, J. S. (1982). *Splitting and Projective Identification*. New York: Jason Aronson.
Horney, K. (1950). *Neurosis and Human Growth*. New York: Norton.
Klein, M. (1936). *Weaning: In Love, Guilt and Reparation and Other Works*. New York: Dell, 1975.
────── (1957). *Envy and Gratitude and Other Works*. New York: Dell, 1975.
────── (1958). On the development of mental functioning. In *Envy and Gratitude and Other Works*. Ed. Money-Kyrle, R. New York: Dell, 1975.
Meltzer, D. (1973). *Sexual States of Mind*. Perthsire: Clunie Press.
Ogden, T. H. (1982). *Projective Identification and Psychotherapeutic Technique*. New York: Jason Aronson.
Rosenfeld, H. (1983). Primitive object relations and mechanisms. *Int. J. Psychoanal.*, 64: 261–267.

Chapter 3

The destructive confounding of intra-uterine and post-uterine feeding as a factor against emotional growth

In the last chapter, I hypothesized that the phantasy of returning to the womb generated anxieties in the growingly stifled, claustrophobic, active ego. I suggested that such anxiety, and its obverse, (the anxiety caused to the passive, return to the womb inclination by the emerging, growing, thinking, and active ego) can only be moderated by the introjection of an "object" which is capable of creatively resolving the conflict between these tendencies. This object, seemingly perceived unconsciously as the breasts of the mother, either mediates, or is the "battleground" for a possibly lethal war between the part of the personality that wishes to stay, forever gratified and unthinking, inside the watery womb, and the part that wishes to break out of such a stifling confinement and become active, separate, air-breathing, open to learning, new experience, thinking and therefore change.

However, I did not hypothesize the emotional changes, or psychodynamics, by which such a creative mediation is introjected. The present chapter is an attempt to explore the vicissitudes of that process.

The first part of the chapter describes a foetus-like state of mind and the potentially adverse consequences of its dominance of the relationship with the breast and the "outside" world in general. The second part of the chapter is concerned with the intrapsychic transition from this state of mind to a more accepting, albeit depressive relationship with the breast.

Under normal conditions, the foetus in utero is provided with a constant supply of warmth, protection and nutrition. Toxic waste products are automatically removed from the foetal circulation, which is continuously replenished with fresh oxygen and other nutrients. Although it is known that various hormonal and other chemical substances can be transmitted to the foetus from the maternal blood supply, in general, the foetus does not have to experience a sense of time delay for feeding or for the elimination of toxins, or separation from the watery, warm maternal environment. Despite the fact that the womb becomes a somewhat confining, constricting environment, especially near to birth, I would suggest that the expectation of such a state of existence and mind does not cease with physical birth. (It may eventually be necessary to postulate the first splitting experience as that between "good" and "bad" womb experience. Again, the split would increase dramatically with proximity to full term.).

This expectation may then form a basis for an emotionally dissatisfying, grudging relationship with the breasts; that is, where they (the "outside" mother) are expected to be a womb. When such a state of mind dominates the personality the necessary emotional adaptation (the depressive position) is averted or attacked. I believe that such a receptacle for emotional elements which are felt to be un-processable by that mind, and capable of returning the processed elements, transformed from emotional toxicity into replenishing "food for thought" and emotional life.

The postulation of the phantasy of the "womb-breast" helps us to understand the wish to get into the breast and steal its good contents.

From a foetal point of view, the breast's contents are felt to be its birthright, because with life in the womb, no acknowledgement of a separate feeder was required. Outside the womb, the so-called foetal part of the personality still expects and lays claim to a floaty, watery environment of constantly available comfort, nutrients and oneness with the mother. Frustration then is experienced as a feeling of being unfairly and violently deprived and robbed of one's essential, vital requirements. Such feelings, of course, must be primitive, being pre-verbal and probably pre-visual. In this sense, the infant does not require teeth in order to imagine the possibility of getting inside the breast, since it experienced such a possibility with regard to the womb: the "being inside." I think that the intensity of rage, disbelief, disappointment, disillusionment and depression that the foetus-like part experiences when the breast (world) does not behave as a womb cannot be overemphasized and therefore I believe that the first weaning is not from the breast relationship, but onto it. Obviously, a more gratifying, comforting and "obliging" breast relationship will make this weaning less troublesome, but feelings about leaving the womb will in turn be a major determinant of such trouble.

It should be noted at this point that I am referring to a foetal mind with its own particular expectations and biology of feelings. I do not want to suggest that there are no other feelings, for example, of relief and happiness associated with meeting the breast-mother relationship outside of the womb. Such feelings, and their behavioural counterparts, have been described and emphasized, for example by Hamilton (1982). But in this chapter, I wish to emphasize the disappointment, rage and disbelief that the foetal aspect of the mind experiences, and it's difficulty adapting to a world where gratification is transient, not under one's control and where active effort (such as crying, reacting, sucking and waiting) is necessary, though not always sufficient, to obtain it The phantasy of the breast as a constantly available "toilet container" of unwanted products and feelings can be seen not only as the yearning and demands for the ideal breast but also as a continuation of foetal expectation and habit.

I suggested that the initial attacks and protests were directed towards the breast relationship, but this might not be the only protest site. It may be, particularly if the mother is absent soon after birth, that the attacks and protests are directed against the infant's extra-utero developmental capacities. In particular, this may be centred on the breathing apparatus, where the desire to re-enter the mother dominates, and the capacity to breathe in air is viciously, suicidally shut down. I believe this to be crucially important for the development of asthmatic conditions, but more detailed discussions about that will not be given here.

At this point, I would like to give two clinical examples.

The first patient had made repeated attempts, particularly at the commencement of sessions, to elicit some sort of theoretical generalization from me by asking such questions as: "What's your theory about why X happens?" Although it seemed that the aim was to control me, it gradually became clearer that his phantasy was of setting me going at the commencement of a session and then sitting back while I filled him with my voice, thoughts and ideas – although it would feel as if he had filled himself.

After I commented on this aim he was silent for a while and then said:

> I was just thinking about when I was twelve, I think it was then: I'd ask some friends of my parents to bring me back a transformer from Hong Kong for my tape recorder.
>
> That was my favourite toy - I loved it - it gave me more pleasure . . . anyway, it meant that I would be able to plug it into the mains, and not have to keep on buying and replacing the two batteries. But when they finally came back from overseas and gave me the transformer it didn't work. I was devastated; but my mother took me outside and told me that I should keep quiet be-cause nothing could be done. When I realized how foolish I was being I hated myself for kicking up such a fuss.

I interpreted that he was very frustrated and disappointed when he discovered that I came in only limited quantities and that I expected him to maintain his relationship with me by paying regularly for new sessions and giving me his thoughts and associations. This seemed disillusioning because he felt that the possibility of a different sort of relationship with me (the tape recorder) where I could just run continuously, with no need for maintenance, cost or disappointment to be thought about. Not only that, but he felt concerned that I would criticize and shame him for having such feelings and expectations of me.

He was silent again and then said:

> I've just remembered a dream I had last week. I don't think it's relevant though (more silence). I was watching a particular type of hippopotamus burrowing into the mud to hibernate - it was a really vivid image. This type of hippo survives under the mud because a termite eats its way into the hide and provides the hippo with oxygen. It seems weird to me. I just remembered it.

I would see the association to the disappointment with the transformer and then the dream as an attempt to describe the kind of relationship the patient was trying to establish with me. That is, where he could feel that he was plugged into an inexhaustible supply of constantly available supplies, via a transforming cord, as opposed to and compared with the come-and-go, exhaustible breast batteries.

With the second patient, the phone rang as I was about to usher her into the consulting room and circumstances made it necessary for me to answer the call. I excused myself and asked the patient to go on into the room. When I returned, she began to describe the following:

> At first I wanted to cut the telephone cord and strangle you with it - but that seemed futile. Then, a sort of eerie calm took over me and I saw myself in a warm bath with my wrists bleeding slowly - I know it sounds morbid, but at the time it felt blissful, I could have almost dissolved into the water - I felt warm, and I didn't care about your bloody phone call. It's frightening to think of how good it felt.

I commented on how frightened she was when tempted by her wish to become immersed in me in the face of her disconnection in the hallway. She responded by remembering a dream in which she was chased by a vampire. Her associations to the vampire were that they needed a constant supply of blood, that they confined to the dark, and that they hate light (which would kill them). "When they drink people's blood the persons stop thinking for themselves and turn into robots. I think they die eventually."

One way of understanding these associations is to suggest that the vampire represents a part of her personality which aims to remain in a dark enclosure and yet be fed fresh blood regularly. At the same time, this is equivalent to launching an attack on the part of her mind which might otherwise be capable of independent thinking. I have deliberately chosen these examples in order to indicate that the wish for foetal connection is perceived differently by different parts of the self. In the first example, the patient identifies with the sluggish, hibernating hippopotamus and it's slightly more active termite – no real cause for great anxiety. In the second example, however, there is an awareness of a murderous vampire which endangers free-thinking, autonomy and life itself, resulting in a dead or robotic mind.

Going through versus getting inside

This section is concerned with the description of a model. It attempts to detail the dynamics of a flux between states of the mind which are dominated by the attempt to re-establish a foetus-like connection with the mother, and states of mind where such demands are given up.

The model consists of the following hypotheses:

1. There is a part of the personality which cannot tolerate or even comprehend the pain and loss of leaving behind the umbilical connection with the mother. In a sense, it "stays behind" in a foetus-like state of mind.
2. This part of the personality exerts great pressure on the personality as a whole, in attempts to coerce it into demands for umbilical types of gratification where

the loss of the womb need not be acknowledged. Any "non-umbilical" relationships, particularly the first with the breasts, are treated with contempt, hostility, disbelief, and attempts to control the breast relationship in order to transform it into a womb-placenta. (This might correspond to what Melanie Klein has called the paranoid-schizoid position.)

3 Alternatively, at the other end of the emotional spectrum, there exists a part of the personality which is able to tolerate and adapt to the pain of the loss of the womb and the movement into the "outside" world, and which, through acknowledging the loss (through mourning) is able to apprehend and appreciate – physically and aesthetically – the beauty and vital quality in the nature of the new relationship, with the breasts. (This might correspond to what Melanie Klein has called the depressive position).

4 In unconscious phantasy, these alternatives are represented as getting inside (the womb) and going through (the womb) respectively. On the visual (or perhaps the artistic) plane, the getting-inside-phantasy is an image of looking or moving into a circular or crevice-like watery darkness from a brightly lit location. The phantasy of going through, on the other hand, presents an image of looking or feeling movement out from a dark place through a tunnel-like opening to "embrace" the outside light, which is softened and muted in yellowy-pink reflection from the mother's breasts.

On a more tactile plane, the phantasy of getting inside refers to a warm, watery but somewhat confined environment, perhaps with an occasional rocking or swaying motion. The going through phantasy refers to breaking through and out of such confinement and emerging out into the open air.

On the plane of psychological development, the alternatives would be paralysis, boredom and superficiality on the one hand, as opposed to the emergence of "Catastrophic Change." I am using the term "catastrophic change" here in the ironical sense that Meltzer (1978) and Harris Williams (1987) developed it from Bion's original application to the interplay between the Individual creative mind and the group's need for stability and security. The irony is that catastrophic change is only catastrophic from the point of view of the "old, limited, stifled" mind. When the catastrophe is "gone through" there is a new mind born from the experience.

5 These phantasies are always in a state of flux. The movement from a state of mind dominated by the wish to get inside the womb to a state of mind where going through to the outside world of the "breast-mother" is sought, is repeated and reversed many times.

There are many phrases in our vocabulary which seem to support this view. We often hear patients say that they feel "in the dark," "stuck," "making no headway," "things look gloomy" and "you don't know what I'm going through." On the other hand, at a moment of progress: "Now I can see some light at the end of the tunnel," "I see the light," "a break through," "seeing something in a new light," "making headway," "going through a lot" and "it was like a breath of fresh air."

Even the word "experience" carries the idea of moving out through, or out from something which surrounds.

I will now give an expanded example of how the model might be understood with regard to a narrative. The main example that I will draw on is Marcel Proust's extensive series of novels "Remembrance of Things Past" (1970).

Of course, it would be ludicrous to attempt any exhaustive study of the whole work here, but I have drawn these examples from a wide spread of the work in the hope that they will elucidate the model and vice versa. The Monty Python team of comedians (1970) has already well and truly warned against summarizing Proust, however, a very brief synopsis is in order.

The "Overture" has Marcel, the protagonist and author, describing a childhood scene which caused him much anguish and pain. Each night he must say goodnight to his mother and cope with not only his jealous phantasies – mother downstairs with father or other men – but also the terror of experiencing his separateness from her. Throughout the book it is the object that he is cut off or separate from which forms the basis of his desire, interest and passion – the object whose presence he has no control over, despite all his efforts and resources. It is perhaps of interest that throughout his life Proust suffered from asthma, particularly following the death of his mother, whereupon he sealed himself up in a cork-lined apartment until his own death soon after the completion of this set of novels.

Now according to the above model, the scenes which describe Marcel's intolerance of separation from his mother (or grandmother or lover) would be associated with imagery of moving into a dark, confined, watery space, perhaps with some rocking or gentle swaying motion. In other words, wanting to never be separated from the mother ought to be linked with the wish to remain inside her as a foetus. On the other hand, the scenes where Marcel does seem more tolerant of separation, where he appears more able to mourn the loss of the constantly available womb-mother, ought to be punctuated with imagery of light, fresh air and movement but from a dark space to meet the yellowy-pink reflected light from the (outside) mother's skin/face/breasts. It is interesting to note just how much of the book is devoted to descriptions of changing light. Certainly, much more of the book is devoted to this than the reflection about human feelings and actions. Of course, it is tempting to suggest that the pages and pages of these descriptive images are padding, or is irrelevant, or serves only to heighten the human drama. But I would rather see it as integral to the human drama. Proust himself, in perhaps a half-joking manner tells us:

> I remain closeted with the little person inside me hymning the rising sun ... and those elements which compose our personality, it is not the most obvious that are the most essential. In myself, when ill-health has succeeded in uprooting them one after another, there will still remain two or three endowed with a hardier constitution than the rest, notably a certain philosopher who is happy only when he has discovered in two works of art, in two sensations a common element. But the last of all, I have sometimes asked myself whether it would not be this little manikin, very similar to another whom the optician at Combray used to set up in his shop window to forecast the weather, and who, doffing

his hood when the sun shone would put it on again if it was going to rain. This little manikin, I know his egoism - I may be choking from a choking fit which the mere threat of rain would calm - he pays no heed, and at first drops so impatiently awaited, losing his gaiety, suddenly pulls down his hood. Conversely, I dare say that in my last agony, when all my other "selves" are dead, if an array of sunshine steals into the room, while I am drawing my last breath, the little fellow at the barometer will feel a great relief, and will throw back his hood to sing: "Ah! Fine weather at last!

(Captive, p. 5.)

Now, in the light of the propositions I have mentioned, here are some examples of the imagery which follows Marcel's having undergone a separation. Marcel's mother has just left his room and he has realized the jealousy he had been nursing for a particular woman has been ill-founded or delusional.

I went to the window and drew back the curtains. Above the pale and misty daylight the sky was red, as at the same hour are the newly lighted fires in kitchens, and the sight of it filled me with hope and with a longing to pass the night in a train and awake at the little country station where I had seen the milk-girl with rosy cheeks ...

(Sweet Cheat Gone, p. 109)

And in conjunction with his mourning for the lost Albertine, who has died:

Without my being previously aware of it, it was now the idea of Albertine's death, no longer the present memory of her life, that formed the chief subject of unconscious musings, with the result that. I interrupted them suddenly to reflect upon myself. What surprised me was not, as in earlier days that Albertine so living in myself could be no longer existent upon the earth, could be dead, but that Albertine who no longer existed upon the earth, who was dead, should have remained so living in myself. Built up by the contiguities of the memories that followed one another, the black tunnel in which my thoughts had been straying for so long that they ceased to be aware of it, were suddenly broken by an interval of sunlight, allowing me to see in the distance, a blue and smiling universe in which Albertine was no more than a memory, unimportant and full of charm. Is it this, I asked myself, that is the true Albertine, or is it indeed the person, who in the darkness through which I have so long been rolling, seemed to me the sole reality.

(Sweet Cheat Gone, p. 85)

Or Marcel's gradual tolerance and realization of the pain of separation from Albertine:

How I suffered from that position for which we are reduced by the carelessness of nature which, on instituting the division of bodies, never thought of making possible the inter-penetration of souls (for if her body was in the power of mine,

Destructive confounding of intra-uterine and post-uterine feeding

her mind escaped from the grasp of mine). And I became aware that Albertine was not even for me the marvellous captive with whom I had thought to enrich my home ...

is followed by:

Meanwhile winter was at an end; the fine weather returned and often when Albertine had just bidden me goodnight my room, my curtains, the wall above the curtains still quite dark, in the nuns' garden next door I could hear, rich and precious in the silence like a harmonium in church, the modulation of an unknown bird which, in the Lydian mode, was al-ready chanting matins, and into the midst of my darkness flung the rich dazzling note of the sun that it could see ...

Now let us turn to moments where Marcel's tolerance of separation from that woman – in particular, the woman associated with a watery environment is weak or non-existent. Here is a scene where Marcel visits Venice with his mother and, at first, cannot bear separation from her;

After luncheon when I was not going to roam about Venice by myself, I went up to my room to get ready to go out with my mother. In the abrupt angles of the walls I could read the restriction imposed by the sea ... in the darkness guarded by closed shutters ...

(*Sweet Cheat Gone*, p. 163)

And, lying alone in bed, Marcel says:

I would feel the satisfaction of being shut in from the outer world like the sea-swallow which builds at the end of a dark tunnel and is kept warm by the surrounding earth.

(*Swann's Way*, p. 6)

Yet, at moments when his grief for the loss of Albertine seems unbearable to Marcel, the appearance of light is unbearable:

From my darkened room the power of evocation equal to that of former days but capable now of evoking the pain, I felt that outside in the heaviness of the atmosphere, the setting sun was plastering the. vertical fronts of houses and churches with a tawny distemper, and if Francis, when she came in, parted by accident the inner curtains, I stifled a cry of pain at the gash that was cut in my heart by that ray of long ago sunlight which had made beautiful in my eyes the modern front of "X" when Albertine said to me "It is restored." It was not enough to draw the curtains. I tried to stop the eyes and ears of my memory so as not to see the band of orange in the Western sky ...

(*Sweet Cheat Gone*, p. 47)

But this Albertine, for whom the struggle of mourning and loss continue to "torture" Marcel, when we look more closely at her imagery, appears to be an object associated with water, rocking and pale light:

> How many times had I crossed, going in search of Albertine, how many times had I entered on my return with her, the great plain of "X" now in foggy weather, when the flooding mist gave us the illusion of being surrounded by a vast lake?
> (*Sweet Cheat Gone*, p. 47)

When we examine one of the rare moments in the whole book where Marcel does seem to have his desire fulfilled, that is where he feels himself to be merged with, and in possession of the sleeping Albertine, the poetic imagery is a kind of seaside, aquatic reverie:

> She had called back into herself everything of her that lay out-side ... her personality did not escape at the every moment, as when we were talking, by the channels of her unacknowledged thoughts and her gaze ... I had the impression of possessing her altogether ... which I never had when she was awake. Her face was submitted to me, exhaled towards me its gentle breath. I listened to this murmuring mysterious emanation. Soft as a breeze from the sea, fairy-like as that moonlight which was her sleep. So long as it lasted. I was free to think about her and at the same time look at her, and when her sleep grew deeper to touch, to kiss her ... Her sleep brought within my reach something as calm. as sensuously delicious as of full moon on the bay of Balbec turned quiet as a lake over which the branches barely stir, where stretched out upon the sand one could listen for hours on end to the waves breaking and receding. When I entered the room, I remained standing in the doorway, not venturing to make a sound, and hearing none but that of her breath rising to expire upon her lips at regular intervals, like the reflux of the sea, but drowsier and more gently ... Her breathing, as it became gradually deeper, was now regularly stirring her bosom, and through it, her folded hands, her pearls, dis-placed in a different way by the same movement, like the boats, the anchor chains that are set swaying by the movement of the tide. Then, feeling that the tide of her sleep was full, that I should not ground upon reefs of consciousness covered now by the high water of profound slumber, deliberately, I crept without a sound upon the bed. I had embarked upon the tide of Albertine's sleep ... was gently rocked by its regular motion.
> (*Captive*, pp. 46–47)

And, although I will not give further details here, the core of Marcel's masturbatory phantasy is of a homosexual couple or group which meets illicitly and plays in a watery environment. It is this phantasy which torments the jealous Marcel, even after Albertine's "external" death, for years.

But when Marcel is able to think about his separateness from Albertine, or indeed, when he is able to contemplate the idea of separating from his old self, and perhaps moving into a new phase of his emotional development, the transition to the outside world of light and fresh air is often made by the fantasy process of "going through." For example:

> Yes, I must go. The time had come. Now that Albertine no longer appeared to be cross with me the possession of her no longer seemed to me a treasure in exchange for which we are prepared to sacrifice every other, for we should have done so only to rid ourselves of a grief and anxiety which we now appease. We have succeeded in jumping through. the calico hoop through which we thought for a moment we should never be able to pass.
>
> (*Captive*, p. 288)

And at the very conclusion of the set of novels, as Marcel is recapturing his past, just at the moment where he is feeling that all is lost, that his life has been futile and nothing of worth exists anymore, that the outside world is full of decayed, ludicrous people, he writes:

> But it is sometimes just at the moment when we think every-thing is lost that the intimation arrives which may save us. One knocks at all doors which lead nowhere, and then one stumbles, without knowing it, on the only door through which one can enter, which one might have sought in vain for a hundred years, and it opens, of its own accord.
>
> (*The Past Recaptured*, p. 129)

It is at this point in Marcel's life that he "stumbles" upon memories of happiness and contentment which focus on a cake soaked in tea, one of his earliest memories of maternal love, or the experience of being offered, and drinking from, the breast. I think the model finds expression in many other artistic contexts. I will briefly use two, more contemporary examples – one from a contemporary Australian writer, and one from the popular American film genre.

Here is the concluding image of Helen Garner's (1978) novel "Monkey Grip," which is concerned with her agonized addiction to a relationship with a heroin-addicted "parasitic" boyfriend, of whom her most ardent feelings are for his marine-coloured eyes. In fact, she is first attracted to him at a swimming pool, which bears the warning "Aqua Profunda." It is only at the end of the novel, that she is able to painfully break this addiction, or perhaps more accurately this "foetal attraction," and therefore to be open to a new form of internal imagery – that of the outside breasts and light.

> In the morning the sky was clear. The sunlight lay on scrubby grass in long pinkish gold stripes …
>
> (p. 272)

And here is the last paragraph from one of her short stories with a similar theme; that is, the anguished, painful giving up of a boyfriend, or let us say "part of herself," which is addictive and parasitic, in the sense that it wishes to live off the life and labours of others without ever having to give anything in return. Again, right at the end of the story she is able to leave this behind and is therefore open to the following internal experience.

> The train slid through a pass beside a jade river. Tremors rose from the depths and shuddered on its swollen surface. After the second border she opened the window. The train passed close to the buildings the colour of old flowerpots ... buildings whose corners were softened with age ... The air had colour and texture. You could touch the air. It was yellow. It was almost pink. She turned back to the compartment and it was full of the scent of sleeping children.
> (*A Thousand Miles from the Ocean*, p. 80)

In another short story, the final paragraph is a rather beautiful description of the swaying to and fro between staying in the pinkish light of the breasts and wishing to return to the watery inside of the mother.

> All night I sleep safely in my bed. The waves roar and hiss and slam like doors. Aunty Lorna snores but when I tug at the corner at her blanket she sighs and turns over and breathes more quietly. In the morning the rising sun hits the front windows and floods the place with a light so intense that the white curtains can hardly net it. Everything is pink and golden. In the sink a cockroach lurks. I try to swill it down the drain with a cup of water but it resists strongly. The air is bright, is milky with spray. My father is already up; while the kettle boils he stands out on the edge of the grass, the edge of his property, looking at the sea.
> (*Postcards*, p. 16)

There are many highly popular films which climax with the hero or heroine breaking through some entrance/exit, air/water light/dark interface in order to end a period of destructively confining foetus-like autistic existence and use of the mother. To name but a few: "Legend," "Tommy," "Alien," "Birdy," "The Wall," "Brazil," "Indiana Jones and the Temple of Doom," and "Altered States," but the brief example I will use here is Spielberg's "Poltergeist."

The film commences by showing us a typical American middle-class family setting. All seems well until we begin to notice the importance and omnipresence of the television. The family appears to wake by it and fall asleep by it – a sort of hypnotically stimulating sedative which barricades the family safely from the "outside" world and each other. One night the little girl of the family (the baby) is watching the television alone (the parents have already fallen asleep by their own television) when it draws her inside and leaves her trapped inside. The tension of the film now pivots on her rescue and the re-establishment of her contact with the parents – particularly the mother. But this involves two tasks. The first is to uncover the reason for the kidnapping and subsequent terrorizing of the family house. The answer is the discovery that some dead bodies have been disturbed near the house by some uncaring, greedy land developers who attempt to cover this up. That is, there has been a failure in mourning what is dead. A seemingly trivial, but parallel cover-up of the need for mourning is when the little girl (just prior to her disappearance) catches the mother removing the dead pet canary from its cage in an attempt to flush it down the toilet. The little girl demands a respectful funeral and burial instead.

The second task concerns the mechanics of rescuing the little girl from her premature tomb inside the "world of the dead." This requires the presence of a "go-between" – someone who seems to understand what is needed to reunite the mother and the child in the outside world of "life." It is here that the film reaches its emotional peak. Trees violently break through the house, doors open and close. Inanimate objects become animated and menacingly intrusive and the whole rescue seems far too dangerous. But the go-between/midwife persists and guides the trapped girl through a lengthy dilemma about whether to move forward towards the light or away from it. Meanwhile, a physical link is established via a stretched rope.

Finally, at a critical moment of decision about moving towards the light, the little girl breaks through, mysteriously and exhilaratingly, and awakens, as if from a sleep, in her mother's arms. The tension is gone, but the epilogue shows the family leaving their house and booking into a motel room from which they promptly evict the television set. I would see the "problem" as one of addiction to a state of mind which attempts to sustain continuously a hypnotic, floaty feeling, and where mourning for the loss of the "foetal" state and the womb are neglected or covered up. The neglect is then falsely rationalized as being in the name of development. The result is a major rupturing of the mother-newborn bond and leaves the personality open to domination by a violently intrusive and baby-snatching force. The bond is eventually restored when, despite all the violent resistance, the infant goes through its womb-like enclosure into the light. Here it can join with the "outside mother" in an engaging and moving way, weaning off the need for the floaty, hypnotic and mindless (television) connection with the inside of her body.

Conclusion

I have put forward the idea that the relinquishment of a pre-natal mode and expectation in relationship to the breast-mother in the outside world might be related, unconsciously, to the phantasy of "going through." This, I think, is connected with the development of capacity to go through one's feelings and experiences – probably the *sine qua non* of development itself. I have stressed the particularly emotionally painful and torrid nature of those feelings and experiences related to the loss of the foetal connection with the inside of the mother's body, even though it seems likely that, particularly as the foetus grows, the increasingly confined space is causing anxiety, and therefore motivation for a new environment – the threshold of "catastrophic change." The alternative seems to be to forcibly, intrusively and manipulatively attempt to control the breast-mother-world into being a "womb." This could be seen as an autistic solution – of destructively sacrificing one's own capacities for functioning and for experiencing feelings and relationships, in order to take one's mother's "arms against a sea of troubles," in contrast with *going through* one's rage and disappointment about the permanent disruption of the foetal relationship.

One way of expressing these ideas is to say that psychologically, part of the personality never leaves the womb. This part is always creating anxiety in the part that has increasingly felt constricted and therefore ready, willing and able to go through the "mental birth canal" (Bion's *catastrophic change*) into the light of the air-breathing relationship with (initially) the mother's breasts and face. In turn, the latter inclination troubles it and this may induce hostile, vicious reactions and protests, which delay or make impossible the work of mourning the "lost world." Emotionally, this means saying goodbye to and accepting the loss of a constantly available, ideally gratifying environment where no effort, thinking or waiting need ever be experienced. The part that "stays behind" in a continuation of foetal "mode," hates this and will do all that it can to tempt, seduce and coerce a foetal re-union. This can be done by attacking or killing vital developmental capacities (such as thinking, feeling or using one's hands, and even breathing) and the relationship with the feeding, loving and beautiful breast-mother.

It may be that the basis for a kind of "incorrect" splitting of good and bad experiences at the breast lies in a confounding of disappointments and failures at the breast per se (unavailability, inciting envy, inadequate flow, smothering, etc.) with an apparent failure to duplicate the style of feeding relationship that was experienced in utero.

References

Garner, H. (1978). *Monkey Grip*. Melbourne: Penguin.

——(1985). *Postcards from Surfers*. Melbourne: McPhee Gribble.

Hamilton, V. (1982). *Oedipus and Narcissus: The Children of Psychoanalysis*. London: Routledge & Kegan Paul.

Harris Williams, M. (1987). *A Strange Way of Killing: The Poetic structure of Wuthering Heights*. Perthshire: Clunie Press.

Meltzer, D. (1978). Catastrophic change and the mechanisms of defense. In *The Kleinian Development*, Part III, Ed. Meltzer, D. London: Karnac Books.

Monty Python's Flying Circus. (1970). BBC Comedy scripts. London.

Proust, M. (1970). *Remembrance of Things Past*. New York: Vintage, 1970.

Chapter 4

What could be better than nuclear warfare?

An essay on the quest for eirenarchic survival

Following on from the previous two chapters, I will now suggest applying their models of intra-psychic conflict to a large group or "global" level. My hope is to generate some new ways of thinking about our anxieties about nuclear warfare and the destruction of life on Earth, and about alternatives.

I want to make clear at the outset that this is a much-simplified hypothesis. The difficulties involved in the leap from a speculative model of the individual mind to a speculative model of a world mind (if, indeed, there is such a "thing") are enormous, as is the possibility of generating nothing but tautological nonsense. However, given the recent exponential increase in anxiety about nuclear warfare and annihilation, its distinct possibility and the relative lack of psychological input to the problem, it may turn out to be safer to err on the side of zeal.

Many psychoanalytical thinkers seem to believe that the task of attempting to understand World War in terms of unconscious processes is inappropriate – that psychoanalysis lies strictly in the domain of thoughts about the transference in the "here-and-now" of a two-person relationship and its repeated, observable patterns.

Those who have ventured to speculate have "bee-lined" straight for Freud's "death instinct." The idea, put in various ways, is that the waging of war is a mentally "primitive" attempt to project our destructiveness, hostility and fear into outsiders and then kill them off. This then allows us to maintain reasonably positive bonds within, "our own" group (see Segal, 1987, for an elaboration of this idea). Another way of putting this might be to say that the mental pain of regarding the world as a group arouses a great deal of "depressive anxiety". The integration of so many richly heterogeneous parts and subgroups, while providing infinite variety and beauty, also strains our capacity for self-understanding and integration to the full. A "simplifying," paranoid state of mind (with goodies and baddies and no capacity for guilt, concern or tolerance of the unfamiliar) is then offered under the group banner of "nationalism."

We have also become experts in selecting "leaders" who are themselves experts in peddling this state of mind. The "chaser" for any spilt remnant of guilt is always the conservative plea that we cannot expect any better sort of integration with our "barbaric" enemies who lack any human or "civilized" values. It is the same "reasonable" plea for maintaining the status quo – no matter how dangerous and perverse – that we hear repeatedly in the course of an analysis, particularly in its early stages, but even to the last session.

From this starting point, I want to take a slightly different direction from that taken by, for example, Fornari (1975). I agree with Segal (1987) that analysts ought to be ready, willing and able to verbalize their observations of certain "psychic facts" such as projection, denial and fragmentation of responsibility. However, I believe that there is also much more work to be done on the detailing of just exactly what is projected, denied and fragmented. Otherwise, as in an analysis, the "interpretation" is too general to produce a really convincing impact. After all, the theory of projection has been around for a while now, but it has probably had little impact on our world group mentality with regard to warfare and conflict.

To think about World War it seems absolutely necessary to hypothesize the existence, at least in unconscious phantasy, of the concept of the "world-as-a-group." Of course we know that, at another level, countries, states within countries, cities within states, families within communities and individuals within families can feel and behave as if they had no connection to any larger group. But that is not the level relevant to this chapter. Externally speaking there is such a thing as a 'global communications network', and the term World War has been used freely to describe conflicts which never have literally involved and threatened (till now) the whole world. Bion (1961) and others have provided some remarkable insight into "group mentality" and its peculiarities, but Rosenfeld (1983) and Meltzer (1983) have shown compellingly that the psychodynamics at the personal level may have some important similarities. It is possible then, that individual and group psychologies might make contributions to each other – especially at an initially speculative level.

Recapitulation of the model

Here is a summary of the model for intra-psychic conflict (repeated here for those reading this chapter as a *stand-alone*) which I am going to review at the level of world-as-a-group conflict.

1 There exists a psychological tendency towards the achievement of a permanent state of non-tension, non-effort, sleep, passivity and oblivion where all the "nutrients of life" are magically provided. The phantasy or mental representation of this tendency is of staying in or re-entering an all-comforting, all-providing womb.
2 With gradual physiological and ego development a new tendency emerges which seeks autonomy, independence and the overcoming of constrictive frustrations through effort and activity.
3 These two tendencies are often felt to be in a state of conflict.
4 The two tendencies exist in the mind as if they were sub-personalities – as if they each had feelings and attitudes about the existence and/or intentions of the other. For example, there may be attempts to dominate or kill off the opposing tendency if it is thought to be threatening the existence of the other.

5 The extent to which one tendency may want to dominate or kill off the other will in turn depend on the degree to which that tendency is being gratified or denied at a particular time. At birth, since the ego is so underdeveloped, it is almost impossible (and unnecessary) for the autonomous tendency to make much opposition or feel too threatened, but as the ego develops it comes to feel that it has more of itself to lose.
6 When the "active-autonomous" tendency (→) attempts to dominate the entire personality it fosters a state of omnipotence, pseudo-maturity and masturbatory attacks on feelings of dependency (Meltzer, 1973). The endpoint is megalomania.
7 When the "passive-sleep tendency" (←) attempts to dominate the entire personality (and therefore to annihilate any desire for autonomy or separateness) it generates a 'morbid dependency' (Horney, 1950) and the expectation of being totally and magically looked after. This masochistically attacks any thoughts of independence, individuation or responsible action. Its endpoint is mortal addiction or catatonia.
8 In early infancy, especially, a viable balancing of the two tendencies (↔) can only be achieved through a mediator (breast/mother/parent/organization) which can set limits to ensure that neither tendency need feel excessive fear of annihilation and will therefore reduce its attempts to dominate. Furthermore, the personality as a whole will feel that the tensions within it have been contained (Bion, 1970) in a way that can be internalized and used later – for example, when the mediating "organization" is not physically present.
9 Objects (both internal and external) which strive to maintain a balance of the tendencies, and therefore facilitate the life and security of both, are felt to be good and inspire feelings of love. On the other hand, objects which seem to be undermining or not promoting such a balancing are immediately felt to be persecutory in the sense that they are assumed to be aligned with a domination or annihilation attempt. Such objects are felt to be bad and inspire hatred and fear.
10 In early stages of development, and also at later stages, there is a fine line between the balancing (life) and "anti-balancing" (death) forces within a personality.
11 When one tendency does dominate the personality, the person will unconsciously yearn for and envy any internal or external objects which seem to display characteristics of the dominated tendency (sub-personality).

When I first proposed this model I was aware that I was using the symbols ← and → not altogether arbitrarily—perhaps with a sort of invocative innuendo in the way that Bion might have used his symbols ♂ and ♀ for his concept of container/contained. I hope that it will become clearer as I continue, that the left and right directions of these arrows might indicate a kind of psycho-political level of abstraction with regard to speculations about unconscious phantasies of the "world-as-a-group." It is interesting to wonder why the terms left and right have been adopted and accrued meaning in the political sphere.

Let us suppose that within the world group the two conflicting tendencies are represented in phantasy (and, at present, in external reality) by two large ("superpower") nations, often referred to as the "left" or the "right." I will call them X and Y, respectively.

Now, the phantasy that Y has about X would be that X wants to force the whole world into a constrictive womb-like enslavement where individual thought and autonomy are either crushed or shrivel up with lack of encouragement in a sacrifice to the group ("State"). The "right" will be willing and able to expand upon the details of this phantasy as applied, for example, to their stereotyped images of the "commies." Contradistinctly, the phantasy that X would have about Y is that Y wants to force independence and autonomy on the whole world with no consideration of the "people's" real needs to be and feel "looked-after." There is no shortage of speeches from the "left" condemning this as rampant Imperialism or Capitalism, or competitive individualism.

Country X prides itself on the idea of everybody being provided with their "true" needs in life—loyalty to this group ideal requiring the relinquishment of unlimited autonomy and individuality.

Country Y prides itself on the freedom of its individuals for which the welfare of the "unsuccessful" is but a "small price to pay."

Both 'sides' view each other as imbalanced, out of control and about to annihilate the physical and mental existence of the other. Compromise or balance seems (and is) unthinkable. For example, the British Prime Minister was recently (keep in mind that this chapter was first written in the 1980s) asked if there might eventually be possible a sort of compromise between Capitalist and Socialist ideologies, to which she replied that this would mean the destruction of the entire "democratic process."

This is, I think, the limit of the mentality of the world as a group prior to any mediating or balancing influence. Polarization is encouraged, and mediation is inconceivable.

I would stress at this point that I am referring to the phantasies that pervade the mentality of the world group, and although I have just outlined these in relation to X and Y, the "rest of the world" would feel the threat of annihilation no less – probably more so. Certainly, at present, the anxiety about nuclear warfare and destruction seems to be more intense in European countries. It may even be possible to locate the front line of tension geographically between X and Y as, for example, a wall in Berlin, outside the national boundaries of both X and Y.

It follows that once these phantasies gather strength and obduracy, X and Y are increasingly felt to be mutually potentially annihilatory, ushering in a "cold war" mentality of killing or being killed as a prelude to a "hot war." At this point, intrusive voyeurism (spying) is seen as a justifiable defence against the possibility of intrusive destruction, as is the tactic of keeping the enemy threatened and frightened. This mentality is reflected in the "arms race." Weaponry (projective and projected) must be developed so as to be capable always of instilling this annihilatory anxiety into the enemy – it must really feel threatened with total disintegration.

The idea that annihilatory anxiety can be warded off by keeping it 'stored' in the enemy is, of course, both mad and stupid. It ignores the obvious outcome of increasing the kill-or-be-killed determination in the enemy, accelerating the onset of warfare. It might even be said that actual "hot" warfare brings great relief to this mental state. Now at least the enemy can be seen and fought as a real physical threat.

One corollary of the model when applied to the world as a group is that the intensity of the perceived death threat or annihilatory anxiety within a sub-group (nation) is directly proportional to the unresolved tensions between and within the sub-group. That is to say, unconscious envy and fear of an "enemy" nation will depend on the degree that balance between → and ← tension has been thwarted by repression of one of either within nation X or nation Y.

It is not difficult to find evidence of these unresolved tensions with X or Y, although the seriousness of the conflict is always denied by the administration of both. For example, country X, emphasizing how everybody is looked after, plays down the protests against lack of freedom and autonomy by many of its citizens. Similarly, country Y, emphasizing its encouragement of freedom and autonomy for its citizens, plays down the protests against lack of welfare and social services made by many of them.

Unresolved and denied conflict between ← and → within countries will always show up in the externalization of the conflict with an "outside" enemy. This process will inevitably and indefinitely delay the resolution or balancing of the conflicting tendencies and may even destroy the possibility.

If, however, we follow the implications of the model through, we are faced with these critical questions: Is mediation of such a potentially destructive international conflict possible? That is, what would be the international equivalent of a mediating, containing, feeding and balancing influence that is provided for a baby by mother's mind and body?

I will argue here that the world as a group does have the making of such structure, (perhaps all too correctly) called the United Nations, but that its functioning is pathologically obstructed. Worse still, the pathological function is covered up by the organization itself. Worse still, that the world as a group turns a "blind eye" (Steiner, 1986) and, therefore, at least unconsciously, wants the U.N. to function ineffectively.

With our individual patients, we are familiar with the expected resistance. The work of Klein, Segal, Bion, Rosenfeld, Steiner and Meltzer has opened up this can of serpents to show that resistance is not just inertia and passivity in the face of change. More specifically, that underneath the "innocent" proclamation of "What can *I* do?" is a bedrock of lies, deception and undercover gang-like terrorization, akin to ruthless dictatorship which aims to destroy the awareness of need and dependence upon dependable, trustworthy, feeding and holding internal objects and organizations (see Meltzer, 1973 for a more detailed account).

Without such awareness, we simply do not develop a capacity for effectively mediating between our feelings and our actions through thought or reverie. To refer to the model, the capacity for internal mediation of the conflicting tendencies,

→ and ←, which depends entirely on experiences with an external mediator, initially the mother, does not develop. Instead, a pseudo-independent, pseudo-mature, gang-like structure develops, but has no capacity for genuinely creative thinking (compared with the constant promulgation of novelty) as the means of resolving both internal and external conflict.

The writer Shirley Hazzard, in her book *Defeat of an Ideal – a Study of the Self-Destruction of the United Nations* (1973), casts a penetrating searchlight on the functioning (i.e. malfunctioning) of the only existing human structure or organization created specifically for the integrated and effective mediation of world-as-a-group conflict.

(I can only give some brief examples of her insights here, as a means of elaborating my argument, but a full reading of her book adds a rich array of detail to the ideas that I am outlining.)

Hazzard notes that the idea of a United Nations seems rational and feasible –

> ... infinitely more rational ... that the series of mass persecutions and annihilating wars that, culminating in the invention and use of atomic weapons, impelled the peoples of the world to call for ...[it].
>
> (p. 58)

But here are some of the points that she makes which indicate that such an idea is either not being pursued effectively, or is actively attacked under a thin mantle or proclaimed innocence, such as "we're doing the best that anyone could."

1 It has been "allowed" that the headquarters of the U.N. be located in one of the superpower nations, which has also been allowed to contribute a disproportionate amount of support and financial backing. This is especially significant since:

> The U.N. Preparatory Commission, meeting in 1945, advised that it should be so situated as to be free from any attempt at improper political control or the exercise of undesirable local influence. As late as 1946, the Yearbook of the U.N. states that the organization 'should not be located in the territory of one of the major powers, in particular one of the five permanent members of the Security Council'. These recommendations were overcome or ignored, and ... doubts as to the suitability of the United States as the site for the United nations have never been allayed in member nations.
>
> (p. 77)

2 There is a massive split in the "functioning" of the U.N. which Hazzard calls **Academism/Legalism versus Life**. This means that:

> Importance has been attached to the formality of government endorsements and declarations in favour of 'humanity' and justice', rather than to insistence on the active use to which these should be put ... despite the face that the

threats to survival, both nuclear and environmental ... do not favour a slow accretion of legislative alleviations evolving without a parallel accompaniment of large-scale vigorous action on behalf of individuals.

(p. 141)

The U.N. is unable to intervene in the domestic practices of its members; and although the public retains the illusion that international bodies exist, like courts, for the redress of individual grievances, these bodies are in most cases powerless to protect petitioners or compel reforms; or even, in many instances, to discuss the questions raised (p. 79). Many of the least active areas of the U.N. emanate exhaustion: it is the fatigue that comes from resisting limitation imposed on capacity, rather than from using oneself.

(p. 96)

Hazzard quotes a Middle-Eastern delegate's observation that: "We are in a beleaguered fortress. The world organization is cut off from the world" (p. 211).

3   The U.N. excludes itself and is excluded from crucially important world conflicts. Of course, the U.N. could not be expected to deal simultaneously with every international conflict, but it seems ludicrous (and suspicious) that it has never been a participant in any "Strategic Arms" talks, the most pressing international event of all world history to date. Hazzard shows clearly the resultant exponential increase in paperwork, resolutions, counter-resolutions and endless debates over less pressing issues that are the tell-tale signs of avoidance, **distraction**, cover-up and denial.

Yet, I would argue, to point the finger at the U.N. organization may itself be a denial of our own allegiance, or the world as a group's allegiance to the latent aim of keeping that organization impotent.

Hazzard notes that:

The public's unexacting indulgence is perhaps the greatest single obstacle that the United Nations idea has had to contend with. Had the Organization and its deliberations been subject from the first to a full measure of public criticism, had it—instead of posing as a convocation of higher beings—been required to justify its procedures in the face of enlightened public comment, or been obliged by its supporters to meet even moderate standards of coherence and common sense, its story would have been more of a struggle and less of a tragedy. Instead, a set of unassailable founding principles has been used as a talisman to ward off self-knowledge. The fact is that the public in general has never been encouraged to take the U.N.'s existence seriously, that is, as an instrument whose ultimate usefulness depends on an implacable public willingness to hold it to serious standards of achievement. It is frequently stated that the U.N. is 'our best hope for peace'. Nevertheless, our best hope for peace continues to rest in the public's determination to have peace; and to create and maintain, by accompanying public insistence, effective instruments for world order.

Public opinion is not 'a factor' in the fate of the U.N.: it is the factor—as it is in all the interaction of contemporary world politics ... A refreshing draught of public indignation over their leaders' performance in U.N. assemblies, a sustained agitation for U.N. effectiveness from a huge body of world opinion, a concentration of unremitting demands for Secretariat initiatives—an emphatic show, in other words, of high expectation—would even now wreak vital transformations in all the deadly circumstances ... as it is, the public has never understood, or been instructed in its power in this respect.

The many sincere and energetic proponents of a stronger U.N. have been unwittingly deflected into putting the Organization's view to the world, instead of forcing the world's emergency on the Organization. The U.N. exerts in such circles the strength of the weak—taking the position that the exposure to any forms of criticism other than the 'agreed' ones would cruelly endanger its frail hope of survival. Thus enfeebled by an ever more liquid diet of obligingness or indifference and demanding a bedside manner from the world, an organization that might have been vitally charged with global life and death, with great issues of right and wrong, has been emasculated into a place of sweetness and light all too closely resembling a sickroom.

(pp. 140–141)

Accordingly, the most insidious, destructive weapon in the world today is apathy, consciously justified as a "realistic" sense of futility, hopelessness and powerlessness about achieving meaningful, effective mediation of "superpower" hostility and lethality.

(The current failure to negotiate anything at all between Russia and Ukraine is but one, if glaring, example of UN impotence because of the way it has structured (idiotically) the workings of the so-called *Security* Council.

But unconsciously, in my view, such apathy indicates a firm and deadly alliance with a mentality that obstructs any effective *mediation* (←—→) – a mentality that attempts conflict resolution by blind, aggressive application of the kill-or-be-killed credo – and which must lead irreversibly to annihilatory (at present nuclear) warfare. An "eirenarchical" world group – one which *actively* promotes the resolution of potentially destructive conflicts – would repudiate such an alliance.

Conclusion

The conclusion to a speculative chapter cannot be "conclusive." To suggest or demand that countries notice and deal more effectively with their internal conflict (→←) through the consciousness-raising of a relocated U.N. more powerfully involved with the most intense international conflict almost misses the point because these things would be the results of the world-as-a-group wish for integration and effective management of its various tensions. Or even, to put it more basically, a wish to prevent total destruction. So these suggestions would have no meaning *without* such a wish.

On the other hand, the various types of public support, commitment and awareness required to activate such changes can be "nudged"; particularly (as with our patients) by bringing destructive impulses into consciousness. As Hazzard puts it:

> It is estimated that there are 27,000 persons in New York City alone associated with the United Nations; and a large number of these have undertaken the task of conveying the significance of U.N. operations to the general public. Why should infinitely more not be done by these groups and individuals to alert the public to adverse developments and deteriorating leadership within the Organization itself, and to press for correction?
>
> (p. 141)

Any re-organization of the world-as-a-group's "mind," as with the mind of an analysand, cannot progress along the path of the relinquishment of destructive, narcissistic and manic-magical organization unless it is fuelled and nourished by the faith, hope, meaningfulness and goodwill that is offered by something dependably better. But how do we become convinced that a reliably better organization is both possible and good for us? I think that such a conviction can only emerge as we watch and experience our feelings in repeatedly familiar situations. We begin to know those organizations of our internal and external worlds which leave us feeling hopeful, loving and alive and those which repeatedly leave us feeling hopeless, indifferent and dead.

If the current organization charged with the safety of the international world is unreliable, un-containing and possibly even irrelevant, then it is possible to re-organize. Mere exposing and denouncing would produce a vacuum. However, I am suggesting that a good, hopeful and reverentially alive feeling would accompany efforts at something better and more durable, but that this feeling is the *sine qua non* of steps towards its creation, providing that the hope is not "blind."

When this chapter was commenced, 35 years ago, a popular Irish musician organized a worldwide communications link-up for a concert to raise money and consciousness about starving people in Africa. He achieved both these aims and also seemed to generate a feeling of concern and aliveness (even if somewhat tinged with idealism) not seen in the "younger generation" since the late 1960s demonstrations against war and victimization.

I have seen stinging attacks launched against this effort of organization – especially by politicians and "intellectuals." Their 'argument' is that only a small proportion of the aid got through because of political problems in the starving countries and that the aid would not be sustained. While I have no doubt as to the truth of these observations, their tone strikes me as very odd. I think that this is because they refused to acknowledge that a threshold between hopelessness and hope was, even if momentarily, crossed. What was achieved, beyond the considerable dollar-pound-food-tonnes-lives saved was the realization that there is a good, warm integrative feeling associated with helping to improve the world as a group's organization. Or, put another way, that the cohesive unification of activity and purpose channelled into the task of establishing a "feeding" concept at a world level might provide a satisfying way of being alive that would render obsolete the always desperate concerns about Gross National Products and military superiority which has us looking down the barrel of Mutually Assured Destruction. Or, worse than that, has us locked into a state of mind which can only wait passively and pathetically for the trigger to be pulled. Or worse still, which robs and deprives us of an alive feeling of interconnectedness with the human myriad which could transcend the brightest nuclear blast. (apologies to Milton).

Summary

This chapter reflects upon unconscious conflicts that pave the way for nuclear warfare and the destruction of human life on a worldwide scale. Attention is drawn in particular to the problem of establishing an effective, publicly encouraged organization which could contain and balance these conflicts without collapsing under their enormously destructive pressures. Some evidence is provided which suggests that the current organization (the United Nations) is not yet strong enough to fulfil this critical function.

References

Bion, W. (1961). *Experiences in Groups*. London: Tavistock Publications.
───── (1970). *Attention and Interpretation*. London: Heinemann.
Fornari, F. (1975). *The Psychoanalysis of War*. Bloomington: Indiana University Press.
Hazzard, S. (1973). *Defeat of an IdealA Study of the Self-Destruction of the United Nations*. London: Macmillan.
Horney, K. (1950). *Neurosis and Human Growth*. New York: Norton.
Meltzer, D. (1973). *Sexual States of Mind*. Perthshire: Clunie Press.
───── (1983). *Dream Life*. Perthshire: Clunie Press.
Rosenfeld, H. (1983). Primitive object relations and mechanisms. *Int. J. Psychoanal.*, 64: 261–267.
Segal, H. (1987). Silence is the real crime. *Int. Rev. Psychoanal.*, 14: 1–12.
Steiner, J. (1986). Turning a blind eye: The cover up for Oedipus. *Int. Rev. Psychoanal.*, 12: 161–172.

Chapter 5

Dreams Grown False

The "cannibalization" of alpha function

This brief chapter is an attempt to further explore, a serious problem of emotional development, where there is a marked disjunction between feeling and "alpha processing" – Bion's (1970) term for the meaningful symbolization of emotionally charged experience into elements that help to provide food for thought and, eventually, action in response to these, often turbulent experiences.

I want to focus particularly on the intrapsychic dynamics of this disjunction and will begin with a description of a vivid short story by Sylvia Plath, and leave a discussion of the more theoretical aspects of the dynamic to follow afterwards. Then I will bring in some clinical observations for further discussion.

My main point about this disjunction between feeling and alpha process is that it involves a polarization between a flashy, impressive but meaningless production of "symbols" (really anti-symbols) and a concrete, sterile wallowing in untransformed "raw" feeling, and therefore no container for the developing self, an hopeless, desperate suicidal state of mind.

These two "poles" may be in a deadly battle for supremacy and therefore eventual physical suicide is a real possibility.

> I will only focus only on certain elements of the whole story here, and just use them to help illustrate and to describe the suffocating transfixion of the relationship that ensues – as a model for the intrapsychic breakdown of the capacity to think symbolically about feelings that I am exploring.

Sylvia Plath wrote her short story, *The Wishing Box*, in 1956, soon after her first suicide attempt, and it is part of a collection entitled *Johnny Panic and the Bible of Dreams*:

> Agnes Higgins realized only too well the cause of her husband Harold's beatific, absent-minded expression over his morning orange juice and scrambled eggs.
> "Well," Agnes sniffed, smearing beach-plum jelly on her toast with vindictive strokes of the butter knife, "What did you dream last night?"
> "I was remembering," Harold said, still staring with a blissful, blurred look right through the very attractive and tangible form of his wife (pink-cheeked

and fluffily blond as always that early September morning, in her rose-sprigged peignoir), "those manuscripts I was discussing with William Blake?"

"But," Agnes objected, trying with difficulty to conceal her irritation, "how did you know it was William Blake?"

Harold seemed surprised, "Why, from his picture, of course."

And what could Agnes say to that? She smouldered in silence over her coffee, wrestling with the strange jealousy which had been growing on her like some dark, malignant cancer ever since their wedding night only three months before when she had discovered about Harold's dreams. On that first night of their honeymoon, in the small hours of the morning, Harold startled Agnes out of a sound, dreamless sleep by a violent, convulsive twitch of his whole right arm. Momentarily frightened, Agnes had shaken Harold awake to ask in tender, maternal tones what the matter was; she thought he might be struggling in the throes of a nightmare. Not Harold.

"I was just beginning to play the Emperor Concerto," he explained sleepily, "I must have been lifting my arm for the first chord when you woke me up."

The narrator of this story goes on to describe how at first Agnes was fascinated by the array of famous people (particularly great American literary figures) or the endlessly "fascinating" visual images – beautiful red-purple deserts

... with each grain of sand like a ruby or sapphire shooting light. A white leopard with gold spots was standing over this bright blue stream, its hind legs on one bank, its forelegs on the other, and a little trail of red ants was crossing the stream over the leopard, up its tail, along its back, between its eyes, and down on the other side.

But soon Agnes, predictably, feels left out and inferior; exiled from the world of really exciting life, and she starts to brood. She is appalled by the gloomy, unflashy and uncertainty of her own dreams, which occur very infrequently anyway. She retained "only" their "stifling, storm-changed atmosphere which, oppressive, would haunt her throughout the following day." She finds her own "imagination" to be very small and inadequate as compared to Harold's;

... so tedious, in comparison with the royal baroque splendour of Harold's. How could she tell him simply, for example: "I was falling," or, "Mother died and I was so sad"; or, "Something was chasing me and I couldn't run.?

The plain truth was, Agnes realized, with a pang of envy, that her dream-life would cause the most assiduous psychoanalyst to repress a yawn."

But Agnes begins to muse wistfully that she did have a wonderfully fertile imagination when she was a child, where wishing boxes grew on trees and, by the sounds of it, her dreams were very effective slaves to wish-fulfilment (perhaps like

Harold's) rather than disappointing producers of depressive, emotionally reverberating pictures of her gloom, which she found dull and ugly.

As a reader, we are already very suspicious of this state of affairs in the blocked dream dialogue/marriage of Agnes and Harold. In fact, it is becoming clear that Agnes has really emotionally meaningful dreams, and Harold's are beginning to sound more and more like idealized "faecal penises" produced for phallic, envy-provoking display and to avoid his own depression about **his** own sense of internal damage. For example,

> Once, at a depressing and badly aspected time of Harold's life before he met Agnes, Harold dreamed that a red fox ran through his kitchen, grievously burnt, its fur charred black, bleeding from several wounds.

But,

> ... last night I was fishing there, and I caught the most enormous pike you could imagine – it must have been the great-grandfather of all the rest; I pulled and pulled and pulled, and still he kept coming out of that pond.

At last Agnes, in desperation, confesses to Harold that she doesn't dream **anything** anymore. Harold, with condescending concern, tries to polish up her dreaming technique by forcibly trying to improve Agnes' power of imagining. This has a disastrous effect on her because it leads her to be even more rejecting of her inner reality – the "gaping void in her own head" – and she turns to superficial, glossy unsymbolic food for non-thought such as newspapers, magazines, catalogues and even the instructions on soap-flake boxes, in a "ravenous hysteria."

Now Agnes feels more desperate because she is trapped in a concrete non-evocative, non-symbolic two-dimensional world where she is nothing but a camera lens; not a feeling human being. There is no meaning left in anything; and the next step is a full-blown addiction to alcohol and television to seal her mental existence into the world of the concrete and the hallucinogenic. She is no longer able to sleep at all:

> Finally a bleak, clear awareness of what was happening broke upon her: the curtains of sleep, of refreshing, forgetful darkness dividing each day from the day before it, and the day after it, were lifted for Agnes eternally, irrevocably. She saw an intolerable prospect of wakeful, visionless days and nights stretching unbroken ahead of her, her mind condemned to perfect vacancy, without a single image of its own to ward off the crushing assault of smug, autonomous tables and chairs.
>
> (p. 52)

After overdosing on sleeping pills, Agnes is found dead by Harold when he returns from work. She is wearing an emerald taffeta evening gown and looks very much like someone from one of **his** dreams. Her "... tranquil features were set in a slight, secret smile of triumph, as if, in some far country unattainable to mortal men, she were, at last, waltzing with the dark, red-caped prince of her early dreams."

He, like Melanie Klein, felt that the infant's early relationship with the holding, feeding and particularly the understanding mother was the key to approaching the psychotic's perpetual misunderstanding of the world, where Knowledge is used for disconnections and for moral superiority (-K) rather than food for thought and emotional growth (K). Bion particularly wanted to look at factors contributing to such wayward development, but also outlined a model of what happened mentally when things went right. He focused on the mother's capacity to dream a reverie about her infant, where its needs and character could be thought about creatively and responded to imaginatively (alpha function). The result of this is not just a decrease in anxiety in the infant but also the provision of a model of an alive, thinking mind for the infant to identify with, particularly if it found itself in distress at a later stage, with the mother physically absent.

Bion puts this in a somewhat mechanical way: "... the container/contained apparatus becomes installed in the infant as part of the apparatus of alpha function" (1962, p. 91).

But, if

> ... the infant splits off the projects its feelings of fear into the breast together with envy and hate of the undisturbed breast, then it will internalize a devouring, greedy breast that strips goodness and meaning from all that the infant receives.

This internal object, sometimes referred to as a "primitive superego" starves the infant psyche from all understanding, and makes any moderation of the fear of dying impossible. It is an antarctic emotional atmosphere (perhaps referred to as *Beckettian* or *Pinteresque* these days), and, according to O'Shaughnessy (1981) this "... Continuing mutual denudation and misunderstanding between mother and infant will leave only-K between them, a cruel, empty, degenerative link of superiority/inferiority" (p. 181).

I think that this is very much the state of affairs between Agnes and Harold in *The Wishing Box*, where the starving infant self is tortured and teased by the show-off, flashy superego, which pretends to have a monopoly of the production of truly creative "symbols."

Bion (1962) writes:

> In so far as its resemblance to the superego is concerned -alpha (-container/contained) shows itself as a superior object asserting its superiority by finding fault with everything. The most important characteristic is its hatred of any new development in the personality as if the new development were a rival to be destroyed. The emergence therefore of any tendency to search for the truth, to establish contact with reality ... is met by destructive attacks on the tendency and the reassertion of the "moral' superiority. This can be seen as implying an

attempt to retain a power to arouse guilt. In this case, however, the guilt aroused is meaningless guilt, and therefore contrasts with a conscience in the sense that this meaningless projected guilt does not lend itself to constructive activity.

Meaningful emotional material is still collected, but instead of being allowed to combine and develop, perhaps symbolically, these elements are "stripped" of their meaning and only the worthless residue is retained. The ego-like function of container/contained is unlike ego function in destroying rather than promoting knowledge. This destructive activity is tinged with "moral" qualities ... asserting the "moral superiority and superiority in potency of UN-learning.

(1962, p. 98)

Ultimately, the patient feels surrounded by meaningless remnants or images of what were once meaningful thoughts, impressions or intuitions.

I now want to elaborate on the clinical picture, as it emerges in the transference/countertransference minefield, keeping in mind O'Shaughnessy's (1981) guiding principles for working in such a field:

The shift from K to -K is a problem of varying seriousness in different analyses. Sometimes all work done is denuded and -K spreads like a cancer over every link between patient and analyst. Sometimes the stripping of K occurs only in pockets. Bion's work demonstrates the necessity for tracing the fate of meaningful interpretations, to see whether they retain vitality and their connection with the analyst. If they do they will be developed unconsciously; but if they become disconnected they will lose meaning and go dead. It is necessary to trace the particular processes which reverse the achievement of K, to ascertain whether the child believes they come from his object or from himself, for whatever reason of anxiety, perversity, pain or envy.

(pp. 184–185)

The following is some case material from a woman who came to see me when she was in her mid-50s, and whose initial complaint was that something was "eating her up inside." She would repeat the phrase, "It's eating me!" many times and rub her hands against her chest. After several interviews where she unwound a somewhat never-ending life story that did not generate more meaning as it went on, some information became clearer, but an understanding of what was "eating" her did not. She readily agreed with this and said that she wanted help to find out what it was before she was devoured by despair.

She was the second of four children – the others all male – and from very early on apparently became the "substitute' mother" (the mother you become when you don't have, or don't want, a mother) to compensate and comfort herself for the inadequacies of her alcoholic, unpredictably absent mother. There were confused innuendoes about mother having been a prostitute and father was, at first, described as a singing, dancing joyful minstrel who gave everyone a zest for life. Years later there were confused hints about his unreliability, promiscuity and irresponsibility, and it appears that all the children were at one stage made orphans. In her twenties, the patient married a sailor, and although he seemed to be absent or drunk for part of the time, she felt it was a very good relationship – except for her annoying mother who kept trying to grab the patient's husband as her own. Apparently, her husband and her mother would sit on the verandah and drink late into the night while the patient felt excluded and belittled but never dared to complain.

She did, however, complain of the awful pain of the traumatic and sudden loss of her female lover, with whom she commenced a relationship a few months after the death of her husband. She wondered whether the horrible feeling of rejection from the homosexual relationship might be due to the incomplete mourning of her husband. But the focus very quickly shifted to feelings about her mother, whose health was deteriorating. Her mother did in fact die, a few years into the therapy, and the patient reported all manner of psychosomatic ailments in identification with what she thought was happening to the inside of her mother.

In the transference, at first, there seemed to be a kind of honeymoon period, where I was seen as the omnisciently clever parent who understood everything about her, and she imagined that she was the ideal, ever-helpful patient bringing an endless array of interesting dreams and colourful material.

At first, this felt like quite a good arrangement – and it took me quite a while – many months – to emerge from a kind of pleasantly flattering, lazy, automatic stupour.

Eventually, this had a rather "sickly" feeling, for me – like having eaten, greedily, too much sugary food at an amusement park.

As I became more thoughtful and less "automatically responsive" she became more and more irritated with my apparent disinterest in her paintings, short stories and poems which she would display – usually verbally, but occasionally concretely.

She would often scream at me – immediately following her presentation of a very elongated dream or experience that it was "all symbolic!" and would then wrap herself up in her own explanations of her "symbols," and gradually became very gruff with my pathetic attempts to clarify her feeling states and her concerns about the limitations of our relationship – particularly that I was not omniscient and was not readily available following any anxiety or distress that she suffered in my absence.

I began to realize that we had, initially, been suffering from what Meltzer (1992) refers to as the "delusion of clarity of insight" and that her so-called symbols were placed as impediments to us thinking about her emotional life.

Although I felt myself as demoted from "Einstein" to the village idiot, nevertheless something more authentic had punctured the initial "sweet paralysis" of our thinking together about her feelings and the great stresses of containment that would invoke invoke, in us both.

This seemed to usher in a quite different phase of the shared work.

Where her "story-dreams" were once being used as "things-in-themselves" – for evacuation through shallow omniscience, and compulsive storytelling, rather than as keys which could open the doors to her emotional depths.

For example, she spoke of realizing that she didn't really **have** to obediently listen to some "doorknock adventists" – that she was free to politely but firmly decline the "enlightenment" that they were supposedly offering.

A change also took place in the countertransference.

Whereas I had often felt quite left out in "twiddling" thumbs mode (she imagined, accurately), especially after I'd made any interpretation about her emotional disconnection from her dreams.

Interestingly, in spite of her conscious annoyance with me, including many innuendoes of leaving – unconsciously she brought a lot of seemingly inconsequential, "… by the way…" material about regaining contact with old friends who were often, surprisingly, in better shape than she had imagined – or quite a few stories of amazement that someone had made a recovery from cancer, or some seemingly hopeless affliction.

Sometimes she would say "shut up!" before I had even finished a sentence. But there was always some part of the session – usually after the therapist used his alpha function against massive regressive forces which seemed to impose mindless sleepiness – where she would momentarily reflect on quite touching images of orphans, street kids and other motherless, homeless sibling creatures.

If I attempted too forcefully, or too quickly, to trace these figures back to her own desolate, isolated abandoned baby feelings then she quickly returned to the lustrous sterility of endless, meaningless "pictures." (Later, we could trace some of this to an erotically charged childhood games of hide-and-seek with her brother, which served as desperate distraction from unbearable feelings of abandonment and rejection, and to fire up excitingly omnipotent phantasies of her becoming the promiscuous, seductive nurse-parent, who helped the poor, needy little brother to survive.)

To provide some more detailed material, I will now focus on three highly condensed episodes of dream exploration, which appeared in stark contrast to the earlier, impressive-oppressive atmosphere of her material. And I present these here because they allowed me the first glimpses of what was "eating" her from the 'inside.'

Dream 1

> She is trying to stuff a brown sausage into the mouth of a hungry little baby, but each time the baby tries to digest the sausage, it burps and the burp smells awful.

She was not forthcoming with associations, so I remind her that in the previous week, we had been looking at how she "smeared" people who tried to help her, by finding fault and then complaining that the help "stank."

She responded with a stubborn grunt, and I added that perhaps she was trying to feed me something long and brown, but wanted to complain about how stinkily I digested what she gave me and that she was also worried that I might complain about how she farted away my shitty, indigestible interpretations. The patient immediately exclaimed: "How dare you make that suppository about me!"

She then denied the slip, but was prepared to explore its implications if I would agree to "eat my words."

Dream 2

This dream stands out as the most emotionally significant experience that she and I had together. She really did seem terrified and jolted by the dream and seemed totally sincere and involved in relating it to me. I felt this dream, as compared with most of the rambling narratives which she had hitherto presented to me.

> She is in the jungle, and it is dark and frightening. Gradually she sees, with total horror, that she's eating something with a group of cannibals. She knows it must be human. At first she thinks it's just a pink flummery or mélange (she must mean blancmange), but she knows, deep down, that it is probably a breast.

This was a very rare dream for her, because of its conjunction of feeling, concern and "nightmarish" image that felt "real." She repeated: "It's just so horrible." Which reminded her of the Marlon Brando "psycho-killer" in the film Apocalypse Now.

Dream 3

This dream came to mind when I confronted her about the way she could change the meaning of what I had said to her in previous sessions, or even in the previous few minutes, and how she then fed her altered meaning back to me as a complaint about my deliberate and cruel misunderstanding of her.

> She has thrown a burning cigarette towards a telephone pole, which catches fire, and so the power and communication lines get crossed and all these sparks are flying; then a Telecom worker tries to fix it, but he says there might be too much damage and maybe it will just have to be left with the wires crossed. She tries to hide so she won't be found guilty of causing the damage.

Meltzer (1978), writing about "the reversal of alpha function," says that the motto of the (manic) defence would be, "If you damage mummy and the sight of it causes you guilt and remorse, smash her beyond all recognition until you feel only horror and revulsion" (p. 123). And Bion (*Cogitations*, 1993), in discussing the retreat from alpha process, from meaningful, associate-able symbols which have links with emotional experiences, notes that:

> ... it is felt that these visual images, by virtue of their suitability for dream-thought, make imminent the depressive position. This carries with it the danger, the certain danger, of the emergence of a murderous superego ("brutal"): and also the problem of the onset of the depressive position, namely depression, a synthesis that reveals the enormity of the destruction already done, and the illimitable vista of the yet unintegrated elements that have not been synthesized.
>
> (p. 113)

As I said earlier, the feeling that somewhere a baby is being left for dead can be covered by delusions of clarity of insight – where the patient cannot see why the therapist thinks there could be anything left to understand after the patient has so charitably explained the meaning of all his or her mental life. Obviously all this can be very seductive to the therapist who is starving for emotional meaning from the patient and eager to fix the tears (and tears) in the linkages between thinking and feeling, infant and mother, and material and interpretation. But, at least unconsciously, if the therapist does treat all of this material as if it is the real thing, the starving infant in the patient will feel rejected. The ambience of such a relationship is cleverness/insincerity and it is the road to impasse, in comparison to intimate development over time through exploration of "real feelings." But the latter must always remain somewhat of an ideal because often the work in a session will involve recognizing and discriminating what is sincere as compared with what "sounds good." The trap for the therapist is to join in with the patient's impatience and greed for precocious (precooked) "symbols" which are not coming from alpha function working on emotional sense impressions of experience, but a greedy attempt to avoid the depressive pain of waiting for this to happen. (Often it is eventually possible to connect this with the external experience of a baby kept waiting for too long for the attentive body and mind of the mother.)

The alpha process can then be hijacked by an envious/deprived superego (internal saboteur) which then produces highly enviable impressive "images" (jingles) which make the "feeling" baby deprived/envious and helpless to express anything. Instead of waiting for "alpha reverie" to produce a containing thought (in identification with a mother who does the same externally), the superego grabs greedily and forces precocious (half-baked) symbols (mental dummies?) into a kind of hallucinatory consciousness, mass-producing "interesting" but meaningless dreams.

This desperate hurry to access a process which bypasses the need for the alpha function being "brought to bear" on painful emotional sense impressions, forms a kind of greed for expression. The aim of this is to expel the pain rather than to wait for the mysterious alpha process to produce a harmonizing "selected fact" or the sighing tears of the depressive position. Perhaps this is conveyed in the biblical story of the Golden Calf, where the group cannot wait for Moses to descend with the inspired words of order transcribed onto two tablets/breasts. Instead, they revel in a glitteringly false symbol of the God-head in a greedy, omnipotent state of mind, or rather, mindlessness.

I remember the artist Brett Whitely looking back on his production of works in the late 1960s and saying that he was greedy and impatient to get ideas and images out of his unconscious, and so used (eventually deathly) copious amounts of heroin. And returning to Sylvia Plath (1983) for a moment; from her journal:

A dream last night of my father making an iron statue of a deer, which had a flaw in the casting of the metal. The deer came alive and lay with a broken neck. Had to be shot. Blamed father for killing it, through faulty art. ... If only I could get it real ... I am so impatient. Yet the one important thing is to pile up good work, if, IF I could break into a meaningful prose, that expressed my feelings, I would be free. Free to have a wonderful life. I am desperate when I am verbally repressed. Must lure myself into ways and ways of loquacity ... My first job to open my real experiences like an old wound; then to extend it; then to invent on the drop of a feather, a whole multicoloured bird. Study, study ... "

(p. 314)

An aimless, desperate and "promiscuous" **imitation** of alpha-coupling-with-emotional-experience reproduces the despair of the infant who has not been picked up and held in the eyes of its mother's mind, nor fed the milk of human kindness and meaning. It fails to gather together the relevant emotional pieces of existence for transformation into thoughts which can modify the fear of dying within a bleak, black, meaningless void.

I think the most tragically beautiful attempt to be one's own receptive container/transformer/eyes of the mother, and its pathetic failure, is conveyed by Sylvia Plath's final poetic offering, *Ariel* (1968). (Particularly; Morning Song, Sheep in the Fog, Night Dances, Poppies in October, Death and Co, The Moon and the Yew Tree and Paralytic Words.) Throughout these poems, the attempt to be both container and contained, but without the life of the mother's eyes breathed into the child's transforming of its emotional experience, cannot be sustained in any hopeful way. They produce a vast and empty internal space, such as comets have to cross – with such forgetful coldness that flakes and peels at mere gestures ... that might have been warm and human in their "pink light."

The "development" which proceeds on false symbols, insincerity and aimless, unhinged alpha, is a kind of "cancerous mental growth" because the "cells" of the mind lack a transform-active element which can reproduce new life or regeneration. Instead, a flat, two-dimensional promulgation of the elements of emotional experience (not alpha-betized, but fragments of beta elements and bizarre objects) are just copied and shuffled, lifelessly, until the experience of life itself becomes a meaningless mortal coil. This is a victory of sorts for the envious self; the non-prophetic soul that hates change and views it as catastrophic. Cancerous growth does not contribute to the growth of the whole organization; so, because it diverts energy away from the organization as a whole, it therefore gradually "cannibalizes" that system. It survives in a medium of contrivance; the pretence of finding some new emotional synthesis (Bion's "selected fact"), but it is really only counterfeiting which stays well within the safe and miserable shallow of what is already known and outgrown, back turned rigidly on the unknown country. What is found through "cleverness" and force "devours" the imaginative and feeling creation of symbolic dreaming and daydreaming.

Harris Williams and Waddell (1992) stress this distinction, made clearly and poetically by George Elliot:

Powerful imagination is not false outward vision, but intense inward representation, and a creative energy constantly fed by susceptibility to the various minutiae of experience, which it reproduces and reconstructs, in fresh and fresh wholes; not the habitual confusion of provable fact with the fictions of fancy and transient inclination, but a breadth of ideal association which informs every material object, every incidental fact, with far reaching memories and stored residues of passion, bringing into new light the less obvious relations of human existence.

(p. 175)

In that sense, to grasp our patients "poetically" is not just providing an occasional grace note to our interpretations. It is a powerful model of rebellion against the sterile colonization of the mind by anti-symbol and imitation feeling, which, ultimately, will perempt suicide. Thus it becomes a matter of life and death that we are not seduced by "interesting" material – even "glittering" dreams. This entails an ongoing vigilance against responding to the patient in a "clever," or even logical manner, before we have really grasped a linkage between the presented material – which may well glitter with expectancy of a "great interpretation" – and authentic feeling.

To me, it remains an interesting question – worthy of further exploration – as to whether the dreams themselves were stripped of emotional meaning at the time of their dreaming – elongated into vast, unending stories with little resonance – or, whether it was her re-composing, re-telling and re-presenting of the dreams to herself, and to me, which unhinged the feeling connections to what might have been, especially in the nights of my absence, a perdurable, meaningfully creative consolation, in a sea of otherwise ungraspable and unfathomable pain and despair.

References

Bion, W. R. (1962). *Learning from Experience*. London: Heinermann.
―――― (1970). *Attention and Interpretation*. London: Tavistock.
―――― (1978). *The Dawn of Oblivion*. Perthshire: Clunie.
―――― (1992). *Cogitations*. London: Karnac.
Harris Williams, M. and Waddell, M. (1991). *The Chamber of Maiden Thought*. London: Routledge.
Meltzer, D. (1992). *The Claustrum*. An Investigation of Claustrophobic Phenomena, Clunie Press, Scotland.
O'Shaughnessy, E. (1981). W.R. Bion's theory of thinking. In *Melanie Klein Today*. Ed. E. B. Spillius. London: Routledge.
Plath, Sylvia (1968). *Ariel*. London: Faber & Faber.
―――― (1977). *Johnny Panic and the Bible of Dreams*. New York: Harper & Row.
―――― (1983). *The journals of Sylvia Plath*. Ed. Hughes, T. and McCullough, F. New York: Ballantine. p. 108.
Shakespeare, W. (1988). Twelfth Night. In *Shakespeare Collected Works*. London: Abbey. pp. 212–276.

Chapter 6

The role of *Disidentification* in the growth of personality and during the analytic termination phase

The psychoanalytic literature on "identification" is vast, and almost every paper makes mention of the concept. One could spend many papers lost in nuances of definition and chronological reference foraging and still not begin to narrow a focus for meaningful discussion. Yet, to write about the rarely discussed concept of **disidentification**, one must say something about identification.

Freud (1933) tried to keep the concept clear and distinct in his New Introductory Lectures:

> ... 'Identification' - the assimilation of one ego to another one, as a result of which the first ego behaves like the second in certain respects, imitates it and in a sense takes it up into itself. Identification has been not unsuitably compared with the oral, cannibalistic incorporation of the other person. It is a very important form of attachment to someone else, probably the very first, and not the same thing as the choice of an object. The difference between the two can be expressed in some such way as this. If a boy identifies himself with his father, he wants to be like his father; if he makes him the object of his choice, he wants to have him, to possess him. In the first case his ego is altered on the model of his father; in the second case that is not necessary. Identification and object-choice are to a large extent independent of each other; it is however possible to identify oneself with someone whom, for instance, one has taken as a sexual object, and to alter one's ego on his model. It is said that the influencing of the ego by the sexual object occurs particularly often with women and is characteristic of femininity. I must already have spoken to you in my earlier lectures of what is by far the most instructive relation between identification and object-choice. It can be observed equally easily in children and adults, in normal as in sick people. If one has lost an object or has been obliged to give it up, one often compensates oneself by identifying oneself with it and by setting it up once more in one's ego, so that here object-choice regresses, as it were, to identification.
>
> (p. 62)

In this deceptively straightforward, somewhat academic account of identification, there are some startling revelations – particularly, that identification is felt to be a kind of weakness (regression), because of its passive ("feminine") origin. By comparison, object choice is seen by Freud to be more an expression of conscious will of the ego, rather than a passive capitulation.

But, considerable complexity was added to the concept of identification when Melanie Klein (1946) proposed that identification could be either introjective or projective – the former producing growth, through psychically taking in elements of external objects to develop and re-sculpt their internal representation. The latter – projective identification – became a cornerstone theoretical concept to explain personality diminution and psychotic processes; although Klein did note that it could also play a crucial part in the capacity for empathy and for love.

With both Freud (1931, 1933) and Klein (1946), identification still remained a mysterious unconscious process, although there was some concordance in the idea of identification being particularly prompted by loss, death and absence of the external object, and Klein reshaped Freud's concept of mourning into her concept of the depressive position. This gave it a mercurial quality, being both a defence against separation anxiety and also a way of bulwarking internal representation of the lost object in order to reduce that anxiety, while simultaneously building and developing the palette of the personality on the steady foundation of the good object.

Although rarely stated directly, the aim of the analysis was to lessen identification with self-destructive elements of the Self and to displace those identifications with the supposedly healthier, growth-enhancing elements of the analyst's character. Freud described resistances to this identificatory process, and Klein (1957) saw unconscious envy as a major limiting factor.

Perhaps the closest term Freud had for disidentification was "decathexis" – but very little was said in explanation of that mysterious process, although frustration was thought to be its instigator.

> Childhood love is boundless; it demands exclusive possession, it is not content with less than all. But it has a second characteristic: it has, in point of fact, no aim and is incapable of obtaining complete satisfaction; and principally for that reason it is doomed to end in disappointment and to give place to a hostile attitude. Later on in life the lack of an ultimate satisfaction may favour a different result. This very factor may ensure the uninterrupted continuance of the libidinal cathexis, as happens with love-relations that are inhibited in their aim. But in the stress of the processes of development it regularly happens that the libido abandons its unsatisfying position in order to find a new one.
>
> Freud (1931, p. 5)

But, not a lot was said about exactly how identifications were relinquished and displaced, and it was not until 1968 that Greenson focused on the process of *disidentification*.

He argued that:

> ... the male child, in order to attain a healthy sense of maleness, must replace the primary object of his identification, the mother, and must identify instead with the father.

The girl too must **dis-identify** from mother if she is to develop her own unique identity, but her identification with mother helps her establish her femininity.

... I am using the term "dis-identify" in order to sharpen my discussion about the complex and interrelated processes which occur in the child's struggle to free himself from the early symbiotic fusion with mother. It plays a part in the development of his capacity for separation-individuation, to use Mahler's terminology (Mahler, 1963), (1981). The male child's ability to *dis-identify* will determine the success or failure of his later identification with his father. These two phenomena, dis-identifying from mother and counter-identifying with father, are *interdependent* and form a complementary series. The personality and behaviour of mother and father also play an important and circular role in the outcome of these developments (Mahler and La Perriere, 1965). The mother may promote or hinder the dis-identifying and the father does the same for counter-identification.

(Greenson, 1968, p. 372)

Greenson was obviously attempting to interweave his concept of disidentification with Mahler's concept of "separation-individuation," and neither author was particularly concerned with distinctions between the internal and external worlds and their corresponding objects. But clearly, they both see that the widening span of identification is crucial to individuation – the developing uniqueness of a personality – and that this must operate in tandem with disidentification from one's previously essential objects of attachment. Blazina, (2004) elaborating Greenson's ideas, agrees that "... the emphasis upon the normal psychological separation/individuation that occurs with both caregivers as a male develops into his own unique person ... is viewed as healthy and normative and is not equated with **disavowing** or disconnecting from either caregiver."

Fast (1999) concludes that a boy's secure sense of masculine identity primarily develops from the quality of the boy-to-mother attachment (not separation) and refers to this developmental phase as **attachment**-individuation rather than separation-individuation.

And yet Mahler (1981) stressed

... the difficulty in gradually shifting primary identification with mother to *selective* identification with her. No mechanism is more important for the achievement of a child's separation-individuation than *selective identification*. This is usually facilitated by dilution, as it were, of the exclusive symbiotic dual-unity stage by distribution of cathexis to father and siblings in the family.

(My italics; Mahler 1981, p. 630)

This takes us back again, full circle, to Freud's distinction between identification and "object choice" and leads me to conclude that a crucial determinant of the success or failure in forming new, healthy, lively identifications is the emotional tone in which the disidentification is made. Later, I will link this tone of disidentification to the sway of the life and death drives.

A simple example might be a rebellious teenager who disidentifies with his or her family. The rebellion may be of crucial importance and allow an eventual geographic separateness and independence of mind, and the parents may have been perceived to be threatening the teenager's attempt to carve out a distinctive identity for him or her. But where there may be an exaggerated denial, denunciation and disavowal of all identification then the separateness becomes quite flimsy, because working through the disidentification is shallow, hurried and incomplete. The supposedly new identity is fragile, being built on a foundation of the triumphant denial "I am not you!", and the internal objects – especially the combined object – have not yet evolved from the withdrawal of projections from the external object (Harris Williams and Waddell, 2011).

Gabbard (2000) has noted the more denying disavowing form of disidentification in the analyst, where there is a failure to accept a "necessary" negative countertransference. He believes that

> ... many suicidal patients are searching for a 'bad enough object' (Rosen, 1993; Gabbard, 2000). It is incumbent on the analyst to resist the magnetic pull to **disidentify** with the aggressor. We must be able to recognize that aspects of the patient are infuriating, annoying, destructive and abusive, and we must be able to own our reactions. It is the analyst's role to be hated and to understand that hatred, not to projectively disavow unpleasant affect states and see them in parental figures (or others) outside the consulting room.
>
> (pp. 124–137)

De Swaan (1997) sees such "projective disavowal" as a key unconscious process in war and hatred, reflecting on the 1994 atrocities in Rwanda – and therefore uses disidentification in a quite negative sense, referring to the processes as a form of denial and projection of one's own negative, hated qualities into the Other. This brings about social exclusion, and "emotional disidentification, with its accompanying affect: hatred" (p. 107). And Daehnert, (1998) recalling Winnicott's use of the term "false self" as a defensive organization formed by the child as a result of inadequate mothering or failures in empathy, suggests that this false self may also form protectively, as a means of "disidentifying" with that mother. Daehnert makes it clear that she sees such disidentification as more of a defensive survival manoeuvre, to put psychological space between mother and child, rather than the healthy outgrowing of the parental identification.

Finally, Tresan (2007) quoting Henderson, in what seems to be the only analytic discussion of disidentification in relation to termination and the "dissolution" of the transference, states:

> "In 1954 Henderson spoke of pre-individuation initiations, (where) the lesson to be learned is that of *disidentification*, the dissolution of identifications:"
>
> Each initiation, in this light, signals the breaking of an initiate's identification with a dominant in his or her life. In Dr. Henderson's model, mother, in both her

personal and archetypal dimensions, is the first such dominant to be depotentiated and disengaged from, then father, tribe, tribal spirit, and lastly guardian spirit. With the subduing of each such identification (or one may say equally 'with the resolving of each identification', as in 'resolving a transference'), one's sense of self becomes less encumbered, more liberated, more itself, its horizons broader. One comes to know one's primary self as other than the child of one's mother, or of one's father, or one's group, etc.

(p. 22)

Thus, we see that whereas some authors regard disidentification in a more positive light, as facilitating and part of healthy psychic growth, others view it as a defensive wrong turn in development, which will have to be readjusted in later life.

It may be that such a conceptual dipole concerning the effects and function of disidentification is somewhat illusory, once we allow for subtle differences in the original definitions of the term. But the issue seems to depend on whether or not disavowal is or is not involved in the move away from the internal parent, and whether or not it is healthy growth, or defensive survival, that largely motivates this move.

The following vignette may illustrate the complexity, anguish and lingering confusion for the growing self in its attempts to forge a creative, authentic identity.

> A patient who was a potentially gifted, but inhibited, writer felt that her creativity was being 'paralyzed' by a friend who kept saying "but, have you read this …?" and so she never quite got around to just writing what she herself wanted to say. After an analytic break, she returned to say that she had "lost contact" with that "friend", but had seen a lot of a new friend (with the same name as the analyst) who instead said "just go with what **you** have to say" and worry about its originality, or not, later. This she did, and produced a short story which was subsequently published.
>
> But, she still had lingering fears that her first friend would threaten to expose her as "an unconscious plagiarist", and she envied intensely those writers that she imagined were totally free of such anxiety, and who could just let go and express themselves freely.
>
> This was eventually also linked to her lifelong difficulties with intimacy – particularly her fears of letting go sexually and in expressing love, as well as a lack of freedom to choose a partner and a job that she found satisfying because of the fear of being too different to her friends, family and analyst.
>
> (Indeed, it took a very long while before she felt able to openly disagree with analytic interpretations, for fear that it would highlight difference.)

Disidentification and disavowal

As I see it, the seemingly divergent views on the importance and nature of disidentification can be summarized as follows:

There are two ways that **identification** can occur – either as an admiring, loving drinking in of the spirit of character of the other, or as an impatient, envious attempt to quickly graft something of the other onto oneself, or to swallow the other whole, with little digestion or getting to know the other.

In the myth of the Garden of Eden, Adam is asked to take time to get to know and to name all the animals, but he is tempted, via Eve, to devour knowledge, as if it just grew on trees.

Likewise, there are two ways that **disidentification** can occur – either as a respectful gradual outgrowing of the limits of a previously admired and introjected object and relationship, or as a premature repudiating, denying, disavowal of the relationship – a kind of spitting out, before the identification has really taken hold in the psyche, and made its full contribution to growth.

Disavowal says, defiantly, "This is not me!" and is based on a manic, envious, denial of dependence and a disavowing (projective) identification. By contrast, disidentification (in the more depressive form that I am using in this chapter) says "This was once me – but no longer." and is therefore an acknowledged parting of the ways, both instigating and a part of a search for the new.

For the creative artist, there is a constant fear that the appropriating, envious disavowal has dominated one's creative productions, as compared with a respectful, but inevitable disidentification.

In Herman Hesse's *The Glass Bead Game* (a game not dissimilar to analysis) the hero Joseph Knecht is constantly burdened with feelings of inferiority and inadequacy on his unknowing path to becoming the new Magister Ludi. This ever-doubting humility, even more so than his intellectual growth, leads to Knecht's eventual transformative growth into a quite different successor to his mentor.

Conversely, Stravinsky (1963) felt that "stealing"[1] aspects of another composer was important, and not plagiaristic, so long as one **loved** the initial inspiration – then something organically new would grow, even if recognizable traces of the original persisted, almost as a tribute.

Plagiarism is mere imitation or photocopying, and there is no development.

To summarize: the "**Death** drive version" of disidentification is envy, intolerance of beauty, and a narcissistic denial of dependence, cloaked in pseudo-originality.

Whereas the "**Life** drive version" occurs through a healthy dissonance within the growing self that requires a re-alignment of its identifications because good objects may become either thwarting or irrelevant to that growing self, or incompatible with the ego-ideal, which is a combined object psychic structure (Meltzer, 1966). I will have more to say about the importance of the combined object in disidentification later, but I do want to stress the depressive pain of mourning in this form of disidentification – as we must relinquish the security of older selves.

Eugenie Grandet and Catherine Sloper

Such pain is illustrated pithily by Balzac and James, in their novels *Eugenie Grandet* and *Washington Square*, respectively.

The fathers in these strikingly similar narratives will not tolerate or acknowledge their daughter's (new) coupling. This is partly because of their narcissistic wish to have their daughters as caged, singing (King Lear with Cordelia) adoring clones – but, also because of their projections onto their daughter's suitor of their own troublesome inclinations – particularly, greed and "sponging parasitism," probably born of their anxieties about vulnerability in old age, and particularly their repudiation of their own infant selves.

The daughter's chosen spouse must prove to the father that he does not want to be pandered to in the way that the father has been indulged in by his (supposedly) slavish "little girl."

The two fathers shown here have been indulged by their obedient daughters, until the time when the daughters' hunger for psychological birth, and a loving, tender, sexual intimacy that the father cannot provide. These fathers believe that the only way to keep the "purity" of their stock is by attempting a graft of their own self onto the next generation.

The extremely brief excerpts below show the tragically doomed heroines of James and Balzac in the throes of their ill-fated attempts to disidentify with (the phantasies of) their heartless, tyrannical fathers.

> "I feel differently; I feel separated from my father."
>
> "Upon my word," said Morris, "you are a queer family."
>
> *"Don't say that - don't say anything unkind," the girl entreated.*
>
> *"You must be very kind to me now, because, Morris, because" - and she hesitated a moment – "because I have done a great deal for you."*
>
> "Oh, I know that, my dear."
>
> *She had spoken up to this moment without vehemence or outward sign of emotion, gently, reasoningly, only trying to explain. But her emotion had been ineffectually smothered, and it betrayed itself at last in the trembling of her voice.*
>
> "It is a great thing to be separated like that from your father, when you have worshipped him before."
>
> (Washington Square, ch. 26) Henry James (1880)

The double irony in James' depiction of Dr. Sloper and his supposedly dull daughter, Catherine, is that the father does indeed appear to be correct in his (projective) assumption that her suitor is merely parasitic. And yet he misses the crucial point that Catherine needs to make her own mistakes in the world, including painful disillusion in her love choices, if she is to develop freely as a human being.

At first, Balzac's Eugenie Grandet appears to be faring better:

> Noticing for the first time the cold bareness of her father's house, the poor girl felt a kind of irritation at her inability to make it appropriate to her cousin's elegance. She felt a passionate need to do something for him. But what? She

had no idea. In her honest simplicity she followed the promptings of her angelic nature with no misgivings about her impressions or feelings. The mere sight of her cousin had aroused in her a woman's natural inclinations; they were all the more intense, as now, at the age of twenty-three, she was fully developed in body and mind. For the first time her heart was filled with terror at the sight of her father; she saw in him the master of her fate and felt guilty at keeping some of her thoughts from him. She began to walk hurriedly, surprised that the air she breathed seemed purer and the sun's rays more invigorating; she seemed to draw from them a spiritual warmth, a new life.

(Balzac, *Eugenie Grandet*, p. 58)

Eugenie feels guilty about keeping thoughts to herself, just as she is on the threshold of disidentification with not only her father but also an old stifled and un-free version of herself. The scene continues to where she is jolted into seeing that her father is cold and ungenerous, as if never before noticing this crucial difference between his character and her own growing, loving self.

There is a moment where Eugenie does disidentify with her father's values and allows herself to be internally critical of him. Her heart-broken cousin is crying for the tragic loss of his beloved father when Eugenie's miserly father says of him

> But that young man is good for nothing. He is more concerned with the dead than with money.
> 'Eugenie shuddered to hear her father talk in this way about the holiest of sorrows. From that moment she began to be critical of her father.
>
> (p. 76)

Tragically, Balzac and James' two young women don't complete the process happily, and to the extent that any such woman does or does not make the leap away from being defined purely by the father's constrictive expectations that she just be a version of himself, or of her mother, she will shape the quality of individuality and new growth, or its stifling, in her new "married" life. For we must also disidentify with what we think our parents want us to be.

However, the girl cannot complete the disidentification process (gaining internal freedom to decide whether or not to identify with the internal parent; not just simple rebellion or defiance or choosing to oppose) unless she successfully combines with her new lover (prince) as he similarly opposes his construction and constriction by the (*dragon-witch*) mother, or miserly, controlling father. Many fairy tales and myths have depicted this struggle – from *Pelleas and Melisande* to *The Little Mermaid* to *Shrek*.

There are also many examples of the equivalent struggle for the male trying to disidentify with his mother, viewed through a particularly macabre humour, in the films of Alfred Hitchcock – for example, *The Birds*, or *North by North West*, and of course the spectacular failure to disidentify with the mother in *Psycho*.

Disidentification, the combined object and the depressive position

The analogous process of disidentification, for the adult parent, is to allow the child to become themselves by growing from, and processing the internal combined object in their **own** way, and not just through the fearful asymmetry of identification with one parent alone.

The internal parent who does allow this benign individuation is always loved, but may need to be augmented by teachers, aunts, uncles, friends of the family, or film or television characters who are able to strengthen the child's faith and courage in the pursuit of the values and ideals of the *combined* object, which may be considerable and onerous. Of course, a single parent can sometimes be a model, in spirit, for an internal combined object – depending on their psychological role – but a less possessively envious or jealous parent will respect whatever the once-child makes of their combined object in the way of its external representation in new relationships, particularly those outside the family.

We need to remember that where Klein's (1928) original concept of the combined object was an internal representation of the parental couple mainly infused with anxious and aggressive impulses, Meltzer, Harris Williams and Waddell (1978, 1988, 1991) had in mind a much more inspirational, rather than terrifying, construction in phantasy.

This is so because the creative inspiring combined object also has in the admixture of its composition the child's Life Instinctual impulses – in particular, the growing reparative, loving, synthesizing and aesthetic capabilities. Maizels (1996) has suggested calling this more benign development of the combined object the ***combining*** *object*, and stresses its more positive synthesizing and integrating qualities for the growing child.

I find it interesting that the Freud-Abraham-Klein focus on drinking in/feeding, as the mind's metaphor for (introjective) identification, hasn't been more widely expanded, at the **whole**-object level of internalization, to the drinking in of the "spirit" of the loved object. In fact, the work of mourning could be seen as the gradual realization that this drinking goes on after separation, physical loss and death.

Elsewhere, (Maizels (1995) I have suggested that this is what allows depressive anxiety to become bitter-sweet remembrance, as we emotionally review the **whole** of our relationship with the one who has been lost. We realize that the physical presence of the other is longed for, but not essential for the safekeeping of the essence of the loved one in the heart of one's mind, nor for continued drinking in of that essence, with strengthened identification over the years. When the lost object is firmly established, internally, a new hope of finding its realization in a new external object brings spring to the wintry depressive anxieties of desolation in the absence of the original loved object.

I am now suggesting that disidentification also invokes such a series of losses and mourning.

If Introjective Identification can be seen as a "drinking in" of the spirit of character of the parent, then incorporation may be equated with a bad "graft," which can only produce imitation and parroting, and never quite takes hold in the growing self as a source of true identity. Therefore disidentification can never occur, because the fragile, false copied-self would fall apart, not having any substantial, psychically alive foundation to build upon – and mourning is not possible. Notably, autistic children have great difficulty with the renewal, growth and supplanting of internal objects, and seem exposed to "black hole" nothingness (Tustin, in Grotstein, 1981) when faced with opportunities to meet new people or establish new relationships, that might augment good internal objects, were they sturdily enough established.

As I said earlier, The **death** instinctual version of Disidentification involves a narcissistic denial of dependence, envy and intolerance of beauty.

But the **Life** Instinctual version has as its basis a growth that requires a re-alignment of the self & its identifications. At this threshold, even previously good objects may become thwarting or irrelevant to the growing self, and incompatible with its ego-ideal, which is a **combined object** (Meltzer, 1979) psychic structure.

If we speculate that the internal objects always hum around a self, which is influenced by them in its formation and judgements – then that self may rebel and change and talk back to those objects – as Britton (2003) has depicted through the way that job questions God, in the biblical story.

It remains a question of ultimate mystery as to whether there was always the existence of a rudimentary, intuitive self which "chooses" its objects of identification, or whether the initial objects of identification oversee and unconsciously select their own heirs. Probably there is a complex, unfathomable two-way influence.

Yet, disidentification proper can only occur when the fledgling agglomerated self has solidified enough, through the *combining object*, to be able to "sense" that the individual parental identifications no longer resonate with its own potential purpose & spirit – perhaps what Winnicott had in mind by the term "potential self," or what Jung just called the self (with the capital S to emphasize its overarching nature).

Whatever we choose to name it, it seems likely that some overarching monitoring-comparative self-agency does this sensing, and "knows" when growth towards the potential self is on or off course, and when the successful path of that self is no longer served by the current identifications with particular objects

It may be that personality characteristics and traits are derived from individual parental identification, whereas one's "spiritual force" – one's dynamic unity of purpose – is forged through the cumulus of combined object identification.

I will try to illustrate.

The Squid and the Whale

Because clinical symbolic representations of the combined object is so personalized, and hence difficult to disguise, in the interests of confidentiality I will make illustrative use here of a cinematic depiction of a young man's struggle to disidentify with his impossibly narcissistic father, as he simultaneously struggles to grasp his combined internal couple. Obviously, what I have to say would be better understood for having seen the film, but it so vividly conveys the struggles and pains of disidentification in the process of "growing up" that I will attempt an outline of its major themes.

The film *The Squid and the Whale*, written and directed by Noah Baumbach (2005), is supposedly based on his own adolescent struggle to come to terms with his parent's relationship. We see a young man, Walt, struggling with the inscrutability, anguish, terror and unfathomability of his parents' failing relationship in order to discover his place in the world.

This combined internal object is strikingly symbolized by the final image of the film, where Walt gapes at a huge museum model of a whale and a giant squid locked in an unlikely, but awesome embrace – an image which terrified him as a child.

The film opens with the dying days of a marriage. Two parents and their two sons are playing tennis – doubles, and the father, Bernard, is taking the game far too seriously. For him, it's clearly not for fun, but to shore up his own pride in being better than his wife. We learn that he is a mildly successful, but waning novelist-lecturer, his wife, however, is about to be published, and her star is on the rise.

Bernard does not cope well with the dawning realization of this – and of her probable affair with a younger, humbler, healthier man – and he tries to clutch the allegiance of his two sons (Walt, 16, and Frank, 12).

As a father, Bernard describes, through an oft repeated anecdote about how his family served up "always one less ..." at meal times – unconsciously describing his internalized ungenerous, depriving breast. This is also a sad, insight into his own difficulty giving of himself, in an unselfish way, to his sons, his wife – and probably even to his own writing creations.

The younger son, Frank, tries to disidentify with this self-destructive narcissism in his father, and attempts a healthier identification with his mother's more recent love object – conveyed by his adopting the lover's phrases, especially the affirming greeting "Bro'!". It forms a verbal bridge to a new type of father, one that values intimacy, encouragement and respect, rather than omniscience and superiority, previously offered by Bernard. (In spite of his claims that he loves his boys, more often than not Bernard lords it over them.)

However, a disturbing tell-tale symptom of his difficulties emerges at school, where Frank has been caught smearing semen, publicly.

But the main focus of the film is on Walt – at 16, feeling the crunch of adolescent hormones, a crisis of creative confidence (he feels a need to publicly pretend that he wrote an already famous Pink Floyd song) and no longer able to just parrot his father's (dubious) aphorisms without being caught out by astute friends.

Gradually, through painfully realizing the limitations of what he can expect from identifications with his father, he manages (is impelled) to confront – through intense anguish, curiosity, and the sheer will to grow – the baffling combined parental object, which is symbolized by the Squid and the Whale – two awesome and frighteningly intertwined, but mysterious creatures, which he sees at the museum.

Walt goes from blindly identifying with his blinkered father (the lie about his having stolen the Pink Floyd song is dismissed as a "technicality" by his father) to a poignant childhood memory, revived when with his therapist, of his mother making the squid and whale less troubling and more bearable.

WALT

And I was glad she let me leave the party early to watch the movie. It's like ... we were pals then ... we'd do things together ... we'd look at the knight armour at the Met, and the scary fish at the Natural History Museum. I was always afraid of the squid and whale fighting. I can only look at it with my hands in front of my face. When we'd get home, after my bath, she'd go through all the different things we saw that day in the museum.

And then we'd get to the squid and whale and she'd describe it for me, which was still scary, but less scary and it was fun.

(p. 91)

Her transforming the fear into something to behold and to ponder – which his therapist is enabling in the here and now of the transference – gives him the courage to go back to the museum at this crucial disjuncture with his cripplingly narcissistic father. I am suggesting that Walt's struggle to find his own identity, which can no longer be grafted onto his father's (or mother's) requires a disidentification with both of the individual parents, and a courageous psychological confrontation with his internal combined object, as represented by the Squid and the Whale at the museum.

He garners this courage after his therapist facilitates, through the transference, a calm holding object, which enables contact with the awful and awesome symbol of his unfathomable internal parental couple.

Here is the final image of the film, as described in the shooting script:

Museum of Natural History

Walt enters the room ... finds the Squid and the Whale that he has discussed with the shrink, earlier.

He approaches it a bit warily. It's dark and scary.

He gazes into the black, finding the squid and then the whale. We STAY on his face as he takes this in.

Very slowly, he leans his head against the glass. And rests.

CUT TO BLACK (p. 111)

Transference and countertransference just prior to disidentification

I have noticed, repeatedly, the presence and intensification of what I will call the *Chameleonic Object* just at the verge of disidentification and just prior to termination.

By this I refer to a rapid and intense oscillation in the self's sense of certainty as to the goodness or badness of that object, especially with regard to suitability for either identification or disidentification.

The presence of this Chameleonic Object also causes immense confusion in the countertransference.

It is an internal object which is repeatedly presented as addictive, obstructive, uncaring and compellingly bad for the patient – but, as soon as the analyst tries to help with the weaning from this supposedly bad object, its **good** side is revealed, and the **analyst** becomes the bad, misunderstanding object who is out to deprive the patient of their most important source of love and security.

The analyst is then left highly confused and unappreciated, because not only is the Chameleonic Object relentlessly attacked and then quickly defended, but vice versa applies to the analytic relationship. The patient is left more (misguidedly) determined than ever to reclaim the Chameleonic Object, and to prove the analyst to be an, interfering, jealous, bullying fool.

It can be a very vexed time, when there is a real danger of the patient terminating prematurely, and the analyst may be left feeling that they are indeed that bad, inept object – incapable of sustaining the intensity of the infantile transference and countertransference.

Above all, patience, confidence in the work, and a non-defensive steady hand, while waiting in uncertainty and under attack, seem particularly necessary in this pre-disidentificatory phase.

Eventually, gradually – the patient will start to fall in love with the **work** (the analytic combined object) and the vexed ambivalence of the "chameleonic transference" is gradually sloughed off. The external representation of that object will start to seem far less important in the patient's life, and curiosity about one's own mysterious choices, in love and in life direction, will take on a renewed zestful energy. The focus will usually, eventually, return to the "Holmes-Watson" working relationship – with its accompanying gentle gibes and helpful hunches, and often a new love or interest appears, out of the blue, in the patient's external world which may make the coming anguish about termination more bearable, soft and bitter-sweet.

Because rapid and fluid disidentification is crucial in the capacity for selective attention, we must be able to decide in a millisecond what to attend to, and what to filter out from consciousness, or we would be paralyzed and overwhelmed by the multitudinous storm of stimuli that we face in even a few seconds of life in the external world. So disidentification and some remnant of skill in thinking about the Chameleonic Object can be helpful in later life – so that we do not become too paralysed by complex or charismatically persuasive personalities, and can think about them.

The type of disidentification that is eventually possible, through the termination process, will heavily depend upon how the initial identification was formed. If it was mainly under envious-incorporative conditions then it will produce in its wake, a hasty, charismatic, enticing-addictive combined object substitute, rather than a warm, resonant, inspiring, renewing combining object identification – and therefore the disidentification will produce an empty, vengeful "Black Hole" (Tustin, 1981), where new experimentation goes dead under the tyrannous rule of an omniscient superego parent that hates liveliness. This often produces, especially in mid-life, fiercely regretful and reproachful fantasies – that one should never have moved on from, or left, relationships where love and growth had died. This serves to rob the mid-life self of a sense of enjoyment of what one **does** have, and has worked for, in spite of its shortcomings. It decries the sense that things are as they should be, even though there will always be many regrets. The popular expression "seeing the glass half full or half empty" captures the emotional knife edge.

Like DNA, infinitely variegating its next generation, so healthy disidentification – through its splicing together of the combined object with the aspirational ego, ensures a new generation with minds only partially formed from their individual parents'.

By contrast, 'psychotic disidentification' – under the influence of the death drive – is an ill-fated attempt to introject a pathological combined object, which is treacherous and sphinx-like in its tormenting of the infant mind. As mentioned above, it corresponds to Klein's original concept of a terrifying and aggressive *combined object,* which is formed from the infantile projection of all of its most jealous, confused and envious oral-sadistic and anal-expulsive impulses. (In Othello, Iago calls this "the beast with two backs.")

Now the disturbed infant is trapped between a terrifying identification with the latter, and increasingly claustrophobic identifications with the individual (probably disturbed) parents. Unless some alternative good objects appear (a frequent theme in Dickens – for example, *Oliver Twist*) then growth will be seriously subverted and diverted by allegiances to feral gangs (including organizations with a veneer of civilized caring), eventually extinguishing all hope of development, and of creative love.

Pathological disidentification can also lead away from one's true self towards an identification (which is constantly failing) with one's **idealized** self-image. In the early stages of analysis, this is transferred onto the analyst and, via a harsh superego, may generate massive feelings of inadequacy and envy (or its denial, in contempt and mockery). Then, the work in the analysis is in re-introjection of the true (infantile) self, and a disidentification with the "impossible" idealized superego and its external representatives. This, in turn, reshapes one's life aspirations and hopefully makes them more realistically achievable. Often in mid-life, these are revisited and may need sweeping alterations, in accord with the reality principle and one's growing apprehension of mortality, with its power to cut all things short, through a (seemingly) ruthless limitation on time.

If successfully negotiated, under the benign watchfulness of the un-ideal analyst, this reworking will lead to a more benign compassion for the imperfection and limitations of other people as they, in turn, struggle with their own imperfections and limitations.

A clinical fragment

Just prior to deciding to set a termination date, and just after a series of dreams in which she was telling a tyrannical old married couple to "stick it!" a patient dreamt that...

She is walking along a cliff-top (overlooking a gorge called "The Gulp") and finds a coin, which looks quite beautiful, and so she wishes to keep it. But, she isn't sure if she has the right to call it her own.

She looks closer at the coin, and sees that her own face is on one side – but, she deliberately refuses to look at the other side of the coin.

Underneath her picture is written: "legal tender if calm and collected."

(She laughs at the pun when telling the dream.)

She eventually does turn over the coin and sees the Australian coat of arms – an emu and a kangaroo, and she wonders why she had never properly taken in this strange and striking image before. She wakes up with a "humble" feeling that there is more to the world than what she had hitherto been aware of, and with an appetite for meeting someone or doing something, new.

The patient had sought analytic help because of a crippling perfectionism, which often left her depressed, and feeling that her life and the world were "without lustre." This became markedly intensified with each analytic break where she seemed, at first, to seek out cool, indifferent potential lovers. She rationalized this by sexualizing the coolness and then protesting to me that I was cruelly insisting that she be attracted to "un-cool" men. This became proof of my perfectionistic aloofness when returning from breaks, and she imagined that I must have a quite cruel, condescending relationship with my wife – even "whipping" her for not being stimulating enough.

Her father had seemed to be a quite niggardly, obsessive coin collector who had barely seen anything good in her and was, apparently, constantly critical of her mother. So the patient was shocked, as a teenager, when her parents – to her great surprise went off for several months on an outback trip, on which they seemed to particularly enjoy the wildlife and each other. I remembered this and linked it to the feeling of surprise when she really looked closely at the coat of arms on the coin in the dream, and she replied: "This stuff we do together, like on my dreams, I can't imagine ever doing that by myself."

I was about to respond with a bland, and blind, reassurance when the patient suddenly remembered her father teaching her to ride a bike. She told him, angrily, that she'd never keep her balance unless he was always there supporting the bike from behind, and he'd said: "Well then just **imagine** that I am there behind you, balancing the bike." After that, she had no trouble riding the bike at all and wasn't so frightened about facing the world.

This association seemed to form the pivot point for confidence in setting a termination date and was referred to many times subsequently.

Disidentification and termination

I see disidentification as a crucial part of the work of termination, as well as a harbinger of its looming on the analytic horizon, and as the process takes hold some graduations of change are discernible in the transference.

I have already mentioned the Chameleonic Object transference–countertransference field, but we can also easily observe an increasing annoyance and disillusionment based on a failure of materialization of the preconception of the perfectly understanding parent-analyst. There is an intensification of phantasies of someone who would understand the patient much better – of being stuck with the wrong analyst – similar to Freud's idea that we all imagine our real (royal) parents will one day be revealed.

Every disagreement with interpretations is now felt to be a catastrophe, much as a young adult needs to find points of wild disagreement to muster a critical mass of annoyance to propel the move out of the home.

Realizations of the shortcomings of the analysis – from annoyance to forgiveness for not being ideal, and especially, for not covering **everything** within the lifespan of the analysis, become more prominent. Often this starts with more conscious complaints about failing external mentors or authorities.

It is an enormous "gulp" to realize the work will have to continue without the presence of the analyst, into later life, and on ultimately to death, so there is a depressive feeling associated with loneliness, but ameliorated with the hope of finding new relationships as external realizations of the internal transformations, post disidentification. This is also aided by the more positive aspects of the disillusionment – that is, the lowering of the expectations of omnipotent protection and of omniscient teaching, which would render all future learning from one's own experience unnecessary.

If the spirit of the analysis is alive then it isn't crucial that every issue be dealt with prior to finishing because one can work on areas not touched on by the analysis without the analyst, with the new help of available understanding objects, through relationships forged in the same spirit.

Lit by the cold fires of impending termination, the emotional focus shifts away from a fear of forgetting important gems or pearls of particular insights and towards the fear of losing this spirit of the sessions. (This may also apply, although usually in a more compressed time scale, to the emotional process in clinical supervision.)

If disidentification is forced prematurely, then there may not be enough of the spirit formed and preserved to successfully form a new identification in the direction of growth, or the new identification may be desperate, idealized and short-lived.

It may become prey to a cultish influence, which may be furnished externally by highly narcissistic charismatic people, who peddle quick pseudo-growth through the magical acquisition (incorporation) of secret magical knowledge. This "growth" may then become a never-ending hunt for newer and more prestigious clubs and associations to join and to conquer, the ultimate danger (and irony) being the loss of all sense of identity in a supposed fusion with a phallic-omniscient godhead who is later, after rapid disillusionment, felt to be a "dick-head".

Meanwhile, back in the countertransference of the termination phase – in a manner that had not heretofore been present in the analysis – the analyst may indeed enact the projection of this "dickhead" and actually try to convince the patient – say, through condescendingly "helpful" aphorisms – à la Polonius – that they are foolish and premature to consider termination.

The mantra becomes "You are not yet ready, you need more insight – you have not yet introjected enough of my containing mindfulness."

The interesting question of how a **training** analysis may complicate this phase of analysis is far too big to be more than raised as an issue, here. However, as a rough generalization, I would suggest that the training process, with its unavoidable emphasis on "joining the club," post-analysis, would necessarily complicate, and probably stifle the disidentificatory processes to some degree, depending of course on the state of the analyst's combined object.

But whatever the case, one must ultimately, at least somewhat, disidentify oneself from the role of "patient."

Paradoxically, when the identification is mourned, even in wilful and energetic disidentification, then the object is seamlessly integrated into the personality. Whereas if the identification was initially more imitatory, or envious, then the disidentification produces an inauthentic mere parroting or parodying of the object, which is set up as a straw dog to be savaged and mocked.

We are usually quite skilled in detecting whether children (or adults) are just repeating the ideas and words of others, not having grasped or digested their meaning. Perhaps we know the ring of inauthenticity and its resultant psychological strain – like watching a bad actor not adequately identifying with their lines.

The analyst must have faith in a capacity to join with the patient in sensing that the time for disidentification is authentic and ripe.

Higgins and Doolittle – separation, disidentification and the depressive position

In Lerner and Loewe's (1968) musical adaptation of Shaw's *Pygmalion*, *My Fair Lady*, Eliza Doolittle's song to Henry Higgins *Without You* gives us an idea of the ambivalence entailed in the above processes – where love and hate bring about a tempestuous showdown, as the necessary prelude to the new mutually adult relationship, for the sake of the brave and the new, and the world outside the cosy, (if fractious) known home. It becomes clearer and clearer to the audience that Eliza is just as important (not "impetant") an influence on Henry, as he supposedly is on her.

They are both, simultaneously, reviewing the entirety of their relationship – as they forgive each other's imperfection and stubbornness – and also revisiting their relationships with their opposite-sex parent, as they attempt to jostle their relationship with each other. This painful, but liberating, mutual realization in both Higgins and Doolittle (actually, she *does* quite a **lot**) of interdependence, and of Eliza's rebellion as a sign of success and development of their relationship, also sets them free from their individual parental identifications – she with her cynical father, and he with his magisterial mother.

In the shared space of the mutually taunting song *Without You*, Eliza exclaims what a fool she was – a dominated, yet elevated, fool – to idealize Higgins. She calls him a *reverberated friend* and declares that he is **not the beginning and the end**.

Unconsciously noosing himself, Higgins replies that she is just an **impotent hussy,** and that it is indeed **himself** who has put every idea in her head and word in her mouth.

Eliza then mockingly derides the "aesthetically-omnipotent breast" – noting with satisfaction that there will indeed still be spring every year without him. There'll be fruit on the tree. There'll be crumpets and tea, and even Keats!

I can do without you. You, dear friend, who taught so well, you can go to Hartford, Hereford and Hampshire! He curses her as brazen, but she continues a lesson in how gravity itself, and the Earth and clouds will still operate without him – but now calls him "Ducky," surely a name of love.

She shall not feel alone without him/can stand on her own without him. But now Higgins is in a triumphal pique about the success of his "creation" and although clearly confirming Eliza's accusations of arrogance, he now seems to notice that she is actually a woman – and a rather wonderful one at that … and Higgins' triumphalism returns to warmer, depressive Earth before long, with his wistful, plaintive: *I've Grown Accustomed to her Face* – the closest he can manage to a love song, even if comically understated. That song allows depressive anxiety to foment a loving, bitter-sweet remembrance of Eliza, which instigates a mutual forgiving of each other's imperfection and stubbornness.

If Eliza's song seems very rejecting – it is a blatant disidentification, at one level – it betrays a residual fondness if not the magnetically charged beginnings of domestic eroticism), and uses some of Higgins' own acerbic wit in humorous criticism. It puts him in his place, but it is without real malice.

Hopefully, there is no need to overly paint the parallels of Henry and Eliza with the intensely ambivalent feelings in the analytic relationship at the arrival of the termination phase, but I do want to stress here that the successful getting through of that process, with all its attendant depressive reworking, is inextricably linked with healthy disidentification. Whereas, its disastrous counterpart, premature termination, is often linked with **destructive** disidentification – a complete revulsion and repulsion with and of the analytic process – a "bulimic" vomiting away of anything good or helpful. (It's very important that Eliza doesn't just walk out on Higgins, but stays to have it out with him, and with the "alchemical" unconscious processes that occur between them.)

In its extreme, that type of bulimic ending will produce a lifelong enemy of analysis, who sees no good in any form of self-examination.

Disidentification and the developing self

To learn anything really new one has to temporarily disidentify with what one already knows, which is very threatening. One would need to be able to disidentify constantly with old selves to live totally in the present – which is impossible, both cognitively, and emotionally, because of far too much depressive pain. And yet, identification must be fluid, or else one's internal world stays fixed and intransigent to modification through new perspectives on experience (vertices) that life (and art) continuously offer up.

Particularly in adolescence, and again in middle age, there may be an awful tension between the need to securely embrace one's known identifications and the need to find new identification with objects that are more akin to the developing self, in spite of the sense of uncertainty and insecurity that they generate.

The falling out between long-time friends, or partners, is often an external indication that disidentification is in process in at least one of their inner worlds. By contrast, in regression, we sacrifice that potential growth, in the hope of a return to the safety of the known, and of the once-relinquished objects associated with that "safety."

Unconsciously then, disidentification may be equated with a form of death, in that previous parts of one's self die, as identifications with internal objects are relinquished. This is probably what Bion (1966) meant by "catastrophic change".

One must disidentify not only with one's previous work but also with the previous self which produced it.

Perhaps there are a handful of actors, barely riding the rim of psychosis, who are able to totally "lose" themselves in a role. Their craft is not just in letting go and disidentifying with their accumulated self, but in then finding a way back to it, after the role has been performed. And it is usually only the very great artist-composer who will continue, ongoingly, this process of identification-disidentification into later life – most being content, having found a style, to stick with it, and to produce, again and again, the "same work."

Further analyst-parent countertransference issues

The combined object – and one's interchange with it – often thrives when the actual parents (or analyst) are physically absent because there has been a spur to symbolize them, and their relationship to each other, as the combined internal object. But, of course, the external parents may not particularly like or agree with these new internal developments, and may put pressure on the young adult to become a clone of themselves, or to opt for security at all costs. If we are totally honest with ourselves, we always hope to lessen parental identifications and increase the patient's identification with our own somewhat idealized analyst selves. Like Prospero with Miranda, and Higgins with Eliza, it is often hard to see the successful parenting sewn in the now grown-up child's mind, when they wish to break free and to love on their own terms. Instead, this may be viewed as disloyalty or ingratitude, and the outsider (ultimately the wide world) is seen as a sordid interloper, counterfeiting love and upsetting the "natural order."

It might be argued that the single-most important contribution that the post-depressive parent/analyst can make is to graciously give their blessing to their transferential progeny – the new Sebastians, Kents, Florizels and even Shreks – or psychoanalytic peers who are very unlike the analyst – yet suitably able to continue inspiring the growth of the child-analysand-no -longer.

Of course, to do this, the analyst-parent must do some depressive work of their own, particularly in the area of omnipotent control – and must, eventually, trust in the internal combined figures now in place to guide the child, beyond their own limited bourn. All of Shakespeare's later plays take on this issue, which has power to sea-change the analyst-parent as much, if not more, than it does the individuating patient-daughter-son.

And certainly this issue was one that Freud had to face, as each of his heretofore loyal protégés drew lines in their own theoretical, and personal, sands. It can be difficult for the parent, or benefactor, not to feel that seemingly ungrateful sand as flung in their own face.

So, the termination phase, in particular, has to be a rather torrid time for both analysand and analyst, as they doubt and redoubt the wisdom of holding on or letting go. The analyst-parent will be tested many times, to see if they care more about their own power or the development of the child, and the "child" will be questioned many times, to see if they have sufficiently internalized the good parent before they begin to disidentify with selected, outgrown, aspects of that identification, for the sake of the (combined object) analytic work.

I hope that I have begun to show that the vicissitudes of disidentification are just as important for mental growth as those of identification, albeit leading ultimately to the final call to disidentification with life itself, in the impossibly mortal coil of mortality.

Summary

I have outlined two different ways that disidentification can occur – one involving great depressive pain in the service of evolving psychic growth. This also involves a movement away from individual parental identifications towards a coming to terms with the internal combined object, which makes great demands on security as it heralds *catastrophic change* and inspired individuality.

Much is also demanded of the analyst-parent, emotionally, particularly during the termination (leaving home) phase of the relationship.

Brief examples – some successful and some not – have been given to illustrate the turbulence and complexity associated with the process.

Note

1 "Lesser artists borrow, great artists steal." & "You must love what you steal, and then it is all right."

References

Balzac, H. (1833). *Eugenie Grandet*. London: Vintage Classics, 1981.
Baumbach, N. (2005). *The Squid and the Whale*. Newmarket. New York: Screenplay & Shooting Script.
Bion, W. R. (1966). *Catastrophic Change*. Bulletin of the British Psychoanalytical Society.
Blazina, C. (2004). Gender role conflict and the disidentification process: Two case studies on fragile masculine self. *J Men's Stud.*, 12: 112–126.
Britton, R. (2003). *Sex, Death & the Superego*. London: Routledge.

Cheever, J. (1946). 'The swimmer'. In *The Stories of John Cheever*. Ed. Cheever, C.K. London: Cape pp. 146–198.
Daehnert, C. (1998). The false self as a means of disidentification: A psychoanalytic case study. *Contemp. Psychoanal.*, 34: 251–271.
De Swaan, A. (1997). Widening circles of disidentification. *On the Psycho- and Sociogenesis of the Hatred of Distant Strangers; Reflections on Rwanda. Theory, Culture & Society*, 14 (2): 105–122.
Fast, E.J. (1999). Early Masculine Identification. *Aus. J. Psychotherap.*, 2: 227–241.
Freud, S. (1931). *Female Sexuality*, SE. XXI, p. 5.
―――― (1933) *New Introductory Lectures on Psychoanalysis*. SE. XXII, p. 62.
Gabbard, G. (2000). Hatred and its rewards. *Psychoanal. Inq.*, 20: 409–420.
Greenson, R. R. (1968). Dis-identifying from mother: Its special importance for the boy. *Int. J. Psycho- Anal.*, 49: 370–374.
Harris Williams, M. and Waddell, M. (1991). *The Chamber of Maiden Thought*. London: Routledge.
James, H. (1880). *Washington Square*. New York: Signet Classics, 1964.
Klein, M. (1928). Early stages of the Œdipus conflict. International Journal of Psycho-Analysis, 9, p. 167–180. Repr. 1975 in: The Writings of Melanie Klein, t. I, London: Hogarth, p. 186–198. (1946). Notes on Some Schizoid Mechanisms. In *Envy and Gratitude & Other Works*. Ed. Money-Kyrle, R. New York: Dell, 1946–1963. pp. 28–53.
―――― (1957) Envy and Gratitude. in the above, 1975. pp. 256–312.
―――― (1975). 'Origins of the transference & on identification'. In *My Fair Lady* (sheet music album), Lerner & Loewe. Warner Music Publishing. (Quotations by permission.)
Mahler, M. (1963). *The Psychological Birth of the Human Infant*. London: Macmillan.
―――― (1981). Aggression in the service of separation-individuation - Case Study of a Mother-Daughter Relationship. *Psychoanalytic Quarterly*, 50: 625–638.
Mahler, M. and La Perriere, J. (1965). Separation-Individuation in Development. *IJPA*, 45: 155–167.
Maizels, N. (1995). Working through or beyond the depressive position? *Aus. J. Psychoth.*, 2: 96–114.
―――― (1996). The wrecking & repairing of the internal couple. *J. Melanie Klein & Obj. Rel.*, 1: 114–129.
Meltzer, D. (1966). Projective Identification and Anal Masturbation. *IJPA*. 51: 212–221.
―――― (1978). *The Kleinian Development*. Part II. *Richard Week by Week*. Perthshire: Clunie Press.
―――― (1979). Sexual States of Mind. Perthshire: Clunie Press. 1973 reprinted.
―――― (1988). with Harris Williams, M. *The Apprehension of Beauty*. Perthshire: Clunie Press.
Rosen, P. (1993). Identification with Bad Objects. *Am. J. Psychoanal.*, 54: 54–65.
Stravinsky. (1963). Radio interview. ABC radio, Australia. Cassette tape – ABC archive.
Tresan, D. (2007). Thinking individuation forward. *Journal of Analytical Psychology*, 52: 17–40.
Tustin, F. (1981). 'Psychological birth and psychological catastrophe'. In *Do I Dare Disturb the Universe?* Ed. Grotstein, J. London: Karnac. 181–196.

Chapter 7

Working through, or beyond the depressive position? Achievements and defences of a *Spiritual* position

In Melanie Klein's "Narrative of a Child Analysis" (1961) there is, to me, a very puzzling moment where both child and analyst are struggling to understand what it is to have a "heart." The analysis is accelerating, somewhat tragically, towards termination, and Richard is discussing his "Lovely Mrs. Klein" drawing.

> Mrs. K. interpreted Richard's struggle between his loving and hating her. He was trying to think that she was nice; beside the drawing representing her at the top of the page he had written 'lovely Mrs. K.'. Nevertheless, he did not actually think that she was lovely, and therefore drew her without arms and hair, and evidently had no intention of making her look nice. He hated her for leaving him and joining other patients and her son and grandson. Richard insisted that Mrs. K. was lovely on the drawing because her tummy was heart-shaped and the arrow in the middle of it meant love. (His face was flushed and he often put his finger into his mouth; the struggle between hate and the wish to control it, and the mixture of persecutory and depressive anxiety, were expressed on his face.) He asked whether Mrs. K. was sorry to go away. Was she going to stay with her son? She was not going to live in the heart of London was she? Richard suddenly became aware of the word 'heart', looked surprised, and pointing at the drawing said, 'But here is the heart.'
>
> Mrs. K. interpreted that her heart stood for the bombed London and was **not only injured by love (the arrow)** but also by bombs. Richard, who wished to love Mrs. K., was afraid that, because she was leaving him, he might turn into Hitler who was going to bomb her. This increased his fear of her death, his loneliness, and his sadness about her departure.
>
> (pp. 412–413)

But what does Klein mean by "injured by love"?

Quite clearly she is trying to convey to Richard, in emotional terms, her theory of the Depressive Position. That is, to bring to his awareness the struggle between love and hate within his mind, and his difficulties in holding both feelings towards the one object.

Richard seems to be saying: "I am trying to find something symbolic which will convey my struggle to love you in spite of feeling injured by your leaving me to be with others. And this symbol, to my surprise, brings together feelings about your tummy, your other sons, and the place you are going to, in the form of a wounded heart."

After briefly tracing some of the complications of the much-used Kleinian terms Depressive Position and Working Through of the Depressive Position, I will explore the usefulness of the old-fashioned term Heart as a symbol for depressive emotional capability.

Particular attention is paid to the development of the "whole-object Father" in the formation of an "observing-ego-in-feeling", and to the development of the "whole-object Mother" (Nature) in the formation of a "metamorphosic," feeling, philosophy of life.

Together, these formations give the mind a "heart", which may come under attack from an omniscient, Tiresias-like internal object.

Some clinical material is used to illustrate these achievements and defences, and to highlight the difference of emphasis (as compared with the working through of the depressive position) that they imply.

In Melanie Klein's "Narrative of a Child Analysis" (1961) there is, to me, a very puzzling moment where both child and analyst are struggling to understand what it is to have a "heart."

The analysis is accelerating, somewhat tragically, towards termination, and Richard is discussing his "Lovely Mrs. Klein" drawing.

> Mrs. K. interpreted Richard's struggle between his loving and hating her. He was trying to think that she was nice; beside the drawing representing her at the top of the page he had written 'lovely Mrs. K.'. Nevertheless, he did not actually think that she was lovely, and therefore drew her without arms and hair, and evidently had no intention of making her look nice. He hated her for leaving him and joining other patients and her son and grandson. Richard insisted that Mrs. K. was lovely on the drawing because her tummy was heart-shaped and the arrow in the middle of it meant love. (His face was flushed and he often put his finger into his mouth; the struggle between hate and the wish to control it, and the mixture of persecutory and depressive anxiety, were expressed on his face.) He asked whether Mrs. K. was sorry to go away. Was she going to stay with her son? She was not going to live in the heart of London was she? Richard suddenly became aware of the word 'heart', looked surprised, and pointing at the drawing said, 'But here is the heart.'
>
> Mrs. K. interpreted that her heart stood for the bombed London and was **not only injured by love (the arrow)** but also by bombs. Richard, who wished to love Mrs. K., was afraid that, because she was leaving him, he might turn into Hitler who was going to bomb her. This increased his fear of her death, his loneliness, and his sadness about her departure.
>
> (pp. 412–413)

But what does Klein mean by "injured by love"?

Quite clearly she is trying to convey to Richard, in emotional terms, her theory of the Depressive Position. That is, to bring to his awareness the struggle between love and hate within his mind, and his difficulties in holding both feelings towards the one object.

Richard seems to be saying: "I am trying to find something symbolic which will convey my struggle to love you in spite of feeling injured by your leaving me to be with others. And this symbol, to my surprise, brings together feelings about your tummy, your other sons, and the place you are going to, in the form of a wounded heart."

This chapter will briefly trace some of the complications of the Kleinian terms Depressive Position and Working Through of the Depressive Position, and will explore the usefulness of the "old-fashioned" notion of having a "heart".

The aim is dual, in that I will not only present a way of clarifying but also of extending these concepts. My reasons for attempting such difficult tasks is that I have grown increasingly dissatisfied about the enormous burden which these terms bear for those who have found value in Klein's work.

So I will attempt to explore the issue of whether or not Klein's conception of the "working through of the depressive position" is adequately differentiated from the "achievement of the depressive position," and further, whether or not the former is still adequate for our current understanding of the farther reaches of emotional development.

Whether or not these clarifications and extensions are actually more useful clinically than the current conceptions of the Depressive Position and the Working Through of the Depressive Position is hard to determine, partly because, unfortunately, almost all "post-depressive" emotional development has, in my view, all too easily been sheltering under the umbrella term Depressive Position.

A clinical illustration will be given as an indication of why I have found it worthwhile to consider some changes to the concepts.

One of the major difficulties inherent in writing about the process of emotional integration in development is that one needs to speak of many different things at once and from different points of view. So my argument will be put more like the branches of a tree rather than linearly, in the hope that its somewhat intangible "trunk" might be revealed implicitly.

The depressive position

It is not possible, in this chapter, to give a complete history of the different shades of meaning that the term "depressive position" has accumulated since Melanie Klein's naming of "it."

Good summaries have been provided by Segal (1964) and Hinshelwood (1989), among others, and although I will underline some aspects of these definitions, I mainly want to show some of the conceptual "indefiniteness" that has accompanied "post-depressive" emotional growth.

Meltzer (1978, p. 114) has noted an array of meanings indicated by terms such as overcoming, surpassing and penetrating the depressive position, where previously the term "working through the depressive position" was more common, and he himself uses the term "threshold of the depressive position" where previously the term "achievement of the depressive position" was more common. In fact, we use the latter term rather than say "the working through of the paranoid-schizoid position". Yet we do not have a term for something new achieved by the working through of the depressive position.

(Perhaps the term which I used above, that is, "post-depressive" is the closest there is to such a term, although some non-technical terms such as mature ambivalence or mature concern have sometimes been used.)

I think that there are at least two reasons why the working through of depressive anxieties has not been given a distinctive new name.

The first reason is that many analysts feel that "the depressive position is never fully worked through" (Segal, 1964, p. 74).

This is the belief that emotional growth consists of the *ongoing, lifelong* struggle to move from part-object, pre-ambivalent, persecutory states of mind to whole-object, ambivalent, concerned states of mind, with some increasing confidence that love for one's good objects can, on the whole, ameliorate or repair one's destructive intentions to them.

The whole relationship to objects alters as the depressive position is gradually worked through. The infant acquires the capacity to love and respect people as separate, differentiated individuals. He becomes capable of acknowledging his impulses, of feeling a sense of responsibility for them and of tolerating guilt. The new capacity to feel concern for his objects helps him to learn gradually to control his impulses.

(Ibid)

The other reason for no new term seems to be that **all** emotional integration and creativity is attributed to the working through of the depressive position.

The infant's longing to recreate his lost objects gives him the impulse to put together what has been torn asunder, to reconstruct what has been destroyed, to recreate and to create. At the same time, his wish to spare his objects leads him to sublimate his impulses when they are felt to be destructive. Thus, his concern for his object modifies his instinctual aims and brings about an inhibition of instinctual drives.

(Segal, p. 75).

Segal then equates all creative, artistic and particularly symbolic mental work with this working through of the depressive position.

The strength of her approach has been to bring a new "test" of emotional depth to creative endeavours.

But this, in my view, has also been a drawback, often giving the "thumbs down" to works of art and states of mind which do not appear to be primarily concerned with the working through of the depressive position, or, more specifically, with reparative intentions towards internal damaged objects through concerned guilt.

I want to explore the idea that it may be useful **not** to group all types of emotionally integrative states under the "banner" of working through the depressive position, although I acknowledge that it is certainly possible, and often helpful, to do this.

I perceive a state of emotional perception and transformation which, although absolutely dependent on capacities such as concern (and gratitude) for the maternal object as separate and with needs and a mind of her own, i.e., the "working through of the depressive position," carries qualities of mind more usefully kept distinct.

Such emotional states seem to have a level of integrity, dream language, and depth of feeling together with defences against the depth of feeling, all of their own.

I will try to argue that a new conception and vocabulary for this – what I will refer to as "the spiritual position" – might be of use clinically, and might also help to unravel some knotted metapsychological issues which are gradually becoming more apparent within that body of clinicians who make use of Melanie Klein's work.

"Transpersonal" psychologists (such as Assagnini, Groff, or Maslow) have addressed the importance of "spiritual growth" and "meta-reflection," but I hope to give more intrapsychic detail than their paradigms have, in my view, allowed.

Working through of the depressive position and catastrophic change

Perhaps I can briefly illustrate the stretch and strain that seems to be evolving between "Kleinian" and "Post-Kleinian" along the theoretical ridge where "depressive position," "working through of the depressive position," "threshold of the depressive position" and Bion's "catastrophic change" vie, by giving two examples.

The first example consists of some very critical comments made by Kate Barrows (1993) in her review of the "post-Kleinian" book *The Chamber of Maiden Thought. Literary Origins of the Psychoanalytic Model of the Mind* by Harris Williams and Waddell (1991), [but]

The 'Chamber of Maiden Thought' seems to represent a place in the mind where not knowing can be tolerated and where there is an intense aesthetic experience as well as increased awareness of dark or painful feelings.

> ... the concept of unconscious guilt frequently seems to be missing in the accounts of literary works; hence awareness of damage to internal objects and the importance of reparation in the creative processes are often surprisingly absent.
> (p. 208)

> Klein suggested that the creative process arises from a wish to restore damaged internal objects; this understanding led to her subsequent formulation of the concept of the depressive position.
> (p. 209)

[but]

> ... instead of awareness of depressive pain and ambivalence, , or 'deities', are often invoked by the authors. It is this tendency to idealisation which seems to obviate the need for recognition of the role of responsibility for unconscious guilt and the importance of feelings of compassion and concern in the transition from omnipotence to the depressive position.
>
> (p. 208)

So, whereas Harris-Williams and Waddell stress the importance of the internalized combined parents as forming a super (Platonic) ego-ideal, Barrows sees this model as a clinging to idealized (that is, part-object) parents.

Although a simple resolution of the differences of perspective does not seem possible, or even desirable, I will try to bring them closer together later in this chapter through some clinical material.

(I have made some further comments on the difference between the Klein/Segal depressive-reparative model of creativity and the Bion/Meltzer/Harris Williams catastrophic change-through-inspiring-ego-ideal model elsewhere [Maizels, 1993]).

A second example of slips of meaning when using the Depressive Position terminology is apparent in the following comments by Hinshelwood (1989) on Grotstein's supposed misunderstanding of the term – that is, of Grotstein's supposed confusion between depressive anxiety and the working through of the depressive position.

Depressive anxiety: The crucial feature of the depressive position, the anguishing over the state of the object, was criticized from a self-psychology point of view by Grotstein (1993):

> Klein has placed too much emphasis on the welfare of the object by the infant and has seemingly sacrificed the right of the infant to have a 'self of his or her own and/or to have recognition of the self's needs independent of consideration of the object's welfare.'

However, what he is describing is exactly the pain of the depressive position in its early stages when the guilt has a strongly persecutory tone that demands extreme self-sacrifice and slavery. It is because of this developmentally early quality of depressive anxiety that the person evades it, defends against it or retreats to the paranoid-schizoid position. It is only by working through this that the infant and older individuals can come to an easier adjustment between their concern for their object and the normal degree of self-respect (a sort of normal narcissism) required to look after themselves.

(Hinshelwood, 1989, p. 152)

In spite of Hinshelwood's criticism, Grotstein (1993) actually prefers a different term of his own for growth "beyond" the depressive position – when it is worked through.

He calls this the "Transcendent Position" which he sees as bringing serenity through a sense of "ultimate reality" (Bion's "O") which nonetheless rests on adequate mourning processes. (This seems similar to Jacques's (1965) conception of the working through of the depressive position as "sculpting creativity" in the service of a serene philosophical emotional achievement). He therefore locates the experience of catastrophic change to somewhere beyond the "working through of the depressive position," whereas Meltzer (1978) and Eric Rhode (1987) locate such "catastrophic" emotional movement (quivering between Ps and D) at the "threshold" of the depressive position?

But in the light of the above crossing of definition, could they (Meltzer and Rhode) mean the threshold of the **working through** of the depressive position?

At this threshold, change of one's emotional values is feared as a catastrophe, which has two, related but distinctive components.

1 The onslaught of **seemingly unbearable** guilt.
2 Fear of the loss involved in the transformation of the self, into a new person, through a "change of heart".

In my conception of a "Spiritual Position," catastrophic change becomes an ironic term, as the self becomes open to transformation and metamorphosis, and this enables and inspires one to have feelings about life, with all its vicissitude and unending change.

(Without this, one cannot experience what the Germans call Vergangenheitsbewältigung – a feeling of coming to terms with one's past – and without that, one cannot come to terms with the concept of death).

Beyond the depressive position

I will now describe the particular characteristics of the "spiritual position," together with defences against it, then some case material and more detailed discussion will follow, where I will make some attempt to resolve some of the theoretical issues mentioned above.

I suggest that there is a level of "meta"-feeling in the spiritual position, where one has *feelings about* one's accumulated feelings.

In a sense, this model resembles Shelley's poetic images of the growth of mind, where accumulations (clouds) of pining feelings are let flow into the accumulations of loving remembrances ().

This "spiritual" state, where one has feelings about all the feelings that one has experienced, feelings about life, *may* be serene, but not necessarily.

The poignancy and plangency of the spiritual position gives it an emotional fluidity perhaps similar to the function of music to film images.

> gives a kind of reverse barometer reading, emotionally, in that it reads the atmosphere that has accumulated rather than that which is gathering.

It may well involve a simultaneous emotional perception of love and hate being brought together towards the one object, in the Kleinian sense of ambivalence. But it involves a level of "emotional abstraction" whereby the "whole-object" is felt, beyond the parental, to be life (or God).

Catastrophic change is therefore the catastrophic annihilation of the part-object mother in order to make her more whole; that is, more in keeping with the whole truth of one's feelings towards her.

Defences against the spiritual position

Part of my attempt to differentiate this spiritual position is to describe emotional defences which seem different in quality and content to the manic defences of the depressive position (see Segal, 1994, pp. 95–96).

This is not an easy matter.

While the latter defensive system centres around the avoidance of guilt, concern and the need to repair the internal good object caused by one's destructive intentions, the following defences of the spiritual position are more to do with the avoidance of feelings towards the repaired, fullyfunctioning, whole-object, when it Is able to grip one's "heart" and bring about constantly metamorphic changes in the self, over which one has very limited control.

These defences may seem similar to some manic or obsessional defences of the depressive position, but here they are present *together with* a capacity for genuine concern and guilt (which is not present in manic or obsessive manoeuvres).

Briefly, the defences are:

1 An obsession with security and habit, repeating only what is "tried and true" and "proving" the propaganda that only what is tried can be true. This keeps "at bay" the emotional realization that

"... only the truest things always are true because they can't be true" (e.e. Cummings, 1958). Therefore the tide (of Change) can never be taken "at the flood".

Or, at the opposite extreme, change is brought about in a manic frenzy in order to give the illusion of control of all change, and to keep its emotional impact "un-new", and uninspiring – an addiction to catastrophe, as opposed to the allowing of "catastrophic change." This amounts to a denial of mystery and illogicality as an unmistakable presence in one's life experiences.

2 Depression is adhered to by repeated futile attempts to "repair" the "old" mother to continuously restore her, rather than to take the helm of the mind's ship and move out into the deep unknown of oneself, as captured in Whitman's

"Oh, we can wait no longer ...

we too launch out on trackless seas,

... sail forth, steer for the deep waters only ..."

["The Explorers"]

and at the same time, to see other qualities in the object apart from good or bad, frustrating or gratifying.

3 Identification is used as a defence against disidentification. By this I mean to include resistance against the extremely painful (but liberating) mental act of relinquishing (perhaps even renouncing) one's allegiance, ego-syntonicity and identification with a **previously helpful** and relevant good internal object which is no longer such to the emerging **new-born** self.

This work usually begins, very tentatively, in the termination phase of analysis or psychotherapy, but continues on well beyond it.

4 Hysterical precedence is given to "feeling" as compared to feelings *about* feelings so that "depth" and "perspective" are never built in the personality (Britton [1989], Fullerton [1994] and Young [1994] have linked the acceptance of the Oedipal Couple by the infant, in the depressive position, with the ability to gain a "third-person" perspective – a kind of detached observer mental stance, in order to reflect).

Here, included as a defence against the Spiritual Position, I am emphasizing the resistance to meta feeling *per se*, in the "heart of the mind."

5 The obsessive activity of trying to change *other* people, to avoid change in oneself, and to remain unknowing of how one really feels about the reality of other people as they are.

6 A "flatulent" juxtaposition of one's life events in emotional memory, as compared with a creative re-combinatory revisiting-for-the-first time from new insight and perspective – perhaps what George Eliot (Waddell, 1986) would call "fresh and fresh wholes."

(A patient continued to paste a deadening "it's just like …" onto my attempts to make living interchanges. But these forced juxtapositions inevitably ground free associations to a halt.)

7 A flight from the *"shock of the* repaired".

This manifests in a stubborn and fearful refusal to accept the "death" of the old in the constant regeneration of the new – what Ovid (1986) illustrated so vividly in his collage of stories of human transformation entitled "Metamorphoses."

In the depressive position, emotional acceptance of the whole-object mother contains the "death" of the part-object mother. But there is a difficulty in accepting the *transformed* and *transforming* aspects of the new, repaired object.

The endings of Shakespeare's "The Winter's Tale" and Hemingway's "For Whom the Bell Tolls," exemplify this struggle in the "spiritual position," while "King Lear" and Alfred Hitchcock's "Vertigo" move us to feel the tragic consequences of literal "reparation" preventing *transfigurational* loss and regeneration – where the "hero" cannot let his loved object "become" herself, but imposes his own limited stereotype on to her personality. Thus he (and those who love and care for him) are paralyzed in a dead-end form of pseudo-mourning – where the spirit of the lost beloved is not recreated in something or someone new. Instead, there is a murderous stifling of interest and curiosity in the Other, by insisting that she remain in purely part-object form, (hair colour, dress and behaviour) with no mind or desire or development of her own.

Depressive loss is only borne and transcended with the acceptance of (perhaps even rejoicing in) the **metamorphic spirit** of life – where regeneration is **never** exactly the same as the "old" which has run its course and been lost in its tomb of absolute uniqueness. The defence against this spirit can manifest itself in an obsession with "fixing" (with its double meaning!) things – to keep them untransformed. This sort of reparation is a defence against letting the object develop into something different and *new*. It has a different quality and intention to it than Klein's mock or manic reparation.

An asthmatic patient dreamt that she was whacking her mother in the head, but the mother kept changing form, so the patient had to whack her again and again until she (the patient) became paralyzed and "hysterical" (Eric Rhode, 1995, notes that hysteria is all about one's feelings about "changing form").

The best description that I can find, at present, for the "home" in the mind for the "reverse barometer" of the spiritual position, is the old-fashioned term "heart," which must be continuously informed and updated by what I would call the *observing-ego-in-feeling*.

But the difficulty and emotional strain of **maintaining** the spiritual position for very long before it cracks into pessimism or an aloof "philosophical shield" is disturbingly registered by Dostoyevsky (1871) in *The Devils*:

> There are seconds - they come five or six at a time - when you suddenly feel the presence of external harmony in all its fullness. It is nothing earthly. I don't mean that it is heavenly, but a man in his earthly semblance can't endure it. He has to undergo a change or die. The feeling is clear and unmistakable. It is as though you suddenly apprehended all nature and suddenly said: "Yes, it is true - it is good ... It is not rapture, but just gladness ... What is so terrifying about it is that it is so terribly clear and such gladness. If it went on for more than five seconds, the soul could not endure it and must perish.
>
> (p. 586)

The miraculous human capacity to risk "having a heart" throughout all one's life is virtually impossible, given that one is always risking the loss of all that one loves and knows – unless one's heart is "tuned," over time, to the metamorphic spirit of transfigurational regeneration. But more often, even in the working through of the depressive position, one's "heart" is in identification with a painful, bleeding breast – wounded in love. (Shelley's *poem Epipsychidion* exquisitely illustrates the to and fro emotional vacillation between these states of identification with a damage, bleeding heart-breast and one which is felt to be radiating new life-bearing musical light, capable of dissolving dull heartache and coldness through love.

I will now try to give more detail and clinical evidence for the spiritual position and its defences. This will also involve some elaboration of the plangent, observing-ego-in-feeling in the formation of the "heart" of the mind, and some evidence for the existence of an internal object whose aim is "heart attack."

Spillius (1994) gives a touching account of a patient's unconscious reaction to termination of her analysis through a dream told by the patient in her final session.

In the dream, the patient was strolling around, and admiring, some particularly "primitive" countryside in New Zealand that she had never seen before. But she gradually became aware that she could not stay, and was saddened to have to leave the place. As she was leaving she had to remind herself to be careful not to damage some particularly beautiful blue trees.

The perspective that I am emphasizing would not understate the importance of the emotional acceptance of separation, loss and the poignant development of a caring and responsible attitude regarding the damage of unique good objects, which are allowed to retain mystery and left to be. (The analyst had been linked to New Zealand in the patient's mind.)

All of these achievements would be seen as the working through of the depressive position.

Nor would the perspective fail to notice the "test" of this working through – passed with "flying colours" – in the patient's ability to symbolize difficult and sad emotional experience – in this case, the loss of her analytic sessions.

What the perspective of the spiritual position might bring to this fragment of material, is the appreciation of the patient's capacity to have feelings about her analysis, herself, and her life, **on the whole.**

A good part of the poignancy of the dream is that it carries feelings of admiration and loss of something that is now seen from a very broad emotional perspective – like stepping back to view a whole canvas – and so the analysis as a whole emotional experience is installed as a place in her mind, inspiring reverence, awe and delicacy.

Moving, in a sense, "backwards" from this example, I will now present a more detailed account of what I see as the psychological evolution of this capacity for having feelings about one's life experience "as a whole." I will try to show this as intimately related to a post-depressive, emotional ability to maintain an intact "heart," and by this, I refer to the old-fashioned concept of the heart as the centre for intuitive, but genuine perception of feeling in the personality as a whole. Therefore the "workings" of the heart remain essentially mysterious and therefore unconscious, although its feeling sensibility is often available through what I shall call "the observing-ego-in feeling." I will return to elaborate this concept after the clinical example.

The case presented here is extremely clipped and shorn of many of its transferential details in order to highlight particular thematic strands, and their development, where this is relevant to my topic of post-depressive emotional capacities – particularly this capacity to maintain a whole functioning "heart."

The patient "arrived" for treatment in an unnervingly dishevelled manner from America – saying that she had heard of me, but couldn't quite remember how, and that most probably she needed help because her life was in a mess. She could see that her move to a new country was both an escape from increasingly chaotic liaisons with dangerous, but, to her, sexually attractive men, and also an attempt to "change herself". She expressed doubts about her choice of career as a Social Worker; partly because it provided too much opportunity for entanglements with highly disturbed men, and partly because it felt too much her mother's choice of career for her, rather than following her own inclinations and talents, which she located in the world of the Arts, particularly film. She had written five film scripts, but they had felt "stillborn" and she had not dared to show them to anyone.

In the initial sessions, she presented as a kind of alluring "Tinker Bell" – not quite "womanly," but pervading an ambience of promising intimacy and budding love, which felt both enticing and suspicious; as if I should be very careful to curb my positive feelings towards her. Or to put it another way; in the countertransference, I felt like a father who wishes to cuddle his daughter, but who stiffens up and feels safer being aloof for fear of inappropriate sexual feelings being stimulated in himself or the child, and this, of course, creates an even more charged atmosphere of **forbidden** (Oedipal) sensuality.

Before long we could trace this field as, in some ways, a retreat from and a revenge on a very limited, depriving internal mother. (Often she would shop for milk before and after a session.)

But in other ways, this emotional field expressed a yearning for a lost, warm playfulness, where the vulnerable infant could feel held in father's lap and stroked by his gaze, consoled for her incomplete engagement of mother's body and mind.

The patient was the youngest of six daughters and felt that she had enjoyed a privileged intimacy with her father until he died of a heart attack in her third year, following which she adopted the role of a Cinderella stuck at home with an insensitive mother and several ugly and stupid sisters.

A rapt attentiveness and responsiveness to my interpretations were peppered with a cool dismissiveness whenever I was felt to be (and felt myself to be) very close. Internally, there was a passionately, if intrusively, attached infant and a fickle, aloof parent.

This internal coupling existed in a highly sado-masochistic state of game-playing and teasing, and was the basis of much of the "cock-teasing" she had played at from teenage-hood, but which was worrying to her in early adulthood.

As we were able to expose some of the cruelty involved in the constant projective identification away of the passionate, hungry infant in herself, she began to become horrified and eventually concerned about what this was doing to other people and to her own development.

She began to recall teenage episodes with her girlfriends in cars, waving provocatively at boys, and then being both excited and shocked when the boys would give chase at high speeds, and she saw how intensely she could stir up sexual and aggressive feelings in them.

This disowning of her own passionate baby-self showed in dreams where a vulnerable baby rabbit (a "bunny") was always left exposed and unprotected against the ravages of a stupid, ignorant dog or wolf. We could also link this to an aspect of her character which came to be called the "wolf in bunny's clothing" – "innocently" devouring the "hearts" of desperate young men.

In one session she was jolted by a slip she made while describing the temptation she had felt during the previous holiday break to play "funny buggers."

Instead, she said "… to play bunny fuckers."

As she began to relinquish these unsatisfying projective identifications and experience more of the "wolfish" in herself, which wished to swallow all parental attention and intimacy for herself alone, she began to feel more kinship with her sisters in the struggle to live without a father. But she also began to feel less "stuck inside" her mother's supposed expectations regarding her career choices.

Complaints about my breaks were about how she couldn't enjoy what **she** wanted to do – expressed in a slip where she said that she felt compelled to have the "stranded" (she had meant to say "standard") break – and was stuck in a kind of depressive claustrophobia. But where this had previously been part of an intensely envious hatred of those whom she saw as free to "follow their own hearts," she now felt free to leave the "compulsive givers" (including that view of her therapist) and to pursue her screen-writing. She also pursued a man whom she had at first seen as "a jerk" but now experienced him as highly desirable and sincere.

(In the transference, I was now experienced as having real feelings of my own, and even vulnerable to illness, accidents and financial struggle, so my interest in helping her was no longer taken for granted).

In fact, her career accelerated at a rapid pace soon after she showed her "stillborn" scripts (which had been kept as stillborn siblings in her internal world) to a "producer-friend" of this man, and. interestingly, nine months later, a new script was bought for a highly successful television drama series concerned with "rescue." She received some critical acclaim, two film commissions, and, for the first time, lived in a "place of her own."

At this time she brought a new openness to sessions, and was able to speak freely about habits she had which she found unattractive, and was not so compelled to always portray herself as the "cute bunny."

One of these habits, she noticed, was a tendency to mindlessly shove bits of ice-cream wrappers into the crevices of her car seat as she was driving.

The name of her favourite icecream, ("Heart") and other associations, suggested that these were unconscious attempts to push away and treat as rubbish, her own heartfelt feelings of love and attachment.

Such "habits" were a kind of masturbatory "cut-out circuit," for whenever she felt enough love to be risking the possibility of a "broken heart."

Sometimes, during breaks, they were enacted more destructively in flirtations with dangerous men, and were always lamented **after** the break with a back-of-hand-on-forehead castigation like "How could I let myself **do** that?"

(If sometimes her self-castigation lacked sincerity, then at other times it seemed to lack compassion).

But the approach to the fourth end-of-year break brought a dream which moved her deeply. After saying, somewhat facetiously, that the dream felt "too deep for tears" she began to cry as she told it. At first, she was immersed, up in the air somewhere, in a puffy, wet grey mist. It felt dull, heavy and very depressing. But gradually she was able to separate herself out from the wetness and saw that she had been in a very large white cloud, which was in the perfect shape of a lamb. When she recognized this in the dream she felt calm and complete and relieved; as if something damaged inside her had been restored, and was working again. Further work in the following sessions linked the lamb with lost lambent feelings (she had been playing with the word lambent in a poem) associated with memories in feeling of playing in her father's lap, and this enabled her to recover some totally forgotten perceptions of her mother as a happy and secure person, prior to father's death.

(Grinberg's [1978] stressing of the importance of recovering the parts of the Self associated with, or in relationship with, the good objects seems relevant here).

Other associations to the dream cannot be included here, along with many other elements of the transference and vicissitudes of the patient's development. But I will conclude the case example by following one particularly prominent thematic strand which was gradually revealed to be central in her flight from "good" relationships.

This theme concerned the emotional struggle to "have a heart."

Although I have not made it explicit so far, the patient commenced in an intensely, if unconscious, suicidal state. The early, often-repeated dreams were of steep, hostile cliff faces, overlooking a cold, rough ocean. Often, in these dreams, she was falling, or wanting to fall onto the rocks below the cliff-faces, wishing to dash her heart against these rocks.

As she developed some trust towards me, a man began to appear in these settings who was trying to both stop her from falling and to take her out on a life-boat towards a ship that would take her to warmer shores. Some associational work suggested the obvious identification with the father who died from an "attacked" heart, but more particularly to a film which had saddened and heartened her. The film was "Papillon," which depicted two prisoners trapped on a prison island, until one of them has the courage to jump into the sea and swim to freedom. She found it sad that the other companion was left behind forever. It was "heartbreaking."

In the session prior to an extended Christmas break, where she was to return to her native country to visit her unwell mother, and also to visit the grave of her father for the first time, she brought up this dream: She was alone in very rough weather, but a man with kind eyes and a lantern held her hand and led her to a helicopter which raised her upwards until she could see thousands and thousands of people similar to herself, even though it seemed to be night. This made her feel more human, and then the helicopter set her down near a warm fire where "the rest of humanity" were gathered and murmuring in a reassuring way. She thanked the man, and asked him what his name was; and he said that he was "Arturo Sclerosa." This unsettled her, but the warmth from the fire drew her to stay.

Her associations were of arterio-sclerosis, heart attacks and feeling homeless; but Arturo the lantern holder must be Arturo Toscanini, she thought. But, she went on, Toscanini conducts with too much military passion, and not enough heart. Then she thought of Mahler as having too much heart. "Didn't he die of heart disease? Wasn't he too much in love with his wife who cause him heartbreak?"

But her thoughts about matters of the heart did not always seem to be coming from the heart. Or they sounded like statements about somebody else's feelings.

The next dream in the "heart series" gave us some further insight into the problem.

An archaeological team was digging up the road in a "lost city" - there was a gaping hole in the road – heart-shaped – but you couldn't get close enough to get a really good look at the site because of "Keep Out" signs all around it.

Her associations were to the Sleeping Beauty, and from there to perceptions of her mother as not allowing her to cry for the lost father. When I encouraged her to look at her own attempts to block access to her feelings about loss and vulnerability she exclaimed, in a tone of deep protest and anguish that; "If I really let myself feel the full love and hate that I **sense** I must feel, I don't think I could bear to feel **that real!** I'd feel human, and breakable..." As her voice tapered out, she let out a long sigh and remembered how puzzled and hurt she was when she broke off the relationship with her first boyfriend, whom she loved dearly. She had no idea why she had felt compelled to stop something that felt so right.

Maybe I just had to break his heart before he broke mine. But it felt like I broke something in myself as well: like my heart cracked ...

But in the following months she seemed to disappear off the emotional radar screen altogether, hiding for sessions at a time under a "we can't really fix anything here, so why don't you admit it!," arms folded rigidly on the couch, type of resistance to looking at anything. Interpretations were met with a minimal grunt, followed by a yawned, sarcastic; "I suppose you might be right then ..." Full stop. No elaboration.

I persevered in linking this to the Keep Out sign in the lost city dream, and then one day (as I was at the peak of feeling rejected and unwanted) she started to cry and to apologize for treating me awfully. She had had a "change of heart" after seeing the preview of an episode in the rescue television series which she had scripted.

In this episode, they used a part of a song by the band *Genesis*, and this set her crying uncontrollably. Luckily her partner was sitting next to her, so it felt safe to cry. She remembered the words as "... someone talking to their own heart, and telling it to hold on to that feeling – and something about how he'll always be with me ..." (I couldn't help but recall her humming in a much earlier session to another song about love being nothing but a *second-hand emotion* – and, *why need a heart when a heart can be broken?)*

Then she said: "I think I can bear the thought of losing you *one* day now. I couldn't before. But I'm not ready *yet*. I better work my guts out so I'll be ready." The work did indeed intensify, particularly so on two fronts, which seemed distinct, yet imperceptibly intertwined.

One front concerned the business of sorting out just what sort of intimacy she could have with someone who was married or sexually unavailable, and yet whom she loved. Sorting out these Oedipal boundaries was very painful to her, but clarifications also produced consolations and new freedom to be adventurous and playful once the boundaries were established. She found new ways of being intimate with both men and women which avoided the habitual problems of flirting destructively on the one hand or denying herself possible intimacy too quickly, on the other.

The other front seemed to arise from her allowing her internal couple to be generative, and for her internal mother to be repaired enough to be both fertile and imaginative in her feeding. It concerned the issue of regeneration\transformation – perhaps even metamorphosis, if we consider the reference to *Papillon* – as alternatives to depressing, claustrophobic stagnation inside the internal mother, with the dubious aim of controlling all intercourse as an "insider."

The first signs In the material of a struggle to take in what Bollas (1979) might call the transformational feeding mother, came at the end of a very frustrating session, when she half-jokingly, but triumphantly, asserted that food was a useless invention because it was only ever transformed into stink. She seemed as surprised as I was to hear this outpouring from her infant self and then admitted that she didn't know how to answer this. I reminded her that food is transformed into growth, and that only the left-over waste is stinky and excreted. Her whole tone changed, and she left the session as if smiling to herself. The following months were filled with death/decay versus transformation/regeneration battles. For example, a pair of plants on my veranda had supposedly died due to my neglect and failure to feed the right fertilizers or trace elements.

In fact, all signs of life *had* disappeared in these pots, but I said to her that it was if she did not hold the possibility of regeneration or of seasons.

She agreed with this, but it was not until the following autumn when the pots were filled with large, orange flowers, that she confessed that she had really thought at the time that I was just bluffing. (The doubting part of myself was also very relieved to see the evidence appear in the concrete form of the flowers.)

This led to her taking a great interest in growing vegetables, and in particular, she was fascinated by a new combination vegetable called broccoli-flower, and by the ways in which plants produced new seeds. She read about exotic means by which seeds were digested by some animals and activated in the animal's gut, to be dispersed and germinated elsewhere. But most rewardingly for her, she discovered that she "was allowed" to be part of creation, transformation and regeneration.

Just before a termination date was set, she made a genuine discovery about herself and her relationships, which seemed to bring together the two "fronts" of analytical work. (That is, the Oedipal/separateness issues, and issues of a "faith" in life as transformational and regenerative). The discovery was that she herself was capable of transforming her loved objects. For example, by offering love to her sometimes withdrawn partner, she saw that she could make him more loving and loveable.

This discovery led to a new way of being in the world for her. Previously, for example, she had seen a relationship as an acquisition, the success of which depended only on how successful she had been in winning the most "powerful, attractive'" partner from competition with other females – a kind of jungle lottery. To some degree this gave her enough faith to envisage a creative and loving life continuing and regenerating after her final session, although there was still much work to be done before termination, particularly on the cynical attack on this possibility.This manifested itself as a mocking sneering tone directed at those, including herself, who were willing to take responsibility for maintaining and protecting the fragile conditions within which life can exist, be enjoyed and regenerate. It was supposedly deeply ironic and comical, but it was also unmistakeably denigrating to herself, and to me.

Discussion

I want to leave the clinical example here in order to say some more about the **omnipotent internal object** which I see as generating this mocking hatred of life, Love and Regeneration.

In my view, the "seer" Tiresias in the Oedipus myth (not the level-headed Tiresias of Sophocles' "Antigone"!) illustrates the sort of internal "prophetic" object that I have in mind.

Grotstein (1980) alludes to a Magus/sorcerer figure who "casts spells on his victims and compels them to follow an enforced scenario from the Magus life" (p. 368). I see Tiresias as having this effect on Oedipus (and, before him, Laius), and one way of understanding Oedipus's self-blinding is that it completes an identification with the blind Tiresias.

Tiresias had a huge Oedipal problem himself. According to Ovid (op. cit.), he once saw two giant snakes mating, struck at them, and was changed into a woman. Seven years later Tiresias again saw the two snakes and again attacked them, and was returned to manhood.

Later, because of his double-sexed experience, he was called upon to settle a dispute between the gods Jove and Juno as to whether women or men get more enjoyment from sex. (Jove teased that women were better off, and Juno denied it.)

> Tiresias declared for women, and as a result was blinded by Juno. But Jove gave him a consolation in the ability to predict the future.
>
> (Graves, op cit.)

Internally, the Magus/Tiresian object says "No!" to the experiencing of the Oedipal feelings of longing, smallness, feeling left out of the parental relationship, and concern about one's murderous feelings towards them. The anti-developmental consequence is the emergence of the child's **whole** feelings towards the mother and father, including the true feelings about them preferring to mate with each other rather than with the child, is prevented. So then, the achieving of a spiritual/philosophical emotional perspective, where one can start to have feelings *about* these feelings, is impossible, if "Tiresias" rules the mind.

In the depressive position, concerns about omnipotent, masturbatory wish-fulfilment are about the mocking and appropriating of the good object.

In the spiritual position, the concern is that omniscient propaganda will block the experiencing of one's true feelings, and therefore the chance of having, at some point, a "philosophical" position **about** these feelings as they accumulate.

Omnipotent, manic masturbatory states of mind not only attack the good internal object; they also prevent true feelings about feelings re life experiences; that is, Spirituality; because they replace the *experiencing of* life, and substitute for it what is *wished* for. And, therefore, one cannot develop and feel *Vergangenheitsbewältigung,* via the Inspirational Combining Object. Instead, one depends on the blindness of the Magus/Tiresian object who hates inspirational, combinatorial, musical mating to produce metamorphoses, and who therefore portrays it as a murderous, humiliating, incestual disaster which *destroys* insight, rather than producing the above-mentioned Shelleyan "light of love."

Tiresias – the voice of omniscience – says something like: "I've looked into/penetrated the insides of the mother, from womb to guts, and can tell you that inside her is a father with a sharp weapon who wants to kill you; but if you kill him and get rid of him first, then the "lost city" inside her is all yours – so long as no one finds out what you've done – and mother will go along with it all, because she really desires you most. And therefore nothing need change in your awareness of your place in the world, and your feelings about the world."

(Suttie [1935] believed that the child constructs the Oedipal myth as a defence against feeling the pain of the mother's rejection of the child as a sexual partner. Apollinaire's (1918) surrealist farcical play, entitled "The Breasts of Tiresias," also set as an opera by Poulenc, depicts the balloon-breasts of the heroine Thérèse floating away on the breeze, revealing her to be Tiresias the prophet, while her husband, by the power of thought alone, brings into being no less than 40,049 babies). Note that the extra level of omniscient defensiveness that the *Tiresian* object brings to that of the *"usual"* infantile omniscience is that the Tiresian aim is to forestall (meaning "highway robbery") *feelings about* parental coupling.

Seneca's Oedipus Tragedy is often regarded as inferior to Sophocles' drama because it gives too much detail to the "blood-and-guts" methods by which Tiresias divines Oedipus's past and future. But I tend to think that Seneca was more "Kleinian" than Sophocles and knew that the earliest Oedipal turmoil was in relation to the fantasized inside of the mother's body, including paranoid anxieties about how she might be combining with the internal father and producing "monstrous" babies with him:

(The lengthy quote seems necessary to convey this.

Tiresias: Had I youth and strength I would receive the power of the go In my own person;
 we must find a way to probe Fate's secrets. Such evil portents in the sacrifice are greatly to be feared.
 Tell me what signs you see in the entrails.
Manto: (His daughter): Father, what is this? ... The heart is shrunken,
 Withered, and hardly to be seen; the veins are livid; part of the lungs is missing,
 The liver is putrid, oozing with black gall. And here – always an omen boding ill,
 For monarchy – two heads of swollen flesh In equal masses rise, each mass cut off,
 And covered with a fine transparent membrane, as if refusing to conceal its secret ...
 The organs are all awry and out of place.
 On the right side there is no breathing lung alive with blood, no heart upon the left;
 Womb and genitals are twisted and deformed. And what is this –
 This hard protuberance in the belly? Monstrous! A foetus in a virgin heifer's womb,
 And out of place, a swelling in the body where none should be. It moves its limbs
 Twitching convulsively its feeble frame – the flesh is blackened with the livid gore ...

> And now the grossly mutilated beasts are trying to move; a gaping trunk rears up
> As if to attack the servers with its horns ... The **heart itself** quivers and quakes.
> Seneca Oedipus the King. (pp. 354–380)

Oedipus's eventual shame might also be his "Tiresian" rage and dismay at discovering that Laius **was** first and **did** have *right of way* inside Jocasta's body.

The emergence of a feeling philosophical value system in the spiritual position

As the influence of the oracular omniscient internal object (Magus /Tiresias) diminishes, a new leap forward seems to occur in the development of "whole object" relationships. I see this as beginning to occur at the time when the child is experiencing not just his or her separateness from each parent and their differences from each other, (working through the depressive position), but is also beginning to realize and feel that his family is not the world. This is a very complex emotional realization, which is certainly a continuation of capacities developed as part of the working through of the depressive position, and rests exclusively on these capacities.

But I think that at this level of development, a cognitive-emotional fusion occurs (perhaps Bion and Meltzer [1978] would say a holding together of loving, hating and wanting to know; L, H, and K which produces a *feeling philosophical value system* – an emotional stance towards "'Me World.")

This would be a *whole* value system, in the sense of it having both complete coherence and meaning to the person. It is deeply felt or rather expresses the deepest feelings. Emotional coherence and wholeness would be developed over a lifetime, in the sense that this depends on sorting out, within oneself, what seems most important to one, and continuously developing ways of being in the world and of understanding the world according to orders of importance. The anti-developmental alternative to this is to adopt a political manifesto or speech or cliché or fashionable doctrine, a pre-formed group value system, and then see how many other people one can "convert," in order to prove its "Truth."

An example of the type of whole feeling philosophical value system that I have in mind would be illustrated by Boethius's (1969) "The Consolation of Philosophy."

This is an ongoing dialogue which gradually evolves by deciding on the supremely important concern (in this case, a sense of "goodness") for the writer, and then reflecting on the relative values and meanings and implications for all other considerations in life, once the importance of a sense of goodness is fully accepted as always being the ultimate, meaningful aim.

Meltzer (1978) sees such ordering of one's values as characterizing a "mature" personality which is motivated by aims, as compared with goals.

Perhaps the tension between the developing whole value system and the auto-sensual part value system is portrayed in the Golden Calf scene in the Old Testament.

While Moses has travelled inward to receive his spiritual values in relation to living a life, the impatient group creates auto-erotic short-term sensual gratification, and live day to day, promise to promise.

Again the evolution of God/Nature, internally, to beyond the parental, does certainly require the working through of the depressive position – where the internal parents are given respect and freedom to be different – but it requires, even more dramatically, that distinctions be made between one's self and one's objects.

At this stage, we know very little about this complex and mysterious achievement, although we do have common expressions like "she's her own person" or "he's his own man" to convey the display of it in personality.

[I have made a tentative attempt to explore the issue in the chapter, on "Dis-Identification"].

The "Merlin-Father" in the transformation of schizoid detachment into observing-ego-in-feeling

Having said something about how the oracular omniscient object substitutes predictive certainty and self-righteousness for the chance to step back from the canvas of one's life and get the "big picture" emotionally – to have an opportunity for "Vergangenheitsbewältigung" – a coming to terms with one's past and one's self, and to piece together what I have called a feeling philosophical value system – I now want to mention the internal object and process which might oppose such omniscience.

Put simply, I see the object which refuses the propaganda as linked to a whole-object version of the internal father. I do **not** mean by this The Law of The Father, according to Lacan, which I see as a much more paranoid, thou-shalt-not-or-you'll-be-castrated construction of the father in the child's mind. What I do mean lies somewhat beyond Meltzer's (1978) model of the development of the internal father, where the child unconsciously experiences him, at first, as possessing a weapon, and only much later in development experiences him as having a "tool."

In the painful, but potentially liberating emotional experience of getting a bigger perspective on the truth of one's feelings about life, the child needs, as it were, to be lifted onto the father's shoulders, in order to be able to face squarely the questions; "Well, how do you feel about all of this?" and "What seems important from up here, in this perspective?" And to feel that the father who once supported the containing mother, can now bear the weight of the child taking its place in the tragicomedy of life. From the case mentioned above, the dream of the "helicopter" function is most pertinent here.

(In fact, a recurring theme in the patient's scripts was the importance of helicopters for getting people out of impossible places where they could not survive for very long.)

The father who provides this rescuing perspective might be called the Virgil father or perhaps the Yorick father, but because I think the process which I am describing here is well captured in the musical "Camelot" I will refer to him as the Merlin father, for argument's sake.

In "Camelot," poor old Arthur is distraught because Guinevere has paired with Lancelot, and seems not to be able to find a way of thinking about how he feels about the whole business. But he turns to Merlin, who tells him that he must become like an eagle, not to escape, but to get a wider emotional perspective on his feelings towards the couple and his values in life. This enables Arthur not to feel so persecuted, and to contain his murderous feelings, and to allow the boy in himself to have the freedom to live. I see this Merlin-like capacity to get the eagle or helicopter view on one's feelings about life as harnessing previously schizoid tendencies of disengagement and emotional distance. In other words, through a trusting link with the internal father, the previously alienating role of the observer is now utilized in what I call the "observing-ego-in-feeling" – the capacity to see the broad canvas of one's emotional world, by standing back at some distance, and to have feelings about the canvas which can be thought about.

This is not quite the same function as "the observing ego" in the Freudian sense, which has a much more intellectualized connotation, whereas the observing-ego-in-feeling has a more "artistic" connotation – in the sense that Art can be conceived of as showing one's feelings about life, or more accurately, one's feelings about all the feelings one has had in life. (Rhode [1987] describes a patient who, in a moment of moving "musical" insight, "... had reached a turning point in his life: a moment, too, in which he could think to look over its entire span." [p. 1181).

The plangent quality of the observing ego-in-feeling, its capacity to put music to one's emotional life, perhaps somewhat like the function of music in a film, gives it a far more active role in the psyche than merely an organ for the perception of psychic qualities.

It may streak a lightning flash of unexpected passion across a train journey, a walk in the park, or the perception of a stranger's face. When it swoops from its broader perspective it sucks in symbols and unifies themes in a maelstrom of meaning which can change a mind.

As Tennyson (1961) versifies it, in "The Eagle":

He clasps the crag with crooked hands; Close to the sun in lonely lands,
Ringed with the azure world, he stands. The wrinkled sea beneath him crawls,
He watches from his mountain walls, And like a thunderbolt he falls.

In Bion's language, the alpha function is acting upon itself (The snake of the One God eats up all the snakes of Pharaoh's conjurer). It may be that the "limitation" of only being able to concentrate or focus on one thing at a time (consciously) is actually an "advantage" emotionally, because it foments a meta/transcendent feelings about feelings state, and therefore becomes a path to "God/Oneness /The Infinite" – Bion's O.

The result is a transformation in O – one's ultimate reality, which can be avoided, ignored and perverted by the self. But if the self has faith in the transformation, that it will not be a catastrophe, but a generation of something new, then the self is transformed. This will increase faith in the next transformation, made possible by the widened perspective of the observing-ego-in-feeling.

In yet another language, the analyst is receptive to a wider perspective on the patient's emotional world first because he or she is (hopefully) less in the sphere of influence of the patient's defences than the patient is, and second because of the augmentation of the perspective due to countertransference feelings. So the analyst may then "lift the patient" to that widened perspective and hold him or her there, as it were, on the analyst's shoulders, until the patient gets the wider perspective, **and** begins to introject the father whose shoulders are strong enough to hold him or her there.

In the depressive position, one pines for the lost good internal mother, and works it through by repairing her and then internalizing her. In the **spiritual** position, one pines for the father who allows the emotional experience and reaction to the loss – who says "How do you feel about not being able to possess mother's body and mind, and how does that help you to decide what's important for the rest of your life?" When the analyst has this transferential significance for the patient, above all others, then the analysis is ready for termination.

Here are two strikingly similar "examples", written almost 160 years apart, of a young man looking – perhaps for the first time – at the need for a coming to terms with his feelings about the world.

Please note that both examples take place following cemetery scenes where the young men have just lost father figures.

The first is from Balzac's (1832) "Old Goriot" (Father Goriot in the original French).

> ... It was growing dusk, the damp twilight fretted his nerves; he gazed down into the grave, and the tears he shed were drawn from him by the sacred emotion, a single-hearted sorrow. When such tears fall on earth, their radiance reaches heaven. And with that tear that fell on old Goriot's grave, Eugene de Rastignac's youth ended. He folded his arms and gazed at the clouded sky; and Christophe, after a glance at him, turned and went - Rastignac was left alone.
>
> He went a few paces further, to the highest point of the cemetery, and looked out over Paris and the windings of the Seine; the lamps were beginning to shine on each side of the river. His eyes turned almost eagerly to the spaces between the column of the Place Vendôme and the cupola of the Invalides; there lay the great world that he had longed to penetrate. He glanced over that humming hive, seeming to draw a foretaste of its honey, and said magniloquently:
>
> 'We'll fight this out, you and I.'
>
> (pp. 237–238)

The second example is from Paul Auster's (1989) "Moon Palace."

> I had come to the end of the world, and beyond it there was nothing but air and waves, an emptiness that went clear to the shores of China. This is where I start, I said to myself, this is where my life begins. I stood on the beach for a long

time, waiting for the last bits of sunlight to vanish. Behind me, the town went about its business, making familiar late-century American noises. As I looked down the curve of the coast, I saw the lights of the houses being turned on, one by one. Then the moon came up from behind the hills. It was a full moon, as round and yellow as a burning stone. I kept my eyes on it as it rose into the night sky, not turning away until it had found its place in the darkness.

(pp. 306–307)

Psychoanalytic and artistic technique

Sincere post-modernism versus technological juxtaposition

Before concluding, I will briefly make two lines of suggestions, as implications of the acceptance of a spiritual position in unconscious emotional life.

The first concerns psychoanalytic technique, and cannot easily, in this discussion, be segregated from considerations of artistic technique.

The second line suggests a minimal revision of the theoretical terms previously, often loosely, applied to the blanket term "depressive position," with the hope of more precision.

(I think that the reader will realize that these two lines of suggestions are better seen as helical rather than parallel).

Bion's (1970) technical suggestions – grounded in his models of container-contained and the dreaming alpha function enabled through maternal reverie – give us an analytic object capable of holding, symbolizing and modifying the infant's anxiety about dying, conveyed in its dread of terrifying, fragmented and un-nameable persecutors.

But Meltzer's (1973) post-depressive combined object is more challenging than being "without memory and desire." It is able to resonate deeply and trustingly with the combined imaginativeness of the internal couple to produce not only the occasional "inspiring" interpretation but also the emotional ambience in which this trust in the combined object's creativity may "work its magic." Meltzer then links this level of unconscious mutual trusting with the weaning process, and although he makes it clear that for this to happen genuinely is a fairly rare business, it is nonetheless important as an indicator of internal growth.

(It also carries the risk of a mutually narcissistic masturbatory activity between patient and analyst).

What I have to say about both analytic and artistic technique, particularly in relation to the "spiritual position" follows on from my thoughts about the transformation of the father inside the maternal container – from threat and rival, to the father who contains the mother's anxieties – in the infant's mind.

The father in the mother must be able to bear the full force of the infant's feelings about being alive.

The **"Anti"** Magus-Tiresias analytic object interprets both the destructive phantasies towards the "combining" internal parents **as well as** the struggle to introject the inspiring ambience, or "music" of that creative, loving couple. This Merlin-like father in the maternal containing function, instils an emotional interest in the patient towards the **whole picture** of the patient's psyche.

This requires a "stance" of the analytic object which fosters the spiritual position in the patient.

Through appropriate "dual" transference interpretations, the patient can have feelings about the object which brings out the **whole** (subjective) truth of the patient's loving and hating phantasies.

Brenman-Pick (1995) describes an "even-handed" approach to the interpretation of both manic narcissistic trends in the patient as well as emphasizing the vulnerability, and Alvarez (1992) stresses the way that a patient's "wild lies" may also have a quality of potential space about them, into which a new self may be born.

So the technique of the Merlin-like object would find a way of combining, with "musically-balanced" stresses of emphasis, both the regressive/resistive elements of the transference and the potentially progressive and imaginative. In this sense then, at the level of the "spiritual position," we might need a "kinder" re-evaluation of, for example, habits of the patient such as smoking or drinking. Where such habits may well have meant some sort of narcissistic fixation or intrusive identification for the patient at the level of paranoid-schizoid position, or denial of guilt at the level of depressive position, in the spiritual position they may well be functioning to give the patient a mental "cave" to "sigh" on feelings about life – feelings about all the emotional experience encountered so far.

In a sense, the analyst or therapist gives the "gift of time" by invoking such a spirituality in the patient, because it is transcendent, emotionally cumulative which gives a sense of time as it bundles good and bad experiences together into a new perspective and gives one the sense of having "lived a life."

(This work moves beyond the internalization of a repaired good object, as in the working through of the depressive position, and yet all the emotional conflicts and defences of the paranoid-schizoid and depressive positions will pertain towards the new "analytic object").

There has been much controversy, especially in the past decade or so, about the value of the artistic "movement" known as "Post-Modern."

If I apply my definition of "the spiritual position" to Art, in the sense that Art could be seen as a sincere attempt to convey one's feelings about a lifetime of feelings, then it becomes possible to tease out two strains of the post-modern ethos.

One strain could be seen as an omnipotent attempt to appropriate all previous Art as one's own – to possess it, by demonstrating nothing more than knowledge of its existence. The end result would be pastiche, or juxtaposition, with no emotional impact on the producer or the audience. At best we might hear a cultist, fashionable flurry of claims that it is "interesting."

The other strain would be experienced as conveying the artist's feelings about life by his or her "choosing" an idiosyncratic array of emotionally endowed "elements" and combining them in a way which produces a "universality," such that others will also be moved to experience their feelings about their lives. Therefore, in both Art proper, and in the artistic interpretation of transference phenomena, in the region of the spiritual position, the only important consideration with respect to "technique" is whether or not the analyst/artist is able to inspire a genuine "feelings about accumulated feelings" sighing-state in an-other. At this level of feeling (a meta-level) the "tried and true" techniques can become a hindrance, especially if the "spirit" of the technique is lost sight of.

A suggested metapsychological revision

The revision which I suggest here is not essential, since it covers aspects of emotional integration already intended by some who are satisfied with the term "depressive position." However, I now find it possible to be more precise, theoretically and technically, due to the aforementioned exploration of a spiritual position, and of defences against its achievements.

I suggest the term "reparative position" to replace the over-inclusive term "working through of the depressive position."

This enables the term "depressive position" to keep its more literal meaning – that is, where love is depressed, and guilt is still experienced as largely persecutory, unhelpful and irreparable.

In the "reparative position" then, one struggles to repair the good internal object, in the face of attacks upon its freedom as a wholly separate entity.

I reserve the term "spiritual position" for an emotional capacity whereby one has further accepted the idea that all people lead separate, but potentially related lives, and that through a growing pattern of repeated feelings, one sees one's own potential, responsibility and limitation for instigating transformations in oneself and others which bring about love and growth.

In the Spiritual Position, one perceives that direct reparation of the internal objects is an omnipotent aim. (Leontes can revive his love and goodwill towards Hermione – but it is not he who brings her "back to Life").

In the "reparative position" one attains a hope that one's love and concern can keep good objects in good repair. In the "spiritual position" one gains "heart" from a faith in regeneration-through-transfiguration, in spite of one's love and hate, and in spite of death.

This process is only possible through ***Vergangenheitsbewältigung*** – an ongoing coming to terms with one's past through the "reverse barometer" of feelings about one's Life, as one moves from pleasure principle to reality principle to psychic reality principle – from paranoid-schizoid to depressive to reparative.

In this sense, the spiritual position is never really beyond the other positions; but more like a "steady lap" where one regains respite, hope, inspiration, faith or even dourness – at very least a sense of humanity through widened emotional perspective, before "plunging" back into the worlds of Ps – D – R. Its full ambience may grip us only occasionally, or even rarely, but its music rings in our souls each night as we clamber up and down Jacob's Ladder.

To recapitulate: the metapsychology of the spiritual position involves three interrelated elements of emotional growth.

1. The whole-object internalized father gives rise to an observing-ego-in-feeling which provides a "whole picture" perspective of one's emotional field.
2. The whole-object internalized mother gives confidence in the re-generational, ever-transforming nature of the internal and external worlds.
3. The internalized creative combined object, which I have elsewhere called the "combining object" (Maizels, 1992), gives one a "heart" to bear the full force of feelings brought on by the whole-object mother and father.

In order to face Death, one needs to accrue a heartening feeling that one's "life energy" has been transformed into a Life. This **feeling** that one has lived a life – not merely the knowledge that one has lived a life – is experienced through the three elements outlined above, which together comprise a "Spiritual position."

Whereas the working through of the depressive position (reparative position) enables the richness and poignancy of an "adagio" in the heart of the mind's music, in the spiritual position the self is heartened to feel this as yet only a "movement" in a whole symphony.

Or as that timeless sage, anonymous, better puts it:

> Low lie the mists; they hide each hill and dell
> The grey skies weep with us who bid farewell
> But happier days through memory weaves a spell
> And brings new hope to hearts who bid farewell.

With thanks to Charles Ives (1925)

References

Alvarez, A. (1992). *Live Company: Psychoanalytic Psychotherapy with Autistic, Borderline, Deprived and Abused Children*. London: Tavistock/Routledge.
Apollinaire, A. (1918). *Complete Plays*. (1986). Paris: Gallimaud.
Auster, P. (1989). Moon *Palace*. London: Faber and Faber.
Balzac, H. (1834). *Old Goriot*. London: Penguin Classics, 1972.
Barrows, K. (1993). Book review of the chamber of maiden thought. *Int. J. Psychoanalysis*, 74 (1): 207–210.
Bion, W. R. (1970). *Attention and Interpretation*. London: Tavistock.
Boethius. (1969). *The Consolation of Philosophy*. London: Penguin Classics.
Bollas, C. (1979). The transformational object. *Int. J. Psychoanalysts*, 60 (1): 97–107.
BrenmanPick, I. (1995). Concern: Spurious or real? *Int. J. Psychoanalysts*, 76 (2): 257–270.
Britton, R. (1989). The missing link: parental sexuality in the oedipus complex. *The Oedipus Complex Today*. Ed. Steiner, J. London: Karnac. 120–141.
Cummings, e.e. (1958). *95 Poems*. New York: Faber and Faber.
Dostoyevsky, F. (1871). *The Devils*. London: Penguin Classics, 1953.
Fullerton, P. (1994). 'The significance of the father for the sense of self'. Paper given to the Victorian Association of Psychotherapists. Melbourne.

Grinberg, L. (1978). The "razor's edge" in depression and mourning. *Int. J. Psychoanalysis*, 59: 245–254.

Grotstein, J. S. (1980). 'Who is the dreamer who dreams the dream and who is the dreamer who understands the dream?' In *Do I Dare Disturb the Universe? A Memorial to Wilfred Bion*. London: Maresfield. pp. 333–380.

——— (1993). Towards the concept of the transcendent position. *Journal of Melanie Klein and Object Relations*, 11 (2): 12–34.

Harris Williams, M. and Waddell, M. (1991). *The Chamber of Maiden Thought*. London: Routledge.

Hinshelwood, R. (1989). *A Dictionary of Kleinian Thought*. London: Free Associations Press.

Ives, C. E. (1925). *114 Songs*. New York: Associated Music.

Jacques, E. (1965). Death and the mid-life crisis. *Int. J. Psychoanalysis*, 46: 502–514.

Klein, M. (1961). *Narrative of a Child Analysis*. New York: Dell, 1977.

Maizels, N. (1993). The chamber of maiden thought. *Journal of Melanie Klein and Object Relations*, 12: 93–103.

——— (1993). Towards the concept of the transcendent position. *Journal of Melanie Klein and Object Relations*, 11 (2): 12–34. (1995). *Dis-Identification*. Unpublished manuscript.

Meltzer, D. (1973). *Routine and Inspired Interpretations: Their Relation to the Weaning Process in Analysis*. Reprinted in *Sincerity and Other Works*. Ed. Hahn, A. 1994.

——— (1978). Catastrophic Change and the Mechanisms of Defense. In *The Kleinian Development*. Part III. Ed. Meltzer, D. London: Karnac Books.

Ovid (1986). *Metamorphoses*. London: Oxford University Press.

Rhode, E. (1987). *On Birth and Madness*. London: Duckworth.

Segal, H. (1964). *Introduction to the Work of Melanie Klein*. London: Hogarth.

Seneca. (1966). *Four Tragedies*. Middlesex: Penguin Classics.

Spillius, E. (1994). *Melanie Klein's idea of the "total situation" in the transference*. Lecture given in Melbourne. Australia, August 25.

Suttie, I. D. (1935). *The Origins of Love and Hate*. London: Kegan Paul.

Tennyson, A. (1961). *Collected Verse*. London: Abbey.

Waddell, W. (1986). Concepts of the inner world in the novels of George Eliot. *J. Child Psychiat.*, 4 (3): 168–191.

Young, R. (1994). New ideas about the oedipus complex. *J. Melanie Klein Obj. Relat.*, 12 (2): 1–20.

Chapter 8

"I'm Miss Red!"

Reworking a premature weaning in a lonely young girl

On the surface, weaning often appears to happen quite quickly. But, I would argue, even the (apparently) smoothest transition from mother's milk to the "food of the world," can take years, or even decades to fully work itself through the emotional tracts of both parents and growing infant. Sometimes this is expressed in an almost benign occurrence which can be observed repeatedly (and not without a good deal of frustration and anguish) by parents of children in the post-toddler age group. The child will appear to happily give up a favourite toy or game or ritual, and then, just at the most inconvenient moment, will passionately demand its reinstatement, knowing full well that it is no longer available, or has been given to a sibling or friend. However, on the whole, weaning often remains a slippery topic, not only for the family but also often for a therapist also, when trying to unravel complex presenting problems and constellations.

Blake (p. 107) after Klein (1926, 1927, and 1928) noted the possibility of a linkage between weaning and Oedipal issues. At first (1926, p. 7) Klein felt that:

… the Oedipus conflict ensues upon the deprivation experienced at weaning …

In fact, Klein thought that weaning was *the* trauma which inaugurates the *Oedipus Complex* – that frustrations by the breast cause the infant to move away from the mother towards the father. But in a later paper (1935) she added that through the achievements of the depressive position, where love and concern grow to counteract feelings of hatred, deprivation and persecution, weaning could be a successful "gateway" to the acceptance of, and interest in, post-weaning substitutes, including the father. In this way, weaning was seen by her not just to be a trauma, but as a crucial focus for the achievement and working through of the depressive position, despite the fact that at weaning the infant is in a confused and labile state of intermingling feelings and impulses, which include oral, anal and oedipal strata of psychological development.

I will now use some clinical material to illustrate in more detail how different developmental levels may become infused and confused with impulses and feelings associated with the weaning process. I will try to illustrate some of the vicissitudes of the process, and its complexity, in a transference and countertransference struggle to rework the first, only partially successful attempt at weaning, in spite of the internal and external pressures to gloss over the issue.

The case

The child that I will focus on was brought to therapy by parents who had become concerned about her friendlessness at school and her frequent mood changes, particularly an often-repeated swing from tantrums to depression. There was also a concern that she could not play with her sister, 20 months her junior, but this was not felt to be particularly important.

The patient, Becky, was seven years old when she was referred by a colleague, who told me that she did not know if the parents would (not could) pay for ongoing therapy. This colleague was aware of the family pressures to appear as thriving and jolly. Becky's first appointment with me turned out to be on her sister's birthday, and the day had clearly been earmarked for the party, which was to follow almost immediately after the session. I was reminded of this several times by Becky.

In fact, the first arrival was somewhat chaotic. Becky and her parents arrived almost half an hour early and ruptured my concentration with another patient. When I ushered them into the waiting room the father excused himself and said that he would return in half an hour. As it turned out, he returned five minutes late for the assessment session and wedged himself in between Becky and her mother on a couch. While they were awaiting Becky's father, the mother was telling Becky to hurry up and finish her lollipop (called a "push-pop") because it was getting too messy. Becky then looked at me for further adjudication and seemed angry that I would not defend her. She said, coldly, "Got a bin?"

Becky then joked that she thought her father had locked himself out.

Before I could say anything, the three of them began to speak at once, but the father, who was the loudest, said that there was no use beating around the bush, and that Becky was just a very, very difficult child. He was not able to say how or why, but the mother then said that there was nothing really wrong, except that Becky got too upset about things that she couldn't have, or which she had to share with her two siblings.

But after a few minutes of awkward looking at feet, a very intimidating atmosphere pervaded, and I felt that I was being ordered to fix something, but with no information to go on. I asked whether anyone could tell me more, but the rigid folding of arms by the parents made me feel that I had no right to ask any questions. I then asked for some information about Becky's arrival into the world and her early life. Instantly, the parents and Becky all exclaimed the same story. That Becky was a delight, at first, and had achieved something remarkable. She had gone from the breast straight to a cup.

All three beamed as if to say "there can't be anything too wrong, with a wondrous start like that."

But gradually, the high and defensive mood became more desperate, and eventually mother said that she was seriously concerned that Becky wasn't developing properly, since about the time of the birth of the next child. The rest of the session was about the parents' parents, and just how difficult it was to please them. Both of Becky's parents said that they always felt like naughty children with their own parents, and that Becky was their salvation because she was so clever. They did not want to tell their parents that she was having troubles.

There did not seem to be room for Becky in the parents' conversation, and it was often as if they were two children desperately trying to engage my attention. Throughout the interview, the father seemed to wish he was somewhere else, and I could feel a very strong sense of humiliation that his daughter (he was a helping professional) might need help.

Strangely, in spite of the awkward, plodding atmosphere, I felt rushed along, and suddenly we were arranging dates. I started to feel angry and pushed around as if there was no time for thinking.

I asked to see Becky by herself next time, and, somewhat surprisingly, the parents seemed very thankful and relieved, and asked whether Becky would need to be seen every day.

Meanwhile, Becky had gone to the toilet, and then the parents walked out towards their car and left her behind, all the while eagerly talking to each other. I was forced to remind them that Becky was still in the toilet, and again the theme of feeling rushed along too quickly suggested itself to me. I was also mindful of Bion's (1962) comments about how an infant might not feel loved and attended to, even if it is given milk from the breast, and of Blake's idea that weaning actually begins "when the mother starts thinking about it." The parents did seem to have difficulty keeping Becky's basic needs in mind, and it seemed that someone in the family always had to be shut out or disregarded.

I also felt extremely thirsty after they had left.

The next day, Becky's mother rang to see if Becky could commence on a different day to the one we'd planned, but I then discovered that the mother had in mind a totally different date and time to the one that I thought I had arranged with her. She rang again the next day to confirm the re-arranged time and made a slip which suggested that she thought herself to be the new patient. At a later date, it was possible to refer the parental couple to a colleague, who, thankfully, was able to work with them so that the boundaries of Becky's therapy were not overly impinged upon and so that they might sort out some very confusing aspects of their relationship with each other.

Initial impressions

The strongest first impressions that I experienced were the juxtaposition of an urgent, "hungry" neediness (both Becky and her parents) coupled with urgent pressures to hurry over such need and appetite. I also felt as if I had been bullied away from inquiring too deeply into Becky's loneliness and unhappiness as if it was supposed to be self-evident, rather than attended too patiently. Perhaps this is why I felt eager to listen to Becky without the commentaries of her parents interrupting and to "get on with" the therapy. I was perhaps over-eager to give her a "good, long feed."

Emerging themes

I will now sketch out some of the main themes and variations that unfolded when Becky commenced her therapy.

Time

By far the most striking feature, right from the first session, was Becky's very serious confusion with time.

She kept getting it very wrong, again and again, constantly checking with me for confirmation. Her watch was set on the wrong time – by several hours. She thought that half an hour had passed, after being with me for a few minutes. She thought that her mother got up at 4 am, to go jogging, but also thought that the parents went to bed at 5 am. When the first session finished she thought that only ten minutes had passed, and she calculated that it would be 40 thousand hours till we met again. She then asked if she could take my clock home with her because she trusted it more than her clock.

Clearly, most of the confusion had to do with Oedipal issues, and with her difficulty waiting. But I was struck by the intensity of her engagement with the therapy process, in spite of the time confusion.

Hunger and rivalry

She made lots of drawings, and they centred on a little girl who was crying out for help, or who was starving. But she had little conscious linkage to these themes. Near the end of the session, she drew a clock with no hands, and I suggested that she wished that there was no time restriction on our getting together. She nodded and then said that she thought we could be friends, but she wondered whether my wife would be angry.

The difficulties with time, as a concept, very gradually subsided in the following months, but most of her drawings were of a very confused, lopsided girl. This girl was drawn over and over again with a markedly asymmetrical, mad-looking cross-eyed face, or one foot was drawn much bigger than the other. Sometimes the hands and feet looked like tail fins of a fish.

Whenever she tried to put two characters into a drawing they became entangled and blurred, and we were able to do some work on the configuration of her "internal couple." and her wish to blur herself into my mind so that we could be one.

Rivalry, merging and separation

As possessive transference feelings intensified, so did the intensity of hunger and thirst in her drawings, as well as a tremendous thirst for knowledge about my home life. How many children? How did I play with them? Who was my mother? Did my wife cook nice meals, or was I left to go hungry at night? Could my children sleep in my bed?

But as we approached an Easter break, the hunger and despair stepped up a gear. It was striking to see just how much of Becky's unconscious life was concerned with feeding and deprivation.

There were pictures of trees with gaping holes in the trunks, a lone figure drifting in a small boat in a big sea, and repeatedly, a starving, deprived little girl. She wrote a story about this little girl, who had given all of her food to her brothers and sisters, but now had none for herself – but she couldn't tell anyone about it, or they would think she was greedy and babyish. Then, a drawing with one solitary girl on the Titanic, just before it sinks, and she cannot cry for help because no one would hear her.

In the last session before the break, after many "help!" drawings, and many interpretations of her feelings of desperate neediness and a wish to have me all to herself, she drew a Neil-and-Becky drawing, and it was left for me to see if they were attached to two balloons with strings, or was it just a trick. It was a clever puzzle, and I had to trace it carefully to find out.

I was able to bring together her feelings about the break, her painful separation from me, and her not knowing whether or not to trust the connection that we'd made.

I said that she didn't want a repeat of her babyhood where she mistakenly felt that she didn't need the balloon breasts anymore, and 'handed' them over to her younger siblings.

Separation, confusion and weaning

She drew a picture of a mother with a huge, pink ice cream, but her little girl couldn't have any. She then promptly tore up the drawing and began a new drawing in bright red.

She entitled it: "I'm Miss Red!"

I linked this to her feeling misread by her mother as to whether she was really ready to give up the breast, and perhaps she felt that I was taking my Easter break without understanding how tied to me she had become.

She nodded quietly and said "I think I know what you mean, and then informed me that it was time to finish the session (which it was). Then she added "Ready or not!" and skipped out of the room, leaving me feeling abruptly cut off, as she may have experienced her weaning.

Denial of hunger, cruelty and despair

Just as breezily, she skipped back into the room, two weeks later, and invented a character called Farmer Straw, who was trying to feed many little chicks – but there were too many to feed, so he ate the food himself, and one of the little chicks was very upset.

The session then became a kind of parody of a feast. Whenever I interpreted her hunger, and her wish to deny it, she drew more and more pictures which alternated starvation with omnivorous gluttony.

There was a bleak picture of a girl who could only talk in holes – and eventually she starved.

There was a cruel Queen, with hundreds of tiaras. When I said that she might wish to be my Queen, and to rule over my coming and going, she shrieked "I'm hungry, slave! Bring me the biggest milkshake in the world or I'll behead you!"

She 'modified' this by adding: "Not really I won't, but I'll cut up this sausage and pretend it's you!"

Her glee in her sadism was quite chilling, but during the next few months much "depressive" work concerning her infantile dependency was done, although it was becoming apparent that her developmental phases were very confused. Hunger for the nipple became a wish to possess my penis and to steal it from my wife, who would grow hungry. But could she still have babies? And whenever she felt like crying, this got confused with urination. There were vivid drawings of a man who cried tears through his penis, and I think she was as surprised by these productions from her unconscious as I was.

(I think, with Blake, that any remnants of unresolved conflicts from anal, phallic and oedipal levels of development are revived and compounded with difficulties in the weaning process.)

Anal control and self-idealization

As the Christmas break loomed, oral and anal phases were confused. Her oral frustration and need led her to idealize her own bottom and its productions. She would fart loudly and then look at me cheekily (so to speak) and seemed to get a kind of omnipotent, sadistic pleasure from her own body. She always said sorry or "pardon me," but this was often followed with a mischievous, derisive laugh.

(Meltzer, 1966, has written about the way a child might idealize its own bottom as substitute for the feeding breast in the face of frustration, loss and envy.)

There was a disproportionate drawing of a man who "couldn't find his bum, and the letter B was snickered at, as the "dirtiest letter of the alphabet" because it meant "bum" even though it looked like breasts, from the side.

She then said: "What does frustration mean?" But before I could comment she told me of a bear that had to shut up its mouth-hole.

I said that she felt she always had to shut up her hunger for love and attention, especially now, since I was about to leave her for several weeks.

Outbreak of love, with depressive and bodily confusion

She drew a picture of a huge goblet full of wine, and said "If the wine is strong then you don't need much." I said to her that maybe that's how love is and that if she could keep a strong feeling of love alive inside her then it might help to sustain her over the break.

In the few sessions before the break, she began making lots of paper packets, with drawings and messages inside them. One was said to have all of my love in it, and she said that she would keep it with her over the break. Then there followed lots of carefully constructed "love packets" but the regressive pull of a retreat to the zonal and developmental confusions from earlier in the year also intensified, and there was a very real struggle between love and hate.

She drew a tape recorder that cried, then said it was piss not tears. She drew a picture of rainclouds falling on a little girl, then added; "At least she'll be clean!"

I think Becky must have experienced her anal/urethral sadism and messiness as responsible for her abrupt loss of the breast, and that the new baby was felt to be good and clean, and therefore more deserving of the breast.

After the break, an immense amount of work went into the construction of a book, called "The Body Book," which listed every part of the human body – male and female.

I suggested that she was starting to put me together in her mind when I wasn't there. She replied loudly: "And me too! It could also be my body!" And so I added that she was putting us both together in her mind. She nodded and seemed happy with herself.

But, one disturbing feature of the body book was a page which she'd dedicated to the groin, and she showed it weeping urine. I said that she often muddled up crying with peeing, and she replied "What **is** the difference? Do you really get thirsty if you cry too much?"

Then she drew a girl singing "I'm singing in the rain …"

I said that it could feel good to cry sometimes, but she drew "Miss Red Number 2" and threw it at me.

I said that she wanted me to know that crying was also painful, and she said "**Yes**"!

I won't describe all of her drawings here, because there were so many, but they included lots of pictures of clouds weeping, although sometimes the sun crept in. There were also several pictures of me just back from a war, and very hungry. But most of her energy went into a massive picture book of the Bible, particularly of Creation.

Jealousy made tolerable. Sharing

It included an apple, and she asked: "What if Eve was just hungry?" I said that sometimes she was truly hungry for me, and I compared this with her sometimes wanting to stop me from feeding my children because of jealousy and the wish to possess me. (She had been asking more and more detailed questions about my other patients.) Rather miraculously, this produced, for the first time, some consideration for her younger sister, and chief rival, Anastasi. She made a paper birthday cake for her, with a cherry on the top, and this culminated in her inviting Anastasi to come along to a session, to see me and the room which we worked in.

She also began to take a real interest in time, drawing clocks and learning how to read them accurately, particularly towards the end of sessions, in spite of the pain of giving up her illusory control of me.

She wrote "I love you" in backwards, mirror writing, and then drew herself inside a heart, which was pierced by an arrow. She said that it didn't hurt … much …

The return of aggression, but as fantasy, not impulse

There was a genuine interest in other children and, for the first time, the idea of sharing. But the intensity of her curiosity and aggression stepped up again as we approached the next break. She asked how many children I had, as she casually drew a picture of my penis being chopped off. She said: "Would your wife be really angry if I actually did it?"

I asked her what she thought, and she answered: "I suppose so. Would she kill me? No, she's probably nice. She's not a vampire, is she?"

I said … not so far as I was aware, and she laughed, with relief.

I said that it was important for her to know that her urges of attacking my couple, with its ability to produce babies and enjoyment, was not going to turn into action. There was a long, hissing sigh of relief from her, and she found the Miss Red drawing again, and said to it: "You don't really want to be …

but you are very angry."

I said that maybe she felt that way when she thought about me getting together with my wife during the break and between sessions.

Following on from this, she spent all of the sessions prior to the break industriously making paper packets. Some of them seemed like little breast-like pockets, with hearts embossed on them; others seemed more like intricate "vaginal" flowers, but they appeared to express a blossoming of femininity and were offered to me in a very tender, delicate way. Some were particularly intimate for her, and were "Private – do not open" packets of "love."

Somewhat understandably, this intimacy, born of reparative urges, collapsed, five minutes before the end of the session before the break. She shifted into a frenzy of manic activity, hastily, and rather sexually, throwing herself into a drawing of a chug-chug-chug train, with a very pronounced nipple-penis protrusion for its funnel. She giggled at it and then glared at me in a seductive, erotic way.

She said, cheekily, "Gotta wet your whistle!" and then snickered to herself. The intimacy was broken by blatant exhibitionistic flirting. As if trying to puncture my attentiveness, she drew very close to me and said, very loudly: "I want to suck your blood," complete with a Transylvanian accent and bulging eyeballs.

But I was quite surprised at her ability to regain the intimate mood, when, right at the conclusion of the session, she said, quietly, but sincerely, "We're all part of the Milky Way … isn't that good?" And she placed in my hand a little note that she'd kept secret throughout the session. It said: "Neil loves his wife and family." I drew hope from this, that she might be able to regain the softer, more intimate state of mind throughout the break. But something was still troubling me.

It had to do with a very strong countertransference feeling that was building up inside me. I had an increasing apprehension that Becky's parents were going to pull her out of the therapy prematurely, and thereby re-create what I feared had happened with her weaning. There was no doubt that the parents had very mixed feelings about the therapy. The arrival times and unscheduled holidays had a strongly chaotic flavour, which seemed to cut across the steady work in the transference. But I was half-expecting the plug to be pulled at any time, and when the parents asked to see me soon after the break, I was expecting the worst.

But, to my surprise, Becky's father, in particular, told me very forcefully that she was **not** ready to finish yet, even though she was now a vastly different girl, and he appreciated the work that I was doing, which he thought was resulting in definite improvement. Becky's mother chimed in that she was able to have more quiet, closer times with her daughter. I was relieved to hear this, but a tone of resentment, and possibly envy, regained momentum at the end of this meeting, when Becky's mother abruptly asked me to reduce the sessions from twice-weekly to once a week, because they used up too much of her time and energy bringing Becky to the sessions.

When I put the idea to Becky she said that it would be okay, because it would please her mother and there would be "less hassle about the whole thing." But later in that session, she drew a picture of a mad woman whose head was in 3 different places at once, and I felt that she had internalized a very frightening version of an inconsistent mother.

The reworking of both oedipal and sibling rivalry

The next year brought repeated waves of working on her oedipal experience of breaks, (the parents had mentioned that Becky's bedroom was right next to their own, and they left the doors to both rooms open all through the night), but also some regression into some fearsome primitive jealousy of the rival babies.

For example, following a break, she drew a picture of a bride and said that it was her wedding day, but the bride had fallen into a big hole and was never seen again. She drew a mummy with a foetus inside, along with sphinxes and skulls, and I was able to link this to her deathly impulses towards her siblings, who she mumbled about while drawing.

She drummed up some controversy at home by insisting on watching the cartoon series "South Park" even though her parents insisted that it was too violent for her. She got her way. But she lost interest quickly after seeing an episode where there was a flagpole that killed Kenny (the child who is (jokingly) killed off in every episode, only to appear unharmed again in the next.) When I mentioned that she was actually quite frightened of destroying her little brother she responded with a made-up story about Bingo the naughty dog who bites the heads of babies. Then she asked "Do you know what happened with Azaria? I think someone dressed up as a dog …" Then she seemed transfixed and lost, before trembling slightly.

I said to her that it must be frightening to be a baby and not be sure whether or not someone might want to eat you. She nodded, but wouldn't look at me for what seemed like quite a long time.

More oral rage and confusion

Then as if suddenly jolted back into the room she screamed "Yes!" And then she launched into an orgy of "baby is hungry" material and pretended to feed sausages and bananas to an imaginary baby, again with a seductive, erotic expression. She said: "But I wouldn't eat you!"

This led to a picture of "Neil's Sausage Shop, where all children eat as much as they like – but some children come back in the middle of the night to get more. I talked to her about her wish to get more than the other children, and her difficulty waiting the now longer time between sessions. (I also took up the issue of confusion between nipple and penis in her perception of me, and her confusion about whether she wanted to eat me or play with my body.)

I wondered if she might have been overwhelmed with these feelings as a baby, and had decided to bypass them by going straight to a cup. She responded in a split way to my interpretations. She drew a very creative picture of a man and a woman kissing, and then, for the first time, some abstract art, which was very accomplished. But when I acknowledged the drawing she immediately regressed to "Goo and Gaa" baby-like sounds.

I was repeatedly astounded at the fluidity and rapidity in her shifting quickly from one developmental level to another.

The beginnings of a good, thoughtful object

I said that it was the baby inside her that was hungry to have me all of the time and didn't like me ending sessions or taking holidays to be with my wife and babies. She "cried" louder, mockingly, and then farted and laughed over-loudly.

She was then silent, waiting for my response, and then said, thoughtfully,

"I'm an angel before I was born."

I acknowledged her wish to be innocent and good back in the womb before all the trouble with feeding and jealousy began. She was silent again, and then snuggled up to me and said :

" I know what you do here! You're the **narrator**!" I was quite taken by the maturity of this comment, which also seemed like a very thoughtful response to my comments, and to the therapeutic process itself.

More links between aggression and separation

She remained quite thoughtful and considerate for a few months, and then, in the lead-up to the next major break, she was able to give full expression to her aggressive impulses. She exclaimed menacingly: "Pretzels are great because you can suck them and bite them at the same time!" She threw paper darts perilously close to my face but denied that she was aiming at me. She began to use scissors, fervently and cut out many nipple/penis shapes and pretended to eat, or rather devour them.

She insisted that she really loved me, again and again, and wrote "secret" love notes to me. She drew a girl saying "Dear Neil, I love you." But she gave the girl no arms with which to express the love.

When I commented on this she hastily drew two plump apples and forced them into my hands. She said, "You have to be my baby!"

She claimed to be joking and then asked curiously: "But who **does** feed you? – Your wife! Did your mother feed you? Do you love your mother or your wife better? I know you love **me** best!" She then laughed and blushed.

In keeping with Klein's (1932) observations, after giving full reign to her sadism she became much more focused on reparative actions and impulses, and seemed to be trying to integrate the many areas of her mind. She made another "Body Book "– which had all of the parts in detail and in good proportion and did not leave anything out.

She drew a "tidy your room" picture, and said with a sigh, "Sometimes you've just got to clean a mess up, and it's no use complaining." She followed the sigh with lots of brown, messy drawings, and I said that she wanted to see if I could stand for her to make messes in the room. She said, "Mum's okay, but Dad would kill me!"

She did, in fact, make some messes in the room, although nothing that could not be cleaned up easily, and was clearly testing my anxiety about the issue. But it took not too much interpretation (and gulping) for this to give way to "fully-flowered" reparative urges.

She cleverly sculpted and drew flowers growing from very brown soil, and the flowers had a rich variety of shapes and colour combinations. When I said that she was growing up and flowering she again blushed, and nodded.

This paved the way for the final phase of her therapy, where her full-blown passion for the breast was unleashed, and this enabled her sexuality and sensuality to burst into expression.

The emergence of passion and sensuality. More reworking

This phase of her therapy was marked by a shameless display of eating delectable food – treats which she'd saved up especially to consume in front of me. She became totally absorbed in this feeding, and I felt like an envious, disgusted, and hungry infant, watching helplessly nearby. It seemed that she was communicating to me just how difficult it was to watch her two younger siblings feed after she had all too quickly foregone her place at the breast. Her involvement was very sensual and involved every possible variation of oral and erotic delight. Often it was accompanied by a rhythmic moaning, interrupted only by the occasional grunt in response to an interpretation. She seemed to be bathing in a sea of voluptuousness, while in the countertransference I was left craving, for example, my favourite gelati, or counting the minutes to my next meal.

I said that she must feel very hungry inside and wanted to eat me and have me inside her and that she wanted to show off this triumph to the world. She burped at this remark and drew a picture which looked like an anus. She wrote "blow" on it, and called the picture the "West Wind." Then she recommenced consuming her food and drink with "orgasmic" satisfaction. I felt tentative about how much of the oral/erotic and anal fusion to put into words – whether to interpret that she wanted to consume me sexually as well as orally. But then I heard from her parents that she was vaginally and anally masturbating, in a loud, exhibitionist manner, in her room at home, and I did start to interpret more graphically. She grunted her responses but did not deny anything.

But there were changes in the following sessions, with an increase in her tenderness and generosity as compared to her self-absorbed feasting. She drew a picture of a chef making two big pizzas, and said, "These are for you." She started talking a little German, which she'd learnt at school – and although she thought I couldn't understand her she sang that I was her yummy little potato.

She drew a picture of Neil catching a big fish, and I felt connected to her again, after many months of underground secrecy. I said that she'd let me catch hold of her again after weeks of playing with herself, as if she only needed her own body and nothing from anyone else.

She said: "I have a great time with you, and you are very kind. Would you like some chocolate?" I said that she did love me, but wanted to be the one who feeds **me**. She then drew a colourful picture (she most usually drew in monochrome) called "Becky loves Neil loves his Wife." She added: "**I'm** your wife ... not really." Oedipal and oral themes were again intertwined, and I said that it was hard to love me when she knew that I loved my wife, who also fed me. She looked inwards for a while and then said that being a little bird could be quite good. "You could visit lots of places, and you wouldn't need much to eat...and you could be looked after by kind people ..."

I said that sometimes she just wanted to enjoy her infant feelings, even though she felt small.

Parental intervention

It was around this time that my worst fear eventuated. The parents had decided, while on a holiday, that "Enough was enough." They were quite aggressive about it, and very insistent that the therapy should stop, even though there was grudging acknowledgement that it was "probably" doing Becky considerable good. But, they would give Becky a few weeks to get used to finishing.

Meltzer (op cit) writes:

> Where parents are not in analysis themselves it is not possible to do more than guess at the motives which lie behind the great frequency of forced premature interruption against analytic advice. I am not speaking of cases which have not seen satisfactory improvement from the parental point of view but of those which have and where the need for further financial sacrifice is not easily apparent to them. Because parents are likely to take a normative and

therefore symptomatic view in first bringing the child to analysis, we need not assume that this is the reason for forcing interruption. In fact the circumstances often suggest that unconscious motives of jealousy, envy and states of mind based on projective identification are the true causes. Similar motives are often suggested by parental behaviour toward their child's analyst, in the form, for instance, of delayed payment, haggling over fees, attempting to reduce the number of sessions, therapeutic interventions of their own with the child, attributing improvement to influence other than analysis, especially "normal maturation".

(p. 51)

I won't describe here all the convoluted interchanges with the parents, but my main feeling was that it was left for me to protect the feeding infant from a repeat of her premature weaning, and there was great pressure on me to feel guilty about this as if I was being overindulgent with a greedy girl.

Blake (op cit) notes that: "In the early months when a mother goes through states of unintegration and disintegration, the weaning process revives in her unconscious feelings about her own weaning. The decision to wean is anything but a conscious one." I wondered what feelings were being revived in Becky's mother as Becky progressed in the therapy.

Becky's depressive reaction

On the surface, Becky adopted a "c'est la vie" attitude to this enforced ending, but she became highly involved in the film "Titanic", drawing endless pictures and describing the tragic dialogue of the two lovers who were to be prematurely parted She said, about the ship; - "The owners were in too much of a hurry to get there! But it wasn't really ready."

We had one small break before her finishing, and Becky's mother rang me before her return session to say that Becky had become uncontrollably upset about the discontinuation of her favourite TV show, and had phoned Kidz Helpline to get a sympathetic hearing from a counsellor.

Becky then told me that this counsellor told her that she also resented the termination of this TV programme. I said that it feels better if she isn't so alone with her disappointments and can feel that everybody has some losses to bear.

She began to cry, and said poignantly, "Everybody has to cry sometimes ..."

Although there was a tragic overtone to the end of the therapy, there was also a strong feeling of closeness, and it seemed that I was internalized as a benign, if somewhat idealized figure, who helped her to think.

She said that she adored Albert Einstein." He must be **your** age." She joked about how he knew everything about **relatives**! And she drew

$E = MC$ squared.

Further optimism about her internalization was prompted by her last therapy drawing. It depicted two females. One was called "outside", and had tiny budding breasts. The other was "inside," and she was given fuller, almost adult breasts.

Conclusion

In retrospect, it seems possible that this lonely young girl was paying the price of an over-hasty and precocious weaning in the midst of the parental decision to have two new babies as quickly as possible, and that she may have unconsciously detected these wishes to hurry up as she took in nourishment from the breast.

Her wish to please her parents, and to become more independent even at a very early age, by skipping the bottle and going straight to the cup, was repeated in good school reports, at the expense of solid emotional development. This glossing over of her basic emotional needs, repeated in her incapacity to find emotional support from friends or siblings, left her mental stability very precariously balanced, and her real development paralyzed. As feared early in the therapy, the drama was replayed in the pressure to finish before she'd had enough.

However, in some ways, the therapy was an improvement on the outcome when she was only one year old. There were words, and a capacity to express her feelings this time around. There was also the opportunity to work through, at least partially, an overwhelming sense of loss, by having some time and space to think about it, and to more securely establish an understanding and nourishing internal breast, before the loss.

The material presented here suggests that Becky's hunger for nourishing intimacy was enormous, and perhaps her parents feared her to be insatiable and her needs boundless. This, combined with her own anxieties about devouring both the breast and the new babies, might well have led to a mutual unconscious agreement to skip the difficulties of the weaning process and to rush along to pseudo-independence and pseudo-eroticism. This might have been particularly the case here, in a family where there never seemed to be enough resources to take care of everybody's needs, illustrated starkly in the initial interview with Becky and her parents, where someone was always left out or forgotten.

Although it is possible for the biological process of weaning to race ahead, by many years, of the emotional process, it eventually catches up as a problem that must be revisited, or else the capacity for intimate relationships will not develop its potential, and will be replaced by confusion and the loneliness of feeling repeatedly *misread*.

It would seem that in cases of a particularly vexed and rushed weaning we find a need for help with further completion of the weaning process. But then **all** weaning is only partially achieved with the transition from mother's milk, and must therefore always be reworked repeatedly **throughout** the lifespan, irrespective of the apparent ease with which it seems to have passed.

One thing that appears to always be the case, is that our individual style in the 'resolution' of the weaning process forever puts its stamp on our character development, for better and for worse.

Blake's more hopeful comment is that apart from its reviving more disturbances of loss, psychotherapy also offers the opportunity for greater integration. And as Edna O'Shaughnessy (1964) puts it:

A child always, in part, *wants* to be weaned. [my italics]

But, according to Emily Dickinson (1970)

Parting is all we know of heaven
And all we need of Hell.

References

Blake, P. (1988). Weaning revisited. *Aust. J. Psychotherapy*, 7 (1 and 2): 97–110.
Dickinson, E. (1970). *The Complete Poems*. London: Faber, p. 702.
Freud, S. (1933). *New Introductory Lectures on Psycho-Analysis*. S.E. 22. New York: Penguin.
Klein, M. (1926). The psychological principles of early analysis. In *Love, Guilt and Reparation and Other Works*. Ed. Money-Kyrle, R. New York: Delta, 1975. pp. 38–54.
—— (1927). Symposium on child analysis. In *Love, Guilt and Reparation and Other Works*. Ed. Money-Kyrle, R. New York: Delta, 1975. pp. 62–74.
—— (1928). Early stages of the Oedipus conflict. In *Love, Guilt and Reparation and Other Works*. New York: Delta, 1975.
—— (1932). *The Psycho-analysis of Children*. New York: Delta Books, 1975.
—— (1935). A contribution to the psychogenesis of manic-depressive states. In *Love, Guilt and Reparation and Other Works*. Ed. Money-Kyrle, R. New York: Delta, 1975. pp. 233–259.
—— (1936). Weaning. In *Love, Guilt and Reparation and Other Works*. Ed. Money-Kyrle, R. New York: Delta Books, 1975. pp. 274–289.
—— (1952). On observing the behaviour of young infants. In *Envy and Gratitude and Other Works*. Ed. Money-Kyrle, R. New York: Delta, 1975. pp. 42–58.
—— (1963). Some reflections on *The Oresteia*. In *Envy and Gratitude and Other Works*. Ed. Money-Kyrle, R. New York: Delta, 1975. pp. 366–392.
Meltzer, D. (1967). *The Psychoanalytic Process*. Perthshire: Clunie Press.
O'Shaughnesssy, E. (1964). The absent object. *J. Child. Psychotherapy.*, 1 (2): 34–43.

Chapter 9

Loneliness and its amelioration through transformations of the Internal Father

In the chapter *Dis-identification*, I mentioned examples of the struggles of patients (and many literary characters) to find an identity of their own when countered by a superego-ish father, who is not sufficiently interested in the unfurling of their child's own unique personality. But, what I did not focus on, in that chapter, was the extremely painful degree of **loneliness** that they faced, with the internal father becoming a harsh, narcissistically unpleasable superego. I will argue that the internal father – for better or for worse – plays a crucial role in the mediation of a particular type of (inner) loneliness, and that the absence, corruption or destruction of this paternal object paralyzes the mind of the child in its ongoing attempts to work with its depressive pains associated with the separation, usually of a more non-verbal nature, from the primary maternal object. This is why an excruciatingly painful form of **boredom** is often part of the emotional experience of loneliness, beyond the pangs of longing for non-verbal closeness with the lost or absent primary maternal object. A clinical example and one chosen from television drama will serve to illustrate these pains, also exquisitely penned by Sylvia Ashton-Warner as she muses that she *"... must burn that letter I wrote to him last; the chronicle of a spinster. I must pick up the permanent things in my life again; my pen box, my piano, my paints, my reading, my scheme, my books, my wood box, my garden, my guilt, my memories, my "reverence for conscience," the gift that God has put in my hands, and my tears. I must take up again my loneliness."*

I will also outline the evolution of the internal father from this harsh part-object superego – threatening castration and permanent exile from the mother – to unhelpfully disinterested, (but not aggressive), to an encouraging, patient and interested whole-object representation – acting as a "lap" for the child to climb up onto (perhaps represented, in America, by Lincoln's huge statue, using sign language – for his initials, A.L, indicating his role in finding language for symbolization.)

Here the child can hear itself think, in the presence of an empathetic and sympathetic **elicitor** of reverie-in-words, if anxiety due to feared maternal jealousy is not overwhelming or distracting. This "lap of the father" is an evolution of the primary reverie initially provided by the mother, although in a more **verbally eliciting** fashion. The father here provides the steady "knees" of his own mind to let the child find its own words for its own inner experiences and shapeless feelings – giving

DOI: 10.4324/9781003364788-9

these a local habitation and a place, in the emerging words of the child, for its own emotional experiences. Therefore, I am extending Klein's very intra-psychic model of loneliness by introducing some notions about the importance of the **paternal** object in strengthening the internal availability of the good feeding object, once **words** can be found for her absence. Much poetry seems to have this function, of finding words for the otherwise painfully ineffable longing for the primal object.

(Currently, it is usually thought (Bion, Ogden) that the main capacity for reverie in the child evolves purely through identificatory internalization of the maternal capacity for reverie, especially about the infant's psychobiological fear of dying.)

While the two examples that I will use focus on the **daughter**-father relationship, there are plenty of narratives – (for example, in Bowles' The *Sheltering Sky* (1949), that suggest both the boy **and** the girl struggle with this internal "guiding" father and his internal absence or unavailability. But, it may be that the task is made more difficult for the little boy because of his oedipal anxiety – in the perceiving of the early (part-object) internal father as such a potentially castrating rival, waiting vigilantly (as Polonius was in Hamlet's bedroom scene with his mother within the most concealed, alluring parts of the mother's body) – is so utterly terrifying. And therefore a genuinely close relationship with father is, felt to be so fraught.

In Bowles' story, Port Moresby (!) is an American writer who travels throughout Africa with his wife, Kit, and their friend, Tunner. When Port arrives in Algeria, he and Kit are all but estranged from each other, in an extremely lonely marriage. They sleep in separate rooms, and Kit and Tunner are waiting impatiently to consummate an affair. One night in Tangier, after a marital fight, Port follows an Arab acquaintance outside the city and has sex with a young prostitute who robs him. After this, Port grows increasingly tired and bored, and becomes saddled with two disgusting Australians, the Lyles – seemingly locked in a disgustingly merged and mutually parasitic mother-son claustrum. They have no real interest in exploring the world for its beauty, mystery or adventure, and Port spirals towards a lethargic, sickly death. But, interestingly, after her husband's death Kit is unexpectedly plunged into a mainly **non-verbal** nomadic tribe, and must strive to gradually learn how to talk again, in a new language, and eventually to internalize the narrator-father-Bowles himself in order to find her new self.

On the other hand, the little **girl** must struggle with her fears of a retaliatory, rivalrous internal mother whom she deems as furiously jealous of any intimate time alone she may have with her father. These themes and anxieties are the "Big bad wolf, Snow White" stuff of fairytales and myths too numerous to detail here.

Chronic loneliness is usually seen as a condition of painful despondency, where one feels cut off from either a person group or experience that would bring them back to life. But different writers emphasize different aspects of that particular emotional experience which we commonly call loneliness. Lucille Spira and Arlene Kramer Richards see the analytic literature on loneliness as beginning with Freud. They suggest that although he never specifically wrote about loneliness, he did talk about the **fear** of being alone in his chapter on "Anxiety" (1916–1917), pp. 392–411).

He illustrates this with a charming anecdote about a child who fears the dark, except when his aunt speaks to him. The child says:

If someone speaks, it gets lighter

(p. 407)

Freud describes Dora (1905a) as unsociable, though not focusing on her loneliness, a condition he associated with hysteria. Freud came to understand Dora's dynamics and symptoms as arising from her longing for the love of a woman (Freud, 1905.) He deduced this from her reporting about the pleasure that she experienced from looking at a painting of a Madonna and Child. In *Three Essays on the Theory of Sexuality* (1905b), Freud generalizes his theory and states that love always has to do with re-finding the original love object— usually the mother.

But what about her great need to lie in the lap of an analyst-father, for months or years, in order to have her longing put into words so that she could move beyond being **frozen** by that infantile longing? Klein (1963) might understand the sensual pleasure Dora derived from phantasies of mother-baby merging as being partly an expression of her loneliness. To Klein, loneliness encompasses a longing for the idealized relationship between mother and infant, where one could be understood without words, a typical fantasy about the early mother-infant relationship, which also reincarnates the longing to return to the womb.

(In chapters 2 & 3 I drew attention to the conflict aroused when these longings collide with the child's push towards development, and how the life and death instincts become entwined in perpetual battle when not presided over by the love of the parental internal objects.)

But, it is the essence of **inner** loneliness that is highlighted when it occurs precisely in the *presence* of friends or intimates. Chekhov, supposedly, wrote:
"If you are afraid of loneliness, don't marry."

Klein developed her crucial emphasis on the **internal** dynamics of loneliness:

"Since full integration is never achieved, **complete** understanding and acceptance of one's own emotions, phantasies and anxieties is not possible and this continues as an important factor in loneliness. The longing to understand oneself is also bound up with the need to be understood by the internalized good object. One expression of this longing is the universal phantasy of having a **twin**—a phantasy to which Bion drew attention in an unpublished paper. This twin figure as he suggested, represents those un-understood and split off parts which the individual is longing to regain, in the hope of achieving wholeness and complete understanding; they are sometimes felt to be the ideal parts **of the self**."

In a deceptively playful way, the comedian Peter Cook entitled his autobiography *Tragically, I was an only Twin* (2002).

One aim of this chapter is to suggest that the father provides a link to this "twin" and fosters a dialogue, of sorts, with it. And so an absent, or narcissistically disinterested father, who fails in this role, may leave the child 'at sea' in the lifelong quest of knowing their own mind, and without the capacity to reflect on what they need for stimulation, growth and nourishing new experiences.

His task is not so much to repeat the more maternal reveries – much detailed by Bion, Rosenfeld and Ogden, but to shape and form the basic canopy under which an interested emotional holding brings about a more verbal, and interactive form of that more primal maternal reverie.

Many others apart from Klein have written about that painful yearning and pining for the lost, idealized wordless at-one-ment with one's mother. And its addictive qualities have been imbued in the German term *Sehnsucht* – which implies, as well as missing and longing, a bitter taste of resentment of any "inferior substitutes" to the pre-natal oceanic oneness, and a contempt for dependency of the infantile self **upon** such an inferior substitute. Combined with envy this can prove to be a very powerful emotional force in turning away from even the most loving maternal object (Maizels, 1992) and towards the omnipotent phantasy of being totally self-sufficient and needing no other.

And Coen (1997) has seen this state of mind as crucial to the formation of **addictions:**

"Sehnsucht represents thoughts and feelings about all facets of life that are **unfinished or imperfect**, paired with **a yearning for ideal alternative experiences**. It has been referred to as "life's longings"; or an individual's search for happiness while coping with the reality of unattainable wishes. Such feelings are usually profound and tend to be accompanied by both positive and negative feelings. This produces what has often been described as an ambiguous emotional occurrence. It is sometimes felt as a longing for a far-off country, but not a particular earthly land which we can identify. Furthermore, there is something in the experience which suggests this far-off country is very familiar and indicative of what we might otherwise call "home." In this sense it is a type of **nostalgia**, in the original sense of that word. At other times it may seem as a longing for a some**one** or even a some**thing**. But the majority of people who experience it are not conscious of what or who the longed for object may be, and the longing is of such profundity and intensity that the subject may immediately be only aware of the emotion itself, and not cognizant that there is a something longed for."

(p. 198)

In some people, this painful form of nostalgia, if chronic, can only be assuaged by a concrete chasing of Sehnsucht **(an addiction** to longing) and may, in addition to drug dependence, become a painful motivator for suicide pacts, including terrorist plots. (See, for example, the films *Brighton Rock,* for a chilling look, and *Five Lions* for a more comic, if no less poignant, depiction.)

F Scott Fitzgerald wrote of the pained nostalgia of Americans abroad:

"His "lonely ache" (p. 62) has all the intensity of Sehnsucht. Only the reader who knows Sehnsucht, and who has not experienced it? Will understand what

I and my characters, Americans, indeed all humans? Suffer from irrevocable loss. Some of the supposed "objects" and attempted means of fulfilment are: the "far off hillside" of childhood and its idealized associations, past events, distant places, mystery and beauty, nature, exotic travels and adventure, romantic tales, a craving for knowledge, and, of course, "the perfect beloved - seeking fulfilment of his "undefinable desire".

(p. 87)

There is little doubt that Fitzgerald drew upon these intensely emotional experiences when writing about his great Gatsby, pursuing his Daisy as the epitome of his deeper yearning for that which he himself cannot put into words. In narrator Nick's observational musings:

There must have been moments even that afternoon when Daisy tumbled short of his dreams? not through her own fault, but because of the colossal vitality of his illusion. It had gone beyond her, beyond everything.

(p. 101)

CS Lewis (1972) used Schiller's term *Sehnsucht* to mean a **frozen** in longing – a clinging to longing, fixated in its attempted fusion with the lost archaic (umbilical) mother, and Owen Barfield saw Lewis as meaning that "… true longing is never fulfilled by anything in the earthly life, but … it's always a disguised longing for God" (1943).

Of course, one can confuse feeling cut off from one's lively internal objects with feeling cut off from the whole (external) human race – and both of these may become confused with the anxious resentment of being cut off, umbilically, from what Wordsworth referred to as our first "paradise."

That resentment becomes murderous in the would-be king Macbeth, and Shakespeare has it that Macbeth can only be stopped by someone born without the usual pains of **birth** – that primal catastrophic change (Bion) where the slings and arrows of outrageous fortune inflict their first wounds on the child's soul.

But, as I suggested above, it was Melanie Klein who really emphasizes the **internal** object relationships in her understanding of loneliness although she, like Freud, and unlike Otto Rank (1924) wavered in seeing the first depressive obstacle for the infant as being the loss of the womb:

"A satisfactory early relation to the mother (not necessarily based on breast feeding since the bottle can also symbolically stand for the **breast**) implies a close contact between the unconscious of the mother and of the child. This is the foundation for the most complete experience of being understood and is essentially linked with the **preverbal stage**. However gratifying it is in later life to express thoughts and feelings to a congenial person, there remains an unsatisfied longing for an understanding without words—ultimately for the earliest relation with the mother. This longing contributes to the sense of loneliness and derives from the depressive feeling of an irretrievable loss."

Although she did think that:

> "... there is a constant interaction between internal and external factors in mental life, based on the processes of projection and introjection which initiate object relations. The first powerful impact of the external world on the young infant is the discomfort of various kinds which accompanies **birth** and which is attributed by him to hostile persecutory forces."

And poets such as Wordsworth, and analytic writers such as Rank (1924) Bion (1977), and Maizels (see Chapters 2, 3) have traced such longings back to the enduring sense of longing for the pre-natal state.

The female poet and her father

A painfully frustrated patient with writer's block returned from a weekend break which she had earmarked for the completion of her latest novel and complained, in tears, that:

> "Inside of me is nothing but wandering shadows ..."

When I noted that although she'd failed to complete her self-imposed edict, the wandering shadows seemed a most apt and poetic image for how she'd felt, she rose from the couch and kicked a nearby bookshelf so that books were scattered onto the floor, and said:

> "Fucking words! Is that that all there is to comfort me?"

Stone (1973), whose heart-wrenching study of Diane Wakoski, Sylvia Plath and Anne Sexton addresses images of absent fathers in "tones of love, grief, and hatred"- thought that each of these poets "... tried to master her early loss of father by manipulating **words** to bridge the gap between inner and outer reality. Stone believes that Plath's father is blamed, in poetry, for leaving her alone with her guilt and fantasies – and for not being present when she needed to test reality. In her poetry, she came as close as she could, if only in fantasy, to the father she so desperately craved, according to Stone. Unfortunately, there is not space enough here to more closely detail Stone's elaboration through examples of Plath's poems. But Stone argues that this intensely lonely struggle to find words for deep and barely containable emotions such as grief and disillusionment "cost Plath" in the creation of poetry. Perhaps, ultimately, even her own life itself was part of the payment.

Plath's father died when she was nine, Sexton's father was "seldom home" and Wakoski's left when she was two.

The latter wrote:

> "My father who made me a maverick – a writer/ a **namer**."

(p. 169)

yet -

"My father did not care if I studied the piano;/my father did not care what I did."

And this flowed

"... through my heart like ink in the thickest nibbed pen, black **and flowing into words.**"

(My italics; Wakoski)

But, I don't think that it is purely words and language that is so important for the young child to "grasp hold of" through the father, it is also that this capacity to find words and language for one's own inner self that is a kind of passport for the child who stands at the threshold between family and the "big wide World". The weaning onto words used expressively, to speak of one's human needs, can be just as important as the weaning onto solid foods, for the growing child. And his or her zest for exploring the world – trying new things, and the joy of experimenting – depend mightily on the successful conveying of **desire**, paramountly to one's **self**.

As Stone wrote:

"Developmentally, the young girl meets her father as the first outsider to help draw her out of the original mother—child symbiosis." The father is "The first stranger, the first representative of the outside world, the first possibility of a secondary-dependent (as distinguished from a primary-dependent or symbiotic relationship) with a separate other."

These poems express the struggle for personal identity and the feeling that identity is that much more unattainable if one misses experiencing the father as representative of wider society

The role of language is central in the description of the fathers in all of the poems. Of course, these are poets, and language is the tool used to recreate their world. Nevertheless, their manipulation of words and ordering of experience through artistic form is a major work accomplishment made in spite of a father's absence.

Naming objects is important to the developing child; it is an expansion of self, a mastery of the unfamiliar through sharing with the parent, the vocabulary like threads woven by the parent and child together to encircle each new object and make it the child's own. Wakoski recovers her father by creating him through the act of naming. Like Adam who achieved dominion over God's creatures by naming them, the poet is able to subdue her feelings of helplessness in the absence of a father through repetition of the word. Naming, as symbolized in the Eden story, gives power, and it is only now that her love for her father helps her perceive that he contributes to her identity.

(Stone, 1973, p. 536)

In the chapter on *disidentification* I suggest that there is an ongoing form of (healthy) loneliness prefigured and necessitated by the need to relinquish various identifications through growth into one's unique self. Part of this is also necessitated by the need to become an individual within a group. In fact, these needs clash and interact and may help or hinder each other in their development. They may also push for some courageous changes to take place, and the above paternal object may be required to help the child to distinguish between courageous acts of independent thinking and reckless presumptuousness.

As I mentioned previously, Klein thought that there was an intimate link between enjoyment and the feeling of being understood – but, she was addressing understanding given by the mother. However, loneliness is not just countered by a remembrance of (good) things (breast) past. There is also, especially when alone or isolated, or experiencing an analytic break, an urgent need to think upon what one needs to continue growing and feeing alive, and to be reinvigorated by new experiences in the **present.** In my view, this requires, additionally, contact with the good internal **father**, who helps promote an ongoing interest in one's current needs – and in the spirit of a benign, thinking father. This is in stark contrast to the stringent, super-egoish (King Lear) father that can only underline the child's duties and obligations; who is very rule-driven, punishment oriented and, above all else, self-centred and focused. The child's mind as an object of fascination and curiosity but which needs a stimulating spark of interest, is not considered – and is felt to be an impediment to his own infantile needs for gratification. He takes no pleasure in watching the child's interests and character unfold or bloom, and is also often physically absent at key moments for the growing child, lest these moments arouse envy.

Klein implied that the child needs to not be frightened by the parents' reaction to its own free associations – both must be interested in where the child's unconscious inclinations lead, without premature judgement or accusations of irresponsibility or destructiveness or chaotic messiness.

Such a child who, in spite of some envy and jealousy, can identify himself with the pleasures and gratifications of experimentation, will also develop that interest in his own unexplored potential, which can provide times of isolation with a powerful antidote to loneliness – it can become a time of opportunity, and even a warm closeness in internal dialogue with the internal father, in particular. But it can bring much depressive pain if the external father (in some ways the representative of the good internal father) dies prematurely early in the child's life.

By contrast, many people **forego** the quest for the interested internal parent and seek one who will provide a comfort-filled womb-like palace and money, a la Madame Bovary.

So, the development of reverie may be a two-stage process. Initially, the mother provides and models it for the child. But later, possibly sometimes even simultaneously, the father "supervises" the development of reverential capacity within the child and encourages and invokes experimentation and self-reflection through words – with their ultimate payload of expressive vocalization of meaning-laden thought.

Ironic then, or is it, that the strong need for psychoanalysis (and perhaps even psychoanalytic supervision) evinced in some people – the current audience probably included – may prove to be quite a most *natural* inclination after all, in spite of its seeming artificiality. And the wish to have someone sit with us for 50 minutes or so at a time, and dedicate themselves to helping us put our deepest (often unconscious) longings into words so that we can eventually reflect on them, is as much our search for an understanding father as for an analytic mother who magnetizes these longings up from the couch and into the reverie of the combined analytic object.

But, of course, I am not suggesting that the mother, **herself**, doesn't help the child to use words. But, I believe that it is the internal father who is in the unique position to encourage words for the frustration and anguished inconsolability of the child's separation from, and disappointment with, its mother, and her limitations. These are particularly intense unconsciously, as we know, in feelings about her attending to a sibling rival or that "old fucker" the father. The **external** characteristics of the internal father, though, are multifarious and protean. He may materialize as a school teacher, a step-parent, a "Yorrick" uncle, of either (or these days, even blended) sex.

The crucial thing about the internal **combined** object, so far as development is concerned, is that both internal parents are infused with love for each other, this love being partially formed, but totally imbued and coloured, by the child's own projections of love – untainted too much by jealousy, envy and an intolerance of their beauty and mystery. (Shakespeare's *A Midsummer Night's Dream* is probably the closest artistic representation we have, in our language, to the intricate unfurling of that tragic-comedy in the child's mind.)

Loneliness and boredom

If longing is clearly fundamental to loneliness, another uncomfortable state of mind is less obviously connected, namely **boredom.**

Flaubert links boredom to loneliness, albeit in a rather cynical tone. In *Madame Bovary* the narrator states:

> "In its less intense or minor form ... we all experience loneliness as boredom; we continually feel that we must keep ourselves occupied lest we are forced to confront the 'nothingness' that is our consciousness."

Greenson (1953), in a paper on boredom, writes that "... the feeling of emptiness, combined with a sense of longing and an **absence** of fantasies and thoughts which would lead to satisfaction, is characteristic of boredom. In patients who suffer from apathy, we also find a feeling of emptiness but here there is no more longing. Or, I would suggest, what we commonly refer to as a "failure of imagination." He goes on to say, in a somewhat remonstrative tone, that

> "... they reproach the world for not giving them the stimulation they crave, while at the same time they reject what the world has to offer. Boredom, then. would seem to be potentially a more vigorous reaction to a sense of frustration or blocking, with anger being close to the surface. Loneliness, as noted above, has a more passive quality, as if one were suffering helplessly, languishing in unhappiness ... but severe loneliness is beyond longing and resignation, and (at least at the outset) ***not reachable through words.***"
>
> (My italics.; pp. 232–233)

Of course, there is also an **unconscious** form of loneliness – where the sufferer seems to successfully keep awareness of painful feelings of loneliness lodged, via projective identification into others. They may, however, perpetually complain of very lonely friends or workmates that seem to desperately need their assistance, or advice, or company and who always seem at a loose end when left to their own devices. One can feel very lonely in the counter-transference with such patients, and "at a loss" about what to say or do, or about the direction of the work. And yet, Cohen (1982) describes loneliness as a painful fragmentation that can occur even when one is loved; it arises from the fantasy of losing parts of the self, as may occur in psychosis. A person's sense of losing particular self-attributes is a variation of Fromm-Reichmann's idea that those who suffer from real loneliness have lost the sense of having had objects in their lives. And this very much accords with Klein's idea that the most painful forms of loneliness are intra-psychic – a yearning for the reunion or re-integration with lost (split-off) parts of one's self. I would argue that the projective identification of loneliness (as with envy) serves as an effective defence, temporarily, but it soon diminishes the self's need and capacity to **think**, and ultimately heightens the feeling of loneliness.

I suggested earlier that there is another element that builds on the maternal capacity to tune in to the infant's unconscious (what Bion calls reverie) but which is more a **paternal function** in providing the patience for, and a stimulation of, a self-reflective curiosity sorely needed to bring those unconscious thoughts out into the light of concepts and **words** (alpha elements), that can be worked on as thoughts.

Zilborg (1938), on the other hand, emphasized missing someone to mirror us, believing the latter to be typical of narcissists. "We have found that for a period of time a person may need to use the therapist as a mirror to assuage their loneliness."

Zilborg, in a discussion of loneliness, says about lovers:

> "I have observed the feelings of loneliness ensue either when the partners fail to understand each other or when they do **no more** than (merely) mirror each other."
>
> (p. 278)

It may be that mere mirroring diminishes a person's self-definition, thereby leaving the person lonely. So, I would see "mirroring," when offered at a certain

whole-object state of depressive development, as being a hugely disappointing misunderstanding of what the child needs, as illustrated by an often repeated sitcom joke about – "I'm hearing that you feel quite angry about me stepping on your toes ..." where a very false form of production line empathy is offered, insincerely and condescendingly. It must also include something from the father's imaginative reverie, offered with patient "loving-kindness" (see the chapter, *The Trees of Knowledge in Thomas Hardy's Woodlanders*) that indicates a sincere interest in finding out just what the little girl, herself, wants, even if it is different to, or outside the scope of, his own dreams or desires **for** her. (A *Lear* father, capable of *Prosperic* transformation.)

An "in-vocation" from the father, impelling and inviting verbalization of his own desire and yearning, particularly for the lost ideal relationship with his mother, is a more depressive need of the father that is far more attentive, involved and complex than mere "mirroring back."

Clinical fragment – Katriona

Katriona presented as a quite tormented and prickly "butch" patient, in her late forties, and from a relatively isolated town, who managed to access very low-cost psychotherapy in a somewhat deceptive, bullying manner. (She deliberately withheld certain information that could well have disqualified her from considerable fee reductions until the therapy was in full swing.) She remained quite secretive and controlling in her manner towards the therapist, and managed to create an atmosphere of careful condescension, thereby parodying what she imagined to be the therapist's attitude to herself. Her tone suggested that she should be treated as offering something quite special, and yet she suspected, with bitterness, that she was not offering anything that would distinguish her from, and above, my other patients – for which she was just barely tolerated by me. (Sometimes, indeed, she provoked just such a feeling in me, by throwing whirlwinds of tantrum, or spirals of intrusive, bullying questions that could never be answered, while simultaneously withholding information that was vital to my fuller understanding of her.) But these outbursts seemed to trouble her enormously, and she would return in the following session convinced that she had "pushed me over the edge" and that I was secretly arranging to be rid of her, and to insert a much more grateful and warm patient in her place. This grew hand in hand with a massive sense of entitlement in all of her relationships, and reading between the lines, it appeared that most of her "friends" preferred to keep a significant emotional distance from her. This led to quite bitter, accusing complaints about loneliness – which, by implication, were aimed squarely at the therapist – although rarely made directly. They were of the type – "X never phones me! I could be dead, and no one would know. How hard can it be to pick up the phone and ask how I am doing, or to check on what I'm interested in at the moment?" (She became very loudly outraged if I ever asked about why she could not make the call herself, but I suspected that she was in far more pain from this sense of loneliness than she was letting on. In the counter-transference, I often felt quite lonely – especially when she seemed to be talking more to herself, in a mumbling, self-justifying tone, should I dare to suggest that she was angry and upset with me for not phoning her in between sessions to ask how she was, or what she was interested in. However, in what she felt to have been a "passably worthwhile session," I was cast in the role of the father who helped her to find words for her rage and inconsolable disappointment with her mother and elder sisters. But this was followed with a session which seemed to fling back at me: "Yes you help console me – but, you are never around when I most need you, you "fucker!" Indeed she did bring a dream where I was Picasso, leading a profligate, endlessly and effortlessly creative life. I was the endlessly gratified infant, in never-ending intercourse with extremely desirable other people. And this led to a painful memory of being humiliated by her father after she'd returned from her first-ever overseas trip, and his ordering her to detail exactly what she'd done, in front of "a table full of his arse-licking clown friends."

From time to time she said that the therapy was of "great consolation", and that she had developed a form of bodily intimacy with a slightly older woman, whom she described as "cuddly and warm." But, apparently the relationship was contingent upon a mutual agreement for minimal talking. She could not bear to share any inner secrets, vulnerability or longings with this woman – who, likewise (I surmised) did not want to hear about such things **from** her.

I want to now focus on a session immediately following a long weekend break (the Melbourne festival of Moomba was held on the Monday public holiday) which was a culmination of growing self-loathing, boredom, indiscriminate envy and a general ennui and discontent about where her life was headed – particularly without a partner. She had massively projected her desperate need for companionship into an apparently sincere, potential girlfriend who had said that she was sitting by the phone waiting to hear from a sister who was going to phone from overseas. Katriona poured acidic scorn on this woman, whom she had at first been attracted to, and now described her as "… pathetically and hopelessly dependent on other people, like a little child waiting for daddy to come home. What a fuckhead!"

In this session, following the long weekend break, she began with quite an effusive, but somewhat hollow and protracted account of what she thought of as a quite wonderful and rich and interesting day she'd had, wandering around all the exhibitions and rides and markets by the river. She repeatedly said "so wonderful – just a perfect day – you couldn't imagine anything better" in such a tone that fomented feelings of irritation and impatience in me. It wasn't so much an envious feeling, on my part, but an annoyance at being kept at a distance from how she really felt, as if I was being suckered, or seduced and distracted.

In the immediately previous sessions she had struggled with the problem of focusing on her own art. She had spoken of this as a demanding but consoling activity that restored her to feeling alive, and that she had something to offer the human race. Yet, she complained that something always seemed to distract her, In fact, she had, almost, established herself as a professional commercial artist and cartoonist, just prior to commencing therapy, but had given it up – following some disparaging comments from her mother and sisters – and taken on menial nursing work (I think mainly to gain some appreciation, but which had left her too exhausted to spend any time on her art.)

With increasing lack of conviction, she continued insistently to speak of what a "great time" she was having out and about in the throng. It slowly emerged in the session that she had actually craved to be back home, to where she could express her longings through painting – but, she had told herself that since it was a nice day, and everyone **else** seemed to be outside, she should be too. This would then also prove to me that she was a wunderkind, optimally progressing patient who was my "star performer" – conquering separation and breaks with consummate common sense and fortitude.

Katriona had, in fact, endured many painful years of an only sporadically available father – but when she reunited with him he was still only interested in brief contact, followed by long gaps of time. In the transference, every pause was experienced as my losing interest in her, and supposedly yearning to be with some highly amusing and attractive, accomplished artist, with large breasts. Of course, this only partially corresponded to my counter-transference preoccupations. But, I did in fact often struggle to keep interested in what she was saying – mainly because she, herself, seemed only vaguely interested in what she was telling me. However, she recounted how when she returned from school or, later in life from a date, her "Hydra" mother would "suck stories" from her, voyeuristically, and wanted to know if anybody had touched her – particularly her breasts. She contrasted this with the brief visits from her **father**, where she craved his interest or curiosity – but he never seemed to ask anything much about her at all.

CJ and the West Wing

I will now turn, by contrast, to a key moment in the "life" of a fairly well-known television character in order to elucidate this vital role of the internal father in helping his child to successfully form their own ego ideal and to reap the sense of life direction that it summons and inspires.

The character is Claudia-Jean, (known as CJ) and is initially serving as the White House press secretary – an extremely difficult job, both intellectually and emotionally – requiring much tact, foresight, precision, judgement and humility. She must think on her feet, without always having support or the luxury of time for deliberation. As the series, *The West Wing,* develops - so does CJ, and she is eventually entrusted with the most influential and senior position in the land, after the President – the White House Chief of Staff. I will focus on how CJ is reaching the end of her term of office, and on the way in which she needs to regress to a little girl, much needing the lap of her father as a place in which to think. In particular, to think about her own place in the world and the direction that she wants to take in the next phase of her life – post-White House. She has at her disposal four men who all love her in their own fashion, but I will show how only one is of great use in firming up and reviving a truly helpful internal father for her.

The first man, unsurprisingly, is the President. He makes it amply clear, on many occasions, that her own needs and aspirations will have to follow on his own coat-tails, and makes no apologies for that – he just expects that it is part of her job not to take that personally, and not to confuse it (too much) with a father-daughter relationship.

The second man is her actual father – approaching death and losing his grip on the world and his own mind – due to intensifying dementia. He tries to listen to CJ, but his own needs and anxieties – many of them quite paranoid or delusional – prevent him from grasping the complexity of his daughter, as she grapples with her conflicted needs.

The third man is Toby, with whom she has had a very close working relationship – but, he has just been found guilty of betraying secrets of state. This issue, and his own narcissism, have made it hard for CJ to fully trust him, and to believe that he may be able to listen to her own struggles without imposing his own issues on her.

But, the fourth man – Danny the journalist – the one that she will eventually settle and have children with – is able to help her contact the little girl in herself and to bring it into the light of day where she can hear what it has to say.

Here are some fragments of vital, but contrasting conversations with (first) Toby, and then Danny, to illustrate the differences in the type of 'fathering' that they are able to offer CJ.

She visits Toby first – and they pick up a semi-flirtatious, fond sibling-esque tone very easily.

CJ   Offers strong drink to T. Thanks.
CJ-   It's not a gift. I need a drink.
T-   Would you like to sit?
CJ-   I sit all day.

T-   Should I be feeding you or just booze? –

CJ   Booze is fine.

I can't eat today.

T-   You sure? I made a chicken.
CJ -   No. So how are you?

The conversation hovers uncertainly for a while, as it dodges and weaves through various pleasantries until it sinks irretrievably into a comically obsessive wry interplay around the equally complex issues of an uncertainty in the Constitution and how to cook a chicken properly.

Toby- So I looked at every English language publication that exists.
        Half of them have the comma, half of them don't.
CJ-   Really?
T-   Yeah.
T-   I called the National Archives and had some woman look at the original. She said she wasn't sure if it was a comma or a smudge.

CJ-	There's a smudge? –
T-	Yeah, a smudge of law.
CJ-	Really? Should we do something?
T -	I'm gonna write it up …

Finally, the two crawl out from the confusing pretence of conversation and declare:

> I missed you.
>   Yeah.
>   We had it good there for a while.
>   Yeah, we did.
>   You should go.
>   You kicking me out?
>   - Yeah.
>   Okay.
>   - Thank you.

In this half-lit, almost-intimate dialogue, heavily wrapped in mere banter, Toby does get quite close to the type of fathering that CJ sorely misses from earlier, much earlier, days with her own father. Toby does, momentarily, manage to remind CJ that she has many options, and tries to get her to think of what she would truly enjoy – but, the joking is also Toby's way of surrendering to his own limits with her. He is far too caught up in his own worries (obsessions) to be able to hold down the role more permanently. (Toby has failed to be the husband that his wife needed, psychologically, and he is tortured with the pain that he will suffer in only having a partial role in raising the twins they produced together.)

But let's move directly (as does CJ in the geography of the episode) to a similar, but crucially different intimate conversation that CJ has with Danny the journalist, who correctly intuits that he can go the full way in a relationship with her.

CJ is tearful and distraught and feels that her hopes for a successful relationship are fading fast. She is being offered some very seductive job opportunities, but is at a loose end because she doesn't know how to focus on her own needs:

CJ	I missed the window.
Danny	That's what's going on here?
CJ	I missed the window to figure out how to do this.
D -	How to?
CJ-	Share my life with another person.
	How to be a partner or whatever condescending way you put it this - I wasn't trying – I don't know how to do it.
	Maybe at one point I did, maybe I never did but it's over now. It's too late. This and skiing, it's too late. It's not gonna happen. You said yourself it's not an accident that this hasn't come together. This is who I am. I'm good at my job, Danny. I'm good at working. I'm not good at this.

D-	You're right. You suck at it. You're gonna need a tremendous amount of training.
CJ-	You're not gonna – D I am, actually. CJ- Train me?
D-	I'll call it something else; that's bad. We'll deal with it.
CJ-	I don't need training.
D-	No, of course not.
CJ-	That's not funny.
D-	No, it isn't. You're gonna get good at it. We're gonna get good at new things.
CJ-	You don't know that. D- I do.
CJ-	Don't make it sound like it's nothing.
Danny-	You didn't miss it.
CJ-	What if I did? D - You didn't miss it.
CJ-	What if we can't?
D-	We'll figure it out. All of it. You - you can be scared. that's okay. But you're not gonna walk away from me because you're scared. I'm not that scary.
CJ-	(Gripped and moved, but somewhat helpless and near tears.) So do you want me to take one of the board of directors jobs? A couple hours a month.
D-	Where did that come from?!
CJ-	I'm trying. You wanna be **involved**.
D-	I'm I'm - I want you to do what you want. Just talk to me about it. I want us to talk about what it'll mean, and how it'll work. I want us to talk like we're gonna figure it out **together**. I want us to talk because I like the sound of your voice. I just wanna talk.
CJ-	Franklin Hollis (a Bill Gates billionaire figure who has met earlier in the day with CJ) wants me to take $ 10 billion and go and fix the world.
D-	That sounds like fun. Does that sound like fun to you? CJ *Nods head in poignant, little-girl manner*. Do you wanna work at the White House? CJ *Shakes head in poignant, little-girl manner*.
CJ-	There's a typo in the Constitution.
Danny-	Well, someone should look into that.
CJ-	Toby's gonna deal with it.
Danny-	Okay.

At this point Danny has taken CJ's little girl past where she got stuck with her own father, and past the point where Toby became jokey and obsessive with her. (The superego, in its never-ending quest for perfection, needs to be remembered, but then put in its place, with gentle but firm humour.) She is now truly un-lonely and simultaneously partnered with both Danny and her lost-child self.

* * * * * *

And so, a definition of the particular state of chronic loneliness that I am addressing in this chapter is beginning to look something like this:

Chronic, paralyzing loneliness is formed and sustained by **addiction** to an internal object which fails to nourish the developing mind of the child and which, instead, manically distracts away from that which may be invoked by the watchful father, who consoles for, and combines with, the lost (but remembered) feeling of being held in the reverie of its mother's eyes, mind and heart.

Melanie Klein was rather sombre in her thinking prognostically about the pains of loneliness, but not without some hope, she thought seriously about which factors might

> "…diminish loneliness. For example, a fundamentally good relation to the parents makes the loss of idealization and the lessening of the feeling of omnipotence more bearable. The parents, by accepting the existence of the child's destructive impulses and showing that they can protect themselves against his aggressiveness, can diminish his anxiety about the effects of his hostile wishes. As a result, the **internal** object is felt to be less vulnerable, and the self less destructive,

because

> … a **harsh super-ego** can never be felt to forgive destructive impulses; in fact, it demands that they should not exist. Although the super-ego is built up largely from a split-off part of the ego on to which impulses are projected, it is also inevitably influenced by the introjection of the personalities of the **actual** parents and of their relation to the child.

> The harsher the super-ego, the greater will be loneliness, because its severe demands increase depressive and paranoid anxieties. The father that can only see the child as conforming or rebelling."

(p. 156)

We need integration in order for the lost, especially "bad" parts of the self to be accepted and acknowledged so that we can feel more wholly ourselves. However, each integrative step brings new depressive pains in the increasing knowledge of our imperfections, limitations and destructiveness. However, we also need **external** experiences and objects that revive and stimulate such integration of our inner objects and their relations with each other.

I believe that many so-called "silent patients" need the therapist to speak first, as a catalytic substrate through speech and inquiring interest, before they are able to speak, and eventually free associate. Not just because of the stimulation to thinking provided, but as an antidote to the poisonous, stifling atmosphere of a perfectionistic superego, for whom the infantile parts of the self are judged as merely pathological, and of no interest to the perfect therapist. If the therapist is patient enough for this process to be repeated, it feeds a hope of reviving even the faintest emotional memory of the lost good internal father. And on this can be built a new universe of possibilities and direction for the growing child.

In conclusion, I have tried to demonstrate a particular element in a particularly painful form of loneliness, which is linked to the absence or unavailability of a paternal function through which the growing child is encouraged to reflect on its own desires and aspirations – in order to encourage and even to provoke the child to ask itself "what is it that I would really like to do, given the physical absence of those that I love (that might truly console the feeling of *Sehnsucht*)?"

I have tried to distinguish this function (with its crucial role in facilitating the separation-individuation from the mother) from the maternal functions of holding, containing and feeding – although there is some similarity, and continuity, with the maternal function of reverie, as described by Bion. The paternal form of reverie is much more verbally-based, and yet far less constricted to the bodily needs of the child. The paternal reverie has a more *aspirational* aim, fostering the child's interests in its own more long-term aims and desires. But, it can never replace the yearning for the primary maternal object, and contrariwise, even the most harmonious maternal object can still give rise to boredom. The combined object, only, ensures a presiding and enduring confidence that one's internal world, and the fruit of its good objects, will provide the manna for a stay in the desert when one's external good objects are unavailable.

(A recent episode of the sitcom *Raising Hope* illustrates this knife-edge flux between the experiencing of a father who is able to transcend his more usual narcissism, in helping his (now adult) daughter to realize her romantic aspirations and fantasies, and the experience of him as deceptively only using her for his own phantastic gratification.)

"Professional" loneliness

I want to conclude with a very brief mention of professional loneliness – not just as another example of counter-transference issues with loneliness, but as part and parcel of analytic work, where we are often engaged in a quest for the good objects of our patients, and not necessarily noticing how deprived we are of any resonance of these good objects, particularly when working with severe borderline or narcissistic patients, who themselves cannot gain access to these parts in themselves.

Klein thought that there was:

> "… one further connection between loneliness and the problem of integration. It is generally supposed that loneliness can derive from the conviction that there is no person or group to which one belongs. This not belonging can be seen to have a much deeper meaning. However much integration proceeds, it cannot do away with the feeling that certain components of the **self** are not available because they are split off and cannot be regained. Some of these split-off parts … are projected into other people, contributing to the feeling that one is not in full possession of one's self, that one does not fully belong to oneself or, therefore, to

anybody else. The lost parts **too, are felt to be lonely**. I have already suggested that paranoid and depressive anxieties are never entirely overcome, even in people who are not ill, and are the foundation for some measure of loneliness."

(p. 136)

Britton, in his paper on *Publication Anxiety* (1999) showed how the wish to belong may be the enemy of writing "truly" since professional loneliness is greatly feared if one does not pander to the imagined (or real) narcissistic needs of one's mentors.

And so, I would underline two major sources of internal loneliness that may be part of the perils of doing psychoanalytic work, especially over decades.

1. The need to bear loneliness in the counter-transference, where one is perpetually gaining an emotional experience of patients' loneliest and unwanted parts of themselves.
2. The need to bear loneliness when asking oneself what is truly interesting, and insufficiently explored, in one's own mind & development. This means reading (and sometimes writing) in areas that may be unfamiliar, or even disapproved of, by one's peers.

The combined effect of the alive, watchful internal mother reverie, with the interest in words reverie of the internal father is needed to endure and to transform feelings of both preverbal loneliness (Sehnsucht), and "loose-end", boredom loneliness. That is, a combined object capable of bearing both the depressive longing for the preverbal mother and for the patient, watching-over of instigatory thinking, father. Therefore, the links between healthy dis-identificatory processes, mourning and loneliness are intimate, and inextricable.

However, inner loneliness, where one's muse, or internal father, is either insufficiently heeded, or absent or undeveloped, is extremely painful. Potential creativity may be counterfeited by a well-behaved, false-self, performing clone. I have explored some of this further in the chapter *Dreams Grown False*. And later in life's crucial forks in the road, such as choosing subjects for a new phase of education, friends, partners and job opportunities, the sitting on father's knee state of mind is very important for initiating a self-reflective taking stock of oneself at such moments – where the good enough father shows a genuinely interested pleasure in the growing child's own choices. So, the providing of a vertex for thought is what counts – enabled and presided over by a benign, open-minded superego. This would be one that can remind of possible recklessness or risk of damage to oneself, but which can encourage experimentation and the unexpected. The beginnings of this capacity need to be securely introjected before some mutually confident setting sail for termination can be embarked upon, without too much fear of the more infantile and needy parts of the self being lost overboard at the first sign of tempestuous weather.

A **touch** of *Sehnsucht* in the night – a longing for the ideal, we call **nostalgia**, can add a touch of piquant reflectiveness and perspective to our task-obsessed lives. But, a drowning in it, leaving us disabled for, and uninterested in, consoling, loving relationships, we call **despair**. In real life, the line between these two states can sometimes seem wafer-thin.

I believe that this prompts a difficult, but interesting, question. Should we see some degree of inevitable failure of the father function, at least as I have suggested it to be, as possibly quite common, and thereby agree with Klein that a certain amount of 'residual' and non-verbal loneliness is a part of the (even healthiest) human condition? If so, could we see this inevitable longing for the ideal (*Sehnsucht*) – a "gap" of longing left by most (even good enough) experiences of one's parents as a kind of "natural" propellant, edging us towards a "romantic-religious" inclination toward the ineffable on the one hand, and towards a love for the imaginative and expressive use of words, and their capability for understanding the outer (and inner) reaches of our emotional experiences, on the other?

In any case, I hope that I've begun to show that the voice speaking in the dark, that can make loneliness lighter is one's own - but enticed and illuminated by an internal father, who understands the pains of the longed-for soulmate mother.

References

Ben Lazare Mijuskovic (2012). *Loneliness in Philosophy, Psychology, and Literature.* New York: iUniverse Books.

Bion (1977). *The Dawn of Oblivion.* Perthshire: Clunie Press.

Coen, P. (1997). When Sehnsucht (desire) leads you up the garden path. *J. Analytic. Psychology,* 29 (2): 141–166.

Cohen, N. A. (1982). On loneliness and the ageing process. *Int. J. Psychoanal.,* 63: 149–155.

Freud, S. (1905a). Fragment of an analysis of a case of hysteria. *S. E.,* 7: 1–122.

Freud, S. (1905b). *Three essays on sexuality. S. E.,* 7: 123–243.

Freud, S. (1963) *Fromm-Reichmann. Loneliness. (1959 & 1990.).* London: Hogarth Press.

Freud, S. (1916–1917). Anxiety. *Introductory Lectures on Psychoanalysis.* S E. 1916: 392–411. London: Hogarth Press, 1963.

Greenson, R. (1953). On boredom. *J. Am. Psych.,* 31 (2): 144–158.

Klein, M. (1963). *On the sense of loneliness. Writings of Melanie Klein. 1946–1963.* NewYork: The New Library of Psychoanalysis, 1984, 300–313.

Kotter-Grühn, D., Wiest, M., Zurek, P. and Scheibe, S. (2009). What is it we are longing for? Psychological and demographic factors influencing the contents of Sehnsucht (life longings). *Journal of Research in Personality* (43): 428–437.

C. S. Lewis (1972) On Joy, Sehnsucht, Longing and True Myth. In *Collected Papers.* London: Bloomsbury Press. pp. 288–298.

Lord, M. M. and Stone, C. (1973). Fathers and daughters: A study of three poems. *Contemp. Psychoanal.,* 9: 526–539.

Rank, O. (1924). *The Trauma of Birth and Its Importance for Psychoanalysis.* Leipzig, Vienna, and Zürich: Internationaler Psa. Verlag.

Scheibe, S., Blanchard-Fields, F., Wiest, M. and Freund, A. M. (2011). Is longing only for Germans? A cross-cultural comparison of sehnsucht in Germany and the United States. *Dev. Psychol.,* 22: 111–143.

Scheibe, S., Freund, A. M. and Baltes, P. B. (2007). Toward a developmental psychology of Sehnsucht (life longings): The optimal (utopian) life. *Dev. Psychol.* 43: 778–795.

Scheibe, S. and Freund, A. M. (2008). Approaching Sehnsucht (life longings) from a lifespan perspective: The role of personal utopias in development. *Res. Hum. Dev.*, 12: 121–133.
Spira, L., and Richards, A. K. (2003). On being lonely, socially isolated and single: A multi-perspective approach. *Psychoanal. Psychother.*, 20 (1): 3–21.
Zilboorg, G. (1938). Loneliness. *Atlantic Monthly*, 161: 45–54.

Chapter 10
Two Vices and a film review

Sometimes a cigar ... on smokers and non-smokers

In 1946, the famous Italian conductor, Arturo Toscanini, was quoted in the Observer as saying:

> I smoked my first cigarette and kissed my first woman on the same day. I have never had time for tobacco since.

This brief chapter is an attempt to understand those not so fortunate as Toscanini – although even he remained addicted to holding a stick (some would say in an omnipotently militaristic fashion) for the rest of his life.

Tobacco was originally used by American Indians as a narcotic drink, but by the time Christopher Columbus arrived, they were smoking it. They used it for ceremonial purposes and believed it to have medicinal properties, which was the main reason it was taken back to Europe. The diplomat Jean Nicot is said to have introduced it to France in 1556. Tobacco was originally smoked mainly in pipes and cigars; cigarettes did not become socially acceptable until the late 18th century. It is usually made from the leaves of common tobacco, but many varieties have been developed and a number of different additives and preparation techniques are used, but the principal narcotic drug in tobacco is nicotine, which is addictive.

Increasing concerns over the links between smoking and lung cancer, heart disease, and other health problems have caused many countries to take steps to discourage smoking – but the taxing of tobacco is a major source of revenue for most governments in the world. In Japan, where smoking generates 20 billion US dollars of tax each year, the warning label on each packet of cigarettes advises:

> Since smoking might injure your health, let's be careful not to smoke too much.

In spite of a downturn in the numbers of smokers in Western countries during the 1970s and 1980s, the numbers have risen strongly again in the 1990s and into the present day.

It was estimated by the WHO (1994) that 68% of the adult Chinese population are smokers.

What I'm going to present here is probably best seen as a kind of "fantasia" on smoking and smokers rather than a formal theoretical paper. Although my speculations have their basis in personal experiences, clinical and non-clinical, particularly with patients and friends who have struggled with the habit over a long period of time, they are offered in a tentative spirit, with the hope of eliciting further thought and discussion, particularly about the unconscious aspects of this sometimes fascinating, often troubling, but persistent human habit. But, I also want to think about the sometimes pernicious emotional field between smokers and non-smokers.

Let's start with a news article from the *Toronto Star*.

Judge rules against prisoner's Penthouse disappointment.

A prisoner in Texas has failed with a lawsuit against Penthouse magazine for publishing what he said was a disappointing layout of scandal identity, Paula Jones.

The suit charged that the December pictorial of Ms. Jones was not sufficiently revealing and caused the plaintiff to be "very mentally hurt and angered".

He sought damages of more than $900,000.

The judge, who was not impressed, wrote a short poem as he dismissed the suit. It read in part:

'Twas the night before Christmas and all through the prison, inmates were planning their new porno mission.

The last line read:

Life has its disappointments, some come out of the blue, but that doesn't mean a prisoner should sue.

The inmate was fined $460 for filing a frivolous motion.

Whilst the judge can never be forgiven for his appalling lack of poetic capability, his bemused and sarcastic tone might quite accurately reflect the feelings that most non-smokers have in the presence of a smoker, in spite of sometimes feeling a smattering of sympathy.

Although it is very hard to make the effort to understand something that we find distasteful, annoying and intrusive, I feel it's important to attempt some understanding of the anguish and pleasure that smokers live with, and arouse – in order that we might get beyond just a grumpy tolerance.

No doubt my wish to gain more understanding has a personal basis as well. My father has been contemptuous of smokers all his life. My step-father smoked heavily until meeting my mother, who went on an all-out campaign – successful – to persuade him to stop. My analyst smoked a pipe during sessions – what more could be expected from someone analyzed by Hannah Segal? – and I too complained until he stopped – or at least that was my fantasy about why he stopped. And many years ago, my idealization of a psychoanalytic mentor received severe bruising when I discovered his total and continuous addiction to cigarettes – the strongest brand on the market.

There is, however, a stunning lack of psychoanalytic papers on smoking, which is all the more striking when we consider that it was such an important lifelong addiction for the 'father' of psychoanalysis. Although it was ultimately responsible for his death, smoking also played a crucial role for Freud as part of his creative ritual in the production of his seminal psychoanalytic works, and of his bedside manner with his patients. (More on the significance of identification with the father later.)

The one paper that does appear in the psychoanalytic literature, was published in the IJPA in 1923(!) with the illustrious title:

"Some notes on smoking", by a G.H. Green.

Because it is really the only paper dedicated to an understanding of *unconscious* factors in the smoker, and because of its quirkiness, I'll quote some of it here.

> The opposition to smoking expressed by parents and parent substitutes, as a result of which the adolescent is compelled to smoke secretly, either in private or in the company of other transgressors, is a fact, which partly serves to determine its place as an onanistic activity.
>
> It is also of importance, I think, that mutual masturbatory acts, smoking, discussion of tabooed subjects are indulged in within the same groups. It is impossible to overlook the relation of such to the bands of brothers who revolt against the father. Expansion of this matter in detail is unnecessary.

(But this doesn't stop Green ...)

> Already one is forced to see in adolescent and juvenile smoking an expression of the death-wish against the father.

Green goes on to describe the case of a son (probably himself) who smoked a pipe – indeed became a connoisseur of tobaccos- in order to defy and defeat his asthmatic father who constantly told him that smoking would have been the death of him.

> One may note that English women still dislike a man to smoke a pipe in the street, but like it in the house. I have heard one woman say that a man does not seem at home unless he smokes a pipe, or that a man does not seem a man without a pipe. All this seems in line with an unconscious identification of the pipe with the phallus.
>
> It is a matter of common knowledge that the French representations of English people in the comic journals, represents the woman with a widely open mouth and exposed teeth and the man with a pipe. It is one of the commonplaces of popular patriotism to represent foreigners as 'dirty', and it is obvious that these popular representations have the significance of exposures of primary sexual organs ...
>
> A fresh set of considerations arises in connection with the attitude of certain religious sects towards smoking. Certain sects of nonconformists object very strongly to a minister who smokes. The Salvation Army, I believe, urges its

> converts to give up smoking, and insists upon its officers doing so. Many Plymouth Brethren object to members of the sect smoking on their way to or from a service, stating as the ground for their objection that a man so devoted to his pipe cannot be sincere in his attitude towards God. If the smoking expresses the wish for the death of the father, the objection that the reconciliation of the smoker with God, the father-substitute, cannot be complete, seems a shrewd one.
>
> Very few men enjoy smoking in the darkness: that is, if the smoke cannot be seen. So little part does the sense of taste play in smoking that there are smokers that cannot be certain, in darkness, whether their pipes be alight or not. This leads us to the significance of the emission of smoke …

Green goes on to equate the white smoke with semen (in the unconscious) and this supports his case for smoking as a form of masturbation.

> If we may write the equation, smoke = semen, we are able to see the connection between huge clouds of smoke and fantasies of potency, and to realise the significance of the furious puffing of the smoker confronted with a difficulty.

Finally, inevitably, Green equates the cigarette with both the phallus and the nipple, and the smoker to an infant at the breast.

He notes that, in Egypt, the expression equivalent to smoking is literally "drinking tobacco."

Well, is there much more to say on the topic after Green's devastating analysis?

I think there might be, but to say more I believe that we need to make use of the Kleinian concept of projective identification, in order to explore not just the physical act of smoking, but the complex states of mind that smoking may evoke in the smoker, and also often in the non-smoker who is in relationship *to* the smoker.

Through our now very complex models of unconscious identificatory processes, including, and especially, *projective* identification, we can see the possibility that the smoker might, for example, be *identifying with* the feeding mother (unconsciously) as he places the cigarette in his mouth, and therefore assumes total control over the feeding process in a way that he never enjoyed in infancy.

So, even to say that the "habit" of smoking can sometimes be understood **just** as a return to the breast, or **just** masturbation, does not do justice to the rich variety of emotional experiences that infants might have, both at, and separated from, the feeding mother. Nor does it do justice to the myriad of unconscious perceptions of, and feelings about, the father who holds, supports and has a mysterious and perplexing intercourse with that feeding mother.

This leads us also to consider the great complexities of the struggles in the infant mind between projective and introjective processes. Perhaps we might even think of the inhaling and exhaling of smoke as sometimes representing these processes, in a bodily way. Especially since, very concretely, it involves a repeated drawing into, and a pushing out from, one's inner body. But, the feeling that a smoker has during this inspiration and exhalation are as varied, and unique for each.

What follows is a very rough attempt to order some of the states of mind – in both smoker and non-smoker-in-the-presence-of-a-smoker. I will try to move from what we might see as the more defensively 'primitive' projective states, to the complex, depressive and expressive states – but, sometimes, in real life, the clarity of this distinction breaks down. My classification of these states is therefore to be seen as a tool for exploration, rather than a "psychiatric" nosology.

Death and the Marlboro

Smoking, at least from the body's perspective, enacts a wish to die prematurely. From this view, it has to be seen as a basic attack on the parts and apparati of our bodies which enable us to breathe in, inspire, life.

The smoker exhales the infinite chain of longing, and – for a moment frees – in phantasy - the shackles of desire, which vanish into thin air.

Sometimes this is a temporary diversion from painful Oedipal struggles. Sometimes it can be seen as a massive regression to a psychobiological foetal state, where each warm inhalation and exhalation mimics a kind of foetal breathing.

Recent studies suggest that the foetus does "breathe" in some of the warm amniotic fluid, and has an experience of this passing through its mouth, throat and gastric tract.

Holding it together: the crippled self and the little glowing cherry

This form and use of the cigarette have the function of temporarily binding together the desperate, fragmented selves of those on the verge of a schizo-psychotic collapse. We see these poor suffering souls in the streets – amongst the homeless (love-less), and those smoking away the hours and years in psychiatric hospitals – in those, probably unwanted souls, whose emotional existence hangs on their clutching lips around a cigarette – the one thing that can never be taken away.

One psychotic man told me once that no one else could ever understand the importance of that "little glowing cherry," and that it made his utter aloneness, particularly in the middle of the night, bearable.

For some, that little red nipple isn't enough to get them through the night, and a yearning for a state of body and mind prior to birth binds them to Thanatos and opiates, in a craving for an existence prior to the impingement of massive, unprocessable maternal projections, or deprivation.

Rosenfeld's (1987) idea of maternal projections before birth is relevant here. He speculates about the importance of a process which works like a physical osmosis but in the mental sphere. He believes that the foetus is completely helpless to ward off the pressure of these projections from the mother, and may become phobic to all maternal situations later in life. I'll return to this idea later when I discuss the projection of this phobic state into non-smokers, who are made to feel something of this projective intrusion into their basic sustaining environment.

Puffed-up Narcissism and contemptuous rage

This is the most obviously projective form of smoking, epitomized, for example, by the late Australian "colourful character" John Elliot.

For those who are not familiar with his antics – a very brief summary. He was a wealthy businessman, a one-time owner of a major brewery, and a self-confessed, nay proud, smoker. He 'owned' a football club and had very public stoushes over his utter refusal to obey smoking restrictions in enclosed eating areas.

He was openly contemptuous of anyone who disagreed with the proclamations spurting forth from his infantile omnipotence.

(To his credit, he was able to laugh at himself, and speaks with half a tongue in his cheek when denouncing the incompetence of any rivals – unlike some recent politicians.)

As he puffed himself up, he puffed out a stream of contempt for the world, and said that he didn't enjoy smoking, but found it "helpful." His smoking was particularly energetic when he was cornered, and his omnipotence threatened. For example, when he was charged with the theft of $66 million from one of his companies, he addressed the press with a puff on a cigarette punctuating each sentence. Rather than proclaim his innocence, he denounced the right of the National Crime Authority to investigate him.

He is an extreme example of this style of smoking, but it can be seen amongst groupings of dissatisfied workers during a lunch or tea break, still called a "smoko." There is a kind of contemptuous posture, perhaps leaning heavily against a wall, or making lurid, ribald remarks about bosses or passers-by. There is scorn for the rest of the world as if it is all *others* that are desperate or pathetic – and there is a particular pleasure with the length and penetration of the stream of smoke that is pressed out through their mocking lips.

I will return to this later when I discuss the so-called "shelter-shed dynamics" between smokers and non-smokers.

There may also be an expulsion of anal sadism in the pleasurable way that the "butt" (sic) of the cigarette is either flicked away recklessly, or squashed and twisted into the ground contemptuously.

Smoking in identification with an admired-and-hated father-figure

We know from our psychoanalytic work that idealization and denigration go hand in hand, and this smoking state of mind has less to do with the actual pleasure of the smoking itself than the anguished satisfaction of becoming the supposedly omnipotent father. Usually, not only is there a delusion about the extent of the father's powers, but the father generally does have that delusion about his own powers, and those of *his* father.

Craig's comments about Freud, and his relationships both with his father and with his loyal follower-sons who are allowed to smoke with him – so long as they adore and accede to his "greatness" – are relevant here.

We also know that the need for an all-powerful father is much stronger in those who have had severe disappointment or deprivation from the "early" Mother, particularly orally.

In an episode of *The Simpsons* (animated TV series), where the young puckish and punkish Bart Simpson "accidentally" joins a crime organization and then sits in Mr. Burns' (the villainous, power-hungry ruler of the town) chair, and smoking one of his cigars. This might fit in with Green's idea about the son wishing not just to identify with the all-powerful father, but also to kill him and take his place.

Smoking is also very important, symbolically, in the initiation of young, ambitious men to the 'council of legislative fathers' – the new executive or business partner has made it when he is invited to join the established fathers after work for a cigar, and possibly other "forbidden" goodies.

There is a kind of mixed homosexual and rivalrous atmosphere in these "boy-into-man initiations" between the new kid on the block and the old guard, which gives it an edgy, uncomfortable feeling. (The sexual and power politics underpinning the apparent camaraderie was explored very cleverly in the film "*Disclosure*" ... Donald Sutherland and Michael Douglas conveyed the tension between the old guard and the new, unguarded, particularly well.)

But the men-and-power dynamic could sometimes be built into family life. There used to be – (in some places, there still is) – a culture of the man wearing a "smoking jacket," in his 'castle', and of the men disappearing after the evening meal into the parlour to discuss – often all too literally – men's *business,* whilst smoking and drinking "spirits."

Oral-oedipal-genital fusion and confusion

In Jean-luc Godard's movie "Work" there is a scene where the big boss of a large factory, sucking on a very large cigar, has a woman employee suck on his penis, whilst she is penetrated from behind by his second in command, who is smoking a cigarette. Smoking is depicted as a symbol mediating sex and power, and I am certain that Jocasta and Oedipus must have shared many cigarettes.

In fact, there is a thriving industry of Erotica, particularly in Asia, which makes use of the supposedly humorous confusion and juxtaposition of images of female genitalia with smoking.

The vagina is depicted as a mouth, and the cigarette, or cigar, is suggestive of a nipple, or a penis.

But if we turn to two 1990s cultural "stories" – both involving male "high achievers," illicit sex and smoking, we have some "dream material" – in the sense that enduring media "stories" (like films) can sometimes be seen as a type of social-dreaming or myth, irrespective of their basis in actual fact.

I'm referring to the Bill Clinton (ex-US president) and Shane Warne (famous Australian cricketer) "stories."

On the surface, they are unlikely comrades-in-arms (or other body parts).

Let's look at the elements of Warne's tabloid myth first.

There is an admired, if somewhat reckless character who has achieved the pinnacle of success in his sport. He accepts money to promote a give-up smoking product, but when photographed by a young fan, in a restaurant, he assaults the boy. Eventually, he gives up the giving up of cigarettes, with mild shame.

He is playing sport overseas, and briefly meets a young nurse in a pub. He becomes obsessed with her and leaves a sexually explicit message on her answering machine. She reveals all to a tabloid newspaper, and then he, his team and his wife are all severely embarrassed.

The content of the phone call is about his fantasy of pouring wine over her body, particularly her breasts, and then supposedly erotically, licking it off. Now, if this was a dream narrative we would probably have quite a lot to say about the protagonist's very oral sexuality, and his desperate difficulty with weaning and growing up. (He met the nurse in the context of drinking, and needless to say, he was very geographically separated from his wife and child at the time.)

But we might also be concerned about his unconscious wish to project a sense of shame and humiliation onto all concerned – particularly his absent wife.

Similarly, on another continent, another, similar, "story."

An American President has been exposed publicly in relation to an illicit sexual relationship (he says it was only an oral relationship) with a daughter-like employee.

Not only that but he has also been exposed as lying about it. Again, there is a humiliated wife (and daughter) and 'team-mates'.

The way that the employee was tricked into betraying her "lover" through a relationship with an exploitative mother- figure is another story, which we won't go into here. But the most prominent dreamlike image of the whole affair is of the President's desire to prove that sometimes a cigar is not just a cigar ...

A complex chain of cross-identifications between infant-mouth, mother's nipple and vagina, father's penis, and the various Oedipal rivalries, impulses and taboos in a modern-day family are all contained in this story. And, not surprisingly, there was a vast array of emotional reactions and an interesting split, not just in Clinton, but in American culture, between those disgusted and offended, and those who were, if not approving, well, at least smiling. The hundreds of Bill'n'Monica jokes – most, incidentally, about the use of the cigar - testify to this.

But are these two stories just aberrations? Or might they indicate the importance of smoking which reaches beyond its significance as a pernicious health hazard, to a complex symbol, mediating intense and unspeakable psychological tension between the generations, the sexes, and the individual and his culture?

The link with the sensual and the erotic

Our increasingly materialistic, possessive society – often bereft of a meaningful link with the world of nature, including our own bodies – deprives us of the capacity to enjoy sensuality as a day-to-day pleasure of being alive. Smoking, for some, especially when it may include stoking the pipe, or hand-rolling the cigarette, might be an attempt to restore some lost link with this important part of being human.

That it can be interspersed with less innocent, more damaging unconscious motivation shouldn't totally expunge some respect for this attempt – perhaps particularly for those who were deprived of this sensual element of parental love in their earliest years.

Evanescence

In a previous chapter – *Working Through, or Beyond, the Depressive Position* – I suggested a model for a state of mind beyond the Depressive Position. I described a capacity to stand back from one's life every now and then, and to have "meta-feeling" – a feeling **about** all one's life experiences and accrued feelings. I contrasted this with the hysteric's all-too-easy flowing over of feeling, and flitting from one feeling to another without any deeper sensibility and capacity to reflect on feelings.

I associated the more reflective state with the ability to sigh.

For some people, smoking seems to help the experience and expression of this state of mind. The slow breathing in and out of the smoke is a kind of sighing, and, in this more spiritual state, the smoker might be better able to emotionally accept and bear the transitory nature of our existence.

The smoker's bittersweet gaze, watching the evanescence of the smoke as it slowly winds and circles upward into infinity, might be likened to the very fleeting moment at New Year's Eve, or at an historical or jubilant occasion peaking with the fireworks.

Yes, there are elements of potency and fertility rights, as sperm-like energetic streams of light rise upward and explode orgasmically – but, there is also a moment of evanescence, as the energy of the lights fades, so quickly, reminding us all of the very limited number of new years that we will have on Earth.

To use a local example, some of you might remember that moment in the Sydney Olympic opening ceremony where the word "Eternity" – in tribute to a man who once wandered Sydney streets chalking it everywhere – was scorched into the crepusculine night.

This mixed state of ecstatic celebration of life, gives some consolation for the terror of our mortality – which we begin to face with our first symbolic journey away from our mother's body and mind – and a depressive acceptance that nothing, including ourselves, lasts forever – is achieved by some smokers, who might, therefore, extol the importance of a 'quiet smoke'.

Plato might describe this as a need to sigh in the cave, in order to gain a wider perspective on the world and one's feelings about it – and although I think it's highly unlikely that the addicted smoker would reach this state with every cigarette, I believe that it does deserve a certain respect for its emotional significance, much as tribal people reserve a special place for smoking which marks a special occasion or achievement.

This reminds me of our own cultural ritual – I suppose more for males, even these days, where cigars are offered and smoked by the new father at the birth of a new child, with its admixture of mourning, narcissistic potency and celebration of life.

And beyond all of this, there is sometimes the attempt to use smoking as a catalyst for the achievement of a transcendent state – such as the emotional acknowledgement of a creator or higher order of nature. Feelings of respect and awe and gratitude which the smoker might access at such moments behoves at least a modicum of respect – in spite of our cynicism and health concerns, and the relative infrequency of such sentiments in the day-to-day life of the smoker.

I am suggesting that, at least sometimes, smoking can be associated with life, and a depressive acceptance of its brevity and fragility.

It may also, sometimes, help a person to emotionally negotiate a difficult life transition, stirring internal fears that change will cause disintegration – what Bion called "catastrophic change," in order to grow through it.

The transitional object vs the addictive object

The aim of the *addictive* object-relation is to pervert (that is, to permanently postpone and waylay) catastrophic, growth-enhancing change in the self.

Whereas the *transitional* object-relation is a segue-way into the next phase of development.

For example, recently there were pictures in that "bible" of unconscious phantasy, *Who Weekly*, of a Hollywood actress with a dummy in her mouth trying (successfully) to give up smoking! *Who Weekly* was obviously laughing at, and cashing in on this woman's attempt to wean herself from an unhealthy habit, but there are many people who do kick the habit and move on in their lives - often in a new relationship.

There are also many people who have needed to use a drug, alcohol or some sort of regressive object experience as a passing phase, whilst re-adjusting to positive changes in their lives.

If there was more time here, I would want to say a lot more about this distinction, and give some clinical examples, but in this short fantasia, I will just note its importance for helping us to be more discriminating in our observations of smoking states of mind.

The need to take the time to carefully understand another person is the only way that we might get to know just which of these states seems most likely at any particular time, or with any particular cigarette.

Therefore, it isn't enough to just say that the cigarette is a nipple or penis substitute – even though that may be true – because it doesn't tell us just exactly what type of relationship the smoker is having with this feeding object and in what state of mind.

Again, a return to smoking at a time of crisis or catastrophic change in one's life might be looked at **both** from the perspective of an addictive regression which attacks the thinking and feeling processes, **and also** from the perspective of an invocation of a more transitional and transitory object relationship. Temporary smoking can be a way to contain intense anxieties sufficiently for a new, much-needed reorganization to be ushered in.

The smoky atmosphere

I want to finish by very briefly attempting some reflection on the states of mutual projective identification between smokers and non-smokers. Unfortunately, these could rarely be described as "spiritual" interchanges. They are often hostile, or at least mutually contemptuous.

As I mentioned earlier, Herbert Rosenfeld (1987) has briefly speculated about the possibility of "toxic" maternal projections being felt, in some way, by the foetus. This, needless to say, would be a very primal, non-verbal sensitivity and revulsion for any contamination of the emotional and or physical environment which we are surrounded by, and immersed in.

Therefore, it might be that some of our rage at those smokers whose exhalations reach the delicate linings of our eyes and nostrils, and those of our children, reflect a "foetal" complaint about the mother's psychobiological intrusion of mood into one's primeval first space.

With regard to the polarizing effect of the Clinton affair, there can be a split, in any culture, between the sexual and non-sexual, so that these can become stereotypes – not just in individual personalities, but in family styles – the *Waltons* cf *American Beauty*.

In the 50s, this polarity was explored cinematically in so-called film noir. The bad, dirty, smoking, sexual, secretive and unpredictably exciting Bogart/Bacal couple, who are free and uninhibited use cigarettes as an essential means of intimate communication. There is a totally sexual poetic dialogue expressed, for example, in the lighting of the woman's cigarette, and the exhalation of smoke towards each other at very close quarters. We can still observe today the way in which some female smokers have their smoking hands raised with the palm opened, – declaring sexual availability.

This posture is forbidden for heterosexual men.

I have already mentioned and illustrated the unconscious equation of the cigarette with the nipple and the penis, and the open hand may represent the available vagina, equated with the infant's mouth. But this doesn't tell us everything about the nature of the feelings in relation to these "part-objects."

And the classic film noir resolution of sexual tension between lovers was a depiction of the couple smoking a cigarette, in post-coital, if anxious, reverie.

But this was set against – to coin a phrase, the Film Blanc stereotype – depicting mainstream unsexual families– what Meltzer calls the Doll's House family – the perfect house, the right schools, the right clubs and holidays and the polite, achieving children.

But passion and imaginative spontaneity – the spirit of Eros – has been killed stone-dead, and can't be revived – not even at the gymnasium!

I remember one year of university, when I couldn't decide whether to study psychology or medicine and was omnipotently

Overburdened with far too much studying. To get through this year I gave myself cigarettes as a kind of "reward" for each hour spent studying in the library.

I also happened to notice the intense sexual "buzz" just outside the library – dozens of students, just like me, sitting under trees and floating sensually in and out of music and sexual fantasy, and sometimes, each other.

(Around that time I also noticed, on my train journey each day, that all the sexy, less inhibited women, were in the smoking compartment. But, then again, that might just have been compartmentalization on my part.)

Mutual projective identification is possible wherever an intimate activity is performed, albeit semi-covertly, in public. It affords the opportunity for the projection of rage at the sexual freedom of the Oedipal couple.

It allows for a primal scene reverberation and evacuation, where someone is always supposed to be left out of the action.

It's the *"shelter-shed"* group psychodynamic – the kids smoking behind the shelter-shed are able to project boredom, sexual immaturity, curiosity, oral disgust and jealousy into the 'good kids'.

The "good kids," in turn, project guilt, shame, greed, desperation and pseudo-maturity into the smokers, and the two groups overtly shun each other but also gossip wildly about each other.

The importance of smoking in this dynamic sometimes carries over into adult life, but is diminishing these days, as smoking becomes more socially incorrect and medically terrifying.

However, fear not, it is alive and well with the culture of the mobile phone – the new accessory for the shelter-shed dynamics – effective even in a crowded supermarket.

It would be interesting to see how many ex-smokers have taken up "addictive" relationships with their mobiles, and earlier this year trains in Britain have some carriages designated as mobile-phone-free. We might chuckle at this bit of millennial madness, but I think this suggests an acknowledgement of the serious intensity of feeling aroused in those who are made unwilling audiences to an up-close display of a type of oral intercourse, and yet be excluded from it.

There is a lot more to be said about the complex mutual projections between smokers and non-smokers, and how these are still being played out in our public culture – recently, there were very heated arguments at Flinders Street Station, in Melbourne, when a station attendant tried to stop passengers from smoking on platforms whilst waiting for a train – but I hope that I've prompted, or provoked, some long overdue thought about this sometimes humorous, sometimes deadly serious "occupation"

(Politically incorrect) Postscript

Months ago, after initially jotting down a few odd thoughts about smoking, I wondered how, or if, I could ever gather them together.

Then, after not having smoked for over 25 years, I found myself sitting on my back steps, pondering these ideas and gazing up at a huge swaying gum tree, whilst enjoying a very mild cigar – no library to be seen.

References

Green, G. H. (1923). Thoughts on smoking. *IJPA*, 4: 323–325.
Rosenfeld, H. (1987). Afterthought. In *Impasse & Interpretation*. Karnac.
WHO (1994). *A Statistical Analysis of World Tobacco Consumption*. New York: United Nations publications.

The significance of Swearing as a *proto-language*

This "lighter" chapter is my attempt to explore an area of semi-conscious behaviour – usually verbal, which we call "swearing." A topic which even, or especially, by its most ardent practitioners – remains little understood, or even thought about. I wondered – if dreams are supposedly the *royal road* to the unconscious, then swearing – the very common use of supposedly taboo words – might be the sleazy plebeian freeway; and it might be worth taking a ride.

The OED defines the word **swear**:

1 state or promise solemnly or on oath. E.g. take (an oath).
2 say emphatically; insist (swore he had not seen it).
3 cause to take an oath (swore them to secrecy).
4 use profane or indecent language, esp. as an expletive or from anger.
5 make a sworn affirmation of (an offence) (swear treason against).
6 appeal to as a witness in taking an oath (swear by Almighty God). b colloq. have or express great confidence in (swears by yoga).
7 admit the certainty of (could not swear to it).

The derivation seems to be Old English – *swerian* from Germanic: related to **answer**.

Interestingly, Bion (*Elements of Psycho-analysis*) often used to quote Blanchot's axiom that: *The answer is the unfortunate consequence (malheur) of the question.* Meaning: don't reach irritably to prematurely resolve mysteries in the material – let them unfold. In other words, swearing is nothing if not **impatient**. In this instance therefore, swearing could be seen as an expression and forced eviction of the accrued frustration with what Keats called the "burden of the mystery."

Most of the people that I asked said that swearing was a way of getting out anger and frustration – and one said it was the "language of the guts." I was interested to know in more detail about what or who the anger was directed towards, and in what shape and form it was "got out." What were 'the guts' trying to express? So – to get the ball rolling, (quite literally, as it turns out) in this far from exhaustive little study – here are a couple of well-known golf jokes – surprisingly similar ... but let's think about, why they might be regarded as funny – well, at least to many people.

DOI: 10.4324/9781003364788-12

A nun was sitting with her Mother Superior chatting.

"Mother Superior, I used some horrible language this week and feel absolutely terrible about it."

"When did you use this awful language?" asked the elder.

"Well, I was golfing and hit an incredible drive, right in the sweet spot, that was going to go 200 metres, but it struck a phone line over the fairway and straight down to the ground after only 100metres."

"And that's when you swore?"

"No, Mother," says the nun. After that, a squirrel ran out of the bushes and grabbed my ball in its mouth and began to run away."

"And THAT'S when you swore?" asked the Mother Superior.

"Well, no," says the nun. "You see, as the squirrel was running, an eagle came down out of the sky, grabbed the squirrel in his talons and began to fly away!"

"Is THAT when you swore?" asked the amazed elder nun.

"No. As the eagle carried the squirrel away in its claws, it flew near the green and the squirrel dropped my ball."

"Did you swear THEN?" asked Mother Superior impatiently.

"No, because the ball fell on a big rock, bounced over the sand trap, rolled onto the green and stopped about six inches from the hole."

The two nuns were silent for a moment.

Mother Superior sighed, "You missed the fucking putt, didn't you?"

II

A farmer and a priest are out on the golf course. On one hole, the farmer misses a twelve foot putt.

"Dammit, missed the fucker!" he swore.

"My son, you really shouldn't swear like that," the preacher scolded gently. "It angers God."

On the next hole, the farmer missed a six foot putt.

"Dammit, missed the fucker!"

"Now, my son, I don't want to alarm you," the preacher said much more sternly. "But if you curse like that again, God is going to strike you dead!"

But alas, on the next hole, the farmer missed a -three- foot putt.

"DAMMIT!" He shouted. "MISSED THE FUCKER!"

The sky suddenly darkened, clouds roiling and thunder booming. The clouds parted, and lightning split the sky, screaming down and striking the preacher, killing him instantly. From the sky came a gusty sigh, and then a rumbling voice.

"Dammit. Missed the fucker."

Apart from the fact that both of these jokes take place in that most Oedipal of places – the Golf Course – they both allow that even the holiest mother and the Almighty father cannot avoid – indeed, do not even try to avoid – the supposed human foible of swearing when frustrated by human foibles. Both jokes relieve our sense of guilt about just needing to "let it out" when the occasion demands.

Although the **main** purpose of this chapter is begin to explore the psychological and emotional functions of swearing, I'll begin with a very brief overview of the history of some keywords in the modern swearing lexicon – partly for interest sake, but also to show how arbitrary the choice of some words are in the collective profanity unconscious, and to show the importance of cultural isolation in the development (or degeneration, as the case may be) of linguistic specificity in swearing.

Robert Graves wrote a little book called *Lars Porsena, or The Future of Swearing and Improper Language*. Writing in the 1920s, he claimed that there was a definite class difference in the use of the words "bastard" and "bugger." He claimed that in the working class, people might well be sensitive about illegitimacy, but were often unfamiliar with homosexuality, and so bastard was a mortal insult and bugger was a much milder term.

The severity was reversed in the upper classes, who had nice traceable bloodlines and a boarding-school education. He claimed that bugger was a much more serious insult in upper-class circles, where people were more likely to believe it. So, even within a particular culture, there might be quite marked differences and lexical boundaries of obscenities between sub-cultures.

Geoffrey Hughes (1994) has provided the only serious study of the social history of swearing in the English language, and I'm using his work for some of the following piecemeal overviews of cultural differences and similarities in swearing. Most swear words derive from childhood slang for anal and genital body parts or products – what we would call "part-objects" – where they are disengaged from the concept of a whole person, and, for example, as Hughes notes:

> A more childish term for penis is 'willy'. This British English word had audiences sniggering in the aisles of cinemas throughout the UK when the first trailers were shown for the film Free Willy. Willie is essentially an innocent playground word, and there was delighted laughter across the land when commentator Brian Johnson referred to two players during a Cricket match, pointing out that 'The bowler's Holding, the batsman's Willey'.

One of the most offensive terms for female genitalia, the c-word, is the ultimate four-letter word in British English, the final media taboo. The first use of the word in a UK TV drama was in Mosley, a drama about the rise and fall of the British Fascist leader Sir Oswald Mosley. This was first shown on Channel 4 in the late 1990s. The word is also the title of a novel by Stewart Home, published in 1999, about the breakdown of a writer as he rather badly loses the plot, both literally and creatively.

The word has Germanic cognates including old Norse (kunta), middle-Dutch (Kunte) and possibly High German (Kotze meaning prostitute), which all point to a pre-historic Germanic ancestor kunton. A Latin word, Kuntus, meaning wedge, might also have been an influence. The word would appear to have entered the English language during the early Middle Ages; in 1230AD, both Oxford and London boasted districts called "Gropecunte Lane," in reference to the prostitutes that worked there. The word has Shakespearian usage, though even he was a little subtle. Hamlet asks whether he can lie in Ophelia's lap, "I mean, my head upon your lap?" and then says "Do you think I meant country matters?" and follows up with "It is a fair thought to lie between maids' legs.' Ophelia answers non-committedly to most of this. A slightly more bawdy use of the word appears in Carry On Don't Lose Your Head, one of a series of British comedy films of the 1960s, in which actress Joan Sims refers to her husband, "The Count," deliberately pronouncing the word "Count" with just enough room to be (mis)interpreted while still getting past the British film censors. A Scottish alternative to these words, little-known even in England, is 'fud'. But the name of the cartoon nemesis of Bugs Bunny, Elmer Fudd, causes no offence to people outside of Scotland.

Intercourse

Although this sounds like the most Anglo-Saxon of all Anglo-Saxon words, the origin of the f-word meaning "sexual intercourse" is actually rather obscure. There is a legend that the old name for the crime of rape was "Forced Unlawful Carnal Knowledge," and part of the punishment was that an abbreviation of the crime would be branded on the perpetrator's head – like a mark of Cain. Hence, people with "F. U. C. K." on their head were known to be rapists. A similar story is that during the time of the plague when it was necessary to increase the population a royal injunction was issued telling the common folk to "Fornicate Under Command of the King." These, however, would appear to be acronyms intentionally spelling out an existing word rather than new creations themselves.

The etymologist Eric Partridge has suggested that the Old German "ficken" or "fucken," meaning 'to strike or penetrate', was related to the Latin words for pugilist, puncture, and prick, or to the Latin "future" which had the slang meaning "to copulate." There are also clearer links to Dutch where "fokken" means breed and is applied to cattle, and to a Swedish dialect word "fokken" which has the English meaning. Interestingly, all the earliest uses of the word in English came via Scotland, suggesting a Scandinavian origin.

Hughes notes: "Records from as early as 1278 identify a man called John Le-Fucker (which, considering people often had names to do with their occupations, makes the mind boggle), and it was certainly in common usage by the 16th Century, appearing in a dictionary, in 1598. By the 18th century, it had become a vulgar term; it was even banned from the Oxford English Dictionary." DH Lawrence's Lady Chatterly's Lover (written in 1928) was the first non-pornographic book in English to use the word accurately and in context and was famously banned for over thirty years. In 1960, US publishers Grove Press won a court case permitting it to publish the book in America, meaning it was the first time the word had been legally used in print, while three years later, the ban was overturned in a British court in the infamous "Lady Chatterly trial." American author Norman Mailer used the euphemism 'fug' in **The Naked and the Dead**, and when Dorothy Parker met him at a party, she said, "So you're the young man who can't spell 'fuck'"?

It has been recognized as one of the most versatile words in the English language and can be put to use as an expletive, an adjective, a noun or a verb. The comedian George Carlin has often shown its variegated, almost unlimited use when expressing anything at all with emphatic passion – positively or negatively. For example, when expressing bewildering curiosity – "what the fuck?" Poet Laureate Philip Larkin famously used the word in the opening lines of one of his poems, writing one of those sentences which is simple, lucid and which cannot possibly be expressed in any other way:

> They fuck you up, your Mum and Dad,
> They may not mean to, but they do.

From the Middle English for "wriggle" or the old French for "rub," "frig" is sometimes used as a euphemism for "Fuck," at other times used to mean "masturbate,"; usually only seen as a gerundive (or verbal adjective) "frigging." The binding of oedipal experience with black hole angst is expressed in the Sex Pistols version of The Good Ship Venus, with the chorus "Frigging in the rigging 'cos there's fuck all else to do."

Hughes thinks that

> swear-words that do not pertain to body parts invariably refer to bodily functions or secretions. It's true to say that the first swear-words most children learn are scatological, focusing on urination ('wee-wee') or excretion ('plop', 'poo'). As we get older, though sexual swear-words tend to predominate, there is still a resistance to progressing beyond what Freud described as the 'anal phase'.

In some **aboriginal** tribes, the worst thing you can say is something like, *you are Satan's shit!* (I find this to actually be quite a complex insult.)

Taboo

Terms of profanity have historically been taboo words. Some words originally considered profane have become much less offensive with the increasing secularity of society, (for example, the word fuck is now a standard requirement in Hollywood action and cop movies - while others, primarily racial or ethnic epithets which can be considered part of hate speech, have become increasingly taboo.

The word "cunt" maintains much of its taboo status at least partly due to the influence of feminism, though other feminists are attempting to "reclaim" a neutral or complimentary status for this word. Shakespeare hinted at the word in Henry V and Hamlet: Hamlet and Ophelia quip about "country matters" when he tries to lay his head in her lap; and the French Princess Katherine is amused by the word "gown" for its similarity to the French for cunt, *coun*.

Interlanguage complexities

In European Spanish, coño (usually translated as "cunt" in English) is very common in informal spoken discourse, meaning no more than "Hey!" or "Christ!". Likewise, in French, *merde* as well as *Scheiße* in German – Boris Becker notoriously escaped tennis fines by using it – is (both translated as "shit") are also quite common as an expletive meaning little more than "Damn!".

Some scholars have noted that while the French and Spanish are comfortable hearing native speakers use these words, they tend to hear the "stronger" meaning when the same words are spoken by non-native speakers. This may be similar to the differences in the acceptability of queer or nigger depending on who is saying the words. Or it may be an example of how it is easier to learn swear words in a new language or dialect than to learn the fine shades of intensity which accompany their use.

A profane word in one language often sounds like an ordinary word in another. Fuck sounds like the French words for seal (phoque) and jib (foc), as well as the Romania word for "do" (I do = eu fac); shit sounds like the Russian for "sewn." Even names in one language may appear as vulgar words in another linguistic community, which causes many immigrants to change their names (common Vietnamese personal names include Phuc and Bich). Québécois French can string a few basic terms from Roman Catholic liturgy into quite impressive strings of invective of up to a minute or more. This is known as *sacre*, and might be seen as the beginning of meta-language.

One thing that I did notice in common with most swear words was that they are **short and sharp**, usually finished with a **hard consonant**, with variations in the length of the preceding vowel. This brought to mind a missile or arrow flying through the air and crashing into something very harshly – like hitting something, with explosive force.

The polarization of attitudes towards swearing is profoundly and comically explored in the animated film '*South Park – Bigger, Longer & Uncut*'. Briefly, the plot concerns a little group of pre-adolescent children who sneak into a puerile, but funny, Canadian animation film and learn the usual half-dozen four-letter obscenities. When, as a consequence, one of the town's mothers hears her child swearing she incites the other parents in the community to declare war on Canada, and (oddly enough) they succeed in convincing America to, in fact, go to war against Canada – risking the lives of millions, including their own children. Eventually, it is only the children themselves who are able to bring sense to the adults – although the film is sharply ironic in the tone of its uneasy ending.

How is it that swearing produces such sharp and intense feelings and polarities in us?

How is it that, for some people, it is felt to be a corruptive evil weapon, taking the 'Lord's name in vain', whereas for others it is seen as a tool for augmenting our expressive capabilities as human

I am going to argue that swearing is a complex, psycholinguistic attempt to process acutely painful emotional states, which are felt to be potentially catastrophically disintegrative – in the perceived absence of an internal parent capable of reverie about mental pain. For most people in our so-called civilized society, this is a very temporary state – jamming a finger in a door, being cut off by another car in traffic, having to wait longer than one is accustomed to in a queue, or receiving a large phone bill. But for some, especially those who have not internalized much capacity for reverie in the face of frustration or pain – there can be an almost permanent state of internal persecution – well beyond "irritability" – where all frustrations and pains are felt to be tormenting and conspiratorial. In such mental conditions, there is a desperate need for an ongoing means of flushing away the accretion of what Bion calls "**beta-elements**" – raw, unprocessed – usually persecutory and terrifying – unconscious elements of emotional perception. I would suggest that this need gives rise to the formation of a "**proto-language**" – which prevents, or at least forestalls, impulsive violent action, but which is not yet capable of processing intense feeling states by reflective symbolic thought, which might eventually produce meaningful communication. This proto-language acts like a kind of buffer, or holding bay, for thoughts in search of a receiver – a mind capable of reverie, and receptivity. (Meg Harris Williams points out how Hamlet is always in search of such a mind – whether he finds it, or not, in Horatio is a moot point. But he certainly doesn't get it from his parents, or friends or girlfriend.)

So this type of swearing can be seen as an emetic, purging of primitive paranoid-schizoid object formations before they terrorize the waking ego. It is akin to a screaming baby before the voice of the soothing, understanding mother arrives on the scene. At the time of the eruption of intense mental pain – the psyche cannot rally the concerned maternal presence that would say something like: "poor thing" – or, "that's terrible, let's think what to do …" Such depressive capabilities are not felt to be accessible quickly enough, and the expletive volcano of beta elements, particularly paranoid terror and black hole nameless dread – blows its stack.

Richard Nixon is probably the most famous public example of someone who had a constant need for an expletive steam valve – an almost constant spray of swearing at internal persecutors, which blinded him to any realization of his own persecuting actions against millions of people in the external world.

Similarly, in the interestingly-titled gangster series "The Sopranos " – I say interesting because most of the characters are like castrati : unable to sing in an authentically male or potent voice – swearing is used as a kind of 'shortcut' to the Real. In fact, most of the characters evade **any** emotional experience, by constantly swearing, and when that is insufficient, violent action breaks out – which only further increases the terror, and guilt, and the need for more defensive toughness in evading it. This type of character, who constantly projects fear and terror into others was also vividly depicted by Dennis Hopper in David Lynch's film "Blue Velvet". His paranoid projection of invasive hatred and voyeurism into the 'fucking couple' was expressed by his ongoing murderous invective: *"Don't fucking look at me!"*

Because the unprocessed beta elements – particles of intense mental pain and fear – are felt to be radioactively deathly and toxic, the expulsion must be with great force and rapidity. (Almost all swear words have a vowel snapped off abruptly with a harsh consonant – almost as if it was a missile hurtling through the air and exploding with a bang.)

But, often in later life, this may sometimes be used as a defence against the experience of O ("O my GOD"!) where overwhelming awe is treated **as if** it was the toxic fecal matter, rather than the nourishing germinal Real, but of which, we can usually only tolerate minute particles.

Swear words have a kind of 'privileged' projective valency – like hand grenades – which are predictably "explosive" in their emotional charge when released. Perhaps in addition to Meltzer's term *intrusive identification* we could add a type of projective identification called *explosive identification* – 'terrorism' would be an externalization and magnification of this psychological process.

However, there are quite permissible "unloaded" words which do not carry these projective valencies, because they "hide" as words for the biological process – for example, "copulation" – or as more playfully evocative – if un-erotic – *bonking*, or *banging* – which could have come from the nursery. That's why we don't consider these words as swear words – in fact, it's quite common to hear prim and proper BBC or ABC announcers using these terms in a very matter-of-fact tone.

Bion (1970) thought that a failure of containment, or understanding, of the persecutory internal object by the external mother is experienced, by the infant, as an attack. I would understand this as an internal experience of the mother as expelling **her** toxic, beta elements into the child. That is, the child projects its **own** need to expel beta elements into the mother - who is then experienced/feared as doing it back to the child. (Notwithstanding the added complexity if the **external** mother has a tendency to actually do that with her child.) Interestingly, there is no culture that I know of that has swear words for the breast or nipple. In fact, we'd probably find it quite comical to even imagine using them. It may be that since, according to Klein, the breast is the first object of infantile love, hate, and envy it is just too anxiety-provoking to openly eviscerate it with public invective. I'm suggesting that swearing can be understood as a **"proto language,"** which facilitates the temporary and rapid expulsion of what the psyche fears as an invading toxically charged, radio-active part-object, which is dreaded for having massive disintegrative power. In our external world, it would be equivalent to a hysteria about weapons of mass destruction, based on a paranoid projection of our own destructive urges. (Tony Blair's slip – where he spoke of 'weapons of mass ***distraction***' said it all, really.)

This proto-language is loaded with raw, unprocessed (un-*alpha-betized*, according to Bion) emotional charge, from where the unbearable frustrations with the breast, meet the emotional shock of the oedipal "primal scene" – prematurely, before a maternal object capable of reverie in the face of panic has been internalized securely – and before the development of symbolic, expressive language has sufficiently matured to bear, name or tolerate such urgent intense emotional states. In practice, none of us ever reach this ideal state – hence the opening jokes about the inevitability of even Mother superiors and Almighty fathers also needing to swear occasionally. The proto-language attempts to forestall the urgency of the impulse to violent and panicky **action**, with destructive consequences that could increase anxiety.

I can remember an all too vivid example of the very fine line between swearing & impulsive aggressive **action** illustrated to me by a patient who automatically interrupted anything I said which could – in her view – gave me a kind of "potency." After a week of cursing and battling with my interpretations about why she needed to do this, she abruptly announced, during a Friday session, that she was giving up swearing – something that had always been 'second nature' to her. On the following Monday, she reported – in a not-too-sorry tone – that she had whacked her new boyfriend in the testicles while playing squash on the weekend. He had to spend two nights in hospital recovering. (I have to say that there are times when a therapist might be very grateful that some things are acted out, rather than in.) Death wishes, and subsequent castration fears, are often held in check by the urge to swear – especially behind the back of the feared parent.

This level of, ongoing, *self-toileting and self-protection* is also invoked in a similar psychological function, in another type of swearing which places a protective barrier between the waking self (ego) and the emotional impact of the **Real**. When this is threatened to be breached, an involuntary outbreak of swearing is used as a temporary wall – for example in the face of the 9/11 carnage, where the same phrases were uttered by many at the scene: *Holy Shit! – fuck-me-dead!* This almost always fuses part-object infantile bodily language with what Bion calls the "Godhead." (Holy Fuck! God all-fucking Mighty! Holy Crap! Sweet Fucking Jesus! God-fucking-No!) These were heard in the live, uncensored reactions to the catastrophe, before network editors moved in to focus on bravery, numbers dead, and political spin.

Ultimately, as Bion suggested, it is the **fear of death** that must be expelled. But he also suggested that an emotionally-receptive maternal mind can modify that fear, over time, by showing that an adult mind can pick up and hold and reflect upon the panicky elements of the fear, and can return that calmness to the infant, who may then internalize not only the calm – but the mother's capacity to bring it about, through her internal reverie.

In proposing that the proto-language of swearing is to protect the psyche from any sudden intense feeling which is felt to be potentially disintegrative or catastrophic I also include feelings of awe – the terror of beauty, and of the suprahuman. I will return to this at the conclusion of the following section.

Levels of the primitive in swearing

- Greed and envy

    An increasingly popular jibe at wealthy men, these days – never aimed at women, is "Fat Fucker". It might be seen as a projection of **greed** into the Oedipal Father, where it is enviously cursed, and also combined with oedipal jealousy. Incidentally, Oedipus might have saved us all a lot of trouble if his father had taught him how to swear properly, particularly at traffic intersections. These days, the sporting fields become the symbolic form of the crossroads, although probably more so for the cursing and swearing spectators than for the actual participants of the sport – although, the latter may be symbolically "castrated" (through bans, suspensions and fines) if they use abusive language. Yet guttural abuse of the umpires by the spectators is what many pay money for, and may form an important part of the spectator's emotional experience.

- Oedipal pain, frustration and hatred
  This type of swearing is usually aimed at the 'fucking couple' (elsewhere in this book I have talked about the depressive growth needed to re-pair the attacked internal couple). The death drive may be projected into the oedipal father, or his genital part-object, or the mother's. For example: "fucking prick," "fucking cunt," or, the rather confused free-for-all "cock-sucking mother-fucker" and so forth.

  In the consulting room a good interpretation which, in the unconscious of the patient, is often experienced as the therapist's coupling, or showing off potency or fertility, might therefore be attacked through jealousy, and not always just envy. Looking carefully at the expletive explosives which follow, is therefore important in trying to unravel what has been triggered in the unconscious by the interpretation. For example: "fuck off!" – or "you think you're so fucking smart," or "I don't give a fuck what you fucking think!" "You fucking say what you fucking like!" One psychotic patient, whom I treated many years ago, had agreed with something I'd said, and then told me – with an unnerving smile - that I should provide "fucking condoms for each session" or else my wife would complain.

  This patient was an extremely intrusive and claustrophobic patient (the former often causing the latter) and, in turn, had a violently intrusive mother.) In one session, following a break – he complained bitterly, and with much exasperation, that he had set up a video to record a television programme, and then told his mother, several times, not to touch the machine. When he returned home from work, she had switched it off, and added indifferently, that it was using electricity. I said, with dubious anodyne effect, that that must have been extremely frustrating.

  He responded loudly: "You don't understand! "I'm in a cunt of a position."

  I was eventually able to link this to his own habit of parking in the senior staff car park at his work, in spite of his being asked not to. And when I encouraged him to look at the part of himself that was somewhat like the mother he was complaining about, he exploded with:

"You can fuck off – you're getting it at home, so the least I can have is a fucking car space, you prick ..." then, with some relaxation of tension and hatred, he started laughing.

"I'm fucked, aren't I? How many years have we got?"

Territorial expletive

Swearing is a primitively aggressive marking of one's home territory, when invasion is feared.

Under various survival anxieties, large groups need to regard and project the dangerous beta particles (which are delusionally externalized and called foreigners) into refugees. However, **swearing** is less violent, and less irreversibly destructive than dropping bombs on a foreign nation. A nation that is insecure in its own identity, will need to hate an enemy to define its own "Axis" of moral goodness hence coining a phrase like *axis of evil* for those who are outside the familiar territory. This is often made corporeal by focusing on some physical feature or disease which is then equated with something parasitic and plague-like – "vermin".

When upset or threatened, youth in the school ground may use "fuck off!" Or in protecting the sanctity of their bedroom – meaning – how dare you stupid, fucking parents impose your fucking on, and into, MY private space. Although it may be a quite psychologically complex expletive, where one's own intrusive impulses towards the oedipal couple are projected into that couple and then experienced as their intrusiveness towards the infant. This is quite common in the adolescent quest for identity, and a private space in which to develop, or incubate, it. Some such invective or taunt is often stuck on a young person's bedroom door – the unconscious says something like: "Now that I've realized that you two parents are fucking away in **your** bedroom, well I can do that too, and **you** can fuck OFF! So get the fuck out of here – get your fucking out of my head please, or my mind feels like a "fucking hell."

As I mentioned before, we have plenty of opportunities to see this dynamic expressed many times over in the transference reactions that many of our patients have when we demonstrate that we are thinking, in front of them, or par excellence, when we return from holiday breaks. Swearing can sometimes be a conduit to express healthy rage at overly intrusive, police-like parents. For example, the word "fuck" itself is used as a dis-identificatory **boundary marker** – saying, in effect, "we are not afraid to go our own way" It can be a catchword for a sane political alternative to war, at rock concerts. Sometimes there is a kind of obligatory swearing – usually very predictable and safe, which says – *we're staying up late and we don't care what our parents think! Make love and not war! What are we fighting for?* Usually, this occurs at the psychological transition point between childhood and adulthood ... where there is enormous internal ambivalence about separating and **dis-identifying** with the parental values, taken on so passively in earlier years. It marks the beginning of the separation of the generations. The latency kids' swearing is usually not malicious or expulsive, primarily, but a way of having a private expressive area away from the "proper" supervision of adults – an initiation into adolescence, and out and away from good-kid latency – or rather the adult myth of latency.

A similar example is provided in the musical *My Fair Lady* – where Eliza is all dolled up and taken to see a supposedly sophisticated horse-racing meet, but the primitive is unleashed through her earnest entreaty to her horse of "move yer arse!". Similar to the supposed naivety of the sister in the aforementioned "fucking putt" joke – *My Fair lady* depicts a young lady – revealed to have passions desires and real frustrations that need to be expressed, as part of their sexual identity and maturity. The adolescent girl is needing to show her parents that she has become sexual, and is no longer a show-doll for display purposes or manipulation. (This dynamic is explored in a really wacky way in many Doris Day movies.) Swearing and other provocative behaviours, help the adolescent girl adjust her father to the fact that she is becoming a sexual being and has a knowledge, and a body, which extends beyond the boundaries of his control.

Eliza Doolittle in fact "does a lot" to bring an emotional dimension of intestinal, gut-real sexuality-with-jealousy to the over-educated and controlled – Henry Higgins, who has no capability to fall in love, until he meets her. She fills a painful dark gap, brought about by the lack of the feminine and sensitivity to feeling in his life, and is educating and transforming him much more so than he thinks he is educating and transforming **her**.

However, many of us have had the embarrassing experience of our adolescent assertiveness backfiring – when we have been caught out using our pseudo-adult swear-barrier in front of parents, or the equivalent authority figures.

(Of course, red-blooded conservative parents will always hope that any rebellious or sexual tension will be simply relieved by all manner of adolescent sport - anything that involves balls, sticks, holes and goals.) The (so-called) penal colonies were said to be rife with swearing – in comparison to so-called peaceful colonies, and Hughes sees this as due to a large proportion of rebellious characters in the population. However, some recent neuropsychological findings – don't ask me what sort of a person studies such things – that parts of the Amygdala – the centre for highly charged fearful responses, is de-activated during orgasm. It would be interesting to see if swearing creates a similar response in temporarily inhibiting the terror and fear circuits of the brain. Nurses know well that patients coming out of anaesthetics, and going into hypoglycaemic episodes involuntarily swear up a storm and we may still have a lot to learn about normal neurological functioning and layers of mental functioning and language development from people with Tourette's syndrome. So, maybe, the question ought to be more "how do we **stop** ourselves from swearing most of the time, in daily life?" – rather than "why **do** we swear?" As the rebellious, sexual anti-authoritarian stance is expressed and worked through, in healthier adolescents, the provocative swearing settles into an esoteric "teen-speak" with its own "cool" words and catchphrases. This teen-speak – or Hamlet-speak, makes them untouchable to the parental generation, and sets a clear boundary that screams "I am not the same as you, and want a self of my own, rather than having to watch you two couple for my only entertainment!"

Swearing as a psychic poly-filler for the Black Hole experience of psychotic despair

ex·ple·tive
   Date: 1612
   1a: a syllable, word, or phrase inserted to **fill a vacancy** (as in a sentence or a metrical line) without adding to the sense;
   2 : one that serves to fill out or as a **filling**. Expletive derivation of: comes from explere expletif old French serving to fill out-occupying space or required to make up a required quantity or number. Meaning an expletive word or phrase one used for filling up a sentence. Eeking out a metrical line without adding anything to the sense – applied to a profane oath or meaningless exclamation. An exclamation or oath, especially one that is profane, vulgar, or obscene.

Swearing as an oath of sincerity, in the face of the Real

Swearing **can** say: "I really mean this and you'd better believe it!" It is particularly effective if the swearer does not usually swear in day-to-day life. "Do that again and I will blow your fucking head off!" is extremely powerful if said by a usually level-headed person, and will, at times, be far more effective than a politely reasoned rational argument. Similarly, it can be used to acknowledge the reality of what someone has said to you – a Fuck or shit – said with an exclamation tone, will say "You've really got through to me, and I am taking what you've said very seriously." It can also express awe because the language of the Real has no words – and the gap must be filled quickly and effectively.

But reverence for awe can easily slip back into fear and persecution – even via the same swear word. Buzz Aldrin caused very mixed emotions in America when he yelled "fucking idiot!" at a guy who challenged the "reality" of his moon landing. But even that wasn't sufficient to prevent him from also punching the man when the latter repeated the taunt.

Swearing can be used as **ejective evasion of the limits of awe** – a protective contact barrier – like a trampoline shield – which keeps awareness and full emotional impact of awe repressed and thrust back into the social ether – passed around like a body over the top of the crowd at an ecstatic rock concert.

Ultimate conflict between the life drive and the death drive

Swearing can express a "breakthrough "moment, or "psychological birth" experience or a sudden revelation. "Bloody Hell' might express feelings about the womb, or even placenta or birth itself. I saw a patient who wished to be "perfectly and permanently anaesthetized," and always said "bloody hell" when forced to look at his real-life situation, which he'd withdrawn from into a trance-like addiction to online poker games. Another patient suffered from a creative writing block, and had lost touch with her real feelings and thoughts. Similarly in her marriage, she no longer knew whether or not she loved her husband, or whether she just felt that she should. In relation to her confusion between creativity-with-feeling vs evacuative "production-line" work – experienced as "psychic shit' – she believed that her authentic feelings (of suffocated rage and hunger for tenderness) could not be contained.

She dreamt that she was looking at some mud thrown against a wall – a man (me) says don't do that – they could be valuable works of Art if you put feeling into it – then she looked at the audience who said – yes, put care into it (like a Greek chorus – she'd loved a Greek grandparent when she was a young girl, but had lost touch with her) - then they turned into colour, and she felt grown-up and valuable herself but was also dreading that this would mean that from now on she would lose control of what came out of her. The next session, she arrived and announced that she was ready to use the couch.

For some patients, the capacity to swear, with feeling and passion, becomes an expressive achievement. For other patients, it can be an achievement for them to cease "automatic swearing" and to contain their frustrations enough to allow them to be thought about. So, the context and meaning of the swearing is very important.

Life instinct affirmation – "healthy" swearing:

Sometimes swearing can make the Real more bearable – and has a sighing, depressive tone – as with a reflective *Fuck yes*. It is affirmative, rather than denigratory, destructive or mocking - or anti-female, or racist or with murderous intent. It **decelerates** the impulse to mindless action. It helps **digest** feelings rather than excrete them from the psyche. It is always tongue-in-cheek and playful, and affirming of life – "Fuck-yes! You fucking beauty!" – to use some Australian examples. It helps traverse the limits of awe, by transforming outbreaks of death drive (especially close to moments of "emergency" – e-merging from the primal object, *psychological birth* (to again use Margaret Mahler's and Otto Rank's term – or what Bion calls "catastrophic change." Swearing can revive a kind of reverie at times like this – internally recalling the mother's Life-drive – transforming something potentially deathly into something humorous – which says – "This is difficult, but it is known and manageable – even death happens ... so we can bear it together."

Death drive spiteful swearing – by contrast, is aimed at the source of Life itself. (Maybe why "cunt" is still a fairly taboo word in our language.) This type of swearing keeps the depressive position at bay – rather than accepting or modifying painful feelings. Therefore it has a desperate, paranoid and violent quality – and is urgently needing a toilet container/victim to pour invective on. It is quite frightening and threatening to be assailed by it.

This is why swearing can be so offensive to some people – it isn't just because they are prudish (although that may sometimes be the case). It's because they feel that the tone and intent of swearing is aimed against life itself, or the Creator. In Kleinian terms, the nipple is seen as being vomited out and fired back at Life/God, with a vengeance and spiteful, envious resentment. This is therefore felt by religious people as the most offensive form of swearing – taking the name of the Lord in vain. It is experienced as a smearing of God's offerings to humans, particularly when these offerings involve pains, frustrations and losses and it is equated with the workings of an envious Satan, or a snake in the garden of Eden, who incites humans into breaking their oath with God, the Life-giver – one's oath to find life sacred and good. So it might well be experienced by some as the equivalent of breaking wind at God and directing hatred towards the goodness of Life – the language of an envious Satan.

But there is a wonderful paradox at work here – something that pokes fun at our simplistic attempts to describe mentality in terms of a simple duality – something that shows just how intertwined our life and death drives are – as are love and hate. In order to curse a God you have to believe in its existence, and omnipotence. Furthermore, you must feel that the Creator is open to hearing complaints.

Thankfully then, the abysmally simple division of swearing motivation falls to pieces when we consider the kaleidoscopic melange of the drives conjured by

Comedy

There is very little profanity on network TV because its aim is anodyne anaesthesia from the Real, to keep any depressing thoughts at bay – and to give the illusion that everything is pleasant and manageable – and simple. Exceptions do break through occasionally.

These days, Hollywood movies almost compulsorily use "fucking" language as a cheap wallpaper effect to make the characters seem "real" – of course, this is a very cheap trick, and the producers have to gamble on not losing too many potential 'proper' audience members. Obscenity is swearing to **off-end** an audience – a large group, or a society or a tribe. It can be either creative, like satire, provoking thought – or it may be to project feelings of humiliation and embarrassment into the audience. Very often it is both.

The Scottish comedian Billy Connolly needs to be singled out, because of the way he has made broadband swearing part of the mainstream. He now successfully combines family television travelogues with the obscene taunting of the local population. His ongoing use of the word "fuck" is psychic glue, at worse – but at best, he provides a gateway for the audience to experience the **Real** in their quotidian existence – especially human inadequacy and buffoonery in coping with Life's serious impossibilities. But he sometimes wallpapers the word "fuck" as a kind of psychic glue to fill a huge vacuum in his own capacity to find words for feelings.

A few years ago, a supervisee came to her supervision session, folded her arms, and then told me that there wasn't much to discuss because all her patient had done was to swear in the past week of sessions. I asked to hear the material, and she said – "it was all just swearing … I didn't write it down!" She was quite uncomfortable when I asked her to try to recall what was said – but it turned out to be a very fruitful supervision – in spite of some of the transferential implications being quite unsettling, The attempt we both made to explore the swearing – almost as if it was a waking dream – allowed the therapist to begin thinking about areas of emotional experience in her patient that were previously unreachable – particularly overwhelming pain and frustration and self-disgust. As a result, the therapist probably headed off a danger of enacting countertransference aloofness and disgust with her patient.

If it is the psychic interplay of life & death drives that gives rise to humour, then it may be that the crucial difference between malicious, stultifying anti-life swearing and the expressive, enlivening swearing which facilitates emotional contact with the Real, is the presence or absence of a humorous playful tone. Just as we hate a sporting contest that is too one-sided, the power of well-timed, if clumsy swearing can bring richness to Life – a sharp reminder of the knife edge we all glide along between our life and death drives.

But, might not we all be forgiven for the often clumsy way we shuffle and fall between playful gratitude and abusive cursing, as we journey along on the painful burden and great gift that we call Life.

References

Bion, W. (1970). *Attention and Interpretation*. London: Tavistock.
Hughes, G. (1994). *Swearing. A Social History of Foul Language, Oaths and Profanity in English*. In the series The Language Library. Oxford: Blackwell.

Life and Death of a Planet in *Melancholia* – a film about depressive cynicism

Melancholia (Lars von Trier director.) A Review.

The artistic merits of *Melancholia* have been debated, and will be debated – probably for many years. Whether Lars von Trier is an out-of-closet Nazi, sadistically torturing his audiences as a way of excreting his own depression (as some reviewers have suggested) or a poetic visionary, cutting through to the core of human suffering, so that it can be acknowledged and thought about, is not what I'm debating here.

Instead, I want to explore a few of the issues that I think the film throws up (in all senses) and which I believe are worthy of some sort of reverie.

The opening of the film is a total piece of dream work. It condenses all that is to follow, and in a few moments of poetry-in-slow-motion, we hear yearning (if hackneyed) Wagner shimmering and aching through a scene of bridal anguish on a golf course, at night. There is almost a sense in which these opening moments make the rest of the film redundant. What words are necessary after we have already sensed the complete ambivalence, apocalyptic anguish and ardour of the marriage ceremony in such a balletic outpouring of intense feeling?

Well – arguably, the rest of the film is there to help us to think about the intensity of this seemingly self-contained prelude, and this is done by the introduction of words, which provide keys to a meditation on the "institution" of marriage. I will argue that these thoughts, or links, about marriage, throw open the doors to a meditation on the whole of capitalist society and its means of reproduction.

Pictorially, the film traces the emotional effects of the end of the world on a very small self- (but un-) contained little group of people. A smugly married yuppie couple – John and Claire – who have everything that money can buy, and their child, Leo – and Claire's sister Justine, who is stumbling at the bridal threshold. She is to marry Michael, a well-meaning, loving man, who is nonetheless way out of his depth with Justine if he believes that love is the only issue for her. And then there are the two pairs of villains: Justine's parents, Dexter and Gaby, whose vituperative invective towards each other show how little they can care for their disturbed daughter, and Justine's boss and henchman – both from the advertising world, and similarly uncaring about the soul of Justine, or of anyone.

The world is ending because a previously impossible-to-detect duplicate planet of Earth, called Melancholia, is on a collision course with Earth. At first, only

Justine notices its presence, but she is dismissed by the smugly scientific, smugly married, and loaded, John. He is rock solid certain that catastrophes cannot occur on his watch and hides his doubts – even unto himself – until the very last minutes when he sneaks a cowardly suicide amongst the stable horses with sleeping pills stolen from his wife. This leaves the two sisters to face the end and the feelings that it throws at them, with the child.

As with the Ancient Mariner, it is a wedding ceremony which prompts the telling of a preternatural nightmare. And the catastrophe itself: a killing of what is rare and innocent, be it an albatross, child or planet Earth, is also an enactment of enormous conflict about marriage.

Part one of the film concerns the aborted "perfect" wedding, in the seemingly perfect location.

From the beginning (with echoes of Alice in Wonderland) – the newly weds are late for their own reception. Their obscenely oversized limousine can barely fit along the narrow rural road to the glorious castle of celebration. Throughout the film, we see that this castle is set amongst many such islands, in a dream-spray of idyllic self-containment. And the metaphor of not quite fitting (continuing on even at the premiere of the movie, with von Trier's risqué Nazi comments not fitting into cultural expectations) reappears – Justine not fitting the expectations of a new bride, and even the two planets not fitting in the same space. Is there, after all, room in our society for the concerns of the melancholic – for misfit souls, who find the world of comfort, property and things unnourishing? Or do they just have problems with ingratitude and envy?

All is perfectly organized – even the cutesy opportunity for guests, upon arrival, to guess the number of jelly beans in a big jar – the message being that we have nothing to worry about – the most pressing problems in the world amounting to nothing but a hill of beans.

But, deeper into the reception, Justine and Claire's parents, become hell-bent on injecting their venomous bile directly into their daughters, with the narcissistic indifference of a self-exiled Oedipus – blinded to all suffering other than their own. Gaby seems not to care at all that her anti-marriage speech will ruin the tone of the occasion and directly damage her daughter on her day of celebration. Mad – Medea, she is more than happy to sacrifice her children's capacity to trust in love on the altar of marital revenge. But Justine's father, Dexter, isn't a great deal better – avoiding his own speech, and later, after Justine implores him not to leave her alone – admittedly on her wedding night – he does just that. His reasons aren't clear, and he does leave a flippant note – but we assume that he must have aroused similar abandonment frustration in Justine's mother.

The cause of the parents' exploded marriage isn't exactly clear, but the one thing that is clear is that disillusionment must have been a central pillar. Dexter doesn't really finish his speech – all he can say is that Justine's mother is domineering, and he provides B-grade humour by humiliating the waiters and calling all the women Betty. He is a flippant Dionysius, floating on the surface of pain and suffering like an oil slick, blissfully unaware of how much damage he is causing.

Justine's mother – in her appallingly honest, but barbed, speech at the wedding celebration – praises "ambition" as being the salient fulcrum on which to attack her ex-husband, and indeed the whole institution of marriage.

For those who don't know who I am, I'm Claire and Justine's mother. Justine, if you have any ambition at all, it certainly doesn't come from your father's side of the family. I wasn't at the church. I don't believe in marriage.

Claire, whom I have always taken for a sensible girl, you've arranged a spectacular party. Till death do us part and forever and ever ... Justine and Michael. I just have one thing to say ... Enjoy it while it lasts.

When Justine tries desperately for a hug, pleading that she is struggling with profound and naked fear, Gaby brushes and crushes her with:

We all are, sweetie. Just get on with it.

From here on we know that Justine will not ever land as smoothly as Lorelai Gilmore in the showdown with deeply scarred, heartless, unhappily-wealthy parents.

And Justine's smarmy, appropriating boss turns his wedding speech into a business function, where he announces that Justine will have a promotion for her good company work. He sees the wedding as an interruption to the working day and later tries to get Justine on the job again, coming up with "killer tag-lines," during her wedding night.

Justine's main outlet for an escape from such an assault on her free will, and on her value as a person rather than purely as a commodity, is in the unadulterated world of nature – especially riding horses. She herself is trying to resist the pressures of being ridden by the will of the capitalist men, who finance her wedding and her career. The notion of the bestial wafts in and out of Melancholia visually, symbolically, antiphonically, and in counterpoint, with the theme of people being used (ridden), in the name of ambition. Her seemingly assertive sexual revolt against the expectations of marriage is to (literally) ride her boss's accomplice as if he were a horse, in the middle of the golf course – thus spitting in the face of the woebegone Michael, and travestying his idealized portrait of the marriage night.

Michael's own contribution to this is in his ignorance of just how important freedom from ownership is to Justine. After showing her a picture of an idyllic block of land, an orchard, that he has purchased for them, and on her behalf, he then sees her shocked and depressive reaction as mere ingratitude, rather than a deeply fissured despondency at yet another male thinking that she can be bought.

The music to the film reinforces and echoes a kind of building claustrophobia with the whole Romantic Illusion. Instead of developing its opening theme (as Wagner did) we just hear the same, repeated segment of music pasted onto the stunning images. It tells us that Justine and Michael's hopes are going nowhere, in spite of the isolated beauty of occasional moments.

Inevitably, in breaking out of her corral, and having this vengeful bout of horse-like sex with the young henchman of her boss, in the middle of her brother-in-law's luscious but sterile golf green, she soon plunges into psychosis.

Desperately, she turns to her father – her only hope of a man who might join the resistance to monetary "ambition" – who promises to stay, to help her through the shock of her wedding night – and yet he is well gone from the scene before the cock crows barely twice. Much as we might understand his reluctance to get involved in his daughter's wedding politics, he is still cowardly in his fear of her dawning psychosis and abandons her to the men who each want a piece of her – including the director, who just barely manages to keep the audience from taking an overly voyeuristic viewpoint during the unfolding of that psychosis in the coming scenes.

* * *

So, in Part II – apparently, several weeks after the un-wedding, Justine's sister and brother-in-law (the owners and choreographers of the opulent of the wedding scene) become the ersatz parents of baby Justine – even foetal Justine – as she regresses into a wordless torpor.

However, Justine has noticed one thing – a seemingly tiny detail – and that is Melancholia – an approaching, encroaching planet, as externally destructive as her own mother internally, but previously obscured, and denied as a significant danger.

Claire is instinctively concerned about Melancholia hitting the Earth's path, and John refutes these concerns – referring her to the infallibility of scientists. The audience must accept that although a simple dose of TV – maybe CNN – would have solved the mystery of Melancholia's potential for destruction – the male capitalist-golfic glorious location is set up according to the holy goals of capitalism. One wrests enough money to become independent of the rest of the world. One gets land, huge private property, the best of everything that used to be communal, a home theatre, a swimming pool and so forth, in order to avoid the indignity of sharing a communal space. (If one does venture out from the castle, then there are private clubs.) These aims are emphasized in the film by glorious shots of the geographical isolation of the wedding place – starkly beautiful, but an island unto itself, amongst many other islands. So we can easily believe that the "normal" rules of watching TV to join in with the rest of the world must not apply here.

Unlike the more blatantly oedipal problem in the 1950s C-grade schlock-buster *When Worlds Collide*, (which Melancholia almost imitates, in plot) the problem is far more complex. The third point in the oedipal triangle is not a rival male. It is the whole weight of expectations of a deeply unwell materialistic society. Even *When Worlds Collide* hinted at the problem, with a crazed wheel-chair bound billionaire who thinks that all life's problems, including mortality, are monetary.

At this vertex, which von Trier seats us at – having unseated us from the wedding party – a psychoanalytic reading of Justine's melancholia falls short.

Yes – she has an awful internal couple to contend with, polluting any hopefulness about her own coupling, and perhaps symbolized by the approaching doomsday planet, Melancholia. And yes, she has a lot of guilt about her own part in this cynical view of love – over-identifying with her "castrating" mother, in a cynical (if deserved) contempt for men. Possibly, she is both envious and jealous of her sister's "catch" – and modulates those feelings with a global nihilism.

But, what about the Culture of blind greed and ephemerality that she is soaked in? The pseudo-human world where mindless consumption and a tabloid appropriation of Beauty reign as Uber-Gods, slaying any trace of the holy albatross – warmth, awe, soul and consideration of the needs of others?

Psychoanalysis sits stumm on that vertex.

Knowing its self-imposed limitation of the analyzable to the individual psyche, it sorely needs the Arts, and social theory, as the blind need dogs and sticks. Thebes had social problems before Oedipus made things more complex. And for Justine and Michael, things go off the rails when they are forced into the awareness that marriage is not just a two-person event. A couple is as wrapped up in wedding guests and their presents, geography, community, banks, and global politics as is a foetus in the womb – and is just as vulnerable.

Justine projects her own guilt onto the Earth, and her own angelic qualities onto Melancholia, viewing it with a wistful, sensual, adoring gaze that was earlier directed towards her new husband, Michael. She thinks:

> The Earth is evil. No one will grieve for it.

She has lived and breathed killer tag-lines and finance, and yet her soul cannot bear for her to be part of the bean counters. And so, from the ashes of her wedding night, she eventually gets past the materialist trappings of comfort, to find a way of 'holding it together' enough to face death, through an act of holding – something that possessions and comfort can never manage. She does manage something beyond easy cynicism (growing beyond her own mother's capability) – and has probably never been so "well". Whether or not we see Justine as a goddess-like Diana, or a Cassandra agonized by futurity, or an Ophelia, unwittingly a part of her own undoing of love, something has tainted her capacity to bear any hopefulness. It is this side to Justine – the narcissistic tormentor of souls – the impenetrable goddess, which links her to the advertising world, which has corrupted her wedding, and her soul. Certainly, she has managed far more than profligate John-the-self-righteous, who can only fling himself to die amongst the horses (an act of contrition, or of identification?) after stealing Claire's stash of sleeping pills – more worried about his own humiliation than about his wife and child. He cannot bear his backlog of guilt.

But neither can Justine. She seems to avoid altogether any guilt about playing a major part in promoting the world that she hates, and which sucks oxygen from her soul. Her haughty contempt prevents her from ever really confronting her own culpability, as a peddler – a damn good one – of addictive advertising slogans which prop up the materialist world of castle building.

And yet, can we expect less cynicism? Can she possibly have a sympathetic or hopeful view of humans and coupling and love or marriage, when they are so linked to her mother's disappointment in her father, and to the grandiose possessiveness of her brother-in-law, which is based on a pseudo-generosity of spirit (he pays for the wedding) without his really getting to know the more horse-sensed sensibility of his wife's sister? How can she have an unsullied conscience, when she is so linked to the propaganda machine by the skills of her own venal imagination?

In fact, von Trier's difficulty with most of his characters (and possibly himself) is that guilt – the mainstay of melancholia, which Freud revealed as a failure to mourn – can **never** be confronted because of the murderous (Old Testament) harshness of the superego. Punishment by death – horrific death – is seen as the only solution for a guilty conscience. There is never any hope of change and reparation, through sincere regret – what Melanie Klein called "The Depressive Position".

This is why so many of his films leave the audience with a feeling of revulsion, rather than sober reflectiveness. There is often little left to think about, being crunched and ground down by unassailable revulsion and horror.

Melancholia does better though, because it slows things down enough, in a semi-compassionate pastoral – if Wagnerian-pastoral – tone, so that we see and feel enough beauty to hold together some state of reverie in our depressive hangover, as we emerge from the theatre back into the world of things, and the still present Earth.

It is therefore an interesting question as to whether Justine eventually emerges, ironically, as a beacon of sanity as the Titanic Earth goes down – or whether she is just injected with so much crazy cynicism as not to be too bothered by what's happening, and won't have to bother with difficult decisions involving suicide. For Justine, the end of the world is not such a bad thing – she knows all too well, through her work in advertising, the corruption of the world and of the word. She cannot be the "happy little vegemite" – selling consumption with one hand, and savouring it with the other – and her brother-in-law and her boss, and even her new husband, will not forgive her for being such a bad little girl. So, she embraces the bad little girl persona, for a bit – refusing to cut the cake, or to swoon at the male gifts on offer, and by horsing around on the golf green – before, ultimately, attending to Leo, and taking over the maternal baton from Claire – who has become lost to despair. (Earlier, Claire showed unending patience with Justine, probably because she sensed that Justine was facing many of her own buried conflicts about marriage and money – not the stuff of Jane Austen.)

But – whatever the case, she alone is able to comfort the child – whose mother is almost comatose with disbelief, shock and a sense of abandon after discovering her cowardly husband has suicided amongst the horses, and taken the 'easy' way out with her sedatives. Perhaps he has acknowledged the triumph of the horse, in the female – but he has fallen in shame and humiliation about the limits of the male-scientist propaganda, in blindly reassuring us that everything is always "okay" and "all right". And, he has betrayed his wife and child by refusing to "bear" the truth, with them – that the religion of capitalist ambition blinds us to the existence of (literally) another world – the world of Melancholia. He refuses to acknowledge it as part of the human condition, and is much more in league with Justine and Claire's mother Gaby, than he dares admit to.

Of course, Gaby's vitriolic speech hints at the complexity – beyond woman as a Natural, Man as (failed) capitalist Pig. Most (but not all) men addicted to money-making, and possession of land-with-a-view, think that they need to provide this in order to assure (buy) the unending love of a woman.

So the ending of the movie – the triumph of Melancholia over Earth, of wild primitivism over controlled male colonial Arcadia – must remain ambiguous, thank heaven(s).

***

But, what then is *Melancholia, in the dream language of the film*?

It is almost too obvious to say.

It is the emerging awareness – catastrophic – that one day – it may have already happened – the capitalist dream or illusion must end, and (like Alice) we must wake up.

There may not ever be endless resources – particularly with endless population growth. And it may not be forever possible to have half that population settling for less, and agreeing to work for less, so that the "lucky countries" may go on "living the dream" – the dream of an island mansion, or Gulag State, bypassing the need for real communal sharing.

To the addicted ambitious capitalist, this is unbearably depressing. What **is** the goal of life if it is not to compete in the accumulation stakes – the Darwinian, private school, horse race – to wrest property, fuel, resources, techno-power, knowledge, money and even other people's babies in order to lure the admiration of prime mates, or to patch over a painful lack of parental love (Rosebud!)?

Yet, the silliest lie of all, still (if unwillingly) believed by us billions, as we watch advertising, and our neighbours, is that enough accumulation – enough possession of an island-state amongst the amiable peasants, will make us happy – when the best that can be gained is a heady, temporary relief from heavy, empty feelings of envy, unworthiness, unlovability and disconnection.

To those who can bear, and even love, the communal experience – who can **willingly** share, and enjoy the sharing – Melancholia is not a problem.

But, at some deep level, the urge of the individual to be special, and to have more than one's neighbours, and to expunge any awareness of the neediness of the Other, still remains in our DNA, even in enforced communism. (The capitalists have not necessarily won, just because enforced communism fails.)

This is how and why Justine is pushed to madness, and why Melancholia and Earth cannot occupy the same space at the same time.

We live in explosive times.

Von Trier sees that some of us see this more clearly than others who hide in the flimsy tent of unhinged techno-science, adhering – like children – to its promise of an endless growth and a brighter tomorrow, while it steels but steals our genes.

Chapter 11

The wrecking and re-pairing of the internal couple

In clinical work and in Shakespeare's *Othello* and *The Winter's Tale*

A model of the progress of the internal parents from a violent, **combined** *object (Klein), with little differentiation, through to a* **combining** *harmonious and differentiated couple, with some examples from Shakespeare's Othello and The Winter's Tale is presented – and some suggestions for the clarification and elaboration of these internal formations are considered in the light of these examples, as is some related clinical material. There is also the hope of an enhanced understanding of the Shakespeare. In addition, the uncovering of a transformation from an infantile-narcissistic-incestuous father into a playful, concerned and Self-eliciting parent is introduced.*

There is a scene in the film *Bagdad Cafe* where the family who runs the cafe gather around the local tattooist (cum sado-masochistic-prostitute) and plead to know why she is leaving Bagdad. They cannot understand. The town has just been transformed from a hopeless, uncoupled, self-denigrating "hell-hole" into a place where people encourage each other, thrive and produce music and art together. All of this through the influence of an uncoupled, 'stray' Bavarian woman on the people of Bagdad, and vice versa.

The tattooist's answer?

"Too much harmony!"

I will trace the importance of the well-being of the internal parental couple for mental life, and the distension and wrecking of this coupling through infantile idealization and jealousy of its creative capacity. But, through references to the imagery of Shakespeare's *Othello* and *The Winter's Tale*, some evidence will be given for the existence of another emotional factor responsible for the wrecking. This is described, in keeping with the above scene from *Bagdad Cafe*, as intolerance of the harmony produced by the loving, creative couple. Othello wrecks his own couple irreparably. The Winter's Tale offers the hope of re-pairing and regeneration, although nothing can bring back to Leontes the lost time with Hermione.

If it is true that the relationship between the internal world and the external world has been a central concern for psychoanalysis since Freud, then it is also true that the pivotal element of this relationship has been the manner in which a child manages to internalize both their own relationship with each parent and their perceived relationship with each other. These processes have been called the

"Oedipus Complex", but today, with the increasingly complex additions and modifications to Freud's original conception, (for examples, see Britton et al., 1989) we are frequently left to wonder; 'When is an Oedipal conflict not an Oedipal conflict? When is it pre-Oedipal or pseudo-Oedipal? Or even "invisible-Oedipal"? (O'Shaughnessy, (1989))

More than anyone else, the person most responsible for the deepening complexity of the complex was Melanie Klein. She saw an "earlier" form of the Oedipal drama in babies. She suggested that when the baby was in the full grip of its oral-dependent attachment to its mother, or more accurately, the breast, it was already exquisitely sensitive to feelings of jealousy. Klein's baby feels something like this:

> If I do not have the breast, somebody else does. If it is not another baby that I can see at the breast, then it must be a baby, or babies inside mother's breast or belly, drinking greedily and endlessly from the inside. And even if I imagine these inside rivals as dead or gone, there will still be something foreign and threatening inside her – dead babies or a vengeful penis.

So now there were two Oedipus Complexes. Or was there just the one, extended back in time, and a forerunner and determinant of the 'Classical' one? The early complex could be shown to underlie the later one. Unresolved genital rivalry, inferiority and jealousy, seen later in childhood, often unfolded into unresolved infantile oral and anal sadistic phantasies, which, in turn, often revealed unresolved unconscious envy of the breast and its feeding capacity, or further, after Bion (1970) of its "holding, containing, linking and transforming" capacities.

But in all of the controversy about 'which Oedipus?' or which couple (mother/father or baby/breast), I believe that Klein's innovation and renovation of the idea of what a couple is, has been obscured. This obscuring of the functional importance of the internalized couple has been partly redressed by the work of Bion (1967) and Meltzer (1978), although Klein herself made it clear that she regarded the internalization of the "good breast" and the loving, harmonious, and differentiated parents to be the 'bedrock' of mental health and life. Nonetheless, Bion elaborated on the importance of the link between baby and breast for the capacity to think, and to learn from, and be transformed by, experience. Meltzer (1978) has elaborated the importance of 'undisturbed' internal parents, in the nuptial chamber of the mind, for inspirational thought and aesthetic apprehension of life's beauty and numinosity – elements essential to creativity and mental growth.

These findings could be added to Freud's observation that the mother and father have to be accepted by the child as the "primal" couple before successful (non-neurotic) romantic/sexual coupling can be achieved in later life. Yet, perhaps because of our need to focus on pathology in mental life, is it possible that we have neglected to give functional importance to the capacity for the experience of joy? A capacity for finding something harmonious in our experience of the world, or, more exactly, for re-creating something harmonious out of apparent noise, chaos and confusion? I will try to show that Klein seemed to be considering these matters, but that she was somewhat limited in their clarification. In particular, I am going to explore her formulation of the "combined parental object," arguably the most difficult of her concepts to grasp. In my view, by the time of *Envy and Gratitude* (1957) and *Narrative of a Child Analysis* (1958) Klein had implicitly traced a line of development of the internal parental couple through three possible configurations.

The first of these was called the **"combined object"** and referred to a part-object (paranoid-schizoid) construction, in phantasy, of a dangerous, bizarre amalgam – totally confused and infused with the baby's own projective evacuations of oral and anal sadism, greed, envy and anxiety. A St. George-and-Dragon mess of blood, faeces, teeth, and an intrusively dangerous penis in filthy, murderous and cyclonic activity with the potential to activate psychotic anxiety in the child, particularly if not counterbalanced by the growing external realization of a good breast and loving parents.

With the dominance of the combined object, the distinction between envy and jealousy is very confused. If the penis lodged in the mother is not endlessly dangerous it might be endlessly gratifying, producing a very enviable object indeed. But since there appears to be a very primitive awareness of the penis as a bit separate from the mother (although it is still felt, mostly, to be part of her), this is also a form of jealousy. (In my view, this primitively gratifying penis in the mother is felt by the child to be a kind of umbilical cord leading to the endless supplies of placenta and womb. Due to massive confusion, it never seems quite clear to the child whether mother is being fed endlessly from this penis/cord, or whether the penis/cord (along with mother's numerous internal embryos) is being endlessly fed inside her.) (See Maizels, 1990.)

I don't think that Klein changed this view of what she meant by the "combined object" much at all after *The Psychoanalysis of Children* (1932). It was a mental monster which needed to diminish if there was to be emotional development as opposed to psychosis. But it was not clearly enough distinguished from what she meant by the "internal couple." In a crucial footnote to the *Narrative of a child analysis.* (Klein, 1958, p. 119) she suggests that as the combined parent figure is gradually transformed into more whole-object identifications rather than part-object identifications, the "monster" begins to resemble two **whole persons** felt to be in a

> ... fighting sexual intercourse. When these anxieties are experienced, the infant has already developed a greater reality sense, a clearer perception of the external world, and a relation to whole objects. However, he is still under the sway of early unconscious phantasies (which, indeed, are never completely given up), of destructive impulses, greed and possessiveness. All this explains why the sexual intercourse of the parents is felt to be so destructive.

So this was Klein's second way that the child unconsciously represented the parents, and for her, it is quite a significant step from part-object muddle to whole object (even if fighting) couple.

Now the next configuration, along the lines of emotional development and stability, is:

> When the child's stability increases, the internal parents are felt to be in a more peaceful relation which, however, does not include a peaceful sexual intercourse. By contrast, as far as the external parents are concerned, we frequently find that very young children desire that mother or father should satisfy each other genitally. This is only one of the instances of relations to external objects differing from those to internal ones, though there is always some connection between the internal and external situations.
>
> (Klein, 1958, p. 119)

In this fascinating paragraph, Klein outlines the third configuration of the parental couple, although it is really only the second one, since the first is not strictly a coupling. The parents are now allowed to "cohabitate" in peace, but this rests on their refraining from sexual (passionate?) intercourse.

It was left to Donald Meltzer (1978) to speculate about the fourth fate of the internal parents. Put simply, what is the consequence of the **internal** parents being "allowed" to have a space for their **private**, mysterious lovemaking? His answer is that this will give us unconscious access to the fountain of inspirational thought – our muses letting us hear the "music of the spheres" for a short while, just long enough for us to perceive (receive?) something truly original, imaginative and generative, so long as we can bear the envy and jealousy and, Meltzer adds, the beauty, which is not for very long.

(The writer Vikram Seth ends his book, "An Equal Music" with this emotional account of hearing a beautiful performance of The Art of Fugue:

> Music, such music, is a sufficient gift. Why ask for happiness; why hope not to grieve? It is enough, it is to be blessed enough, to live from day to day and to hear such music – not too much, **or the soul could not sustain it** – from time to time.

One painful realization for the child is that it cannot directly repair the internal mother. All that can be done – all that needs to be done – is to repair the internal couple so that the internal father can be left to revive the internal mother with **his** penis, in creative intercourse with her. It follows, as Klein suggested, that one essential ability the child must develop (or allow to develop) is the ability to discriminate the individual qualities of each parent as separate, both from each other and from the child. It is probably this achievement, really the relinquishment of (mainly) projective identifications in favour of introjective identifications, which helps to "move" the child along through the three or four developmental configurations mentioned above.

Or, as Goethe has his Oberon say in the little send-up of Shakespeare's *Midsummer Night's Dream* contained in *Faust:*

> Wedded couples, seeking bliss,
> Let example guide you,
> The recipe for love is this,
> *That first we must divide you.*[1]

Part II

I will now present some material from two of Shakespeare's plays, as well as some clinical material, for two reasons. First, I believe that the complex working through of these configurations, and the failure to work them through, was a central concern of Shakespeare's work, particularly in the later plays and the sonnets, and that in these works he provided some masterly psychological and poetic insight into the difference between a loving, lively coupling of human beings and a dead, shipwrecked uncoupling.

Secondly, along these lines, I will use the Shakespeare to return to the problem of 'intolerance to the harmony' produced by the loving internal couple. I see this factor as somewhat different from the problems of envy and jealousy, and would locate it, developmentally, at the point where, for the first time, the child notices that the parents not only provide food, protection, pleasure and frustration but that they also create an emotional field when they combine. This field is not just a creator of babies, it is a creation in its own right. It is a site (particularly felt to be the mother's genital region, in unconscious phantasy) where chaos and violence seem to be miraculously and repeatedly transformed into harmony. For this reason, I would prefer to call the harmonious internal couple the "**combining** couple," as distinct from the Kleinian "**combined** object" or the slightly vague term "creative couple" (where the emphasis seems to be more on what is concretely produced). I think that the term "combining" reflects the dual elements of bringing together, and of synthesis.

I hope to show that Shakespeare not only demonstrated the existence of an antiemotional force, totally intolerant of the combining couple, but also a particular form of narcissistic defence against it. This might be called "imitation" combining – a form of masturbatory mental activity, but specifically centred on the denial and denigration of the harmony produced by the combining couple. This is then poorly mimicked through an appropriated, "hermaphroditic" self-production. This self-production is often a thin cover for murderous and suicidal intentions, as Shakespeare makes obvious through the character of Iago in ***Othello.*** Iago is generally seen as the villain who seduces and corrupts the "innocent" Othello, who would otherwise not be 'given to jealousy', and certainly not given to murdering his own wife. Most literary and psychological discussion of the play has taken

Iago's motivation as the central emotional puzzle. I am more interested to see what it is in Othello that predisposes him to 'fall' into collusion with Iago's voyeuristic malevolence.

Here, I turn to the newlyweds' first intimate time together.

> DESDEMONA   The heavens forbid
> but that our loves and comforts should increase,
> Even as our days do grow
> OTHELLO   Amen to that, sweet Powers!
> I cannot speak enough of this content;
> It stops me here; ***it is too much of joy.***
> (They kiss)
> And this, and this the greatest **discords** be
> That e'er our hearts shall make.
> IAGO (aside)   O, you are well tuned now!
> but ***I'll set down the pegs that make this music,***
> As honest as I am.
> (11, 1, 186) (Author's emphasis)

Note that **Othello** cannot bear the joy of the music, it stops him (and "stops" also refers to the playing of a fretted musical instrument) **before** Iago plots to slacken the strings of love that are beginning to vibrate too harmoniously both for him **and** Othello. It is as if Othello feels his own heart to be a stringed instrument being played by someone else (the sweet powers) and therefore too much beyond his military control as if it was a kind of drunkenness, which is hinted at in a juxtaposed scene where some of his men lose their self-control due to an excess of alcohol, thanks to Iago's engineering.

Othello is ripe for Iago's taking, and I think that events proceed this way: Iago launches a full-scale attack of mockery and innuendo on what he believes to be the site of potential harmonious lovemaking between man and woman – the vagina and womb – equating this female site with a sewer, and the penis with a flatulent, useless noisemaker, so that their **musical intercourse** becomes, for him, more like a slimy creature writhing in tangled filth.

For example, earlier, Iago denigrates Desdemona and Othello's coupling and tells Desdemona's father that:

> IAGO   I am one, sir, that comes to tell you, your daughter
> and the Moor are now making ***the beast with two backs.***

(Perhaps just exactly what Klein meant by the infant's unconscious perception of a 'combined object'.)

And when Iago is cursing to himself about Cassio's three-fingered kiss to his own denigrated wife, Emilia, he says

> Yet again your fingers to you your lips?
> Would they be clyster-pipes for your sake![2]

Trumpet
(aloud) The Moor! I know his trumpet.

These lines convey both his disgust with the unclean, blocked, vaginal passage, and with the annoying, unwanted penis that is felt to be within – the theme of the penis in the vagina being equated with a flatulent, dissonant annoying thing is taken up again when a Clown ridicules the efforts of a musician.

CLOWN   Why, masters, have your instruments been in Naples, that they speak i'th'nose thus?[3]
FIRST MUSICIAN   How, sir, how?
CLOWN   Are these, I pray you, wind instruments?
FIRST MUSICIAN   Ay, marry are they, sir.
CLOWN   O, thereby hangs a tail.
FIRST MUSICIAN   Whereby hangs a tale, sir?
CLOWN   Marry, sir, by many a wind instrument that I know. But, masters, here's money for you: and the General so likes your music that he desire you, for love's sake, to make no more noise with it.
FIRST MUSICIAN   Well, sir we will not.
CLOWN   If you have any music that may **not** be heard, to't again. But, as they say, to hear music the General does not greatly care.
FIRST MUSICIAN   We have none such, sir.
CLOWN   Then go put up your pipes in your bag, for I'll away. Go vanish into air, away. EXEUNT MUSICIANS.

The comedy and tragedy here do indeed hang on the word-play tail/tale. Is the penis an animalistic, farting noise when it meets lips, or is it capable of producing a melodious tale of love? The tragic overtone rings through the setup of imagery which has already shown us the forces at work which would destroy musical coupling.

Emilia and Desdemona, however, do try to preserve a type of music – the music of the dying swan.

EMILIA   ... I will play the swan and die in music.
(V, ii, 247)

As Iago is already busy infecting the musical atmosphere, the next step, first instigated in the "I'll set down the pegs that make this music ..." scene, is to make himself into a self-conceiving, hermaphroditic imitation-couple, and to infect Othello with its seductive anti-music. Yet that is what Othello seems to **prefer** to that other type of music with Desdemona, which is "too much of joy."

I mentioned previously that this hermaphroditic "coupling" could be seen as a type of narcissistic defence against the experience of the "musical couple." But Iago does have an extreme sensitivity to the beauty of women, and their fragility, as his mock praise of Desdemona in another scene shows. After all, he can only mock what he recognizes as beautiful.

Desdemona, perhaps already smelling the rotten atmosphere of insincerity, asks Iago to compose something in her praise, although one can easily detect that she is checking on Iago's ability to praise **any** woman, or to praise anything which he acknowledges as good.

After confessing that he is "nothing if not critical" (much truer than he imagines) Iago prefaces his "pregnant" denigration of all women with:

> My muse labours,
> And thus she is deliver'd.
>
> (II, i, 128–129)

Desdemona accurately, and probably dangerously, diagnoses Iago's perversion of poetry as "... a most lame and impotent conclusion".

(11, i, 162)

She gets right to the central connections between Iago's sexual insecurity, his intolerance of beauty and goodness, and his inability to even sustain a rhyming couplet, let alone a meaningful intercourse with a woman.

Elizabeth Sacks (1980) suggests that;

> ... the little failure to satisfy Desdemona does not matter much, since Iago is bent on proving his fertility in other ways. As in the exchange with Roderigo in Act 1, scene iii, the figurative language which he uses in '**playing** creative' provides him with the idiom to develop his idea and persuade others of its plausibility.

Like the invention of his little ballad, Iago's invention of the slander on Cassio is also a pregnancy. In these words, he sets about convincing Roderigo:

> ... nature **will** ... compel her to some second choice. Now sir, this granted, as it is a most **pregnant** and unforced position
> who stands so eminent in the degree of his fortune as Cassio does?
>
> (II, i, 236–241)

We are reminded of Iago's earlier omnipotent Macbethian pronouncement;

> There are many events in the womb of time which will be delivered.
>
> (I, iii, 376–378)

When Iago "conceives" the idea of abusing Othello's credulity; and exclaims:[5]

> I have't. It is engendered. Hell and night must bring this monstrous birth to the world's Light.

he anticipates Victor Frankenstein.

Jealousy of the couple, of their faithfulness, or togetherness, is melted down into the hermaphroditic self-conception of a scalding plot which is flung at the "innocent," and at the principle of faithfulness itself. It is indeed a monster, of which we are reminded by Emilia in her famous words;

> ... but jealous for they're jealous. It is a monster begot upon itself, **born on itself.**
>
> (III, iv, 155–162)

Klein talked about the *green-eyed monster* of envy, but perhaps we can now understand jealousy and envy as inseparable because the object of envy always seems to be perceived unconsciously, and primitively, as engaged in some perpetual form of coupling. And it is not just a question of feelings about the supposed pleasures and gratifications which each member of the couple enjoys, from each other. There are also feelings about the coupling itself, which not only produces "babies," but in a more profound way emanates love or harmony; an antidote to the nothingness which so permeates Iago's tormented soul. But in his immense rivalry with the loving couple he wants to believe that he can procreate alone.[4]

Where Iago does "succeed" in coupling, it is with his alter ego, Othello.

I have already suggested that Othello is intolerant of the music of his own coupling with Desdemona, but by the end of the play, he has become as much Iago as Iago.

> OTHELLO O, curse of marriage!
> That we can call these delicate creatures ours
> And not their appetites! I had rather be a toad
> And live upon the vapour of a dungeon
> Than keep a corner in the thing I love
> For others uses
>
> (III, iii, 265–270)

Obviously, he hadn't heard William Blake's little poem about Eternity:

> He who binds himself to a joy
> Does the winged life destroy;
> But he who kisses the joy as it flies
> Lives in eternity's sunrise (From Blake's 1792 notes)

But more to the point, he is speaking the language of Iago – "partobject" denigration of women, and particularly the part that might be *used* by others – he cannot imagine *loved* by another.

(Can this be the same Othello who said that he would "... climb hills of seas, Olympushigh and low as hell's from heaven," just to be with Desdemona? But then perhaps we should have been suspicious of the exaggeration.)

This is followed by desires for murderous revenge as a perversion of the harmony that he himself cannot endure. After hearing that Cassio has killed Roderigo, rather than vice versa, he exclaims:

> Not Cassio killed! Then murder's **out of tune**, and sweet
> revenge grows harsh.
>
> (V, ii, 116)

Again, these are lines that might have been Iago's. And when Othello harshly dismisses Emilia with:

> Leave procreants alone!
>
> (IV, ii, 28)

he seems to be commenting, unconsciously perhaps, that he is now, as Sacks says; "procreating his own disastrous conception" in the style of Iago, and prior to his murder of Desdemona, Othello makes clear that nothing she says could

> remove or choke the strong conception that I do groan withal.
>
> (V, ii, 53–56)

He therefore ends up choking Desdemona, and thereby his own chance of a happy, creative coupling, instead of removing or choking, perhaps aborting, his own misconception, and this brings us to the closing act.

Does Othello eventually mend his ways? According to my argument, which follows the course of his own imagery, he cannot. At best he might be forgiven because he knows not what he does.

The doomed Emilia says;

> I will play the swan and die in music.

to which Othello responds, in a remarkably sensitive way(!), by announcing that he has a weapon, and is prepared to use it. (Words that might have come from a Clint Eastwood gunslinger.) On this matter of the father's weapon, Donald Meltzer (1978) writes;

> It is only relatively late in development that the aesthetic of the father and his genital enters as a force in development, through the emergence of introjective identification with the internal mother's view of him. This limited apprehension of its aesthetic quality greatly facilitates the conception of the import of the male genital as a weapon rather than a tool.
>
> (p. 63)

I would add; or an **instrument for combining**, to produce intimate harmony.

Othello has murdered not only Desdemona, but his own faculty for receiving inspiration and enjoyment both from his inner muse and the world of the loving feminine other.

He has become like William Blake's impotent, uninspired man who pleads to the Muses:

How have you left the ancient love
  That bards of old enjoy'd in you!
  The languid strings do scarcely move! The sound is forced the notes are few!

(Author's emphasis)

Leontes, in *The Winter's Tale*,[6] manages better. But how and why?

He too, suffers delusional jealousy. He too demands the death of his faithful and beautiful wife – even the death of his daughter as well, and indirectly he causes the death of his young and promising son. The list doesn't end there either. He banishes both his lifelong best friend and his most trusted advisor, Camillo. Yet Leontes manages a partial recovery because he has some capacity for self-examination, and through this capacity, he can eventually 'remove and choke' the misconception that groaned within him – that his wife and his best friend, Polixenes, had formed a sexual union.

The following exclamation from Leontes, just as his jealousy is heating up, has often been described as containing Shakespeare's most incomprehensible lines. But what a different mind it is that grapples with delusional jealousy here as compared with Othello's ' *O, curse of marriage!*' speech:

LEONTES Affection! Thy intention stabs the centre:
Thou dost make possible things not so held,
Communicat'st with dreams; – how can **this** be?
With what's unreal **thou coactive** art,
And fellow'st nothing: then 'tis very credent
Thou may'st **cojoin** with **something;** and thou dost,
(And that beyond **commission**) and I find it,
(And to the infection of my brains
And hard'ning of my brows.)

(Author's emphasis)

To which Polixenes, God bless his puzzlement, says (for us all);
  What *means* Sicilia?

The first thing of note here is that Leontes, unlike Othello, turns inward, to where ideas are forming in his own mind to look at his awful problem and its diagnosis. Goddard (1951) says of Leontes' puzzling speech: "Emotion brings within the realm of possibility things non-existent. But he hopelessly confuses cause and effect" (p. 651).

That is, since emotion can give reality to "nothing," he argues, it seems credible that "nothing" should join onto 'something' in the external world (that the conception of a faithless Hermione secretly and lewdly coupling with Polixenes should actually fit the actuality of their relationship). And this "conception", he says, infects his brain.

Yet the truth seems more that his sick mind has forced his phantasy onto the real world. He cannot hold the thought of a couple, other than his own, engaged in sexual intercourse, as a **possibility.** It is an ongoing **certainty** which must be disproved, not proven. Clearly, his internal, perpetually fornicating parental couple is interfering both with his own sexual coupling, and also his capacity to bring possibilities together in his mind for thought and consideration, or as Bion might have put it, his capacity for linking, or perhaps for "conceiving."

And yet he does seem, for a moment anyway, to want to know about this confusion between internal couplings and external ones. But the moment is brief, and he is soon overtaken by the conviction that he lives on a "bawdy planet" and begins to speak of a seweranimal spawning woman in a way that matches Othello's language very closely, and also that of Lear *(**King Lear** is thought to be Shakespeare's next play after **Othello**)* in the storm of his madness:

> LEAR   … Down from the waist they are Centaurs,
> Though women all above:
> But to the girdle do the gods inherit,
> Beneath is all the fiend's.
> There's hell, there's darkness, there is the sulphurous pit,
> Burning, scalding, stench, consumption; fie, fie, fie! …
> (IV, vi, 123–128)

But unlike Othello and Lear, he defers his final judgement (albeit far too belatedly) to a couple which he believes can be trusted not to become as confused as himself. Yet when Cleomenes and Dion declare, via the oracle, Hermione's innocence, this is taken as the pronouncement of the Gods only after Leontes is told that his son Mamillus has died of grief, and that Hermione has collapsed. Is truth to be spawned from the thinking couple being allowed to come to their own conclusions, or from the terror of Divine retribution? By contrast, near the end of the play, we hear of Leontes's reunion with Perdita and his re-coupling with Polixenes, and of Perdita's coupling with Florizel (Polixenes's son) through a news-bearing couple, said to be *"delivering the 'pregnant truth."*

> Every wink of an eye, some new grace will be born:
> Our absence makes us unthrifty to our knowledge. Let's along.

It is almost as if these are two previously unpaired (perhaps unimpaired) thoughts in Leontes's mind, rushing off to tell him about the goodness of coupling if it can be given his trust and freedom. Leontes tells how he

> ... lost a couple that "twixt heaven and earth Might have thus stood, begetting wonder
> As you, gracious couple, do ...
>
> (V i, 131–133)

His wonderment at the couple allows him to eventually appreciate what he lost with Hermione; or is it the other way around? Shakespeare allows for both together. Hermione is now valued more like a priceless work of art rather than the "thing" he owns, but further still, she is a priceless loss because she is the one with whom he could **feel** himself to be in a wondrous couple.

One of the recurring themes throughout Shakespeare's work is that those who fail to value and appreciate the love that is offered "freely" (perhaps as a kind of grace from the nuptial chamber of the Olympian parents) will have what they love stolen from them.

> 'Beauty provoketh thieves sooner than gold'. (As You Like It).

But, according to Shakespeare, the most energetic and unstoppable of all thieves is time.

> Time is the thief that comes 'stealing on by night and day'.
>
> (Comedy of Errors, IV, ii, 60)

> The inaudible and noiseless foot of Time which steals, and which brings growth and decay'
>
> (All's Well that Ends Well.)

Even Richard II bends his knees.

> I wasted time and now doth time waste me.
>
> (V, v, 49)

The point is brought home continuously in The Winter's Tale through the comical, but highly relevant roguishness of the petty thief and slanderer of women, Autolycus, who is always relieving people of their unappreciated and unprotected goods. And yet his antics are linked to spring and regeneration, just as time-the-thief, in depriving Leontes of his wife, acts to regenerate his valuing the time of the life of his couple. A new generation of couples is born, determined not to waste a second of time together;

> Your hand, my Perdita: so turtles pair,
> That never mean to part.
>
> (Florizel)

Coupling and regeneration are restored as the monarchs of human life but both Leontes and Polixenes have to learn through the coupling of their daughter and son that the couple cannot be voyeuristically controlled (as Othello and Iago attempt to do), but must be seen as a willing union of two free souls – not statues, and not perfect clones or imprints of their parents.

It is my impression that coupling is still just a little controlled by Leontes at the play's conclusion, albeit that he has the better interests of others in mind, namely Paulina and Camillo. And, although we know that Hermione needed time to heal her own wounds, and that Paulina had this in mind alongside her wish to teach Leontes a lesson that he'd never forget, her keeping the royal couple separated for such a long period does have the faintest ambience of controlling jealousy about it.

Marsh (1980) suggests that "One of the most profound implications of the play is that what has been lost through the destructive power of evil can never be **wholly** regained" (p. 158).

The aged Hermione and Leontes move towards the end of their lives together, repaired, and in forgiveness, and graced with a beautiful daughter and worthy son-in-law, but nothing can bring back the years together that Leontes allowed time to steal.

Shakespeare seems to have moved more freely into the problem of what interferes with happy coupling and regeneration after that carnivalous cavalcade of coupling and uncoupling, *A Midsummer Night's Dream,* where 'combined' bestial objects alternate rapidly with loving free spirits.

However, *Othello* shows us the tragic consequences of the persistence of the 'combined parental object', whereas *The Winter's Tale* points the way towards a somewhat depressive, but more life-giving possibility, what I have called a tolerance of the "combining internal couple" and the love and harmony that it can produce.

But it is possible that it was left to Prospero, in *The Tempest*, to travel that further painful, but liberating path, of letting the internal couple have their total freedom.

> PROSPERO   ... *Go, release them, Ariel.*
> *My charms I'll break, their senses I'll restore,*
> *And they shall be themselves.*

Not until Ferdinand and Miranda are given his blessing to the couple and enter into the brave new world can Prospero (and the reader) identify with and enjoy the beauty of the babybreast couple.

> Where the bee sucks, there suck I ...
> In a cowslip's bell I lie;
> There I couch when owls do cry,
> On the bat's back do I fly
> After summer merrily:
> Merrily, merrily shall I live now
> Under the blossom that hangs on the bough.
> (V, i, 88)

Although there is no time (it steals again …) in this chapter to more fully explicate and explore it, I want to mention something that seems very important in later Shakespeare, and sometimes in clinical work,

It involves the transformation of the incestuous-narcissistic-baby father into a more adult form of concerned, loving but not controlling for his own gratification, or trying to use his daughter to magically restore what damage he is done to his own couple. This is made very obvious in Lear's disturbing stranglehold on Cordelia's affection, and with Leontes' attempts to control Perdita, in the context of having destroyed his own wife in psychotic jealousy. The dynamic is shown intensely, but more indirectly, in *Pericles* – where an incestuous king has doomed his daughter, and Pericles must re-find a different type of father-daughter relationship, both for her sake and for his own sanity in avoiding becoming a perpetual Flying Dutchman, roaming the world restlessly, from woman to woman.

This theme will be taken up in more detail in a forthcoming paper – ***Transformations of the Internal Father – from Lear to Leontes to Prospero.***

I will conclude with some material from a clinical case, the patient being a sensitive, intelligent, suicidal "drop out" with a marked propensity for disconnection between his thoughts and his feelings. I cannot say that the material is a neat example of the ideas which I have presented thus far, but I have found it helpful to think of the way his "combined object" hinders his thinking and creative capacities, and his struggle to allow the existence of a "combining internal couple." through which he might think, and enjoy life. His "combined object" gives rise to a kind of omnipotent, "hermaphroditic," narcissistic union with his own projective conjecturing.

Some repeated themes emerged:

1 He cannot bring my thoughts together with his own. He either "loses" my thought or his own.
2 He forms an "unconsummated" relationship with an older woman who lives directly opposite to his father.
3 He gets together with a friend of his who has the "professional capability" to help him to aurally spy on the father and the woman when they are alone together in a particular room.
4 He gradually reveals that this "professional friend" enjoys beating people up, whenever he gets the chance, which is not infrequently. He reveals that just recently this friend had been severely reprimanded for manhandling and humiliating a couple who were parked down a lovers' lane. The patient says, almost hysterically: "I had to laugh, even though I knew it was an awful thing to do to anyone." But when asked why he has not seriously questioned the value and meaning of his relationship to this 'friend' he shrugs the issue away with; "Good question!" and then continues to talk about nothing in particular, till ten minutes later he stops himself and says, as he often does. "I've totally forgotten what you've said."
5 He meets many women who show genuine interest in him, but he ends the budding relationship just prior to sexual intercourse, or, on the rare occasion when it does go further, the first sexual intercourse is unsatisfactory because: (a) he is

too worried about his potency – meaning that he is worried about his capacity to maintain minimal emotional contact with the woman. (b) he begins to sense that the woman's genitals smell awful and are putrid, which disgusts him and "turns him off" but he is not sure whether he imagined the smell or not.

6 The one exception to this pattern is a relationship which ended just prior to his first serious suicide attempt. He feels, despairingly, that he wrecked this relationship because he couldn't stand how good it was.

"She smelt beautiful."

7 He says that he is "uncoupled." He would like to study how to make films, how to "put them together" but he feels compelled to complete a Law degree, seemingly because his father failed his attempt at a Law degree, and so he must succeed, in spite of feeling dangerously suicidal each time he fails to produce an essay or assignment. He is convinced that his interest in film is an "impossible dream" but he has never checked to see what serious study of film would involve and whether or not he could be admitted to a course.

8 He cannot remember my holiday dates, because they are my "business," not his. (For him, "business" means an exchange of money in mutual exploitation, defaecation and squalid sexual intercourse.)

9 While describing a fantasy that he has seen my wife in a "milk bar" near my rooms, he says that he wonders what it would be like to drive my car but then adds that my car would be too complicated for him, and that he'd write it off reducing it to just a mangled piece of junk. (He laughs almost hysterically.)

He has damaged his own car, mainly through negligence, four or five times since seeing me.

10 He cannot imagine being happy, because he believes that true happiness can only come from "getting hitched" and having children and that would be "the pits" – a stinking prison hell hole that you'd never get untangled from. He says:

"Even I can see the contradiction in that, but I can't think about it. It just won't come together."

11 He describes a recurring experience, in one form or another, where he is approached menacingly by a couple of dangerous figures who are hard to distinguish from each other because it is dark, or because they seem huddled together.

An example of this experience is: He is walking home alone at night and two people are walking a huge dog – a horse of a dog – they look like two men (the **people** do, he adds), he couldn't be sure, but he crosses to the other side of the road, but so do the "disgusting trio." He sees them as one big animal. They say hello to him but he's not scared (he insists). "The stupid fools think I'm scared, but they just don't realize that I want to get away from them because I'm disgusted by them. They are animals."

He describes a similar sort of experience quite regularly and eventually admits that he seems to actually want some sort of confrontation. He imagines a bloody, chaotic fight, with limbs and organs flying everywhere.

12 His mother has physically tried to interrupt our sessions. (She could not have done this without his co-operation.) After insistently ringing the doorbell, which my wife had to eventually answer, his mother yelled continuously at her

that she must use our telephone because her son the patient – must have broken her car, which she could not start. My strong feeling in the countertransference was that I was failing to protect my own marital couple.
13 His (external) parents have been separated for many years – he cannot bear to ask if they are actually divorced or not – and apparently often fought in front of him. He once attacked his father because he thought that his mother was in danger. It is difficult to get any sort of picture from him about his parents as individual people, differentiated from each other.
14 He frequently makes definitive statements where he is absolutely certain of his knowledge and judgement. He says: "I'd back myself on that one!" Very often, it turns out that he is wrong, although this is quickly glossed over.
15 In three years, he had brought one dream. He says that he cannot "come at the idea" of regularly bringing his dreams. He describes them as "master messes."

When I ask him what he means by this (he is a master of non-elaboration) he says that he intended a pun on "masterpieces" and then goes on, in a far-away voice, as if dreaming aloud, to "master bedroom". This is followed by ten minutes of silence, which is ended abruptly with his self-diagnosis, admonition, and proscription that 'nothing connects!'

This is the dream:

He is sitting in a producer's (no, director's) chair for the preview screening of his own movie but the movie being shown is a "corny love story" with lots of kissing and cuddling – not at all like the movie that he'd thought he'd made (a spy thriller). He turns around to tell me that the wrong film is being shown but I too am apparently kissing some 'stupid' woman. Then when he turns back to the screen it is totally black, except for some bad scratching, and there is awful, distorted, screeching music on the soundtrack.

His reluctant associations centre on a film that he actually walked out of (close to its beginning), on the day before the dream. He thought that it was too predictable. It was called **The Object of Beauty**. He hated the couple. They were yuppie, materialistic "… dead-shits, who cut and thrust over each other, without one saving grace. Their values were fucked."

Did he really *say* "cut and thrust? … Of course he'd meant "clucked and fussed." He'd wondered if he was like the censoring priest in another film called **Cinema Paradiso** who cut out all the love scenes in films, supposedly on high moral grounds, but really because he couldn't stand for people to enjoy life.

The soundtrack in the dream reminded him of a string quartet that a friend had played to him recently. He'd thought the music to be obscure and too dissonant, and couldn't make "head or tail" of it.

I will not detail the various transference interpretations that were suggested by all of this material, but I hope that it can be seen that parts I and II of this chapter – rethinking Klein and Shakespeare, helped me to think about the inner struggles with coupling, of many sorts, that this patient had. Eventually, beginning with the transference relationship, he was more able to enjoy some degree of intimacy and love in a couple.

However, in concluding, I want to draw attention to the 'screeching music' of the patient's dream. Harris Williams and Waddell (1991) describe the inner transformation of the doomed and imprisoned Richard II at the moment where he hears some distant music.

> ... the music is not harmonious but awkward and jarring, and it takes Richard a while for the meaning of the symbol to penetrate ... that this inharmonious, uncourtly music ... is in fact a sign of 'love' ... The music 'mads' him, but it is the appearance of madness which accompanies the first steps toward insight, with their initial discordance.
>
> (p. 14)

Similarly for the patient, it seems that the emotional "sounds" heralding the shift from the violent, jarring 'cut and thrust' **combined object** to the harmonious creative, synthesizing, poeto-musical **combining couple** are, at first, perceived as a dissonant cacophony – a strangely out-of-time, "screeching music', not yet recognizable as a beautiful, if possibly "corny," love story played by a brave new poetic self.

This new, feeling and synthesizing self is described beautifully, again by Goethe, in his overture to *Faust:*

> POET ...   Whence, but from chimes that in his soul will start, to *harmonize* the world that would betray him?
> When Nature's thread, that filament neverending,
> Is nonchalantly on the distaff wound,
> When unrelated things that know no blending
> Send forth their vexed, uneasy *jarring sound*
> Who then bestows the rhythmic line *euphonious,*
> The ordered pulse, to stir or soothe the soul?
> Who marshals fragments to a ceremonious
> And splendid music, universal, whole?
> Who rides the flood of passion at its height?
> Or sings the glow of evening, solemn, sweet?
> Who strews the spring's dear garlands of delight
> In petalled path for his beloved's feet?
> Or who can twine the wreath for honour's portals,
> Can insignificant leaves with tongues invest,
> Assure Olympus, and unites immortals? -
> The might of man, in poets manifest.
>
> COMEDIAN Well, use the wondrous inspirations, pray,
> And set about the business straight away.
> Approach it as you would a loveaffair (Goethe's *Faust*)

Notes

1 In my opinion, many couple therapists confuse this need for separateness in the patient-couple with a need to commence seeing each partner separately, at some difficult point in the therapy. A move which, in my view, enacts violence towards the couple, which usually wrecks hopefulness about the therapy.
2 Compare this with the following, similar speech by Troilus, *from Troilus and Cressida,* supposedly written a couple of years before *Othello*.

> I am giddy; expectation whirls me round.
> The imaginary relish is so sweet
> That it enchants my sense: what will it be, When that the watery palate tastes indeed
> Love's thrice ruptured nectar? death, I fear me, Swooning destruction, or **some joy too fine,**
> **Too subtlepotent, tuned too sharp in sweetness,**
> **For the capacity of my ruder powers:**
> I fear it much; and I do fear besides.
> That I shall **lose distinction** in my joys;
> As doth a **battle,** when they charge on heap, the enemy flying.
> (III, ii, 19) (Author's emphasis)

Nor does Shakespeare confine the issue to men. Both Portia and Ophelia are pained by the problem of a 'surfeit' of joy.

3 Clyster-pipes refers to both a vaginal and anal douche.
4 Neapolitan disease and nasal impediment refer to venereal infection.
5 As well as proving to himself that he is capable of self-conception, Iago also prefers to "pull strings" (manipulate the feelings of others) rather than to be "played" as a stringed musical instrument himself. This is referred to often in the imagery of the play. In the opening paragraph, for example, Roderigo objects.

> I take it much unkindly
> That thou, Iago, who hast had my purse
> **As if the strings were thine,** shouldst know of this.
> Othello (I, 1) (Author's emphasis)

6 Leontes, king of Sicilia, has a groundless suspicion that his pregnant queen Hermione has committed adultery with Polixenes, king of Bohemia, who is paying a visit to his court. Camillo, an old Sicilian lord, warns Polixenes and flees with him to Bohemia. Leontes, taking this as proof of the queen's guilt, has her imprisoned, humiliated and tried. He also wants to kill their newborn daughter, Perdita, who is abandoned to "Nature," but found and cared for by a kindly shepherd. Meanwhile, in Sicily, Mamilllius, their little son dies of grief, and Paulina stages to the king the death of Hermione.

Sixteen years pass as Perdita grows up and is courted by Florizel, Polixenes' son. Because Polixenes strongly disapproves of the match, the young couple flees to Sicily, aided by the exiled Camillo, who wants to return home. The old shepherd eventually reveals evidence that Perdita is the lost princess, and Polixenes now approves of her.

Paulina arranges for an end to Leontes mourning for his wife by having him inspect a statue of Hermione, which "comes to life" in front of him. There are then a series of touching re-couplings – not only Leontes with Hermione and Paulina to Camillo, but most poignantly, Hermione with her long-lost daughter, Perdita.

References

Bion, W. (1967). *Second Thoughts*. London: Heineman.
────── (1970). *Attention and Interpretation*. Tavistock. London.
Blake, W. (1792). 'Notebook & for the muses', ed. Ralphson, J. in *Selected Poems*. Vermont: Everyman, 1982. 116–128.
Britton, R. (1989) The mising link. in *The Oedipus Complex Today* ed. Steiner, J. Karnac. London.
Goddard, J. P. (1951). *The Meaning of Shakespeare*, Argus, London.
Goethe, J. W. (1812). *Faust, Part One*. Middlesex: Penguin Classics, 1949.
Harris Williams, M. and Waddell, M. (1991). *The Chamber of Maiden Thought: Literary Origins of the Psychoanalytic Model of the Mind*. London: Routledge.
Klein, M. (1932). *The PsychoAnalysis of Children*. ed. Money-Kyrle, R. New York: Dell, 1975. 28–112.
────── (1957). Envy and gratitude. In *Envy and Gratitude and Other Works*. New York: Dell, 1975.
────── (1958). *Narrative of a Child Analysis*. New York: Dell, 1975.
Maizels, N. (1990). The destructive confounding of intra-uterine and post-uterine life as a factor opposing emotional development. *Journal of Melanie Klein and Object Relations*, 8 (2). 24–46.
Marlowe, C. (1593). *Tamburlaine*, in *Elizabethan Tragedy*. Cambridge: Cambridge University Press, 1953.
Marsh, D. R. C. (1980). *The Recurring Miracle, a Study of Cymbeline and the Last Plays*. Sydney: Sydney University Press.
Meltzer, D. (1978). *The Kleinian Development*, Part II. Perthshire: Clunie Press.
Meltzer, D. (1988). *The Apprehension of Beauty* (with Harris Williams, M.) Perthshire: Clunie Press.
O'Shaughnessy E. (1988) The invisible Oedipus Complex. in ed. E. Bott-Spillius,. Melanie Klein Today, Vol. 2. Mainly Practice, pp 191–205, London.
Sacks, E. M. (1980). *Shakespeare's Images of Pregnancy*. London: Macmillan.
Shakespeare, W. (1961). *Collected Works*. London: Abbey.

Chapter 12

Trees of Knowledge in Thomas Hardy's *The Woodlanders*

This chapter is an attempt to think about a process that we all, pretty much, take for granted. It is the process of how we come to know, or to feel that we know, another person, and I'm going to try to explore the issue from different angles.

What does the writer Thomas Hardy have to say about how we succeed or fail in getting to know, other people?

Keep in mind that Freud was not only reading Sophocles. He was a big, though understated fan of Thomas Hardy – so it's interesting to know that Hardy was writing about "transference" in 1887, in The Woodlanders, where he speaks of the capacity for love in his anti-hero, Dr. Fitzpiers, undergoing "division and transference" onto many different women. (p. 265)

The Woodlanders is the novel of Hardy's which most readers tend to leave alone – probably because the story seems so plain, on the surface – but I experienced it as a profound and detailed meditation on the different ways that characters seek to know or to **avoid** knowing each other, often with lifelong, tragic consequences. I'd even suggest that the worst tragedies in the lives of all of Hardy's characters ("Jude" and "Tess" par excellence) are caused by failures in really getting to know the hearts and minds of others, particularly of their beloved. But, for the purposes of this chapter, I'll confine my discussion of Hardy's views on the matter to his own favourite novel, *The Woodlanders*.

I'll now explore *The Woodlanders*, and Hardy's evocations of the **interplay** between knowing and loving.

At first sight, the plotline of the novel is very simple, even perhaps with a glimmer of "Mills and Boon."

The story accrues through the interplay of a small group of characters who inhabit a densely treed little woodland byway called Little Hintock, and these characters are linked together in various psychological pairs and triangles of obsessions and passions which rarely find direct satisfaction, or even fulmination, but as soon as the reader tends to pick a central character, Hardy's kaleidoscope of observation turns, and we then see that character in a different shape, context and light, and not necessarily at the "centre" at all. (This can also happen in reverse.)

There is Grace Melbury, a not-so-simple country girl, treated condescendingly and controllingly by her father, who seems to have a guilty obsession with the manner in which he felt that he stole his first wife (Grace's mother) from another man.

To assuage this apparently Oedipal guilt he pledges his daughter to Giles Winterbourne, the son of his defeated rival, and also the local cider-maker, who lives life amongst the seasons, the trees and the fruit. (What better setting for a novel which so often hints at the modern-day subtleties of the Tree of Knowledge story?)

As it happens, Giles does love Grace, and Grace is very fond of him, at least until after she is sent away by her father for 'betterment' through an expensive education, where she learns about etiquette, fine clothes and the big-housed lives of the comfort-loving, worldly city dwellers.

When she meets Giles again after her years of education he seems, to her, quite bland, naive and lacking in means and mystery. So she is in conflict. She now feels a painful gap between her new ideal of an educated, sophisticated man, and the apparently glum reality of life with a man who is her father's choice **for** her.

But she tries to please her father, who, in the meantime, after having "invested" so much money in her "improvement," is also starting to renege on his own pact with himself, supposedly out of concern for Grace's future happiness.

Meanwhile, in the background to all of this – or is it the foreground? – there is Marty South, a poor but dedicated, skillfully hard-working girl, who has loved Giles secretly for many years through her working contact with him in the woodland.

At first, Hardy depicts her as a very pathetic figure. She is forced to sell her beautiful long hair in order to support her dying father, who can no longer work because he is in the grip of a brooding paranoid depression about a large tree which he feels certain is draining away his life force, and which he believes will eventually fall and crush him.

And Marty holds no real hope of Giles even noticing her, let alone reciprocating her affection. But she is also painted by Hardy in a literally glowing, even angelic, light, and psychologically speaking, she is the only character who has established a firmly-loved and respected internal object by the novel's close, where her hopeless love for Giles is eventually transformed into a poignant vigilance in her keeping his spirit and her love for him alive after he dies.

And Giles' death is constructed with symbolic complexity by Hardy.

Ostensibly, his noble – or is it masochistic? – refusal to sexually consummate the relationship with Grace, even when they are all alone in the depth of the woods, leads him to sleep in the cold rain, with insufficient shelter, and this finishes him off, physically. But he has already been suffering from a broken heart ever since Grace's marriage to the dubious Dr. Edred Fitzpiers.

In fact, Grace's conflict, partly inherited from her father, between "sophisticated," "educated," civilized, best-of-everything values and the supposedly simple, straightforward dedication and asceticism of rustic communal values is played out in her indecision about Giles versus Fitzpiers.

Dr. Fitzpiers is a restless soul, who is himself in conflict between the pursuance of lofty philosophic generalizations about life, reading till all hours of the morning, (much to Grace's tantalization) and the practical life of being a G.P. in a small community, happy to love an apparently straightforward, pretty young woman like Grace. But he cannot stop from projectively wishing all sorts of grandiose qualities into her, wanting her to possess all the charm, wealth and status of a woman he has heard some gossip about – the lonely, hysterical and pathetic Felice Charmond, who married an older man for wealth and security, but is now widowed.

He cannot choose between these two women – marrying Grace, but then having a tortuous affair with Felice, as well as the odd, mindless fling with one of his patients.

Hardy's architectural balancing of characters and their alter egos (or projective identifications) makes it clear that Felice Charmond represents the hysterical, shallow, materialistic, showy and fashionable side of Grace. It is Charmond who has purchased Marty's hair, in order to make herself appear more natural and youthful and enviable – but Hardy subtly shows us these same leanings in Grace's character at times.

Quite clearly, Hardy wants to explore what narcissistic affluence and loveless materialism do to the possibility of sustained intimacy between men and women. But even more so, he shows again and again the knotted tragedy of being blinded by the projection of one's own ideals onto and into another person, and then finding it impossible to retract the projections, or to humbly dissolve the relationship as a case of mistaken identity.

(These difficulties were to be explored even more intensely and painfully in *Jude the Obscure*. 1895.)

Hardy locates the problem partly as society's need to keep stability by shaming couples into staying married, no matter what, and partly as the individual's guilt about unresolved Oedipal matters, leading one to unconsciously equate a change of marriage partner with a breaking of the incest taboo. This is most painfully illustrated by Grace's feeling that she <u>must</u> stay with Fitzpiers, because she is married to him, even if it means continuing to believe in lies, false ideals, the humiliations of his distant affairs, and the loss of her "true self."

It is simultaneously illustrated by Giles Winterbourne's misplaced "nobility" in not 'pressing his point' with Grace, even when he knows what a sham her marriage has become. Everybody eventually feels impotent, paralyzed, unhappy and resentfully bound by obligation rather than love, and Hardy hated this in his own society, although he felt deep compassion for the human vulnerability to this kind of unhappiness.

I will now try to outline a spectrum of the different levels of <u>knowing</u> something or someone that I think Hardy adumbrates in *The Woodlanders*.

Listed briefly, they are:

1 Gossip.
2 A <u>cursory</u> view - based solely on wishful, omnipotent projection.
3 Seeing – but 'merely observing', without any feeling of interest in what is seen.
4 Drinking, or sucking in, sensually, with the avidity of a <u>feeding</u> infant.
5 Discerning and appreciating through "watchful lovingkindness" – where loving and knowing "talk" to each other, dialectically.

6 "Following," with a hope of lively intercourse, in order to explore the reality of the other, and of oneself, as compared to innate, preconceived Ideals.
7 Patiently, humbly and lovingly exploring mutuality and difference through many and various types of intercourse, in a "sympathetic interdependence," which creates long-term intimacy through "old association."

Although it is 5. – attending in "watchful lovingkindness" – that will be of particular interest in relation to the issues I want to raise with Bion and my patient, Alexander, I will now give some brief illustrations of the comparisons and interplay between each of these ways of getting to know, as depicted by Hardy.

The first, and 'lowest' form of getting to know another person is really a way of avoiding getting to know them. It is through gossip.

Being attracted to gossip as a means of getting to know others does allay envy and jealousy and awe, through stereotypical denigration, but it can also increase envy and jealousy and awe, through stereotypical idealization. It means giving over one's experience of another person to the Basic Assumption mindlessness of the herd, so it is even more primitive than projection because it "borrows" the projections of others.

I won't quote an example from Hardy, because we are all familiar with gossip and its tabloid/magazine vapidity, as well as its damaging effects; but he does describe its workings many times in the novel, where groups of villagers quickly size up anyone who behaves unpredictably or outside strict norms.

Gossip also carries an air of omnipotence, because the denigrations or idealizations can never be challenged by the real presence of the object of propaganda. (Many of Alexander's perceptions of me were composed of snippets of gossip infused with projected negative aspects of himself.)

Klein (1946) did mention the importance of projecting loving feelings as well as destructive feelings in the process of projective identification, but Hardy implies that this **exploration** of the object through projective love, or as he calls it, "watchful lovingkindness", is a crucial tool of understanding and getting to know another person.

Perhaps the following quote will clarify how Hardy contrasts this with what he refers to as a "cursory view."

> There was nothing remarkable in her dress just now beyond a natural fitness, and style that was recent for the streets of Sherton. But had it been quite striking it would have meant just a little. For there can be hardly anything less connected with woman's personality than drapery which she has neither designed, manufacture, cut, sewed, nor even seen except by a glance of approval when told that such and such a shape and colour must be had because it has been decided by others as imperative at that particular time.
>
> What people therefore saw of her in a cursory view was very little; in truth, mainly something that was not she. The woman herself was a conjectural creature who had little to do with the outline presented to Sherton eyes; a shape in

the gloom, whose true quality could only be approximated by putting together a movement now and glance then, in that patient attention which nothing but <u>watchful loving-kindness</u> ever troubles itself to give.

(My italics) (p. 79)

Dr. Fitzpiers has great difficulty in getting beyond the wish to know only the idealized, projected version of his own narcissism in another person – particularly Grace. Hardy calls this projective, wishful-omnipotent illusion of getting to know another person "conjecture." (Although in other parts of the novel Hardy sometimes confuses this with the more "mature" type ....of conjecture involved in maintaining an intense interest by thoughtful reflection.)

Fitzpiers sat down to the book he had been perusing. It happened to be that of a German metaphysician, for the doctor was not a practical man, except by fits, and much preferred the ideal world to the real, and the discovery of principles to their application. The young lady remained in his thoughts. He might have <u>followed</u> her; but he was not constitutionally active, and preferred a <u>conjectural</u> pursuit.

(My italics) (p. 162)

Hardy further describes how Fitzpiers seems cut off from the satisfactions of an "<u>old association,</u>" built on the repeated accretion of 'local' knowledge through living intercourse:

Fitzpiers ... had lately plunged into abstract philosophy with much zest; perhaps his keenly appreciative, modern, unpractical mind found this a realm more in his taste than any other. Though his aims were desultory Fitzpiers's mental constitution was not without its creditable side; a real inquirer he honestly was at times; even if the midnight rays of his lamp, visible so far through the trees at Hintock, lighted rank literatures of emotion and passion as often as, or oftener than, the books and matérial of science.

But whether he meditated the Muses or the philosophers, the loneliness of Hintock life was beginning to tell upon his impressionable nature. Winter in a solitary house in the country, without society, is tolerable, nay, even enjoyable and delightful, given certain conditions; but these are not the conditions which attach to the life of a professional man who drops down into such a place by mere accident. They were present to the lives of Winterbourne, Melbury and Grace; but not to the doctor's. They are <u>old association</u> – an almost exhaustive biographical or historical acquaintance with every object, animate and inanimate, within the observer's horizon. He must know all about those invisible ones of the days gone by, whose feet have traversed the fields which look so grey from his windows; recall whose creaking plough has turned those sods from time to time; whose hands planted the trees that form a crest of the opposite hill; whose horses and hounds have torn through that underwood; what birds affect that particular brake; what bygone domestic dramas of love, jealously, revenge, or disappointment have been enacted in the cottages, the mansion, the street or on the green. The spot may have beauty, grandure, salubrity, convenience; but if it lack memories it will ultimately pall upon him who settles there without opportunity of *intercourse with his kind.*

In such circumstances, maybe, an old man dreams of an ideal friend, till he throws himself into the arms of any imposter who chooses to wear that title on his face. A young man may dream of an ideal friend likewise, but some humour of the blood will probably lead him to think rather of an ideal mistress, and at length the rustle of a woman's dress, the sound of her voice, or the transit of her form across the field of his vision, will enkindle his soul with a flame that blinds his eyes. The discovery of the attractive Grace's name and family would have been enough in other circumstances to lead the doctor, if not to put her personality out of his head, to change the character of his interest in her. Instead of treasuring her image as a rarity he would at most have played with her as a toy. He was that kind of man. But situated here he could not go so far as amative cruelty. He dismissed all deferential thought about her, but he could not help taking her somewhat seriously.

He went on to imagine the impossible. So far, indeed, did he go in this futile direction that, as others are wont to do, he constructed dialogues and scenes in which Grace had turned out to be the mistress of Hintock manor-house, the mysterious Mrs Charmond, particularly ready and willing to be wooed by himself and nobody else.

(My italics) (p. 172)

The next quote illustrates the contrast between 3. (*seeing, but 'merely observing'*), and 4. (*sucking in experience with the pleasure and avidity of a baby at the breast*), as it compares Graces' style of perception with that of her father's.

It was a day of rather bright weather for the season. Miss Melbury went out for a morning walk, and her ever-regardful father, having an hour's leisure, offered to walk with her. The breeze was fresh and quite steady, filtering itself through the denuded mass of twigs without swaying them, but making the point of each ivy-leaf on the trunks scratch its underlying neighbour restlessly. Grace's lips <u>sucked</u> in this native air of hers <u>like milk</u>. They soon reached a place where the wood ran down into a corner, and they went outside it towards comparatively open ground. Having looked round where they were intending to re-enter the copse, a panting fox emerged with a dragging brush, trotted past them tamely as a domestic cat, and disappeared amid some dead fern. They walked on, her father <u>merely observing</u> after watching the animal, "They are hunting somewhere near".

(My italics; p. 131)

But sometimes Grace's father is not even capable of "merely observing.". When asked about Grace's health, he responds:

> 'Grace is not at all well. Nothing constitutional, you know; but she has been in a low nervous state ever since that night of fright. I don't doubt but that she will be all right soon ... I wonder how she is this evening?'
> He rose with the words as if he had too long forgotten her personality in the excitement of her previsioned career.
>
> (p. 335)

<u>"Following"</u> – with a hope of 'intercourse' – (cf <u>collecting</u>, with no pleasure or intention for intercourse itself) and with the aim of further discerning and loving both the similarities with, and the gaps between one's Ideal pre-conception and one's actual emotional experience in the presence of the other. This means a loving but depressive relationship with the loved one, because the Unfulfilled Intention in another and in oneself is always apparent and sad. But there is also consolation, and sometimes unexpected joy, when instinctual or Oedipal disappointments are transformed into the satisfaction of getting to know oneself and the other, through the accretion of 'old association'.

Hardy's concept of the <u>Unfulfilled Intention</u> refers to the everpresent gap between instinctual stereotypes (Jungian archetypes) and the 'fruit of K' (Bion's term for getting to know one's emotional experience of people and things, through curious interest.)

> They went noiselessly over mats of starry moss, rustled through interspersed tracts of leaves, skirted trunks with spreading roots whose massed rinds made them like hands wearing green gloves; elbowed old elms and ashes with great forks, in which stood pools of water that overflowed on rainy days and ran down their stems in green cascades. On older trees still than these, huge lobes of fungi grew like lungs. Here, as everywhere, the Unfulfilled Intention, which makes life what it is, was as obvious as it could be among the depraved crowds of a city slum. The leaf was deformed, the curve was crippled, the taper was interrupted; the lichen ate the vigour of the stalk, and the ivy slowly strangled to death the promising sapling.
>
> (p. 93)

Hardy then shows us just how unwilling Dr. Fitzpiers often is in accepting this, emotionally, as a principle of Natural and Mental Life.

For example, he says to Grace:

> I fancied in my vision that you stood there,' he said pointing to where she had paused. 'I did not see you directly, but reflected in the glass. I thought, what a lovely creature! *The design is for once carried out. Nature has at last recovered her lost union with the Idea.* My thoughts ran in that direction because I had

been reading the work of a transcendental philosopher last night; and I dare say it was the dose of Idealism that I received from it that made me scarcely able to distinguish between reality and fancy. I almost wept when I awoke, and found that you had appeared to me in Time, but not in Space, alas!'

(My italics) (p. 179)

But if Fitzpiers is unable to love, or even to respect this principle of Unfulfilled Intention, then it is totally noxious to the hysterical Felice Charmond.
(She is remonstrating to Fitzpiers about life's miseries.)

'O,' she murmured, 'it is because the world is so dreary outside! Sorrow and bitterness in the sky, and floods of agonized tears beating against the panes. I lay awake last night, and I could hear the scrape of snails creeping up the window glass; it was so sad! My eyes were so heavy this morning that I could have wept my life away. I cannot bear you to see my face; I keep it away from you purposely. O! why were we given hungry hearts and wild desires if we have to live in a world like this? Why should Death alone lend what Life is compelled to borrow – rest? Answer that, Dr. Fitzpiers.'

'You must eat of a **second tree of knowledge** before **you** can do it, Felice Charmond.'

(p. 252)

Felice doesn't want to let in reality because it seems too harshly glaring and depressing, in comparison to her "foetally-Oedipal" triumph over her rival, Grace.
Here, for example, as Fitzpiers is attending to her 'illness':

He drew back the window curtains, whereupon the red glow of the fire and the two candle-flames became almost invisible under the flood of the late autumn sunlight that poured in.
'Shall I come round to you?' he asked, her back being towards him.
'No,' she replied.
'Why not?'
'Because I am crying, and I don't want you to see my face in the full sun's rays.'
He stood a moment irresolute, and regretting that he had killed the rosy passionate lamplight by opening the curtains and letting in garish day.

(p. 254)

And yet there is also something of this depression about the 'light of reality' in Grace. For example, here, Grace realized that she is not as jealous as she would be if she still really loved her husband, Fitzpiers.

In truth, her ante-nuptial regard for Fitzpiers had been rather of the quality of awe towards a superior being than of tender solicitude for a love. It had been based on mystery and strangeness – the mystery of his past, of his knowledge, of his professional skill, of his beliefs. When this structure of ideals was demolished by the intimacy of common life, and she found him as merely human as the Hintock people themselves, a new foundation was in demand for an enduring and staunch affections – *a sympathetic interdependence*, wherein mutual weaknesses are made the grounds of a defensive alliance. Fitzpiers had furnished nothing of that single-minded confidence and truth out of which alone such a second union could spring; ...

(My italics) (p. 258)

And later, when Grace does get a chance for such a union, with Giles Winterbourne, upon meeting him at an apple mill where he is working, she rejects it, and clings stubbornly to her loveless marriage as a pretext.

He looked and smelt like Autumn's very brother, his face being sunburnt to wheat-colour, his eyes blue as corn-flowers, his sleeves and leggings dyed with fruit-stains, his hands clammy with the sweet juice of apples, his hat sprinkled with pips, and everywhere about him that atmosphere of cider which at its first return each season has such an indescribable fascination for those who have been born and bred amongst the orchards.

Her heart rose from its late sadness like a released bough; her senses revelled in the sudden lapse back to Nature unadorned. The consciousness of having to be genteel because of her husband's profession, the veneer of artificiality which she had acquired at the fashionable schools, were thrown off, and she became the crude country girl of her latent early instincts. Nature was bountiful, she thought. No sooner had she been cast aside by Edred Fitzpiers than another being, impersonating chivalrous and undiluted manliness, had arisen out of the earth ready to her hand. This, however, was an excursion of the imagination which she did not wish to encourage, and she said suddenly, to disguise the confused regard which had followed her thoughts, 'Did you meet my husband?'

(p. 258)

Hardy implies, through this imagery, that the real fruit of the Tree of Knowledge is in coming to know and to love, or love and know, all the realness of the object in its "imperfect," but "juicy" difference from our ideal expectation. This **difference** can imbue the loved object with an "earthiness," and therefore could be a powerful consolation in mourning the loss of the ideal, which, as Hardy says, is never fulfilled – at least not in reality, though it may **seem** to be, in Fancy or Hallucinosis.

Of all the characters in *The Woodlanders*, only Marty South, supposedly the most pathetic and deprived, has achieved an acceptance of this principle, which is reflected in her patient, humble method of working intricately in comparison to the impatient, superior, phallic-medical dissection of trees by the male barkers.

As soon as the tree ... had fallen the barkers attacked it like locusts, and in a short time not a particle of rind was left on the trunk and larger limbs. Marty South was adept at peeling the upper parts; and there she stood encaged amid the mass of twigs and buds like a great bird, running her ripping-tool into the smallest branches, beyond the furthest point to which the skill and patience of the men enabled them to proceed – branches which, in their lifetime, had swayed high above the bulk of the wood, and caught the earliest rays of the sun and moon while the lower part of the forest was still in darkness.

'You seem to have a better instrument than they, Marty,' said Fitzpiers.

'No, sir,' she said, holding up the tool, a horse's leg-bone fitted into a handle and filed to an edge; "tis only that they've less patience with the twigs, because their time is worth more than mine.'

(p. 185)

Indeed, Marty does have a better instrument than the impatient men, and that is her **mind**.

The tragic irony of her plight is that through her humility and total lack of self-interest, she actually gains a far deeper, more patient, long-lasting knowledge and loving relationship with her beloved, albeit internally. Her bond with Giles, which rests on her complete understanding of him, will far outlive Grace's and Fitzpiers's charade, where they are only able to see and know each other through the mirror of their own idealized and idealizing selves.

Although Fitzpiers eventually does **seem** to realize the delicate inter-relationship between loving and knowing, (when he is trying to win back Grace after returning from an unhappy escape with Felice Charmond) this remains a purely intellectual insight, because he doesn't really mean it, and also because he is not really totally convinced as to whether it is Grace or his idealized model of her that he truly loves.

'And yet I love you more than I loved you in my life.'

Grace did not move her eyes from the birds, and folded her delicate lips as if to keep them in subjection.

'It is a different kind of love altogether,' said he.

'Less passionate; more profound. It has nothing to do with the material conditions of the object at all; much to do with her character and goodness, as revealed by closer observation. **Love talks with better knowledge, and knowledge with dearer love.'**

'That's out of Measure for Measure,' she said slyly.

'Oh yes – I meant it as a citation,' blandly replied Fitzpiers.

'Well then, why not give me a very little bit of your heart again?'

The crash of a felled tree in the depths of the nearest wood recalled the past at that moment, and all the homely faithfulness of Winterbourne.

'Don't ask it! My heart is in the grave with Giles,' she replied staunchly.

(My italics) (p. 409)

Bion

I now want to sketch out some of the similarities and differences between Bion's explicit model (really models) of how we come to know ourselves and each other, and the above model which I have derived from Hardy.

Bion's model of knowing is very complex, and that isn't all that surprising, because first Freud, and then Klein, also seemed to have rather complex and ambivalent relationships to the topic.

For Freud (1909) "scientific" curiosity was a form of sexual curiosity about the primal couple, but it could also be seen as a defensive, inhibited turning away from anxieties about one's libidinal drives through excessive intellectualization.

> The histories of obsessional patients almost invariably reveal an early development and premature repression of the sexual instinct of looking and knowing (the scopophilic and epistemophilic instincts; ...
>
> (S. E., x, p. 245)

Then Freud goes on to define the perversion of these instincts. He suggests that this occurs when sexual energy is diverted away from the **content** of thoughts and into the **process** of thinking itself.

For Melanie Klein (1946), curiosity was "epistemophilic instinct," and was derived from the unconscious phantasy of penetrating to the inside of the mother's body, partly for intrusive reasons, such as jealousy and envy of the inside babies, and the parts of the father that are felt to be indulgently feeding and fertilizing there, but also partly for reparative aims – wanting to see what is and what isn't damaged inside the mother, in order to face, and thereby to alleviate, guilt about destructive phantasies.

Examples of the mixed feelings of aggression, anxiety and the wish to know about damage are drawn lucidly by Klein in her *Narrative of a Child Analysis.* (1961)

She describes, for example, (p. 398), how Richard hammers the floorboards violently because he wants to know what's underneath them, and Klein interprets this as his wish to break into her to find out whether she contains a good or a bad father's penis that puts baby seeds into her.

She gives other examples where Richard imagines using a submarine periscope both intrusively, and also as a wish to see and know about torpedo damage.

So, epistemophilia, the thrill of getting to know, can be connected to facing guilt, and to finding out about damage caused by one's intrusive feelings of wanting to stop mother from having intercourse and babies. But it can also be an expression of that intrusive impulse, by forcing oneself inside, detective-style, irrespective of the needs and boundaries of the mother. And because this type of intrusive identification or action creates even more persecutory guilt and anxiety, it has to be secretive, quick and interrupted. Therefore knowledge gained is always felt to be unsatisfying, incomplete and stolen.

(I would also add, that one misses out on feeling the loving generosity of the mother and the experiencing of her "watchful lovingkindness". Therefore, an eventual identification with that aspect of her is blocked.)

Through Klein, there is the implication that projective identification can be used either intrusively, in the phantasy that one has gotten inside and taken over the body and mind of the mother, with the illusion of getting to know her, or empathically, derived from the genuine wish to feel with another person.

How this latter happened was left as a mystery, until Bion (1962, 1970), extended Klein's theory of projective identification, with his models of container-contained, **and** of K and minus K. This gave the desire to know an instinctual importance all of its own. Furthermore, in keeping with the beginning of the Old Testament, disturbances in the way we ingest knowledge were seen by him as the genesis of all other problems, particularly the Oedipus Complex. Bion (1962), and also Grotstein (1981), Gold (1988) and many other psychoanalysts view the Tree of Knowledge story as being about a prohibitive, omniscient limiting of human knowledge, which is projected into a primitive God who cannot bear for humans to know about suffering and pain and the harshness of the world, and, presumably, guilt about sex.

But, in my view, this interpretation of the story might miss its spirit.

I think that the Tree of Knowledge emerges as an issue for Adam **after** God asks him **to get to know,** and then name, all of the creatures of the Garden. (There is a beautiful engraving by William Blake which depicts Adam looking inwardly as he contemplates his task of getting to know the Creation, while using his hands to subdue the serpent.) It seems to me that the tree represents an oral-narcissistic temptation which offers a shortcut to the process of "getting to know" – an alternative to patient, loving exploration.

The serpent claims that knowledge can be had just by incorporating it as if it was an apple that could be taken in with just a few quick bites.

The symbolism of the serpent also suggests a parallel distinction between phallic, lustful, carnal sex and the process of getting to know, through repeated loving intercourse. The former might bear on Adam's and Eve's sense of guilt and sordidness after eating from the tree, thus spoiling the process of exploring Eden. (It is interesting how, in the Old Testament, the word "know" means both familiarity and sexual intercourse.) It is as if the God within says:

> If you treat Creation as a miraculous unending mystery which will occupy you for your whole life, then the world will be like a Garden of Eden to you. But if, instead, you grow impatient and ungrateful in this process of getting to know, you will miss the beauty of the world, and your life will become a frustrating hell of possessing and devouring one forbidden fruit after another, with little satisfaction, and you will have only a fake, perfunctory feeling of gratitude to the Creator, as did Cain.

Bion (1970) added another peril in the building up of knowledge, which he often equated with the attainment of critical conditions in a nuclear reactor. He suggested that, eventually, K becomes a <u>defence</u> against a "Transformation in O" – later referred to as "catastrophic change," or, at a group level, the "messianic idea" (1970).

If K is clung to as "mere knowledge" which doesn't actually change a person, through growth and development, from the mental digestion of emotional experience – what Bion refers to as *Becoming through Achievement* – then it is only, in Hardy's words, "merely observing."

In Bion's Grid, Action is the most "evolved" aspect of thought – that is, thoughtful action, as compared with the mindless acting out in psychosis, and Bion (1992) was fond of the phrase: "Thought as a prelude to action," which is similar to Freud's idea that the thinking process should always be an aid to instinctual gratification and not an end in itself. Freud also saw thinking as a kind of "experimental action."

Or, as the Chinese proverb puts it;

"To know, and not to act, is not yet to know."

As you get to know another person, (in Kleinian terms, from part-object idealization/denigration to whole-object ambivalence), there is a depressive pain associated with the Immanent emerging from the ideal, because mentally, the ideal is always "strangled." But the original prescience is always felt and remembered as a pre-conception, or archetype or Platonic ideal.

I think that the change in the self which occurs when we emotionally digest all the accumulated knowledge (K) as we get to know another person, and ourselves, is what Bion meant by the transformation of K into O, the unfathomable real, and Bion says that this change in the self is resisted as if it were to be a massive catastrophe. But I think that it is the transferring of love to the **gap**, that is, from Hardy's *Unfulfilled Intention* to the 'real' Other, which is crucial. This shift to loving both another and also one's own, real self, as compared to the idealized, "perfect," preconceived form is felt as a disruptive "catastrophe," at first.

If, however, knowledge **is** emotionally digested, then, in fact, the mind experiences a growthful re-birth, and, so does the relationship between the self and another person, who can be

Perhaps this perfunctory attitude could also be called 'negative **incapability**', and the point I want to make is that it can sometimes defensively masquerade as "negative **capability.**" This means that one might be very attentive, and open to all associations and countertransference thoughts and feelings – but in a sort of narcissistic reverie – in love with the analytic role rather than perceiving the patient with "watchful lovingkindness", with a real emotional interest in wanting to find, restore and have intercourse with the patient's lost good internal objects.

Negative Capability needs to be in the service of this watchful lovingkindness, or else we might become like lonely, addicted Sherlock Holmes – solving everything, but moved by nothing except our own theoretical violins. Hardy would call this "merely observing" our patients, and patients like Alexander, starved for genuine love and interest, can unconsciously derail us from **feeling** the desire to make contact with and rescue their contact with good objects, and cannot feel our interest with love, or our love with a genuine interest. Then we are in danger of becoming soullessly interested in "how the mind works." I see Bion's concept of "reverie" as incomplete if it includes only the capacity for containing the infant's fear of dying, and even if it also includes the capacity for negative capability – which I would paraphrase as being like Walter de la Mare's (1953) *The Owl*, who waits until it is dark enough to see.

I think that reverie, particularly with patients like Alexander, with severe narcissistic disturbances, must also comprise Hardy's quality of "watchful lovingkindness", as a more active analytic quality, which emanates a kind of infra-red light of love so that the patient can see and feel his or her own good objects, and only **then**, through identification with our interest, begin to sincerely care about their fate, at the hand of damaging narcissistic defences. If a patient cannot feel **in touch** with their good objects, then interpretations about the damage to them only arouse a persecutory, intellectual guilt, rather than an energised concern, and a wish to use analytic help for their restoration and future protection.

Bion's initial (1962) concept of 'reverie' did suggest both an openness to loving projections from the patient, as well as the capacity to provide love and understanding.

> ... reverie is that state of mind which is open to the reception of any "objects" from the loved object and is therefore capable of reception of the infant's projective identifications **whether they are felt by the infant to be good or bad**.
> (My italics) (p. 36)

But in his later writings his **emphasis** was more often on the processing of emotional pain associated with the dread of dying, and the capacity to think.

> Normal development follows if the relationship between infant and breast permits the infant to project a feeling, say, that it is dying into the mother and to reintroject it after its sojourn in the breast has made it tolerable to the infant psyche.
> (1970, p. 116)

If the projection is not accepted by the mother (in a state of reverie) the infant feels a nameless dread.

By 1970 Bion is referring much more to his models of "container-contained" and "negative capability" and his concept of "reverie" has disappeared from his writing altogether.

An analyst once declared that he'd at last realised that "... we don't really have to like our patients," and maybe there is some truth in that. But I think that we have to be able to emotionally conceive of finding something likeable (ultimately good internal objects), to sense their latent presence in the patient, beyond the defensive shadow of the negative transference.

If we cannot even intuit their presence, then, I would argue, we are not truly *emotionally* motivated to get to know the patient – in spite of "scientific interest" or the need to earn a living.

Then we are not just in danger of projecting envy into the patient, but worse still, of not seeing, and therefore not helping the patient to feel, the love that is being stifled, and which needs "liberation" for the psyche to be healed and creative.

In 1936, Joan Riviere wrote that, particularly with patients whose love is severely stifled;

> The very great importance of analyzing aggressive tendencies has perhaps carried some analysts off their feet, and in some quarters is defeating its own ends and becoming in itself a resistance to further analytic understanding. Nothing will lead more surely to a negative therapeutic reaction in the patient than failure to recognize anything but the aggression in the material.
>
> (p. 142)

My impressions of some of Bion's comments about some of his patients is that sometimes he was capable of using "negative capability" to say to himself, as he listened to his patients, "What's wrong with this story?" – so intent on catching out the liar or psychopath in the patient, that he forgot to ask "Where has Love disappeared to with this patient?" My point is that sometimes this produces a certain callousness in the analyst, under the guise of disinterested helpfulness, and being without memory or desire. But **is** it actually possible, or helpful, not to have a desire to make contact with the loving aspects of another person (perhaps especially a narcissistically crippled patient) in the course of a relationship with them?

When there is a propensity to see a propensity for love in another person, (that is, when we can projectively imagine the existence of good objects in the mind of another person) then we gain an entirely different **type** of knowledge about the person. This is where Hardy's stance of "watchful lovingkindness" – true to Bion's original model of "maternal reverie" – holds loving **and** knowing together in a synergistic, helical, dialectic, as illustrated in Peter Porter's (1994) poem *Into the Garden with the Wrong Secateurs*, where he says:

> Theory One: we need language to invent King Lear.
> Theory Two: we need King Lear to invent language.

And I think it does make a difference if the L-link and the K-link are working synergistically with each other.

The pictures drawn of Richard Nixon, for example, in films by Robert Altman and Oliver Stone invoke totally different levels of emotional responsiveness in the viewer. In the latter, we get to feel Nixon's losses and narcissistic injuries, so we get to "know" him in a more sympathetic, whole-object way, rather than just as the foul-mouthed, bad, screaming infant of Altman's version.

Hardy's "watchful lovingkindness' is not the same as gratifying a patient's instinctual demands, nor need it be unquestioning of tricky or destructive aspects of a patient's narcissism. But it does see things in a person that impatience, dogmatism, and even tolerance and concern and open-mindedness might miss. It works through imaginative loving – an emotional expectation of finding something loving and loveable – as a healthy mother automatically reaches to find the key which unlocks her infant's smile. It seeks out, and contributes to the good objects, through a lively, interested and eliciting intercourse.

"Container-contained" and "negative capability" as concepts are very useful, but, with some patients, they can also 'blind' us because they emphasize the mother's capacity for finding <u>trouble</u> and <u>anxiety</u> in her infant, and then calming it down by processing it emotionally, through her alpha function – the symbolic transformation of psychic pain into the stuff that dreams are made on.

But Hardy's "watchful lovingkindness" is a cognitive-emotional lens, which seeks out, is sensitive to, and focuses on, the loving potentiality in the infant psyche, which needs to be brought out into the light of emotional day by the living responsiveness of further watchful lovingkindness. So if we want to truly know another person we must faithfully give something of ourselves – something more than just observations or open-mindedness – something which will bring about a meeting at all levels. From this perspective, Love has a psychoanalytically functional role which is much more than just a lubricant for a therapeutic alliance, and Bion's concepts of K and L cannot be kept separate. For Bion, we "inherit," through identification with the thoughtful, loving mother, a capacity to process and bear our feelings and for thinking.

For Hardy, we inherit, through an identification with the "watchful lovingkindness" of the parents, the seeds of the ability to take an interest in getting to know the worlds of personality.

Hardy has helped me to think more about exactly how I had to struggle to "grasp" my patient, and through facing this painfully interdependent nature of loving and knowing, I know that I felt better resourced for the next difficult narcissistic patient that I saw after Alexander's termination. I was also able to be more thoughtful about taking on patients where I felt, through the assessment sessions, that my emotional interest would probably stay perfunctory for many years, without "watchful lovingkindness" really being there spontaneously. There was some relief in being able to relinquish the omnipotent idea that I ought to automatically feel this for all potential patients, and in allowing for the possibility that the patient might be "grasped" better by a colleague.

My stance with the severely disturbed narcissistic patients has benefited from my infusion of Hardy's ideas into Bion's. Although difficult to define, it feels something like a recognition of the importance of a psychoanalytic capacity to change the atmosphere between adult and child, where it seems stuck in a mutually defensive disinterest, through increased awareness and emphasis on the living interplay between L and K, which is so subtly and poignantly depicted here by Italo Calvino (1976):

> "The darkness is punctuated with tiny spots of light; numberless fireflies are flickering over the hedges.
>
> 'Filthy creatures, women Cousin …' says Pin.
>
> 'All of them …' agrees Cousin. 'But they weren't always; now my mother …'

'Can you remember your mother, then?' asks Pin.
'Yes, she died when I was fifteen,' says Cousin.
'Was she nice?'
'Yes,' says Cousin, 'she was nice.'
'Mine was too,' says Pin.
'What a lot of fireflies,' says Cousin.
'If you look at them really closely, the fireflies,' says Pin, 'they're filthy creatures too, reddish.'
'Yes,' says Cousin, 'I've never seen them looking so beautiful.'
And they walk on, the big man and the child, into the night, amid the fireflies, holding each other by the hand."

References

Bion, W.R. (1962). *Learning from Experience*. London: Heinemann.
——— (1970). *Attention and Interpretation*. London: Tavistock.
——— (1992). *Cogitations*. London: Karnac.
Calvino, I. (1976). *The Path to the Nest of Spiders*. Trans. W. Weaver. New York: Ecco Press.
de la Mare, W. (1953). In *Collected Poems*. London: Faber and Faber. 1979.
Freud, S. (1909). Notes upon a Case of Obsessional Neurosis. S. E. 10.
Gold, S. (1988). Psychoanalysis and the Acquisition of Knowledge. *Aust. N.Z. J. Psychiatry*, 22: 71–77.
Grotstein, J. (1981). *Do I Dare Disturb the Universe? A Memorial to Wilfred R. Bion*. London: Maresfield.
Hardy, T. (1887). *The Woodlanders*. Penguin. London. 1981.
——— (1895) *Jude the Obscure*. Penguin. London. 1985.
Klein, M. (1946) Notes on some schizoid mechanisms. In: *Envy and Gratitude and Other Works. 1946–1963*. London. Hogarth Press. pp. 1–24.
——— (1961). *Narrative of a Child Analysis*. New York: Dell. 1975.
Meltzer, D. (1988). *The Apprehension of Beauty*. Perthshire: Clunie.
Porter, P. (1994). *Millenial Fables*. OUP. Melbourne.
Riviere, J. (1936). A contribution to the analysis of the negative therapeutic reaction. In *The Inner World of Joan Riviere*. Ed. Hughes. London: Karnac. 1991.

Chapter 13

Distraction – as both an important manic defence, and yet also as a creative unconscious consolation when facing immense depressive or disintegrative states

*Freud wrote to a friend that "I conquered my depression with the aid of a special diet of intellectual matters and now, thanks to the **distraction**, it is slowly healing." But, Pascal's view was that ... "Distraction is the only thing that consoles us for our miseries, and yet is itself the greatest of our miseries. For it is this (distraction) which principally hinders us from reflecting upon ourselves, and which makes us insensibly ruin ourselves, (but) without this we should be in a state of weariness, and this weariness would spur us to seek a more solid means of escaping from it. But diversion amuses us, and leads us unconsciously to death."*

Such is the contagiousness of distraction that it is difficult to discuss without experiencing a blend of the ultra-serious with the seemingly facetious humour of the trivial. This uneasy humour is expressed exquisitely through Tony Blair's ridiculously revealing slip – "weapons of **mass distraction**" – made as the then British prime minister was trying to rationalize an unjustifiably destructive war involvement, to an increasingly sceptical world. So, the idea of distraction as a blatant avoidance of painful or humiliating political truths, is hardly unknown to most people. We even had an apparent virtuoso of this technique tweeting his art out, from his Oval Office. And the internet is full of such gems as: "**10 Ways to Defeat Distraction.**" Of which, my personal favourite is the suggestion that we "… seek out all distracting sites on the internet and block them." (!)

Well, good luck with that.

There are also prayers asking for deliverance from distraction in worshipping God, and so forth. For example, an American pastor/counsellor writes:

> "Our fundamental and most dangerous problem in distraction is in being distracted from God — our tendency to shift our attention orientation from the greatest Object in existence to countless lesser ones. The Bible calls this idolatry. This fundamental attention shift disorders us in pervasive ways. We find our tendency to be distracted from the more important to the less important cascading down, detrimentally affecting our relationships and responsibilities. So, at the deepest level, we are distractible because of our fallen, selfish nature; we have evil inside us."

But, he then, with a somewhat kinder-toned superego, suggests that;

> Our attention often runs to what's important to us. So distraction **can** reveal what we **love**.

I will follow through this apparent two-faced nature of the workings of distraction in, and on, the mind – but there has been surprisingly little attention paid to distraction in the **psychoanalytic** literature, and it is not usually included in our clinician's "checklist" of manic defences, alongside the usual triumvirate of denial, triumph and contempt.

In this chapter I will argue for its (long overdue) inclusion as a manic (or manic-obsessive) defence of significant importance in the disruption of depressive, whole-object (Klein, Bion, Meltzer, Rosenfeld) thinking and of the capacity for mourning and reparation.

However, I also hope to show that there is another side, or vertex, in which the defence of distraction may have a life-protecting, and even creative capability if it is not too cursorily condemned, or dismissed as **merely** destructive, or always serving the manic-destructive cause.

And, as clinicians – with a supposedly free-floating, evenly suspended Freud-Bion-Sherlock reverie-inducing state of mind, we are deliberately focusing our attention away from the specific, to the broader canvas – to hear the unexpected pattern or theme or ringing of far off bells in our counter-transferential minds.

Which of us have not found it useful, even essential, at times to turn away from the detailed content of what a patient is thrusting at us, in order to hear the tone of voice in which it is offered? Is it rushed and manic? Laboured and painful? – as with a difficult birth? Or, stilted and inhibited – with great fear and anxiety? As we listen, we must, somehow- know when to change the "gears of our attention" - without too quickly labelling this as always a purely destructive distraction of mind.

Keeping in mind my suggestion that distraction may be seen as Janus-faced – both as seriously effective manic defence, but also, sometimes, as a helpful guiding light from the unconscious towards what is truly important – I will proffer a brief excerpt from the unnerving social observation comedy *Curb Your Enthusiasm* (2018) which illustrates, amongst many other things, this under-explored manic defence of distraction.

(Of course, it would be better to watch this clip in real time – to get the admixture of comedy and seriousness, and their intermingling rhythm.)

The anti-hero Larry David (a "schlemiel" who is an awkward, stupidly obsessive and "unlucky" person, shaking his fists at the world) is in a therapy session and has just recalled a dream where he is proffered 72 virgins – but, in his typically obsessive way, he counts them and can only see 71. This stops him from enjoying any of the virgins, as he repeatedly counts them, again and again, and again. Then, just as the therapist tries to engage him on this very point, Larry suddenly and urgently states that he cannot abide by the perceived difference in comfortableness between the therapist's chair and his own – the patients.' This, on the one hand, is used as a distraction from taking in and thinking about anything that the therapist confronts him with – but, on the other hand, it may be understood as a creatively unconscious deepening of, and association to, the very issue that the by now exasperated (pseudo)therapist is trying to focus on.

I see this as an interesting **apparent** paradox about the workings of distraction, and its differing conscious and unconscious manifestations.

In this particular, fictitious, example the therapist, (interestingly, but also a distraction, the therapist is played by the same actor whose very fine line of moral corruption is exposed in the series *Breaking Bad*) is way out of his depth – seemingly having no knowledge of, or expertise with, the concepts of transference-countertransference, and unconscious references to the here-and-now patient-therapist relationship. But, nonetheless, for illustrative purposes only, I will use this unlikely, but concise example from a fake consulting room in order to discuss distraction as not **only** an important manic defence which may also play a crucial role in obsessional states of mind (or mindlessness).

In fact, before Melanie Klein's model of psychic "positions" was dovetailed into the typology of *paranoid-schizoid* and *depressive*, she had included "manic-obsessive" as a midpoint – before full depressive guilt was tolerated by the infant mind. But I also want to make a plea for tolerating the actual content of the seeming distraction, as potentially a pointer to further understanding of the **unconscious reasons** for the distraction.

For example, although the Larry David example makes clear the need to retreat from thinking about an obsessive oedipal rivalry, (needing to have every woman for himself before he can enjoy even one) it also illustrates, simultaneously, the opportunity for an unconscious deepening of the **source** of the obsessional anxiety. His immediately distracting focus on the differences in comfort of the chairs reveals an **envy** of the primal object's breast chair, leading to an attack on the worth of what the therapist offers and a sense of begrudging unfairness in the world.

Of course in real life we all dip in and out of distracted states – for better and for worse. (In fact, a few colleagues that knew I was working on this chapter half-joked about offering examples from their own personal lives.) But, a **chronic** inability to stay in touch with, to concentrate, and to reflect upon one's more difficult, complex and painful feelings may seriously impair one's capacity to work through life's immense frustrations, disappointments and grief – and to emotionally develop and grow through the use of thinking to modify one's frustrations, or to avoid endlessly repeating them.

Some clinical examples will further illustrate these issues, where (as with the Larry David snippet) the patient always seems to be focusing on the "wrong" things, in order to avoid thinking through her seemingly most important issues – but staying focused on those issues which would invoke the experience of depressive pain, such as guilt, loss and regret – and I have already briefly alluded to some political uses of distraction as a "convenient" manic defence.

The changing concept of *Manic Defences*

But, first, just a little background on the way manic defensiveness has been construed over the last century. Freud in his paper "On narcissism" (1914), introducing the concept of ego ideal, discussed the relationship between "ideal ego" and the "actual ego," i.e. one in which "ego is measured and secured by one's ego ideal" (p. 93) and that we all need fairly constant **distraction** away from the pain of our falling short of the demands of this ideal. Karen Horney made much of this ongoing failure to actualize our ideal selves, and like Freud, thought that we may spend years **distracting** ourselves away from this pain – as if it meant castration. She felt that liberation from the demands of our (often grandiose and unachievable) ideal selves could free us to accept, or even to love, our **real** self and those of others.

Hinshelwood has attributed the notion of *manic defences* to Melanie Klein, as an extension of Freud's thoughts on mania.

By adopting a triumphantly scornful attitude toward psychic reality the patient uses this kind of defence to avoid the depression associated with the conviction of having destroyed a (good) internal object.

In Mourning and Melancholia" (1916–17g [1915]), Freud wrote:

> In mania, the ego must have got over the loss of the object (or its mourning over the loss, or perhaps the object itself). The manic subject plainly demonstrates his liberation from the object which was the cause of his suffering.
>
> (p. 255)

Karl Abraham elaborated on Freud's view by attributing manic triumphalism to a liberation from the impossible perfectionistic demands of the ego ideal.

In the context of her theories on the depressive position, Melanie Klein emphasized the importance of manic defences for mental life and enriched the Freudian conception of mania by adding the idea of the subject's feelings of guilt concerning the disappearance and destruction of the object.

The manic subject tends to downplay the power of the object, to disdain it, while at the same time maintaining maximum control over objects. Manic defences are typified by three feelings, namely **control, triumph,** and **contempt**.

In her later work (1957) Klein also made it clear that these manic defences were also of major importance in alleviating the awareness and pain of envy.

But importantly, Anne Alvarez (1992) with particular attention to psychotherapy with autistic patients, has stressed the "healthy necessity" and liveliness of that which may first appear as a manic retreat from psychic reality – crucial not to throw out the bathwater of filigree development, and genuine joy, with the gurgling baby's need to protect itself against the overwhelming shock of an "uncompliant" mother and her strangely indifferent world. Indeed, I would go further, and propose that distraction can be an essential ingredient of the creative process – in that, when the conscious contribution is exhausted it may be enormously recharging, and essential, to invigorate the process with contributions from the unconscious mind – something that Jung referred to as *self*, and Freud only hinted at through *sublimation*. I am suggesting that to "distract" oneself – say with a walk, or an inane television programme, or some music – will often allow the unconscious aspects of creation to bring in more subtle connections and links with work that has seemingly halted – what we often call "writer's block". Far from being a genuine block, I believe that this is actually a nodal point, where the creative self is asking to be immersed in unconscious inspiration – where the internal coupling is forging new linkages, beyond mere consciousness and linear, sensible thinking. This is the "stuff" on which dream thoughts are liberated and allowed to merge with, and to infuse, the stuff of ego-logical thinking, with all its causal confinement and paucity of symbolic (Bion calls it *alpha*) enrichment of imagination.

Similarly, before Jung, and later Paula Heimann, *counter-transference* was considered to be a distracting impediment to the analytic process, rather than an extra lantern in the dark cavern of transferential emotional fields with which to see new possibilities, often beyond words.

> Heimann conveys the notion that unconscious transmission in analysis is a two-way street and that the analyst's countertransference should be reconceptualized as a source of knowledge rather than as a mere hindrance to the analytic process.
> Rolnik Jama (2008) (with thanks to P. Maxwell)

Before Melanie Klein simplified her conceptual framework into Paranoid-Schizoid and Depressive Positions (1935) in her *contribution to the psycho-genesis of manic-depressive states* she had initially believed in the existence of a **Manic-Obsessional Position**. In this state of mind, there was some awareness of guilt about the damage to one's good internal objects, but as yet inadequate maturity in bringing to bear one's reparative capabilities. And so, the guilt was experienced more as a persecution, or accusation, rather than anything helpful in mobilizing one's love and concern for the welfare of the loved figures.

The child was tormented by guilt and so had to project blame and responsibility outward into external objects rapidly, or else risk becoming paranoid and filled with the terror of retaliatory punishment. These days we would call this feeling persecuted by guilt. Freud thought that guilt about one's ambivalently loved objects could be channelled healthily into sublimation – which he also saw as the creative foundation of civilization and an expression of Eros in the wider family of humanity.

Sublimation allows emotional work to be done, through symbolic-emotional alpha work, whereas **manic distraction** only allows signposts to the problem, but doesn't continue the working through of unconscious guilt about destructive impulses toward the object of ambivalence. It is always interrupted, in a retreat from the depressive position, where guilt can be evaded by projection onto others (Steiner, 1998).

> There is a massive caravan of destructiveness headed towards our borders – we need to build that wall before good people are destroyed!
> D. Trump (2017)

Manic Denial compared to sublimatory reparation

So, I would propose a necessarily blurry, but crucial, distinction between "sublimatory" distraction which attempts to further the symbolic work of mourning and creation, and true "manic distraction". Always blurry, however – for example, what we call "escapist entertainment" may be used to further the work of sublimatory symbolism where the workings of conscious ego logic have been blocked for fear of being overwhelmed emotionally. I will say more, later, about the implications for thinking about all unconscious defences as having this dual nature – but, only a careful, patient, understanding of detailed associational thinking and transferential linking in the consulting room can clear, or at least think about this apparent blurring in the nature of distraction – between a shallowing manic defence and a deepening associational expanding of the clinical material.

Clinical example of an architect who could only experience, and think about, his feelings when viewing them on a screen, and preferably in the sci-fi mode. He even called this process his "inner sci-fi channel" – where feeling was "indulged" so long as it seemed many light years away from his daily life – which was highly conflicted and confused. But, when highly engaged watching his "Star Trek Discovery," for example, he was deeply emotionally involved and could think about all sorts of emotional conflict – including sexuality, and his ongoing struggles with intimacy vs independence. It would have been quite brutalizing to label this as mere distraction. In fact, he had left a previous therapy because he had been told that he was "too easily distractible."

I would also want to link the use of distraction to Bion's concept of an ***attack on linking***, as being a fundamental breakdown – deliberately so – of the thinking process, whenever this might produce an emotionally painful response – particularly if it is painful or conducive to the discomfort of depressive guilt – and all our usual suspects and adumbrations, such as Oedipal rivalry, separation pains and the need for weaning off one familiar source of nourishment onto a newer, but uncertain one, such as with birth and weaning and leaving home, and so forth.

Thus, it can be seen that while distraction may **seem** like a fairly harmless defence, if it sets in chronically, as a major avenue for avoiding psychic pain, then it will begin to have a distinct effect on one's capacity to think. This is problematic because thinking is also our major way of reducing pain and frustration. But again, if there is a **temporary** use of distraction – which is then used for reflection on one's feelings and defences – then the temporary distraction may, eventually, **aid** thinking and self-reflection, albeit at a more unconscious level.

But, if the distractions accumulate, and become a chronic diversion from the capacity to think about one's feelings, this unconsciously leads to a feeling of deep despair – that one's emotional problems can never truly be thought about or understood.

A patient spoke of never catching up on her tax returns, (immediately following a session where, for the first time in her therapy, she acknowledged not being happy in her marriage, but felt that she had become "addicted to the distraction of buying new things" so couldn't afford to leave) and that this created a deep feeling of disconnection with those around her. She tried to compensate for this by constant involvement with "social" media – but she nonetheless felt others could see that she was always sweeping things under the carpet, and that she wasn't giving to the culture that nurtured her. She produced a dream where she was, indeed, sweeping something under the carpet – but couldn't bear to lift it and see what was under it. She wanted to but each time she tried, a little Eddie McGuire (a well-known spurious quiz show host) kept grinning at her and offering her more and more seductive prizes to lure her away from looking under the carpet. He offered to remove the "trouble" for a "modest price" – but, he wouldn't tell her the price of his "service." His evasiveness made her very suspicious of him, and she had the thought that she could save herself a lot of "trouble" if she just looked and faced down whatever horrible thing might be there. But "Eddie" just kept glaring at her – making it clear that he was not going to give up without a fight. He was very intimidating.

If there is a lifetime of chronic, habituated use of distraction – somewhat like the massive island of plastic, the size of Queensland that lurks in the Atlantic ocean – I believe that a psychic island – perhaps equivalent to Steiner's idea of a "psychic retreat" or Rosenfeld's and Meltzer's idea of an internal perverse narcissistic gang – can form as an enduring unconscious "bypass" structure in the mind, and the capacity for tolerating emotional pain and conflict is drastically curtailed. It is probably a crucial component in the maintenance of bipolar states of mind. But, in real life, distraction and sublimation may often appear in a rather blurred mix of distraction and sublimation – mania and depressive depth, somersaulting over each other in Jack and Jill style, tumbling over each other, again and again – broken crowns alongside pails of quenching water. It is why a work of art can serve as both a working through function for the artist, and yet also as a "weapon of mass distraction," which then only allows **others** to work through with full emotional engagement in the work that has required so much energy and involvement from the artist, writer, or composer. The potential hybridization of life and death instinctual motivation may prove endless, and distraction can work for either side as a "triple agent."

Bernstein maintained that the deployment of attention at any given time is of great importance to analytic work; and he thought that the patient's ability and willingness to pay attention to fleeting thoughts is often a reliable measure of his analytic progress.

> Attention is a very important tool in overcoming repression. The approach of the unconscious toward consciousness elicits a reinforcement of repression. At the same time, there is a deflection of attention toward the outside. This deflection of attention constitutes an important aid to the maintenance of repression. The impelling quality of action, then, may be not only a measure of the instinctual pressure seeking discharge, but may also reflect, from the side of the ego, the urgency of the need for **distraction** as an auxiliary function for the maintenance of repression.

The interpretation of action as distraction fosters the introspective psychic stance so basic a requirement for analytic work. It is this that eventually leads to an understanding of the meaning of behaviour at a given point in time and avoids the possible error of assuming that the significance of an action lies only in its content meaning.

Distraction in socio-cultural matrix

The child in the family in the community in the global village

A couple in their late forties sought my help for an apparently dual-natured problem. Their sexual-romantic life had become an almost non-existent background to their "impossibly busy lives." And also, their son at high school was becoming increasingly "distracted" at school – and in spite of his natural intelligence, was in danger of failing. He was sleeping less and less and would become very threatening if told to stay off his media devices after 11 pm. When his parents tried to disconnect him from these devices, he did – once – punch a hole in his bedroom wall.

Summarising the family's psychological domain in a few bullet points

All are addicted to phones/computer games

- Dad tried to lure me into a conversation about my laptop – which his eagle-eye had detected under some books in a far corner of my room – "they're pretty good those ... have you tried the ...?

    Randolph – wanted to see if I would allow his phone in sessions. I asked him what he thought. He will leave it on standby in case we reached any "dead spots."

    In fact, there had been two recent grand-parental deaths, and Randolph (named after the Hearst-like, money-obsessed father of his father) had been told not to attend either funeral, in case he became "too intense."

- Mother couldn't choose a further learning course, because always she saw a better one – which then distracted her.
- Both parents were always distracted away from intercourse – of any sort.
- Phones seem much more of a threat than potential affairs.
- Both grandmothers were alcoholics – the grandfathers were absent "on the road."
- Mother's mother always told her that children were the biggest distraction in life – you gotta get out from underneath them.
- Mid-session her phone ringer went off loudly with the (very loud) song: *Don't stop thinking about tomorrow!*

We can but only **curb** our distraction – never totally eliminate it - after all – which parent of a curious and zesty toddler could survive a whole day without resorting to some form of distraction, both for the child and for themselves?

But Abrahams noted an interesting difference between the two types of parenting:

"As parents adapt themselves to the proclivities of their infants, quite early parents ... discover that 'fussiness' can be diminished and **distractions** achieved by offering 'things' for inspection and engagement; parents of the second group, on the other hand, discover that they need to offer themselves. When seeking to assert their authority or impose controls, each parent group knows precisely what affective string to pluck and what kind of threat to pose."

(Abrahams, 1978)

And, as I mentioned earlier, even Freud (writing to a friend, as he tries, distractedly to work on his *Interpretation of Dreams*, says:

"I conquered my depression with the aid of a special diet of intellectual matters and now, **thanks to the distraction**, it is slowly healing."

(Freud, 1983. Letters)

"It is a session before a holiday break and on a Monday. The patient asks me if I know someone called "X"—then quickly adds "never mind, don't tell me, I will explain it all to you later." Such a remark was highly unusual for this patient. He went on to complain that his homosexual companion was looking worried and distracted, and "does not seem to know what is going on." He had asked him a question and he complained bitterly that his companion was impossible, because the reply he received suggested five different possibilities. The patient immediately added that he had been to see a doctor about a complaint in a particular area of his body, but the doctor had said that the cause of the complaint was elsewhere. As an aside, he added that this doctor had rooms in the area of my previous consulting room, where the patient used to see me. On impulse, he had gone there because he thought he remembered that a certain friend who practised homeopathy had lived there. He explained in a rambling fashion that the bells indicating the various consulting rooms in the building were not working. By chance, a man who worked in the building came along and told him that his homeopathic friend was no longer there. This man turned out to be working in my old consulting room as a psychotherapist. My patient was amazed and said "this is the man 'X'", and he added "he was dressed most informally, seemed very disorganized ... not like you, very professional and organized in the way you put things to me." It is of course difficult to convey a rather long series of ideas such as this and the atmosphere of it. The analyst's reaction was an awareness of a change in that for this patient this was a lively exchange of ideas, that left the analyst somewhat bemused. He was drawing my attention to a number of related events. He was aware of a companion looking worried and distracted, who gives five different possibilities to an apparently simple question; a doctor who when confronted with one problem suggests the trouble is elsewhere; his memory of a homeopathic friend who seemed to have "self-cures" or one for each separate aspect of the body and finally a rather disorganized and informal psychotherapist. A great deal of work had been done on his sense

of distraction and worry, that he could only feel fleetingly, which gave him the feeling he did not know what was going on.

In this state of mind, he had the greatest difficulty in being able to concentrate and get to the point of a situation. *My patient was not aware that the "worry and distraction" that he described in this situation were* **his**, *and this caused difficulties in his appreciating the nature of his anxieties about the coming holiday break. He had told me that he could not believe he was so worried.* **He located such events in the analyst by projective identification. What he feels confronted by then are those aspects of himself that break up connexions between events and are disorganized, so he is not sure what is going on.**

He broke up the previous week of analytic work that had been related to his anxieties about separation so that he felt that he was presented with five separate possibilities. He found difficulty also in understanding his doctor's advice that one area of his bodily complaint could be **related to another**. *He was able to tell me that* **what he feared most was that he confused everyone around him, i.e. he felt that he had done this to his doctor and to the analyst causing them to appear confused, and what they said to be** *unrelated. His thoughts do not "ring a bell," he cannot make contact with parts of himself or the analyst. He does however feel that an organized aspect of the analyst and his self remain, that allows him to continue the analytic work."*

Goldberg (1987)

Distraction can often, certainly, be a contributing element of K – however, depending on the capacity to **examine** one's distraction – it may eventually lead to a furthering of K – the wish to know more about one's unconscious issues and conflicts. Far from the madding crowd of bread-and-circus manic distractions, there is also the behind-the-scenes bespoke tailoring of dream work and creative defences, readying us for the next day's call to battle with slings, arrows and heartache through the magic repairing of deflated narcissism and love, eternally rejected, disappointed and eventually lost.

My conclusion, therefore, abstracting the ideas in this chapter, and the work of Alvarez (op cit.) – is that **the life and death instincts are not diametrically opposed** – but are helically en-coiled and entwined– and in endless interplay. This means that the whole conception of defences as "enemies" for psychic growth may have to be made more complex. Where a defence is in place, it does shield consciousness from anxiety and pain. But, it may also allow psychic work on that pain to proceed, unconsciously.

Therefore, the role of interpretation is not merely to make one more aware of destructive impulses and diversions – but to also give the patient a chance to join forces with the unconscious's attempt to find the **sources** of potentially crippling emotional pain.

Needless to say, patients arrive at therapy because they are unable to do this for themselves.

I think that too harsh a superego-ish response to distraction can intensify a vicious circle – where manic defences are used because guilt is felt to be unassailable and un-processable, and then the therapist is perceived (usually in identification with a very harsh internal parent) as criticizing the use of manic distraction, rather than aiding in the understanding of its need.

I would like to underline the distinction and similarity between the words *distraction* and **destruction** – almost sonically identical (language never happens by accident – but by perfectly over-determined co-incidents condensing and shaping meaning through sound, culture and deep layers of unconscious resonance with "dancing" symbols and a rhythmic sharing of emotional experience and nuanced intention and purpose. Also, "**distraught**" (also meaning intensely distracted) which suggests that the psyche can be "pulled apart, in anguish" if manic distraction is allowed to totally dominate one's state of mind or mindlessness. So, I don't take lightly my task in also indicating a potentially helpful and positively creative side of the "distraction coin."

Although it is true that (Bion, 1959.):

> "Attention and distraction are simply two morally and culturally charged terms referring to what in reality is the same behavior. We label this behavior distraction when we disapprove of its objects and objectives; and we call it attention when we approve of them."

After all, we say "Free associate! – let your mind become **distracted.**" when we guide our patients towards helping us to understand them. We see this sort of distractedness as allowing faith in the unconscious mind to steer us in integrative directions, and not as getting away from difficult feelings and conflict.

Distraction is a very important, even essential, element of how we tiny humans manage to keep our nerve in such a volatile, fluid and often dangerous world, where the irreversibility and starkness of death and impermanence is sewn into the daily fabric of our lives. I have argued for the clinical dialectical approach of regarding it with caution, but also with respect for the opportunities it may open up if explored patiently.

As a crucial way that we tiny humans manage to keep our nerve in such a volatile, complex and often dangerous world, where the irreversibility and starkness of death and impermanence are sewn into the daily fabric of our lives, it may be time to give distraction due recognition, not only as a major manic defense but also as a potential bridge of light between the conscious and the unconscious in that impossibly human struggle to embrace the wider world.

References

Abrahams, B. (1978). Enduring personality characteristics or adaptations to changing life situations? *Dev. Psychol.*, 14 (4): 39.

Alvarez, A. (1992). *Live Company*. London: Routledge.

Bernstein, S. B. (2015). When the Analytic Patient has Attention Deficit Hyperactivity Disorder. *J. Am. Psychoanal. Assoc.*, 63 (2): 213–245.

Bion, W.R. (1959). Attacks on linking. *Int. J. Psycho-Anal.*, 40: 308–315.

David, L. (2017). *Curb Your Enthusiasm*. CBS-DVD. Roadshow.
Freud, S. (1983). *Complete Collected Letters*. Harvard Press. Boston.
―――― (1914). On narcissism an introduction. In *Standard Edition of the Complete Psychological Works of Sigmund Freud*. Trans. Strachey, J., et al. London: Hogarth Press.
Goldberg, P. (1987). The role of distractions in the maintenance of dissociative mental states. *Int. J. Psycho-Anal.*, 68: 511–524.
Heimann, P. (1950). On counter transference. *Int. J. Psycho-Anal.*, 31: 81.
Hinshelwood, R. (1989). *A Dictionary of Kleinian Thought*. London: Karnac.
Klein, M. (1935). A contribution to the psychogenesis of manic-depressive states. In *The Selected Melanie Klein*. New York: Macmillan. pp. 116–145.
――――(1940). Mourning and its relation to manic-depressive states. *Int. J. Psychoanal.*, 21: 125–153.
――――(1957). *Envy and Gratitude*. London: Penguin.
Meltzer, D. (1973). *Sexual States of Mind*. Perthshire.
Pascal, B. (1979). *Pensées*. (1656). New York: Norton. pp. 164–165.
Rolnik, E. J. (2008). Why is it that I see everything differently? Reading a 1933 letter from Paula Heimann to Theodor Reik. *J. Am. Psychoanal. Assoc.* 56 (2): 409–430.
Rosenfeld, H. (1987). *Impasse and Interpretation*. London: Karnac.
Steiner, J. (1998). *Psychic Retreats*. London: Routledge.
Trump, D. (2017). *NY Times*, New York. January 24, 2017.

Chapter 14

Narcissus Rejects

Unbearable Beauty and the urge to destroy it, in *The Comfort of Strangers*

It seems both a great pity and yet fully plausible that the huge significance of the Aesthetic Conflict (as propounded by Meltzer and Harris Williams in their co-written book "*The Apprehension of Beauty: The Role of Aesthetic Conflict in Development, Art and Violence*" (1988) has not easily been assimilated into "mainstream" psychoanalytic theory. In some cases – for example, Bergmann's (1992) astonishingly misguided review of the book –it has aroused bemusement, bewilderment and annoyance. But such is the magnetic pull and beauty of the theory of aesthetic conflict itself, that an opportunity to speak of its impact in the consulting room must also afford an opportunity to engage more closely with that theory, and to grapple with its implications and interaction with other theories. As with Melanie Klein's theory of unconscious envy, it is a very complex, yet far-reaching concept – affected by, and affecting, almost every aspect of the psyche. Like unconscious envy, the stifling of our capacity to be moved by beauty impinges on the capacity for giving and receiving love – indeed, for faith in the whole world as a benevolent and generous creation of which we are invited to drink in and to enjoy. If we are unable to find, or to enjoy, beauty in our daily worlds, then like Iago, we are doomed to a faithless life of wrecking, cynicism, scavenging and spoiling – a truly joyless and fringe-dwelling experience.

If Marlowe and Shakespeare knew that Beauty was incapable of not provoking,

Your beauty was the cause of that effect;
Your beauty: which did haunt me in my sleep
To undertake the death of all the world,
So I might live one hour in your sweet bosom.

GLOUCESTER (Richard III) Shakespeare

then Chaucer was not all so melodramatic in declaring:

Your two eyes will slay me suddenly
I may the beauty of them not sustain,
So wounded, hit throughout my heart keen ...
Alas! that nature has in you compassed

So great beauty; that no man may attain
To mercy, though he starves for the pain.
So has your beauty from your heart chased Pity
that it avails me not to complain.
For Danger holds your mercy in his chain.

Merciless Beauty Chaucer

Freud intuited, in 1919, that

> "It is only rarely that a psychoanalyst feels impelled to investigate the subject of aesthetics, even when aesthetics is understood to mean not merely the theory of beauty but the theory of the qualities of feeling. He works in other strata of mental life and has little to do with the subdued emotional impulses which, inhibited in their aims and dependent on a host of concurrent factors, usually furnish the material for the study of the aesthetic."
>
> Freud, S. *The Uncanny* (1919, p. 219)

Ovid (*Metamorphoses*) was aware of Beauty's transfixing and metamorphic capability, for if we truly apprehend Beauty then we must bear the provocation of our rawest feelings, without destroying the aesthetic impact – which becomes the lifeblood of our growing selves – our capacity for love, hopefulness and gratitude. But the ability of Beauty to transform and to work its effects in an emotional way, were rarely mentioned in the transference/counter-transference field of psychoanalytic "nuts and bolts" work until Donald Meltzer and Meg Harris Williams introduced *The Apprehension of Beauty*.

> The ordinary devoted mother presents to her ordinary beautiful baby a complex object of overwhelming interest, both sensual and infra-sensual. Her outward beauty ... bombards him with an emotional experience of a passionate quality, the result of his being able to see [her] as 'beautiful'. But the meaning of his mother's behaviour, of the appearance and disappearance of the breast and of the light in her eyes, of a face over which emotions pass like the shadows of clouds over the landscape, are unknown to him.
>
> Meltzer (1988, p. 22)

With the scent of such troubling "aesthetic doubt" in the wind, the baby might instead reverse the gears of development and dismantle (Meltzer – autistic states) such a differentiation by sticking only to the surface and physical appearance of the beautiful mother in what Meltzer calls "adhesive identification." However, this will always interfere with what Grotstein calls the quest for the *Object of Destiny*, which I take to mean, an aesthetic, loved object who inspires awe, but who also **reciprocates** the feelings, so that one gathers a similar interest in one's **own** internal mysteries – probably the most important factor, apart from mental suffering, that brings a patient to analysis. Such an object may never be found externally, but its beatific Beatrice-Muse qualities, internally, give not only eternal hope and faith but also an inspirational fuel to explore and to enjoy the mysterious, in both the external and internal worlds.

Hamlet and, more recently, Inspector (Endeavour) Morse do experience great difficulty in believing the sincerity of such reciprocation. With Morse – his aesthetic response to certain women (particularly their musical voices) blights his capability for clear reasoning and deduction about murder investigations, in the face of serious danger to his life. It also interferes with his capacities for successful long-term intimacy, because he is too much in awe to attend to both his and her "lesser" needs. Alcohol then serves to dull the aesthetic pain.

Hamlet cannot bear to identify with Ophelia's pain (of unreciprocated love), which she succumbs to in regression to the womb of watery death.

In this chapter, I will try to adumbrate some primary component hues in the white light of the Harris Williams-Meltzer concept of "aesthetic conflict," and then give some very condensed examples of each of these – both clinically and through film and literature. I will also make a few comments about the inter-relationship of aesthetic conflict and narcissism.

Theoretically, the emotional wellsprings of aesthetic conflict can be segregated, artificially, although in the real life of the mind, they always mix and flow and congeal in varying admixtures and proportions for each individual, and in each new moment of passionate engagement, and its avoidance.

The particularly important strains of aesthetic conflict that I will illustrate here are:

1 The transient, evanescent, ephemeral nature of Beauty invokes **depressive** pains of loss and an apprehension of mortality and limitation in the face of Death and time and Oedipal restriction.
2 The fear of **submitting** and helplessly **surrendering**, to Beauty – in order to apprehend it. One must submit to faith in O(Bion) and therefore lay oneself open to "catastrophic" change. This may be experienced as wounding or castration.
3 One always risks the yearning, anguished pain of **un-reciprocation**.
4 Beauty may lead to **danger** – unleashing the terror of losing one's self, soul (Faust) or even life.
5 Envy and **awe of the *Creator*** must be born, in the light of a realization of the fearful asymmetry between oneself and the "Godhead."

I will now sketch out some detailed descriptions of these components, using some clinical material and a mélange of examples from film and literature. Because every clinical struggle with aesthetic conflict is highly personal and idiosyncratically esoteric, I have taken the risk of using an accumulation of varied snippets from all of these sources to build a picture of the above five components in gestalt form. But the reader must be prepared to take a kind of magic carpet ride, in good faith, rather than be presented with very lengthy, or inappropriate, case material from a single source.

Two clinical examples

I want to briefly describe a session with a patient who had been fighting her own curiosity about using the couch for two years – saying that she couldn't possibly use it because my room was so ugly that it was impossible to properly trust me. (Further elaboration was firmly resisted.)

She had arrived as a somewhat lost soul – although very confident and assertive on the surface. There was something about her, and her rather meandering way of speaking, together with a meandering choice of non-career (as a "puppet-master") that led me to see her as somewhat indulgent, and this was indeed her worst fear of how others might see her. She felt very emotionally deprived of parental interest and of physical affection of any sort – yet strangely, I struggled to **feel** much pity for her seemingly quite sad struggle to find love in the world. But she had fallen in love intermittently in her twenties, which enabled her to move out from her constricted, un-giving family and make some lasting friendships. This gave her a great deal of confidence, and she felt, at last, that she was important, as a human being – and that some people in the world experienced her as beautiful.

But her closest friend had recently made a serious suicide attempt, and it got her thinking that her own life was "passing her by," and that she needed to know herself better, to find out what she was "really like."

She had recently become extremely interested in puppets – that they could help her to "get things out". Indeed, I often felt used in this way by her in the countertransference – although she often accused me of treating her this way as someone to be controlled and at the whim of another person. I suggested that a move to the couch (her physical gesturing had become quite stifling for my capacity to think about what she was saying) would deepen that concern, and she grinned: "You betcha."

It eventually emerged that what had really brought her towards help was the suicide attempt of her best friend. She had imagined that this was because of her own wanting to be with a lover, (who was felt to have particularly beautiful skin), and had mentioned a planned holiday with him to the friend, just before the friend's attempt. She had told her that she was "smitten like a kitten!"

When after several months of work on her confusion about who wanted to control whom, she finally steeled herself to make the leap into hyper-trust, and as she hit the couch she turned to face me – beaming, as she looked around, and said that she'd been a fool because from the new perspective the room looked quite beautiful – and why had she never noticed before!

Then she produced a dream, seemingly in the wake of finally ditching the now "extremely parasitic" boyfriend with "immaculate skin."

Dream

She climbed up into an attic that was "undiscovered" – but everything was covered in a dusty decrepit imitation velvet coating which was a lurid green colour, and crawling with parasites. She knew that the objects under the coating were very valuable and beautiful, and potentially her own, but she needed someone to help her carefully remove the coverings so that the objects wouldn't be contaminated – and this reminded her of farm animals who lick the sticky stuff from the womb of their newborn babies, or newborn kittens. She was clearly moved by the dream and was crying.

Then she had a massive sneezing fit and asked if I had any tissues.

She said: "Sometimes I just feel soaked in sad!"

And for the first time, I started to really imagine her as loveable – something that I hadn't really felt so confident about before that moment – I wasn't really feeling that we were "on the same side." Although, from time to time, I was still tempted to see her as ridiculous, particularly when she described her "performance art" – her latest project being to dress as a Dodo, and to flap her wings at passing strangers. She had spent quite a bit of money handing out protest stickers, with quite nondescript slogans on them, and pasting them on lamp posts in various suburbs, including my own. One such, for example, was: "Birds are beautiful and useful."

Example 2

My second brief clinical note concerns a middle-aged doctor who suffered for many years from what he called a "low-level, grey depression". His tone of voice was perpetually flat and deadening, (quite literally, mono-tonous) and he complained quite bitterly that he had a dead-grey car, with "no grunt – its boringly reliable ... I have grey everything!"

He said that his mind was "suffused" with a very painful, excruciating memory. It comprised his father coming home from work one night and going straight to bed, complaining of an awful headache. He was left ("alone") with his mother, who explained that it was a special wedding anniversary, and she looked inconsolable. He felt utterly "desolate."

"She just kept looking **through** me."

Immediately following an incident at a beach, where I had apparently walked straight past him with no acknowledgement, he brought a "ghastly" dream of dreading his mother, who had her back turned to him – she was seen to be nursing a very deep gash in her belly, but the patient didn't know whether to walk away or to help – or whether or not he had in some way **caused** the wound. She was turning grey, and near death – and he was very relieved to wake up, and to hear birds chirping "so enthusiastically."

He was very reluctant to associate with this dream, and I was left wondering whether, in fact, his mother had lost a baby before his birth, severely impeding her capacity to enjoy him and be enlivened by him. But even months later, he was groaningly reluctant to ask her such a potentially "knifing" question.

In my counter-transference, over several painstaking years, I often felt painfully bored, and that the relationship had become a tediously contractual relationship. Every interpretation seemed correct, but never particularly enlivened him – and was either met with a robotic "but ..." or "yes, but how is that supposed to help me?" If I occasionally asked why he wished to continue, he would plead that I was at least making things endurable. When I asked if that was necessarily a good thing, he said that it had to be, because death was "nothing at all" and that when he left each session he felt a little bit better and more "charged up to face things." He apologized for not properly conveying any gratitude or sense of progress. I responded by saying that he found it hard to imagine that he had anything good to offer me that could potentially enliven us both. He placed his thumb in his mouth and was silent for the remainder of the session. But it was a very full silence.

In the following session, close to an approaching holiday break, he brought another dream. But the dream was remembered only after some restless thrashing on the couch and a very atypical outburst. He was usually quite composed, but the night before he had watched a documentary about sex addicts and Donald Trump.

> *... Not many people could actually stand to look at a beautiful woman and just enjoy her beauty – it has to lead to sex and lust and wanting to DO her – it absolutely **must**, or you can't be a real man. I know this is sort of fucked – but beauty is actually destructive, you know – it stiffs (meant to say "stuffs") up people's lives and just ruins simple pleasures – its God's worst invention – I mean why would you DO that to us? We're just innocently trying to enjoy our lives and then you get skewered by this whole new dimension – that's just – just impossible to manage! I can see why people want to become soldiers ... I really can! He noted his surprise at seeming to defend Trump.*

Then, immediately, he remembered a dream.

Dream

The scene, he slowly realized, was in Hong Kong, and he realized that he was on holiday and free to roam wherever he pleased. He had been there many times in real life, on business, and always found it "samey" after the first day. But this version of Hong Kong was "suffused" with stark, purplish El Greco skies – and was utterly fascinating, and every turn of his head brought a new and surprisingly stunning vista. There was a mysterious form of lightning moving across the city, which kept showing different facets and highlighted ever new things to look at, and it was all quite stunning. He was totally gripped by the scene, unlike ever before in his life.

(He paused telling the dream to note that, in fact, he'd looked up the word "vista" in the morning, and was interested to see that it could mean either an interesting view or a new life horizon – like a new career path opening up – a total contrast to how he usually felt – which was to be weighed down by sameness and lack of interest in anything.)

But then, back in the dream –

There had been a death, perhaps a murder – and he started to feel guilty and furtive and wondered whether or not he should hide from the authorities or "come clean" – even though he didn't really know if he had murdered anyone, or not.

In the next session he talked a lot about an old friend from school with whom he'd lost touch, but who was now staying with him – and he spoke of how he saw

Melbourne quite differently when showing the friend around – the city seemed much richer, subtle and more interesting than when he wandered around aimlessly by himself. (He had spent a lot of time in his twenties doing such in Europe – visiting many places that he'd thought he should see, and which should have inspired or stimulated him and literally brought him to life – but he always heard a voice in his head saying "Is that all?"). I reminded him of the dream, and again he put his thumb in his mouth and became thoughtfully silent. However, this time he was nodding – which let me know that he was reflecting.

In the ensuing months, he began to take more of an invigorated interest in the relationship with his daughter, which had previously been mainly a dutiful relationship – as was his own "contractual obligation" marriage. He said, "I don't think I ever realized that she is **actually** quite beautiful. I was always suspicious of people saying that about their own children – like it was part of the deal – you just have to see your kids as beautiful – to force you to look after them … I now even feel a bit guilty for enjoying looking at her. I think she's noticed, and she gives me this smile. Sometimes it cracks me open."

Also, rather astonishingly, he had commenced Roller Derby training over the break, and said that it was exhilarating to "throw my weight around." He had not previously told me that the one place he felt free as a teenager was roller skating at his local rink. Apparently, he was very talented but stopped suddenly after accidentally knocking over a woman. His best friend had yelled at him that "she could have been pregnant!" Interestingly, it was only after throwing his weight around in the session with the rant about Beauty that he felt free to revive this robust sport.

When I mentioned that he now trusted that I was robust enough to handle his aggression, he joked (half-joked): "Watch it buddy!"

I hope that this very condensed example shows clearly, particularly with the *Hong Kong* dream, that progress in one's experiencing the world as containing more beauty and interest (K) immediately summons the superego police and intensifies anxiety about one's (unconscious) destructive "anti-beauty" impulses and their consequences. Such impulses are aroused usually through a very idiosyncratic mix of jealousy (as Meltzer stresses – the infant mind cannot trust that the physical beauty of the object is fully concordant with its inner "fickleness," envy, fears of letting go, separation pains of dependency and needing to submit, and massive fears of being changed, forever, by experiencing the full, thrilling impact of the aesthetic object.

I would like to mention here, in passing, a particularly thought-provoking, moving but disturbing film by Spielberg (2001), *Artificial Intelligence,* which tells of a futuristic android-child that is programmed to feel. This means that it attaches to its human mother, and feels exquisite pain if his love for her is not reciprocated, or is given to his rival brother. He spends a lifetime (in fact thousands of years) searching for this lost, non-reciprocating mother, who has in fact died many years before him, but he is eventually "granted" his wish to have her live again, although only for one day. Some analysts (Gabbard, for example) view this day – where he is, at last, given his mother's full reciprocated love and attention, as a blatant Oedipal transgression, a mere "wish-fulfilment" – but it could be seen as the child's need to revisit the aesthetic mother, to have her reciprocate, so that she can be internalized as a **beautiful, dreaming object.** It is significant that only after experiencing this day, the android (Pinocchio-like) now-real boy begins to **dream**, and thus becomes truly human.

But, in contrast, we now turn to a very different cinematic and literary situation, where Beauty leads to mortal danger.

Dangerous beauty in *The Comfort of Strangers*

Ian McEwan (writer), Harold Pinter (screenplay), Paul Schrader (director)

A couple (Colin and Mary) are revisiting Venice where, four years earlier, they had fallen in love. They seem now to be at an impasse, in the midst of an unspoken conflict that has kept them undecided about long-term commitment – mainly about struggles with autonomy, commitment, independence and jealousies. – They become entangled (both physically and through projective identification) with a malicious, psychotic and sadomasochistic couple who masquerade as good Samaritans – but who, in fact, are their enthralling executioners. The centre of gravity of both the story and the film is the exploration of Colin and Mary's fascination with the perverse couple – whose lack of aggressive expressive inhibition is both aphrodisiacal and terrifying for Colin and Mary. But the issue of concern for this chapter is how the two couples try to deal with the problem of Beauty – how to contain the urge to control and to destroy the aesthetic object, within the bounds of exciting sexuality, and sanity. None of the four succeed – but, arguably, the writer, the director and the screenplay author (Harold Pinter) do, in that they allow us a reflective, highly emotional (if upsetting) space to reflect on these issues.

Both the story and the film explore the (literally) knife-edge struggle between admiring and enjoying beauty, and its mutual acknowledgement of us, and wishing to maim or to destroy it.

Colin and Mary begin to discover the perversity of the older couple – it is made very clear to them that they are endangered – that they are being "hunted" and stalked and that it is Beauty itself which is the prey. But we soon learn that encounters with the older couple are aphrodisiacal to the younger couple, and that the latter are indeed harbouring quite similar, if not more cruel, and fascistic fantasies about each other's beauty. They do not just wish to control or maim each other, but to destroy each other in a cruel sexuality of torture.

> "They took to muttering in each other's ear as they made love, stories that came from nowhere, out of the dark, stories that produced moans and giggles of hopeless abandon, that won from the spellbound listener consent to a lifetime of subjection and humiliation. Mary muttered her intention of hiring a surgeon to amputate Colin's arms and legs. She would keep him in a room in her house, and use him exclusively for sex, sometimes lending him out to friends. Colin

invented for Mary a large, intricate machine, made of steel, painted bright red and powered by electricity; it had pistons and controls, straps and dials, and made a low hum when it was switched on. Colin hummed in Mary's ear. Once Mary was strapped in, fitted to tubes that fed and evacuated her body, the machine would fuck her, not just for hours or weeks, but for years, on and on, for the rest of her life, till she was dead and on even after that, till Colin, or his solicitor, switched it off. Afterwards, once they were showered and perfumed and sat sipping their drinks on the balcony, staring over the geranium pots at the tourists in the street below, their muttered stories seemed quite tasteless, silly, and they did not really talk about them."

In a sense, then, it is ultimately made clear that the hesitation in their commitment to each other as a couple is their fear of mutual destruction, in the face of being tortured by each other's beauty. But they need not have worried – since the perverse couple enacts murder for them.

So – while Meltzer stresses the agony of non-reciprocation, there is also the (Kleinian) dreadful anxiety of engaging intimately and passionately with the aesthetic object and facing one's (unconscious) wish to destroy it – particularly its "unity of form" with its beautiful, if transient, integrity – its capacity to transfix our soul, which provokes and musters an intense, usually unconscious, wish to retaliate. (As the goddess Diana wished to hunt the man Acteon, who hunted her beauty, resenting his intrusion as stalking foray, not foreplay.)

But there are numerous vivid examples from Marlowe and Shakespeare:

> ... *his love was an eternal plant*
> *Whereof the root was fix'd in virtue's ground,*
> *The leaves and fruit maintain'd with beauty's sun,*
> *Exempt from envy, but not from disdain ...*   Warwick (H6, part 3)

> *O happiness enjoy'd but of a few! And, if possess'd, as soon decay'd and done*
> *As is the morning's silver-melting dew against the golden splendor of the sun!*
> *An expired date, cancell'd ere well begun:*
> *Honour and **beauty**, in the owner's arms,*
> *Are weakly fortress'd from a world of harms.*   Richard II

Ultimately, I believe this to be (Milton's) Satan's problem with creation – he is ultimately a very envious baby who cannot stand for God and the infant Job to gaze lovingly at each other – much as Iago cannot bear to see Desdemona and her twin admirers Othello and Cassius to be producing such an intense field of admiration and beauty – and Oberon (*MSND*) is similarly overwrought by thoughts of Titania and her changeling infant.

As we know – the Iago-part of Othello gives way, and together they do destroy their beautiful wives, together with their rich and rare and much-needed admiration of themselves as "beautiful babies."

Oberon holds back from the brink – and Leontes (*WT*) bursts the brink, seemingly losing all that he loves as beautiful, but is given a second chance at reparation by his (somewhat condescending) Paulina superego.

Unconsciously, Beauty – with its capacity to disarm the "male" and to bring the conquering Troilus–Greeks and imperialistic Rome-Caesar-Antony to their knees and inward swords – may be perceived as a kind of "castration" of the Will. And the male mind must either submit, whereby the submission itself is both enlivening and beautiful (*Parsifal*), or alternatively, regress to narcissistic, or autistic states of mindlessness in order to keep the beauty at the surface, thereby destroying the inner depths of its mystery – like Ahab. Meltzer (1988) noted that this is akin to destroying one's inner compass, sextant, and Muse.

The vulnerability of baby Troilus (in Shakespeare's *Troilus and Cressida*) to swooning over mother Cressida is made plain here:

TROILUS

O that I thought it could be in a woman
*... Outliving beauty's **outward**, with a mind*
That doth renew swifter than blood decays!
Or that persuasion could but thus convince me,
That my integrity and truth to you
Might be affronted with the match and weight
Of such a winnow'd purity in love;
How were I then uplifted! but, alas!
I am as true as truth's simplicity
*and simpler than the **infancy** of truth.*

Her bracing answer is:

In that, I'll war with you. **CRESSIDA**

This shines backward onto, and is illuminated by, the whole metaphor of warring mistrust between the Greek and Trojan nations, in the face of their war of pride over who rightfully "owns" Beauty, in the form of Helen as property-wife. It is a more serious form of war than Oberon and Titania's mock war over possession of a changeling child. And so anxious mistrust is borne of the infantile awareness that the beautiful exterior of the mother's body, may not run exactly parallel with her inner thoughts and desires – just as Leontes (*The Winter's Tale*) cannot bear this massive tension at the point of his wife's preoccupation with her young (Mamillius) son, and the growing daughter inside her, and her friendly overtures to his childhood friend (and rival) Polixines.

The wish to damage the beautiful object derives from its unreliability and impermanence. In its original form, the breast, being the solution to the rupture of the birth, now becomes a traitor and is revealed to be part of the conspiracy of nature as a constantly teasing and beguiling impermanence and evanescence. But the issue of the beautiful object's fickleness, I think, is often driven by one's beginning to notice that one's **own** feelings of love can be somewhat tidal or unpredictably volatile – and so it dawns that perhaps the loved object's love is just as fluid. (This might be illustrated, for example, by the ever-changing light moving over the vista, in the *Hong Kong* dream.) The loving eyes of the beautiful mother will always blink.

So – the Aesthetic Agony consists of a strange brew of envy, love, admiration, jealousy and passionate, vigorous wishes for physical engagement, where the reciprocity cannot be waited for, through faith. And thus, the knife-edge between surrendering to Beauty (to let oneself be "slain" by it, and to fully submit to the catastrophic change that it magnetizes) and slaying the object by dismembering its unity, and therefore dampening it's aesthetic impact – for example, from beauty to porn, or from artwork to entertainment. We sometimes call the tension between the passionate impulse to engage, and the wish to destroy the beautiful object of desire "sexual tension". But sexuality is only part of it. Similarly, we describe the intensely aggressive wish to penetrate the mystery of beauty, Lust. The "remembered form" of the breast becomes a source of hope for new relationships and loved objects – but it is probably never fully trusted again. The hands that forged the Tyger are always feared – whatever has been created can be removed – and the story of Job is an attempt to come to terms with just that sort of a God. Faith in its "re-newness" takes a lifetime of love and loss, and runs parallel with one's internal capability for renewing love in, and from, one's good objects.

Envy of the Creator Tyger Tyger, burning bright...

I noted earlier that Milton's Satan has a big problem with creation. But William Blake's *Tyger* poem really lays bare those feelings that were unbearable, in the face of infinite creative might. Of course, the fearful beauty of Blake's little poem is in the way that it creeps up from out of nowhere, like a tiger, and pounces on the unsuspecting reader, who is thinking that the poem is about the tiger.

It is not.

It is about (feelings for) the Creator, and the awesome force of creative-combining imagination which forges with its *immortal hand-eye* – its unimaginable beauty and hammer-firing trembling power, its furnace mind, far beyond any fear of a mere tiger's bright symmetrical eyes. This is truly awe in the face of the most unimaginably fearsome conceptual beauty of all - the mind of the Creator – only sensible to our finite minds through gulping reverential terrible wonder, or wondrous terror.

At a **later** (more Oedipal) stage of development, in comparison to the earliest need for godlike parents to be a massive container of nameless dread, this Creator is experienced, unconsciously, (see Harris Williams and Waddell, The *Chamber of Maiden Thought,* 1992) as the *combined parental object*, or internal couple, and will therefore always arouses some degree of Oedipal longing and limitation and guilt about the wish to intrude into, or to destroy, the couple.

I want to pause here, briefly, to recapitulate the array of cognitive-emotional factors that demand apprehension so early in life, and that seem to constitute the heart of "aesthetic conflict." These are core pillars of aesthetic "resistance" of which the aim is to anaesthetize the emotional impact of the aesthetic object – particularly, since one's feelings are not under rational control.

1 **Depressive pain,** because Beauty is always experienced as symbolic of the ephemeral, and therefore presages our own mortality.

Turner (says Ruskin), " ... was without hope: he could not conceive final victory; he could not conceive the rose without the worm, beauty without decay. The ... smaller serpent-worm, it seemed, he could not conceive to be slain. In the midst of all the power and beauty of Nature, he still saw this death-worm writhing among the weeds." (7.420).

As the notes to the Turner Bequest point out:

There seemed through all his life to be one main sorrow and fear haunting him - a sense of the passing away, or else the destructive and tempting character, of beauty. The choice of subject for a clue to all his compositions, the 'Fallacies of Hope,' marked this strongly.

(p. 159)

2 We must submit by **surrendering** the urge to possess or to projectively (and protectively) control the **mystery** of the Beauty. To submit fully to the passions of love and hate and curiosity is to leave our narcissistic infant selves openly helpless, and, unconsciously, we often experience this as a form of castration.

In Shakespeare's *Pericles*, brave (or foolish) knights submit to (likely) death in order to claim the possession of beauty.

"I live in Hope" Is Pericles' motto – and he is neither slain totally by beauty nor wishes to slay it. But he has faith in Goodness and "divine will." Unlike the torrid, tempestuous, stumbling King Lear:

You nimble lightnings, dart your blinding flames
Into her scornful eyes! Infect her beauty,
You fen-suck'd fogs, drawn by the powerful sun,
To fall and blast her pride!
     King Lear Act III

Even more vengeful courses are plotted, obsessively, by the castrated captains, Hook (in *Peter Pan)* and Ahab (in *Moby Dick*.) Both, in turn, projectively experience Beauty as a voracious, devouring and vengeful water beast.

3 Toleration of (almost) **unbearable jealousy** and the gnawing suspicion that adoring admiration of the beauty may not be **reciprocated** (and certainly not continuously). It can leave one feeling painfully alone and unlovable, or ugly.

(Iago, Richard III, *Beauty and the Beast*, or Oberon-Bottom – feeling like an "ass".)

Mitrani (2008), however, notes:

In part, as a result of that last conversation with Tustin, I have arrived at the conclusion that the resolution of what Meltzer called "the aesthetic conflict" might be predicated, at least in part, upon the capacity of the mother to contain the baby's reverence and awe of her, along with her own capacity for tolerating her baby's hatred, envy, and terror of loss. It might be said that the apprehension of beauty (Meltzer 1988) is linked to the existence – at the core of the inner sphere of the personality – of a container, not just for our painful experiences, but for those joyful ones as well; a containing object with the capacity to endure not just our feelings of hatred toward the object (and therefore toward the self), but one that is enduring of and resonating with those loving feelings felt toward the perceived external object, one in which the capacity for realistic self-love and esteem are rooted.

But,

4 Even when Beauty does reciprocate, the impulses it arouses are felt to be very **dangerous** as they threaten to destroy the object of beauty, and oneself – as I have illustrated above, with *The Comfort of Strangers*.

Love is a breach in the walls, a broken gate,
Where that comes in that shall not go again;
Love sells the proud heart's citadel to Fate.
But they know love grows colder,
Grows false and dull, that was sweet lies at most.
Astonishment is no more in hand or shoulder,
But darkens, and dies out from kiss to kiss.
All this is love; and all love is but this.
Rupert Brooke (1912, p. 112)

5 Unbearable envy of the awesome *Creator* of Beauty – and/or jealousy of the combined couple.

I have written in more detail about the latter in the chapter *The Wrecking and Re-Pairing of the Internal Couple,* and see the above Blake poem re the former.

Fortunately, the healthy enough infant will rapidly develop capabilities for symbolizing these horns of the aesthetic dilemma, and as Meltzer and Harris Williams have prefigured – it is in the grip of Beauty that L, H, K and the terrifying but wondrous need for faith in O are first roused and aroused – and in that wake, dreams may come, and fresh new wholes may be born. But under the pressure of the five components of aesthetic conflict that I have outlined, the negative grid is engaged – the world of anti-feeling.

This may even become **minus faith in O** – epitomized by Milton's Satan, taunting and mocking the God who creates even Tigers.

There is a truly wondrous scene in P. J. Hogan's film of Barrie's *Peter Pan* where the repressible Captain Hook (usually depicted as the split-off envious, jealous, uncoupled father – forever persecuted by a voracious crocodile of time and insatiable oral greed – catches Peter and Wendy in wonderment of their discovery of a beautiful fairy-like couple dancing in the centre of a forest glade. He is not just mildly bemused by it (the double couple) he is utterly bewildered – incomprehensive, and inapprehensive. All that comes to his impoverished orphan (lost boy) mind is that he is all alone – while Peter has found "a Wendy." Later, in the same scene, Peter and Wendy are inspired into love for each other and also begin to dance. But when Wendy asks Peter to say what he really feels, he denies that he has swooned into love with her, and insists that he doesn't even know what it is, and has never ever been in love. (Indeed, never-land could easily mean **never** fall in love with a mother who might abandon you, or fall in love with someone other than you, and leave you feeling like a "lost boy.") He becomes very Hook-ish in his retreat from untrustworthy Beauty.

But, more hopefully, a budding adult part of the mind will expand its grasp of whole objects and will begin to apprehend a more far-reaching meta-level of integrated aesthetic appreciation. When feelings of awe foment (as perfectly illustrated in Blake's transfer of awe for tiger into terrified gratitude for the Creator in his famous poem) feelings towards the source of the beauty, we experience some form of spirituality or religious reverence. For many, this may become a need to worship a deity or Mother nature – but the true sense of awe and reverence and gratitude that this summons in the ever-forming self is always threatened by the regressive, charismatic, seductive, golden calf pull of a political (fascist) with the "star-quality" of a magazine (graven) image idol. Under that sway, every promise is excitingly "awesome" and depressive tears are "walled off" in Trump-ish triumph of a pseudo-Godhead, who has no head at all. The combined object of inspiration is replaced by a narcissistic donkey, promising everything and braying "greatness."

This recalls, for me, the seemingly odd addendum that Meltzer made to the conclusion of "*The Apprehension* ..." where he seems aware that alpha function and mindlessness are also worthy of a place when considering the "array" of mixed anxiety and inspiration that Beauty provokes in the growing mind of the baby. I'd speculate that Meltzer must have been increasingly aware that the aesthetic conflict underpinned so many other mental-emotional capabilities, and that he could only outline an intimation of these, by the end of the book. Interestingly, nearer to the end of his life he became interested in thought disorder. Hook (and Iago and Ahab) are not just annoyed by Beauty – they are also made stupid (struck dumb) in its face – to the extent that they destroy what they love – their daily beauty. Meltzer's

(1987) paper, *Concerning the Stupidity of Evil* indicated that in the face of unbearable Beauty, Iago-Othello and Ahab-Hook, become self-destructive idiots, sans K, sans L and sans faith in O.

Insofar as individuals have sacrificed their capacity for passionate response to the beauty of the world, they are prey to envying others who have a "daily beauty in their lives," an inner beauty. But here again, stupidity mistakes outward form for inner beauty and sees "secrets of success" instead of a "heart of mystery."

Finally, a few brief comments about the aesthetic conflict and narcissism.

Narcissus rejects

It is worth noting something painfully obvious by now. The mother who is herself narcissistically damaged will always find it somewhat difficult to fall in love with her baby. The enjoyment of mutual love – swapping smiles and musical phrases – (like Leontes in *The Winter's Tale*) may then be viewed suspiciously, as if the baby is "stealing" love for its own greed or gratification, without giving its radiant joy and newness back to the mother. In the consulting room, this is often felt to be the greedy, selfish therapist – taking money and praise, while denuding and exploiting the helpless baby, who is asked to give up everything of value to the therapist. Furthermore, these valuable gifts from the patient are felt to be shared with someone else (a partner, or rival children) with great and never-ending enjoyment, like stolen booty from Aladdin's cave.

Narcissus cannot conceive of himself as being an enticing beauty to Echo, or to anyone. He has not known maternal reciprocation of his infant self – and thereby is prey to falling in love with himself, without realizing that it **is** indeed himself. Thus, he cannot identify with Echo's falling in love with an other. (Mind you, her communication skills are fairly limited.) It takes a great adult maturity – often unachieved – to continue enjoying the beauty of the loved object in spite of its indifference to our needs. It is extremely difficult, at times, to discern the difference between such maturity and self-destructive masochism in martyring oneself to the object for the supposed self-glorification that is seemingly promised – submission to a mindless tyrant who charismatically summons one to "the cause."

To enjoy mutual love, we must – at least somewhat – be able to enjoy sharing our own beauty with another – to, however briefly or incredulously, enjoy that another being enjoys us. But we may try to spoil that enjoyment – being unconsciously envious of it – or see ourselves as an ass, beguiling the spell-bound Titania. **Or**, we may just not believe it, or even see it, when we have never been able to identify with, or bask in the eyes of, an adoring mother, if deprived of it in infancy. It is harrowing music of lost love, which turns out to be the incapacity to fall in love because the narcissist rejects it. But the narcissist is not fully **aware** of their rejection of love from others – and yet tragically, and ironically, love seems to be all that they crave, or want to know on Earth. The unconscious projection of rejection into others is a way of attempting to ease the pain of feeling the vulnerable infant gaze unmatched in the eyes of the mother. The aim is to unceasingly "echo" (projectively identify with) that pain in others, and some as fragile as Ophelia do not survive, or are turned to stone or ice internally, and dead to Beauty and its inspiring passion.

I hope that I have begun to show that the Meltzer-Harris Williams conception of *aesthetic conflict* not only extends Melanie Klein's work on the stifling effects of unconscious envy but also puts envy in its place, alongside the other sometimes crippling, sometimes inspiring, facets of which the conflict is comprised. I conclude with a reminder of the exquisitely apt, yet ambiguous, choice of the word "apprehension" in the title of Meltzer and Harris Williams' navigational pointer in the vast star field of Psychoanalytic Aesthetics that is yet to come. We must live with, or at least partly **subdue** our apprehension about what Beauty will bring about and potentially change in us, in order to at least partially apprehend its sublime essentiality for our emotional existence and development. To do this unceasingly throughout life necessitates – as Klein (and Robert Louis Stevenson, Dostoevsky and Melville, to name but a significant few) knew all too well – a constant acknowledgement of the "beastly" and the murderous responses to Beauty in the Ahab-Iago-Hyde of our deeper selves. Although the risk of this knowledge is always breakdown, there is also the hope, and urgency, of breakthrough – to a place where fully **feeling** inconstant Beauty in our lives transforms us into creatures rich and strange, even if "soaked in sad."

Kafka's statement that

"He who keeps the idea of beauty never grows old."

might be slightly amended to

Without the idea of Beauty, one never grows.

References

Bergmann, M. S. (1992). The apprehension of beauty: The role of aesthetic conflict in development, art and violence. *J. Amer. Psychoanal. Assn.*, 40: 885–888.
Brooke, R. (1912). *Complete Poems*. London: Penguin. 1985.
Harris Williams, M. and Waddell, M. (1992). *The Chamber of Maiden Thought*. London: Routledge.
Hogan, P. J. (2003). *Peter Pan*. Universal. Film.
Mitrani, J. (2008). Unbearable ecstasy, reverence and awe, and the perpetuation of an "aesthetic conflict". *Psychoanal. Quart.*, 67(1): 102–127.
Meltzer, D. (1987). Concerning the stupidity of evil. *Melanie Klein & Obj. Rel.*, 7 (1): 156–165.
Meltzer, D. and Harris Williams, M. (1988). *The Apprehension of Beauty: The Role of Aesthetic Conflict in Development, Art and Violence*. Perthshire: Clunie Press.
Schrader, P. (1999). Film. *The Comfort of Strangers* (screenplay by H. Pinter).
Spielberg, S. (2001). *Artificial Intelligence*. Film DVD. Los Angeles: Amblin.

Chapter 15

Inconclusive Conclusion

The resilient persistence of the Life-Death instinct through variations in its relationships with the drive to Death

Melanie Klein's conception of mental-emotional development in the child centres on some complex interdependent achievements whereby the movement from paranoid-schizoid splitting of the internal mother-breast into good and bad to a more integrated, but painfully complex relationship with her as a "Whole-object" who is both loved and hated for being both frustrating and **gratifying** – because if she is not frustrating, then the gratifying feed may provoke envy. As underlined in the previous chapter, Meltzer and Harris Williams have also augmented this emotional complexity by underlining the aesthetic conflict that intimate contact with a mother will arouse in an infant.

I see the achievement of "Whole-object **thinking**" as a lifelong development, and utterly pivotal for the process that this book has explored – the struggle between expanding and yet consolidating the integration of the Self.

By developing Jung's concept of an evolving Self, and re-configuring Bion's grid to supplant mathematical (calculus) integration with **feeling** integration, through emotional-symbolic abstraction, a growing poetic Self is seen to unfold – capable of, and thriving on, a melding of thinking and feeling. (Not unlike a giant space telescope unfolding to receive new data of a more revealing deeper natural universe, except that the incoming data is of emotional experience about being alive.) This combining and melding of thinking and feeling, as a type of freed-up, exploratory thinking – often called intuitive, or inspirational – which most major "scientific-deductive" systems and artistic creations are originated from, is practically the only way forward in the evolution of a civilization capable of learning, through the abstraction of experience.

An example of the type of curious, reverent, widening of abstraction might be William Blake's achievement in whole object thinking as applied to a *Creator* in his awe-filled *Tyger* poem. At first, we think that he is in awe of the tiger itself – then we are impacted with the realization that he is actually addressing his feelings towards the one who *created* the tiger. This enables a whole new level of awe and reverence apart from admiration and awe and fear for the mere tiger itself.

Authentic whole-object thinking-feeling cannot be faked, because it is intimately interwoven with the emotional apprehension of beauty and awe – irrespective of whether or not this invokes some systematic religious enthusiasm or a fleeting, deep sigh of reverence towards a Creator.

That so much violence has ensued from fighting over the details, rather than feeling a commonality of feeling is perhaps humanity's greatest tragedy and stupidity.

For the moment, I propose four basic templates for the interrelationship-entwinement of life and death drives. These are:

1 **Unified-Cooperative**. Promoting exploratory intercourse not only produces creative artistic gestation but also brings in the risk of Self-envy and internal sabotage. The life and death drives are in tandem – intertwining and leapfrogging, almost like teasing lovers in a temporary unity that brings about a highly charged erotic-electric emotional field.

2 **Sabotaging-Fearful**. When the drives become totally split apart, and fear each other as annihilatory enemies, such as I have detailed in the earlier chapters of this book.

3 **Provocative-Catastrophic**. Where one drive pushes to the extreme, in a desperate attempt to get the other to take hold. This is very dangerous, (risking all-out war) but sometimes felt to be necessary, for the sake of integration. Chapter One detailed the dynamics of this life-death struggle through *Strangers on a Train* and *Dr. Jekyll and Mr. Hyde*.

4 **Transcendent-Spiritual**. The soul-sighing attempt to reach emotional integration through revering the ever-recombining, creative couple. Although this is often hijacked by a pious, cynical lack of faith (minus F, in Bionian) in the strength of life's reparative-renewing force. (The biblical story of *Job* is but one example of the harrowing struggle between Job and God and Satan.) This dynamic is detailed in the chapter which proposes a *Spiritual Position*.

Emotional growth involves perpetual mourning for lost Selves, as well as for their external, fleshly, representatives, as a cognitive-emotional development in the formation of an authentic identity. And, with each new person we are about to meet, we juggle an ardent desire to expand and change our Selves together with the terror of unknown destruction or dismantling of what we have thus far attempted to hold onto, and all that we yet know.

In this way, Faith is absolutely necessary for the work of mourning – it forces one to realign from the good **object** as the total source of life and love and creativity, to its highest whole object **spiritual representation** – that is, one's God or belief or philosophy. (Notwithstanding Hamlet's elbow to Horatio.) This fourth, transcendent-spiritual, dance of the instincts, in my view, forms a bridge with whole-object thinking and feeling. If one truly ascends one's level of abstracting to a more whole seeing of the *tree-for the-forest-for-life*, one doesn't just have an intellectual revelation but also an emotional epiphany.

Regretfully, there isn't the space here to further illustrate these four types of interplay amongst the basic drives through the use of mythology. Indian mythology, in particular, vividly evokes the psychodrama of these – and makes use of such ambiguously destructive-creative figures as Shiva and Brahma.[1]

I don't claim any final knowledge of the unity and interplay of these two drives. But nor do I think that the Freud-Klein abstraction of these ultimate psychic forces (Eros and Thanatos) that sculpt and fire the mind was trivial, senescent or ill-thought. In this book, I am pushing for us to further reflect on the nature of their *interrelationship* – and to explore the clinical usefulness of conceiving these instincts as unified in aim (a life-death instinct), even if they may at times seem to be at war in the mind. But I do know that my understanding of all this is quite incomplete and beyond my full grasp. And that whilst the never-ending drive towards integration is relentlessly and at times brutally determined, whole object abstraction towards the Godhead in the mind is ostensibly more a direction than a reachable destination.

Within that multiply-charged flux of psychic transformations, defences and growth-reversing *minus*-formations (Bion) *something* (say an impulse, or phantasy or action), is always at the same time, *something else*. In other words, the spiritual is nothing if not ambiguous – and the tolerance of ambiguity is crucial. It is a poetic capability. (I hope that I have illustrated this in the chapter on Distraction, being both a manic defence, but also, simultaneously, a chance for enriched Self-integration.)

Instinctual aims are magnetic compass threads, but not themselves the overarching composite organic growing-forging fabric of the Mind's **purpose** in guarding the Self from stagnation, and from over-wrought iron filings of psychotic disintegration and Self-alienation – the most painful form of all psychic loneliness.

"Whole-Object thinking" is a lifelong development, since the indefatigable drive to integrate is a hallmark and purpose of the Life instinct. And so extending Jung's larger concept of Self into an expansion of Bion's grid (supplanting his Algebraic Calculus as the highest form of abstracted thought) to embrace a growing poetic dimension of the Self – where feeling and thinking and abstracting are given free play to combine and permute into *fresh and fresh wholes* (Elliot/Waddell) brings us to the brink of a capacity for abstraction, and the beginnings of dream-thoughts.

The freshness of transformation is
The freshness of a world.
It is our own, It is ourselves, the freshness of ourselves,
And that necessity and that presentation
Are rubbings of a glass in which we peer.
                                 Wallace Stevens, *Notes toward a Supreme Fiction*

(At the conclusion of Ridley Scott's film *Blade Runner*, there is a life and death physical and psychological struggle between an android, who wants to live forever, and his hunter-assassin who is charged with defeating this aim. But, at a crucial moment, the android ceases to struggle, and becomes **poetic** – allowing him to emotionally reconcile his terminal life force through the (grateful) acceptance of all the beauty that he has seen in the universe.)

And of course, whole object thinking and feeling are essential in sustaining an analytic capacity for perceiving patterns and themes in clinical narrative and for exploring the stuff that dreams are made on, in order to decipher and hone the ever-unfolding nature of the transference relationship, and in fuelling and sustaining long term love in general.

> After many years, I have understood that love is not an end in itself, but a process of learning to know another fully.
>
> *Up Against the Night* Justin Cartwright

Because whole object thinking is never-ending, I have kept this concluding chapter extremely short. But, in my view, we require a constantly revitalized perspective on the concept of primal instincts or drives – to perceive and to respect their sacred commonality of purpose in the survival and promulgation of Earthly, mental, emotional and spiritual life.

This is likely to be wholly important for *the combined melding of thinking and feeling,* as a type of freed-up, exploratory thinking – we often call it *Intuitive –* which most major scientific-deductive systems are actually founded on. Freud, Einstein, Newton, Feynman and Shakespeare were all fluent in the *experi-mentality via speculative projective identification*. The French composer Pierre Boulez often stated that he aimed for unity of thinking and feeling together in his music. Because Whole object thinking embraces and thrives on ambivalence –as a fourth dimension of the mind – where something is always something else again from a different perspective, then the role of death instinct is in keeping this "real" and making it impossible to shirk – a kind of *fidelity to one's Self, in the* refusal to dumb-down emotional complexity by *overly Disney-fying it.*

Anorexia and Bulimia are a bodily expression and excrescence of the starvation and hungry unquench-ability of the Self for digestible identifications to assimilate and to grow from when the available adult models are impossible to digest, assimilate and grow from.

The chapter on *Disidentification* showed the necessity of being helped past that stalemate of the unfolding, evolving Self.

This involves turbulent thrills and spills in the painful struggle to evolve a mind of one's own through the formation of a highly individualistic, personally selected internal family. This is in comparison, and sometimes in opposition, to the compulsion to complete one's **parent's** unfulfilled life quests. It highlights the sometimes awful violent conflict between the individual's life-quest and those of parents, grandparents and even ancestors, real or imagined.

Birth and the increasing knowledge of death become the caesural opening-closing valves and spurs for these processes. The unknown bourns that round and disrupt our sleeping souls, where mind, body and spirit reconfigure and remould the basic instincts as they give them a local habitation through the formation of habits. Our attempt to make the new world our home, in the face of primeval knowledge that it can only ever be temporary, is both reassuring and terrifying. And yet, we are gifted as humans with an organic capacity for a dialectic interplay of instinct and free will as the fuel of our emotional-cognitive development in bearing the unknown.

But, every attempt at whole-object thinking and feeling must end somewhat abruptly in its arbitrary incompleteness. And yet, an incomplete whole-object beckons through its eternal mystery – and that is our human calling.

The mind's inclination to growth, through the development of Whole-object thinking and through ever-widening abstraction, suggests the probability that the unconscious mind is a continuous cognitive-emotional processing array whereby all dream thoughts, including dreams themselves, are "indexed" according to **emotional meaning** and stored and pooled for potential matching through "alchemical" réactivation with every new emotional experience.

Thereby interactive emotional dream elements form fresh and fresh wholes, (Bion's *alpha narrative*) every night, and continuously.

A decent analytic session will bring some of this into consciousness, which forms a part in the array - but which is limited in its access to the full store of alpha elements. However, with help, the array can accessed indirectly through free associations, emotional replication and verbal ambiguity.

This living, organic repository itself is in renewal through dream-linking and integration of multifarious emotional responses to one's experiences. And this functioning of the unconscious mind is constantly shaping and reshaping its responses to the other major element of the unconscious mind – one's instinctual impulses. (In many ways this resembles Freud's proposed eternal struggle between ego and id - but here, in accessing links in the array, the unconscious aspects of the ego play the major role – not just the conscious ego's quest for control over unruly id impulses.)

This book is not, or ever will be a whole truth – but on the whole, it is a sincere hologram of my merely individual attempt to grasp a perspective. Or, more simply – I have tried to be honest about what I really think about what it takes to grow a mind – on the whole.

Note

1 see the *Mahabharata* for example.

Index

Abraham, K. 66, 219
abstraction xvi, 39, 86, 244, 246, 248
addiction xv, 3, 17, 33, 35, 49, 86, 124, 137, 144–145, 168
agoraphobic anxiety 18–20
alpha function 10, 47–57, 99, 101, 130, 163, 214, 220, 241, 248
Alvarez, A. 102, 219, 225–226
ambiguity, when something is also something else x, 246, 248
array of emotional experiences 42, 52, 82, 102, 150, 239, 241, 248

awe, of creator xvi, 89, 163–164, 168–169, 176, 202, 206, 229–230, 238, 240–241, 243, 244

Balzac, H. 63–65, 77
Bandigung 1
Baumbach, N. *The Squid and the Whale* (film) 67, 68, 77
beauty, as dangerous surrender 164, 169, 176–177, 180, 182, 191–192, 204, 210, 215, 228–230, 233–244, 246
binding, as expansive inter-connective quality of life instinct i, 3, 147, 160
Bion, W. xiv–xvii, 3, 10, 12, 17, 19, 28, 36, 38–39, 50–51, 56–57, 76–77, 99, 101, 104–105, 122–126, 140, 156, 202, 208–215, 217, 220–221, 244, 246, 248
Bion's grid xvi, 211, 241, 244, 246
birth, going through symbolism 3, 14, 24–25, 36, 39, 64, 108, 125–126, 140, 147, 151, 168–169, 221, 232, 237, 247
Blake, W. xvi, 48, 106, 108, 111, 118, 120, 187, 189, 210, 238, 240–241, 244
Boethius 97, 104

breast 13, 15–19, 21, 24–26, 35–36, 39, 50, 54, 68, 75, 88, 96, 106–108, 110–113, 116, 119, 146, 163, 180–181, 204, 212, 237–238, 244
breathing in the spirit of the feeding object 24–25, 32, 36, 96, 147, 151
Britton, R. 67, 77, 87, 139, 180
Bronte, E. 12
Bruno (*Strangers on a Train.*) 7–10

Chamber of maiden thought 83, 104–105, 180, 191, 198, 238, 243
cinema, as public dreaming xi, 195
claustrophobic anxiety 18–20, 24, 57, 71, 93, 165
combined object 61, 63, 71, 74, 76–77, 138–139, 64, 179, 183–184, 192–193, 196, 238, 240–241
combining object 66–67, 71, 95–96, 101–102, 104, 179, 183, 188, 192–193, 196, 238, 244–247
Comfort of Strangers, The 235, 240, 243
countertransference 51, 53, 61, 69, 70, 73, 76, 90, 100, 106, 113, 116, 171, 195, 211, 218, 220, 231
creative clinical moment 56–57, 62–63, 82–83, 87, 104, 115, 193, 196, 212, 216–217, 219–220, 225–226, 238, 245

David, Larry, *Curb Your Enthusiasm* 217–218, 227
death instinct 2, 8–10, 12–19, 103–105, 122–123, 164–165, 168–178, 205–206, 222, 225–226, 244–247
defence, as ambiguous x, 11, 23, 40, 54, 59, 83–88, 96, 100, 130, 163, 183, 212, 239, 221–225

De la Mare, W. (*dark enough to see*) 100, 167, 211, 215
denial 19, 38, 43, 61, 63, 67, 71, 86, 102, 110, 183, 217, 221
dependence 13, 17, 19–21, 41, 63, 67, 71, 124, 234
depressive anxiety 37, 66, 75, 73–106, 216–222
depressive pain transformed 55, 63, 75, 77, 84, 121, 128, 137, 211, 218, 230, 239
depressive position 2, 3, 16–18, 25, 28, 54, 55, 66, 74, 79–90, 100–105
dis-identification 58, 60–63, 65–78, 87, 128, 247
distraction, as manic defence 43, 53, 163, 216–227; as Freud's cure for depression 216, 224
dreaming 14, 49, 56–57, 101, 149, 195, 235
dreams which reference other dreams 247–248

envy, as self-correcting xvi, 19, 39, 50–51, 128–130, 243–245
epistemophilic instinct, Klein. 209
evanescence 151, 230, 237
exploratory projective identification 211, 244–245, 247

father, from incestual to facilitating 126–129, 134–135, 173–176, 179–180, 193–195, 199–200, 204–205, 209, 241
false dreams 47–57, 61, 67
feelings about accumulated feelings 79–81, 83–93, 98, 102, 95–104, 168–170
feelings, indexed in retrievable array 226, 229, 248
Fitzgerald, F.S. (*The Great Gatsby*) 124–125
Florizel (*The Winter's Tale*) 76, 190–191, 197
foetal 19, 24–25, 27, 33, 35–36, 147, 153, 175, 206
Freud, S. 1–3, 10, 13, 58–60, 66, 73, 77–78, 122–123, 145, 177, 179–180, 209, 211, 215–216, 219–220, 224, 246–248

God, as personal symbol for fearful awe 67, 86, 98–99, 125, 146, 163–164, 169–170, 210, 233, 238–241, 245

goodness 13–23, 19, 50, 70, 97, 166, 170, 186, 190, 208, 239
grid (Bion) needing Poetic abstraction xvi, 211, 241, 244, 246
Grotstein, J. 16, 18, 67, 84, 95, 105, 210, 215, 229
growth, as aim of life-death instinct 3, 10–11, 23–24, 58, 62–63, 67, 73, 76–77, 81–85, 103–104, 152, 210, 225, 246, 248

Hardy, Thomas (*The Woodlanders*) 131, 191, 199–215
Harris Williams, M. 28, 56–57, 61, 66, 83–84, 105, 162, 196, 228–230
heart (symbolic-emotional meaning) xiii, 65–66, 79–81, 85–93, 108, 126–127, 137, 143, 184, 200, 207–208, 228, 239–240, 242
helical entwinement of instincts 101, 213, 225
Hermione (*The Winter's Tale*) 103, 179, 190–192, 197
Highsmith, P. 9, 11–12
Hitchcock, A. 1, 4, 7, 9, 12, 65, 87

Iago (*Othello*) 71, 183–197, 228, 236, 240–243
injured, by love 79–81
inoculative identification 1, 4, 10–11
integration 1, 3, 9–11, 23, 37, 44, 81–82, 103, 118, 120, 123, 130, 137–138, 244–246, 248
internal couple 10, 68, 93, 101, 109, 165, 193–198, 238
interrelationships of life and death drives, types xv–xvii, 245–246
intra-uterine 14, 24–38
Ives, Charles 104–105

Joy-Jouissance 127–128, 135, 140, 180, 184–185, 187, 197, 205, 219, 242

King Lear 64, 87, 128, 131, 190, 193, 213, 239
Klein, Melanie. 2, 4, 11–16, 18–19, 57, 66, 71, 78–81, 105–106, 116, 122–125, 137–138, 179–182, 195, 202, 209–210, 220, 217–220, 227–228, 243–244, 246
knowledge 43, 50–51, 63, 73, 102–104, 159, 167, 195, 199–215, 218, 220, 243, 246–247

Index

lap of father as space for reflective reverie (*Hamlet*) xiii, 90, 103, 121, 123, 133, 159–160
Leontes, (*The Winter's Tale*) 103, 179, 189–193, 197, 237, 242
life-death instinct 9, 245–247
life instinct, expansion of mind through loving curiosity 2, 3, 13, 18, 37–40, 66, 94–95, 169, 233–234, 245–247; at cellular level x, 4, 11, 56
loneliness 73, 79–80, 108, 119, 121–141, 203, 246
love 8, 10–11, 18–20, 33, 39, 59, 66, 74–77, 111–113, 123, 126–127, 138–140, 166–167, 170, 199–202, 206–208, 228–231, 234–242, 245, 247

Maizels, N. 66, 78, 84, 98, 101, 104–105, 124, 126, 131–132, 181, 198, 224
manic defences, as ambiguous 54, 63, 86, 102, 113, 120, 216–227, 246
Marlowe, C. 198, 228, 236
Melancholia (film) 172–178, 219
Meltzer, D. 3, 5, 10–12, 28, 38, 41, 52, 54, 63, 66, 82, 97–101, 111, 117, 153, 163, 182, 227–230, 234–244
meta-feeling 151, 161, 241
metamorphosic 80
miss red, premature weaning vi, xiii, 106–113
mourning 28, 30, 32–36, 52, 59, 63, 66–67, 85, 152, 197, 207, 209, 221, 227, 245
murder of Beauty 87, 189, 230, 233, 236, 243

Narcissus, unconscious rejecting of echo 36, 207, 228–243
narrative alpha 11–12, 248
nuclear warfare 37, 40, 43–44, 46, 210

Oberon 183, 236–237, 240
Oedipal longing 205–206, 238
Othello 71, 179, 183–190, 236, 242

paternal function 130, 138
paternal object 121–122, 128
Perdita, (*The Winter's Tale*) 190–191, 193, 197
Pericles 193, 239
Peter Pan, (PJ Hogan film) 239, 241, 243
Plath, Sylvia 47, 55–57, 126
poet (female) 56, 126–127, 160, 196
poetic, self 9, 32, 56, 85, 126, 144, 153, 196, 244, 246

pre-natal 36, 124, 126
premature weaning 106–120, 128, 209
projective identification 4–6, 12, 15, 61, 63–64, 78, 90, 118, 130, 146–148, 153–154, 163, 181–182, 193, 201–203, 209–210, 212, 225, 235, 247
proto-language 156–171
Proust, M. xii, 29, 36

Rank, O. 125–126, 140, 169, 203
re-pairing, of internal couple 179–180, 240, 244
romantic illusion 125, 138, 140, 174, 180, 223
Rosenfeld, H 3, 5, 12, 23, 38, 41, 46, 124, 147, 153, 217, 222, 227

Sehnsucht, longing xiv, 124–125, 138–141
self-envy 11, 12–23, 244–247
sensuality 90, 116, 150
Shakespeare, W. 57, 77, 87, 125, 129, 159–160, 179, 183, 189–193, 197–198, 228, 236–237, 239, 247
Shakespearean types of fathers 64, 126, 127
sighing, as post-depressive indicator xiii, 55, 103, 151, 169, 245
sincerity accessible through feeling 55, 91, 105, 186, 229
smoking (and vaping) 102, 143–155
Spielberg, S. (*Poltergeist and Artificial Intelligence*) 34, 52, 234, 243
spiritual position 62–63, 66–67, 73, 83, 87–88, 97, 100–104, 245–247
Stevenson, R.L. 12, 243
Strangers on a Train v, viii, 1–12
swearing, as a proto-language 156–171

taming, of instincts (Freud) 1–3, 10
termination, through *disidentification* xii, 61, 69–80, 87–88, 94, 100, 118, 139, 214
Tiresian, attack on coupling 95–97, 101
Titania, *A Midsummer Night's Dream* 236–237, 242
transcendence 88, 102, 138, 152, 206, 245
transformation 3, 9, 44, 56, 73, 83, 85, 87, 93–99, 101, 103, 131, 179, 193, 196–214, 246
transience 25, 57, 230, 236
trees of knowledge 63, 199–215
Tyger, The (William Blake poem) 238, 244

un-symbolic dreams. cf *narrative alpha* 49, 51, 61
United Nations, failure 41–46, 141, 155

vaping *see* smoking
vergangenheitsbewaltigung 85, 95, 98, 103

Waddell, M. 56–57, 61, 66, 83–84, 87, 105, 196, 238, 243, 246
watchful lovingkindness (Hardy) 71, 137, 139, 201–203, 209, 211–214
weaning 15–18, 23, 25, 35, 70, 101, 105–120, 127, 150, 221
West Wing, The (TV show) i, xiii, 133–138
whole-objects x, 66, 80, 82, 86, 98, 104, 121, 131, 181, 211, 213, 217, 223, 225, 228, 241, 244–248

whole-object thinking 82, 98, 244–248
Winter's Tale, The 87, 179, 189, 191–192, 203, 237, 242
womb 13–25, 28, 35–36, 38, 95–96, 115, 128, 168, 176, 181, 184, 186, 230–231
working through, of depressive position 9, 10, 17, 61, 78–106, 134–135, 151, 158, 183, 200, 207, 213, 218, 220–222, 224
Woodlanders, The (Hardy) vii, xv, 131, 199–215
World War 37, 38
wrecking of internal couple 179–198, 228, 240

yearning 25, 90, 124–125, 130–131, 133, 138, 147, 172, 230